MAN, MORALS AND SOCIETY

MAN, MORALS AND SOCIETY

a psycho-analytical study

J. C. Flugel

Duckworth

Reissued 1973
Reprinted 1945, 1948 and 1955
First published March 1945

ISBN 0 7156 0235 7

Printed in Great Britain by Butler and Tanner Ltd. Frome and London

PREFACE

AT the time when the present writer and his fellow-students (a very small band of them sometimes regarded as distinctly eccentric in their choice of subject) first approached the study of psychology it was customary to distinguish between psychology and ethics by saying that the former was a positive science, the latter a normative one ; that is to say, psychology described the actual facts of mental life and of behaviour, without passing moral judgement on them, whereas ethics endeavoured to discover how we *ought* to feel and act. We could have said much the same thing by calling psychology a pure science, ethics an applied one (indeed, the most generalized of all the applied sciences). Since that time the distinction in question, though still valid at the highest level of generality, has become somewhat less easy to apply in detail. This is mainly due to two developments in psychology itself ; in the first place to the rapid growth of applied psychology—in medicine, education, industry, vocational guidance and selection, criminology, and other fields ; in the second place to the fact that psychology has increasingly concerned itself with those aspects of the mind which play a leading part in what we might broadly term the moral life—with conscience, will, mental conflict, value judgements, self-control, our loves and hates, our impulses to construction or destruction. In doing so it has provided ethics with a mass of fresh data which it must take into consideration—in much the same way as progress in physics or physiology must have profound repercussions on engineering or medicine.

When the present book was written, during the later stages of the Second World War, there were, so far as my knowledge went, very few works dealing with the relations between psychology and ethics, and these were becoming rather out of date, especially since most of them had taken no account of psycho-analysis, that branch or school of psychology (one in which the pure and applied approaches were so intimately blended) to which were due so many of our new insights into the mental factors concerned in moral or immoral conduct. A book dealing with the relations of psychology and ethics especially from the psycho-analytic point of view seemed therefore to be called for, and since I had already, as long ago as 1917, attempted a short survey [1] of what seemed to me to be the ethical bearings of psycho-analysis, I felt justified in approaching the theme once more, this time on a broader basis and in the light of the immense additions to psycho-analytic knowledge made in the intervening years.

Even from the point of view of pure psychology, apart from its relations to ethics, there seemed to be an urgent need for a synoptic presentation of the findings of psycho-analysis as regards the psychological factors which enable man to be a moral animal, conscious of ' good ' and ' evil ' ; in short, of the doctrine of the super-ego—a part of psycho-analytic theory which was far less widely understood than were the earlier formulations concerning the nature and manifestations of ' libido '. This indeed was one of the main tasks attempted in the book, which apparently succeeded in its purpose if reliance can be placed on the statement of one kind (but very competent) commentator,[2] who said that it is ' almost a super-ego encyclopædia, since it includes practically everything that has been formulated concerning super-ego development and function '.

Had I but known it, this double task of describing the super-ego doctrine in all its fullness and of relating it to the general problems of ethics had already been attempted by my Swiss colleague, Dr. Charles Odier, whose valuable book on the subject [3] covered much the same ground as the present work, but which, owing to the war, was not available in this country till several years after publication. The two books are, however, in some respects different in their approach, Odier's being more clinically and less genetically and sociologically órientated, while at the same time it deals more thoroughly with the problems involved in the relations between the psycho-analytic and the religious points of view, a matter as regards which a number of critics have found the present book to be deficient.

In the Preface to the original editions of this work it was suggested that the very real need to consider the moral implica-

[1] ' Freudian Mechanism as Factors in Moral Development ', *British Journal Psychology* (1917), viii, 477.

[2] Marjorie Brierley, *Trends in Psycho-Analysis*, London, Hogarth Press, 1951.

[3] Charles Odier, *Les Deux Sources, Consciente et Inconsciente, de la Vie Morale*, Neuchâtel, De La Baconnière, 1943.

tions of psycho-analytic discoveries would soon give rise to other publications on the subject. This expectation has shown itself to be amply justified. Since 1945 there has appeared a steady stream of relevant books, articles, and addresses, some of them expository, others critical, still others dealing with some special application (e.g. their bearing on political problems or on the aims of the psychotherapist or educator) or connected with special features of the authors' own psychological theories. In so far as my book has played a part in stimulating such discussions, I have every reason to be satisfied with what at the time seemed to me a pioneering effort. It only remains for me to express the hope that a constantly growing circle of readers may reflect upon these problems in their many and varied aspects, upon some one of which at least each reader will have some special knowledge or experience. Only by serious reflection on the part of many minds can we hope to enjoy the full benefits of increased psychological knowledge as it affects human conduct in the individual or the group ; and only in this way can the limitations imposed by our ignorance or prejudice (including that of psychologists and moralists themselves) be gradually reduced and the many social problems which beset humanity be approached with a correspondingly more hopeful prospect of finding a solution.

J. C. F.

March 1955.

CONTENTS

CHAPTER I

PSYCHOLOGY AND MORALS

THE present is an age in which it is difficult for the psychologist to escape some feeling of embarrassment, inferiority, or downright shame. Like others, he is conscious of the fact that society, through failing to solve sundry of its major problems, has got itself into a tragic tangle from which it can extricate itself only by a great effort of readjustment. More than others, however, is he aware that both the failures of the past and the problems of the present and the future are to a large extent psychological in nature: that they are to that extent a direct challenge to him, and that he is ill-equipped to meet this challenge —for, in spite of the progress that psychology has undoubtedly made during the last half-century, it is still lamentably backward when compared with the physical sciences, and provides at best a puny weapon with which to attack the vast and complex evils from which society is suffering. At such a juncture he must, if he is sensitive, feel somewhat like a doctor compelled to watch the life-or-death struggles of a patient whose malady he cannot fully diagnose and for whose treatment he can prescribe, if at all, from intuition rather than from insight. Like the doctor, however, he knows enough to understand something of the general nature of the disease and to realize that with further advance of his knowledge more competent diagnosis and prescription would be possible. Meanwhile, not without searchings of heart, he is likely to attempt some review of the relevant facts and theories at his disposal, all too conscious of their inevitable inadequacy, but with some hope that such a scrutiny of available data will reveal him, both to himself and to his fellow-men, as one who is not altogether doomed to gape idly and uselessly at the scene of human tragedy, but rather as one who can at least here and there make a promising suggestion or lend a helping hand in the work of salvage and of reconstruction.

It is pretty generally agreed that the problem of rebuilding our tottering society upon a sounder basis is to some extent a moral problem, in the sense that its solution depends upon an appeal to the moral impulses of men. If we are to make this appeal successfully, it would seem that we should know something of the origin and nature of these impulses. Now it happens that in the last twenty years or so psychologists do appear to have increased their knowledge concerning just these impulses. It is our task here to examine the nature and implications of this knowledge. Since, of the various 'schools' into which psychology is still so unhappily divided, that of psycho-analysis has contributed most in this field, it is with psycho-analytical concepts and with the psycho-analytical approach that we shall be mostly concerned, though we shall also deal sometimes with the work of other schools so far as it appears to be helpful and relevant. If our initial hopes prove to be justified, we shall, as the result of our examination, succeed in showing that, fragmentary and uncertain as much of our information in this field still is, it is yet of such a kind as to deserve the earnest attention of those who hope that the history of mankind during the second half of the twentieth century may be less violent and bloody than during the first.

It is true that such facts or theories bearing on this field as psychologists have so far thought themselves in a position to present have not always been readily welcomed or easily accepted by their fellow-men—and this applies particularly to the school of psycho-analysis. In the earlier days of its history many people were profoundly shocked by the findings and formulations of psycho-analysis within the sphere of sex. Their cries of horror and expostulation have, however, for the most part now died down, and the fact that Freud, a few years before he came to this country as a refugee at the end of his life, was granted the high distinction of Foreign Membership of the Royal Society may be said to have set the seal of scientific respectability upon psycho-analysis as a method of approach to the problems of the mind. But there is still a considerable fear in some quarters of the influence of psychology in general, and of psycho-analysis in particular, on just that field that concerns us here—the field of values. It is felt that psychologists in their attempts to understand the motivations underlying values, ethical, religious, or æsthetic, are in danger of destroying these very values, or that they are indeed actively seeking to destroy them. Hence an effort, inspired by the fear of desecration, to put these psychologists firmly in their place, to disprove their evidence, to undermine their arguments, and to show them up as meddlesome intruders in a field with which they are incompetent to deal. With this end in view, it has been said that psychology is still a young and undeveloped science and that such crude conclusions as have sometimes been drawn from it in its present state should be accepted with the greatest caution, especially if they seem to threaten ancient and venerable institutions or beliefs. Furthermore it is said that psychologists themselves are by no means free from the very complexes about which they love to talk, and that their conclusions are therefore likely to be biased, as well as based on insufficient knowledge. Again it has been argued that psychology has been unduly influenced by psychopathological studies and that generalizations have all too frequently been made from the abnormal to the normal mind, so that psychologists have acquired a jaundiced and distorted view of human nature.

We do not propose to deal here with these first three objections; their adequate consideration would take us much too far afield. But there remains still another argument which seems to have some special relevance to our present undertaking and which therefore cannot be so lightly dismissed. This last objection is to the effect that psychologists, puffed up with the pride of a few recent discoveries, have forgotten the limitations imposed by the very nature and definition of their province. Psychology, we are reminded, is a positive, not a normative, discipline, that is, its business is to describe, classify, and (if it can) explain the facts of mental life, just as physics and chemistry deal with the facts of the material universe. Like these latter sciences, it has no concern with values as such; it must take the facts as it finds them and must not presume to pass judgment on their desirability or undesirability.

Few if any psychologists would wish to quarrel with this general position. Nevertheless the contention in question raises certain points which must be cleared up before we can proceed to any detailed consideration of the bearing of psychology upon ethical problems. These points can perhaps most conveniently be summarized under four main heads:

(1) When compared with the other sciences, psychology is in a special position in this matter. Values happen to be facts of *mental* life, and psychology, since its task is the study of mental life, is also concerned with the examination of values as parts or aspects of this mental life. In this respect it differs from physics and chemistry, which are not thus directly brought into contact with values in any part of their field, since value does not appertain to matter as such.

(2) As regards all branches of knowledge we must distinguish

between pure and applied science. Whereas pure science is concerned with things as they are, its only aim being knowledge for its own sake, applied science seeks to use this knowledge for the attainment of certain ends, ends which are assumed to be desirable and which therefore imply certain values (over and above the mere value of truth or knowledge). Thus medicine or engineering imply values in a way that physiology or physics do not; they imply that it is desirable to achieve and maintain a person's health or to construct and keep in order a machine. Similarly there can be pure or applied psychology. The latter has been used considerably in the fields of medicine, education, and industry. It is entering the fields of criminology and war, and there are some who hope to see it soon established in the wider spheres of sociology and politics. In all such cases—as with the physical sciences—certain values (e.g. mental health, efficient learning, reduction of fatigue, the rehabilitation of delinquents, victory in war) are assumed, and our psychological knowledge is put to use in the service of these values.

(3) This brings us to another distinction, that between 'instrumental' and 'intrinsic' values—or more popularly 'means' and 'ends'. The values implied in the applications of science are for the most part instrumental values only. The doctor and the engineer assume that it is desirable to keep the human body or the machine in efficient working order—they do not ask for what purpose the body or the machine is to be used. Such questions they leave to those concerned with 'higher' or more general values, and ultimately to the moral philosopher. It is the business of ethics to decide what these higher values are. Applied psychology therefore, like other applied sciences, is concerned with 'means' rather than with 'ends'.

Nevertheless the distinction between means and ends is nearly always relative. There exists a whole hierarchy of values, each of which is a means to the value that stands just above it in the hierarchy. What from one viewpoint is an 'end' becomes from a wider viewpoint but a 'means'. Thus a city business man may set his alarm clock so that he may wake in time to catch an early train. The waking is a means to catching the train, which is the end. But catching the train is itself only a means of getting to his office, which is a higher end. His work, however, is only a means to a still higher end—earning a livelihood or, if he is more ambitious, acquiring wealth. And this last, he would perhaps maintain, is itself sought only because he regards it as an essential means of being happy. Indeed the distinction between means and ends, though often convenient for the consideration of some relatively narrow problem, is largely arbitrary. At best there can only be a few unquestionably intrinsic values at the top of the hierarchy, such as Truth, Goodness, Beauty; or, if we press the matter further, there should strictly speaking be one only, a *summum bonum* or supreme value, to which all the rest are means—and, as we know, moral philosophers are not yet in agreement as to what this supreme value is.

Furthermore, while we are engaged on a means, we may make some discovery or have some flash of insight which may modify the end at which we are immediately aiming. While getting up, our city worker may remember that a neighbour is driving his car to the town that morning and that, if he begs a seat, this may provide a quicker and more convenient mode of transport than the train. While driving in the car he may learn from his neighbour that an important business acquaintance from another town, whom he is anxious to meet, is staying at a near-by hotel; in which case he may proceed straight to this hotel instead of to his office. At the interview in the hotel he may come to the conclusion that another line of business, or work in another city, may offer greater prospects of acquiring the wealth for which he hopes; and his whole life may be changed accordingly. Finally, while seeking wealth in this new way, he may decide that happiness is not the highest aim in life, but that fame or power or civic service constitutes a better goal.

Similarly in the field of applied science, when we begin to study the means to some desired end, we may be starting a process which will terminate in a profound modification or extension of the end that we are seeking. The inventors of the internal combustion engine sought to build a horseless carriage, but found eventually that they had gone far towards solving the problem of human flight. Advances in medicine or economics may lead to a radical revision of our notions of the true nature of health or wealth. In psychology, too, we have no right to be astonished if, while dealing with a means (e.g. the cure of a neurotic symptom, the discovery of more efficient ways of learning, or the relief of industrial fatigue), we find that we have modified our attitude towards the end (acquired some new insight into the nature of mental health, the rôle of education, or the place of work in human life). When it is objected that psychology can have no concern with values, it is of course meant that it is not in a position to state what are intrinsic values. But in view of the relative and fluctuating position of intrinsic and instrumental values it is hardly possible to say exactly at what point in the hierarchy of values its influence must cease. Psychology, particularly clinical psychology, has shown that there are many high goals, such as Love, Power, Riches, Virtue, Security, which are regarded by an individual, either explicitly or implicitly, as good in themselves, the adoption of which, however, has been largely determined by influences of which the individual is at best but dimly aware. A greater understanding (brought about by psychological treatment) of the origin and cause of their adoption may then sometimes lead to an appreciable modification of their value to the individual.[1] It is here that those who fear the inroads of psychology upon certain spheres of ancient privilege with regard to what are usually considered intrinsic values may have a certain amount of justification for their alarm. But it is in this way also that psychologists may perhaps hope to see a fresh field opened to the beneficent influence of the knowledge that they have laboriously gathered.

(4) In so far as psychology may in this way invade the sphere of what would usually be regarded as intrinsic values (and therefore the domain of ethics) there is involved a further subtle change, which is of great importance for our present purpose. The substitution of the psychological for the moral point of view in any matter implies also a change in mental attitude—a change from a relatively emotional attitude to a relatively intellectual one. Scientific judgment is primarily a cognitive process, moral judgment—in this respect like judgment in matters of religion or æsthetics—primarily an orectic process.[2] But with regard to difficult and delicate problems, cognition is often more effective than orexis. We have come to recognize

---

[1] In his two books, *Goals of Life*, 1939, and *A Guide to Mental Health*, 1939, H. D. Jennings White has well brought out the importance of such individual intrinsic values and at the same time their dependence upon the particular course taken by the mental development of the individual and the methods by which he seeks to adapt himself to his environment (methods which we should sometimes have little hesitation in regarding as pathological).

[2] Here and elsewhere I propose to follow a number of modern writers in using the convenient Aristotelian term 'orexis' (with adjective 'orectic') to describe the feeling, striving, and wishing aspects of the mind, as distinguished from the reasoning, knowing, and perceiving aspects, which, in accordance with customary usage, I shall call 'cognition'.

that with regard to the material world moral judgments are out of place. It is useless to become morally indignant with a motor-car that refuses to move; we have to discover what is wrong with the mechanism and to put it right. When we possess the necessary skill and knowledge, there will be little temptation to pass moral judgment on a mechanical contrivance. But when the task is beyond our skill, we easily adopt an animistic attitude, address the machine as though it were a living being, and resort to profanity and moral censure. Indeed the verb 'refuse' that we have just employed indicates such a lurking animistic attitude; an attitude which is common enough in primitive societies and at primitive levels of the mind, and which sometimes persists as an anachronism into civilized legal codes, as in a modern law in New Jersey according to which a car that has been involved in a fatal accident must be destroyed.[1] We are still more tempted to apply moral judgment to animals, and even legal trials of animals are not unknown.[2] In general, however, with regard both to inanimate objects and to animals, there is clearly a tendency to adôpt a cognitive, cause-and-effect attitude rather than an orectic, moral attitude; and it is now only with regard to a few domestic animals that we regard moral indignation as at all appropriate. With the development of psychology, this restriction of moral judgment and the substitution of judgment in terms of psychological insight is rapidly increasing, even in our dealings with fellow human beings, and for much the same reason as elsewhere, namely that it is so often more effective.

The mentally deranged (sometimes, too, the mentally defective) were formerly treated in much the same way as criminals, that is from the moral point of view, but, since Pinel in 1792 struck off the chains from his patients in the Bicêtre, it has become ever more recognized that the insane should be regarded as ill rather than as vicious, and that they are better treated by medical science than by moral condemnation. In more recent times education also has seen an attempt to substitute understanding for censure; it is recognized that it is better to find out why a pupil is lazy or stupid than to blame or punish him. Still more recently there has been a similar change in the treatment of criminals and delinquents; more particularly in the case of the young offender, but to some extent also in that

---

[1] R. Allendy, *La Justice Intérieure* (1931), p. 35.
[2] See, for instance, E. J. D. Radclyffe, *Magic and Mind* (1932), p. 86.

of the adult. Finally we find suggestions that the psychological point of view is applicable to the field of politics, and that even in political questions insight is preferable to indignation. To take a concrete instance, it is now being suggested, not only by psychologists, but by some students of politics themselves, that the only satisfactory way to conclude a peace is one in which the victors will take sufficient account of the feelings and suscepti- bilities of the vanquished to ensure a relatively willing co- operation, rather than one in which, giving way to their own feelings of moral outrage, they demand revenge, punishment, or reparation, regardless of the psychological effect that such measures may produce.

In all these, and in other ways, the psychological is thus tending to replace the moral point of view, and there is little doubt that, in so far as the new approach proves effective, the process will continue. It is indeed only an aspect of that more general change in virtue of which methods based on scientific knowledge come to replace the less certain and accurate, but more emotionally toned, methods to which men are wont to resort in the absence of such knowledge. Magic, divination, sacrifice, and prayer may relieve our feelings and reduce our fears when we are ignorant and impotent, but as our knowledge and our power increase we tend to abandon these practices in favour of others which we can see to lead more surely and directly to our goal. Science may never give us ultimate values; it may indeed, as is often argued, be precluded from doing so by its very nature. Nevertheless, as it advances, it may be of help in ever higher levels of the hierarchy of values; and in this increasing usefulness of science psychology will inevitably have its share.

CHAPTER II

CONSCIENCE AND WILL

MORAL action is action in accordance with values. Funda- mentally these values are determined by our biological nature and our innate psychological equipment. As an animal that lives more or less continuously in the society of his fellows, and as one that spends the first few years of his life in a state of almost utter dependence upon others, man possesses many natural tendencies which fit him for harmonious social life and for the protection of the young and helpless. Much moral conduct is therefore instinctive and spontaneous, and some students of ethics would regard this natural morality as the most valuable of all, and as providing a model of easy, happy virtue, which we should regard as an ideal. All would agree, however, that, strictly speaking, it is an unattainable ideal, and that, in order to live well in the complex social environment he has created, man needs, in addition to his natural virtue (which in any case varies considerably from one individual to another), a superimposed factor of acquired direction and control, a factor which is in a sense less 'natural' and 'spontaneous' than instinct, and which bids its possessor now to proceed more vigorously in some direction than his instincts would dictate, now to desist from some action which to his instincts would appear desirable. True, the more satisfactory his moral development, the higher his ethical technique, the less this factor of control may be in evidence; but in itself it is no less indispensable than the control underlying the technique of the artist, however spontaneous and effortless a great artistic creation may appear.

Our first task then must be to examine the nature and origin of this factor of moral control.

We may begin with a reference to an interesting recent study of this moral factor (or at least of some aspects of it) as it presents itself to introspective consciousness.[1] Two Viennese psychologists, Frenkel and Weisskopf, asked a number of persons trained in psychological introspection to call to mind what they would regard as certain characteristic 'wishes' and 'duties' respectively, and then to describe the differences between them. These differences as found are hardly of a kind to cause astonishment, but they amply confirm the general view that wishes are in a certain sense more spontaneous and natural than duties, which latter seem to involve the calling up of reserves of mental energy and which often seem also as though they were imposed upon our reluctant selves by some relatively extraneous force. The five chief features of wishes that, according to these results, distinguish them from duties are as follows:

1. They are accompanied by more lively feelings and emotions,

[1] Else Frenkel and Edith Weisskopf, *Wunsch und Pflicht im Aufbau des Menschlichen Lebens*, Wien, 1937.

B

especially those of a kind which seem to possess some bodily resonance.

2. They impel more vigorously to action. There is in fact usually a desire to translate them into action at once.

3. They appeal to the imagination in a way that duties do not. They are often imagined as actually in process of fulfilment, whereas in the case of duties there is no such imagination of the actual process of carrying out the duty; in so far as imagination operates at all with regard to duties, it occupies itself either with the consequences of not fulfilling the duty or with the situation as it would exist after the duty had been carried out.

4. There are, in particular, far more visual images connected with wishes than with duties. This reminds us of the important part played by visual imagery in day-dreaming and wishful thinking generally, whereas it has been found that such imagery recedes at moments of strenuous effort or intensive thought.

5. Whereas wishes appear as immediately and inherently desirable, the necessity for duties is often questioned in inner thought. Reasons are sometimes produced why they should be performed, though at other times there is only a sense of compulsion or necessity, often accompanied by such phrases as 'I must', 'I should', 'I mustn't', in inner speech. The fact that a duty is in a sense something that impinges on the self from outside, whereas a wish emanates directly from the self, was symbolized by one subject in contrasting imagery. A duty was represented by an arrow shooting in towards a circle (the self), whereas a wish was represented by an arrow shooting away from the circle. A further important point, however, is that, in spite of its external origin, we may recognize the justice of a claim that duty has on us and make this claim our own. This process is often brought about by subsuming the particular duty under some general principle; but, however accomplished, once the duty is made our own, it becomes as it were a part of our self, so that its fulfilment becomes at least as much the concern of the self as the fulfilment of a wish. This fact that a duty, though originally in a way extraneous to the self, becomes adopted by the self, so that its fulfilment is essential to our mental well-being, is one of the central features of the development of the moral life, and we find references to it, in one or other of its aspects, in practically all the psychological literature concerned with moral conduct, no matter to what school the

writer belongs and with what particular problem within the moral field he is immediately concerned.

In another part of the investigation to which we have just been referring it was found that with older people the sharp contrast between wish and duty tends to get obliterated. The duties the older people think of are, at least for the most part, those that have been so long adopted by the self and have grown to be so intimately a part of the self that they have become 'second nature' and almost as spontaneous as wishes; indeed wish and duty often appear intimately fused, though in this fusion it sometimes looks as though the duty, once it is adopted by the self, has the capacity to draw a wish to it, to clothe itself in the form of a wish. 'More like a self-appointed task which one gladly fulfils', says a wife of her household duties. 'I've come to an agreement with myself that I shall do gladly everything I have to do', writes a middle-aged professional man. Still older subjects are apt to be even more emphatic as to the relative absence of an external compelling quality in duties. Thus they can even say: 'things are wished because they are my duty'; duty is 'something *a priori*, contained in our very protoplasm, something immediate, like affection or love'; or 'duty is my innermost self, my very life'. A great contrast indeed with the clear-cut distinction between wish and duty drawn by most of the younger people! Lest it be thought that the older subjects consisted exclusively of prigs, it may be mentioned that at a certain stage in life, according to this investigation, people seem to be able more or less definitely to reject such potential duties as they are not able to adopt and assimilate, and that it is only duties that have been successfully assimilated that are referred to as though they were obvious and *a priori*. Thus we find such statements as: 'I refuse to do things which one can't understand or assent to'; or: 'Duties! I don't think I want to recognize that I have any. True, I want to behave decently; I don't know quite why, but that's something *I* have set myself to do, not something that is imposed on me from without'. Duties that the subjects have themselves adopted are contrasted with those they have been unable or unwilling to assimilate, and these latter are often rejected. 'Duty! It sounds so external, as though it came from one's parents (my mother used to talk a lot about duties!).' Thus, men and women in later life behave as though they had come to some sort of decision as to which kind of duties, of all those that originally made a claim on them, they will accept; these they have adopted, so that, if not exactly indistinguishable from wishes, they are willingly and ungrudgingly performed. In this respect the lives of older people who have come to terms with their duties are smoother and freer of conflict than those of younger ones, and it is interesting to note that those of the sixty-five subjects (of between 17 and 80 years of age) taking part in this portion of the investigation who did not show this typical change with increasing age (provided they were old enough to do so) also gave signs of being maladjusted or of suffering from nervous symptoms. The cynical reader may be tempted to think that as we get older we grow either smug or neurotic—or else (as is often suggested) that psychologists themselves are apt to confuse prim self-satisfaction with normality. In defence, however, both of the psychologists and of their subjects, three further facts brought out by these data should be mentioned.

In the first place, it would appear that, as we grow older both our wishes and our duties refer more and more to external things and persons and less and less directly to ourselves. Furthermore, this seems to be a natural and almost inevitable tendency, associated with the biological and social conditions of our life; whereas in early years we are chiefly occupied with the development and equipment of our own personalities, and are looking forward to the more important rôle that we shall shortly have to play, in maturity we are largely occupied with work, with our dealings with fellow-men, or with our families. This diminishing ego-centricity of our wishes probably makes it easier for them to be harmonized with our duties. We can easily see that this is likely to be true if we compare, by way of an extreme instance, a successful professional man of 45, thoroughly interested in his work, and desirous of the well-being of his family (which between them are the occasion also of his most important duties), with the boy of 5 or 6, most of whose 'wishes', however natural and innocent in themselves, are liable to cause inconvenience and annoyance to his elders, and most of whose 'duties', imposed on him as they are from without, seem at best necessitated only by the pointless pedantry of adults and often in addition cruelly at variance with his own natural interests and desires.

In the second place, many of the subjects make certain

exceptions to the general rule of 'adopting' duties, i.e. there are certain tasks which they recognize are, or might become, duties, which they cannot reject but which at the same time they cannot wholeheartedly adopt, or even pretend to find pleasant or interesting. Thus the married woman who speaks of 'gladly fulfilling' her household duties seems to be not without qualms about the future, for she adds in eloquent aposiopesis: 'Perhaps when one's been married ten years . . . !'; while the professional man who seems to have so successfully applied to himself the injunction 'Do it and like it' does in fact exclude a few chores (especially those connected with his mother-in-law!) from the general rule of doing gladly everything he has to do.

Finally, it may be noted that in the definitely elderly, there is a return to a feature of earlier life; i.e. a great preponderance of wishes over duties in the number of those brought up for consideration by the subjects. This agrees with the general tendency to retire, in whole or in part, from active work in later life, and to devote much of one's spare time to hobbies or other occupations that come under the heading of wishes rather than of duties. This tendency, as well as that relating to the decrease of ego-centric wishes and duties already referred to, is brought out in the following small table:

Age	Wishes to 10 Duties	Ego-directed Wishes and Duties to 10 Externally Directed Wishes and Duties
17–30	20	27
30–45	17	13
45–60	10	3·8
60–80	20	2·3

We have dwelt at some length on the results of this investigation, both because it is, so far as I am aware, unique of its kind, and because it brings out conveniently, at the descriptive level, some points which are in general harmony with the results of many other lines of research in general and experimental psychology and in psycho-analysis. The two most important of these points, about which a little more may be said here, concern respectively: (1) the distinction between duty and wish, and (2) the adoption of a certain course of action by the self. The former of these is, of course, only an aspect or consequence of that special factor of moral direction and control to which we referred at the beginning of this chapter.

The distinction between this guiding moral power (whatever it be called) and the more natural and spontaneous propensities, wishes, appetites, or instincts, is one which has forced itself on the attention of psychologists from the earliest times. It found vivid expression in Plato's famous simile of the charioteer controlling the two fiery steeds corresponding respectively to the nobler and the baser passions. Under the influence of the associationists in the last century (or indeed of their modern equivalents, the more extreme behaviourists) the distinction tended to become badly blurred, only to reappear in recent years in two typically modern forms: as a quantitative ' factor ' of the mind, accounting for some of the differences between one individual and another; and as a vital element in the act of will revealed introspectively in various experimental studies of the processes of will and choice.

The classical research of Webb [1] brought to light a factor in virtue of which one individual would quite generally tend to be more consistent, conscientious, persevering, and principled than another, who was more likely to be carried away by transient whims, passions, or enthusiasms. As a result of a detailed analysis of his data, Webb did not hesitate to give this factor a moral interpretation. The factor corresponded, of course, not to the spontaneous play of generous or kindly impulse, but to the deliberate process of control. Indeed Webb called his factor 'w', to indicate its apparent close association with the will. After a time Webb's results began to be called into question, because they were based on *estimates* of character qualities, and although it was not doubted that the estimates were carefully made under exceptionally favourable circumstances by judges well acquainted with the persons concerned, psychologists were not at the time fully aware of certain subsequently discovered general tendencies which often make such estimates invalid. Later on, however, Webb's results received a remarkable corroboration by objective methods. In a most extensive and elaborate investigation called the Character Education Inquiry,[2] an ingenious series of actual life tests of various kinds of 'goodness' (such as truthfulness, conscientiousness, co-operativeness, spirit of service, perseverance, power of resisting temptation, honesty, generosity, self-sacrifice, and self-control) was devised and applied to large numbers of

[1] E. Webb, 'Character and Intelligence,' *Brit. J. Psych. Mon. Supp.*, No. 3, 1915.
[2] H. Hartshorne, M. May, J. B. Maller, *Studies in Service and Self-Control*, 1929.

American children. As a result there appeared once again a general factor of integration or consistency which seemed to play a part in every form of 'goodness'. True, there was here also at first some considerable dispute as to the way the findings should be interpreted, connected partly with the psychological presuppositions of the investigators and partly with questions of statistical method. Further consideration of the data,[1] however, has shown that these findings (which are free from the difficulties and sources of error inherent in estimates) agree very well with those of Webb. In the upshot we may say that the existence of something corresponding to the popular idea of 'conscience' has been demonstrated by the most precise methods at present available, that this controlling moral agency in the mind operates over a wide field of human activities, and that it tends to function more regularly and consistently in some individuals than in others. As minor results of this and comparable investigations may be mentioned two further facts: (1) A tendency to good conduct is apt to be more general in its application than a tendency to badness. Badness is seldom consistent; even the most dishonest children are honest sometimes, whereas goodness in its very nature appears to tend towards consistency—a matter which is probably of some importance in dealing with the 'difficult' and the delinquent. (2) Knowledge and intelligence have only an indirect relation to moral conduct. They are of course of immense help in the establishment and understanding of principles, which we have seen to be of great importance in the performance of duties, but it depends upon orectic factors whether they are directed to this end or not. A mere knowledge of what is considered right, or even mere intellectual acceptance of this generally acknowledged rightness, is not sufficient to guarantee good behaviour, though there is generally a low positive correlation between knowledge and intelligence on the one hand and moral conduct on the other—probably because knowledge and intelligence make it easier to foresee the full consequences of actions and to take the long view which shows that on the whole morality is justified by its results.[2] In general, however, moral precepts or principles have to appeal to the impulses or to the will before

---

[1] J. B. Maller, 'General and Specific Factors in Character,' *J. Soc. Psychol.*, (1934), 5, 97. See also C. Spearman, *Psychology Down the Ages* (1937), ii, ch. 42.
[2] A review of the whole literature bearing on this subject will be found in C. F. Chassell, 'The Relations between Morality and Intellect,' *Columbia Univ. Contributions to Education*, No. 607, 1935.

they become thoroughly effective, and research along the lines of 'factor analysis' throws little light on the way in which this appeal can successfully be made.   To study this, other methods must be used.

The work of McDougall probably contains the most consistent attempt to present a psychology of the moral life at all levels. Beginning at the simplest level with a doctrine of a limited number of relatively specific instincts, supplemented by a few general tendencies (such as play and imitation), he shows that some of these instincts and general tendencies may of themselves lead to behaviour in a moral sense—more particularly the tender or maternal instinct (which he often seems to regard as the font of all altruism).   The essential condition of developed morality, however, lies in the organization of the instinctive tendencies (and their correlative emotions) through their direction to particular objects in such a way as to form 'sentiments'.   The object of a sentiment tends to arouse different instinctive tendencies under different conditions.   Thus a mother will feel fear if her child is in danger, anger if it is threatened, joy when it prospers, and (passing to more complex states and 'compound emotions') gratitude to those who assist it, remorse if she herself has harmed it, and so on.   In the course of mental development the sentiments themselves are built into something like a hierarchy, and the interrelations within the hierarchy give order, consistency, and predictability to behaviour, over and above that afforded by instinct, habit, or isolated sentiments. This consistency may be further increased by the fact that one may develop sentiments, not merely for concrete objects or classes of objects, but for abstract ideals, like generosity, courage, or fair play.   Moreover, dominating in some ways the whole hierarchy, there is the 'sentiment of self-regard', a sentiment which has the self as object and which determines what kind of acts and wishes befit the self and are worthy of it (a concept to which we shall refer again in Chapter IV).

The stress that McDougall lays on the importance of organization and integration for moral conduct is thus in complete agreement with the results of such entirely independent investigations as those of Webb and the Character Education Inquiry.   But a well-knit organization of instinctive drives into a hierarchy of sentiments, though necessary, is not in itself sufficient for the attainment of a high moral character.   Such character depends on content as well as form; in other words, the objects, aims, and ideals which form the cognitive aspects of a sentiment must themselves be of a moral kind. A master sentiment of hatred, revenge, or self-aggrandizement, dominating a well-organized character, will only make a master criminal. Fortunately such persons are rare, though where they exist they can work incalculable havoc. But where the master sentiments are directed to great and noble ends (or as, with our British love of understatement, we should probably prefer to say, where these ends are sound and decent) we get the highest type of character. McDougall describes character of the finest type as 'that which is complex, strongly and harmoniously organized and directed towards the realization of higher goals and ideals'. Here the importance of both form and content is adequately recognized.

When we turn to the individual moral act, as distinct from the permanent organization that constitutes the moral character, we find ourselves in the domain of will. The characteristic moral act is the will act, and this, according to McDougall,[1] consists in just such a process of adoption by the self as we first encountered in the work of Frenkel and Weisskopf. For him the essential element of the process commonly called an act of will lies in the incorporation of an impulse or tendency within the system of the 'self-regarding sentiment'. In other words, we make the impulse or tendency our own, we endow it with the interest and value that we attach to the idea of the self as an object with which we are vitally concerned, and we put at its disposal the energy that is always ready to be mobilized on behalf of the self. This, he maintains, is the secret of that ability to tap some reserve of energy, which has always been recognized as a feature of the will.

McDougall's account was formulated in 1908, admittedly as a 'theory' of the will. But since that time it has received corroboration from a whole series of experimental researches in which Ach and Michotte were pioneers, but in which a number of British investigators working under the inspiration of Aveling produced the most extensive data.[2] In all these researches, in

[1] W. McDougall, *An Introduction to Social Psychology*, 1908, and numerous subsequent editions. See also McDougall's various later textbooks.

[2] N. Ach, *Über die Willenstätigkeit und das Denken*, 1905. *Über den Willensakt und das Temperament*, 1910. A. E. Michotte and E. Prüm, 'Étude Expérimentale sur le Choix Volontaire,' *Arch. de Psychol.* (1910), 10, 119.

For a short account of this work and further references, see F. Aveling, ' The Psychology of Conation and Volition,' *Brit. J. Psychol.* (1926), 16, 339. Also 'Emotion, Conation and Will,' in *Feelings and Emotions: The Wittenberg Symposium*, ed. by M. L. Reymert, 1928, and *Personality and Will*, 1931.

which the subjects (highly trained in introspective analysis) were asked to carry out a difficult task or to exercise a choice between two alternatives, it has consistently been found that there is a heightened awareness of the self and a deliberate adoption by the self of the imposed task or of the favoured alternative, and that this reference to, and reinforcement by, the self is the common and essential feature of the will process.   McDougall's theory was thus triumphantly vindicated.   As we shall see, this theory also fits in well, so far as it goes, with the conclusions derived from psycho-analytic sources.

Though the will act constitutes, from the psychological point of view, the climax and supreme achievement of the moral life, it has disadvantages which make a very frequent resort to it under ordinary circumstances a sign of weakness of organization rather than of strength.   In particular, involving as it does some degree of conflict, some process of deliberation (however short) and a calling up of reserves of energy, it makes great economic demands upon the mental life.   While it is occurring, consciousness is not free to deal with other matters.   For the general routine of life, even above the purely instinctive level, it is therefore desirable that resort should be made to other less expensive methods.   Two such methods are available: those involving the processes generally known to psychologists as habit, and as 'determining tendency' or 'mental set' respectively.

Habit is so well recognized a feature of our mental life, and has been the subject of such innumerable descriptions and discussions, alike from the layman, the moralist, and the psychologist, that practically nothing need be said about it here.   We need only emphasize, as others have done, the immense moral value of habits that are in harmony with our conscious moral aims and the moral handicap of habits that are incompatible with them.   From the strictly behaviourist point of view indeed nearly all psychotherapy, nearly all moral struggle and endeavour, have as their aim the breaking of bad habits and the substitution of desirable ones.[1]   But for the rest it will be sufficient to refer the reader to the inimitable little sermon on the subject contained in William James' *Principles of Psychology*.[2]

The 'determining tendency' or 'mental set'[3] is less well known, and it was a considerable achievement of experimental psy-

[1] See E. R. Guthrie, *The Psychology of Learning*, 1935.
[2] W. James, *Principles of Psychology* (1890), i, pp. 120 ff.
[3] H. J. Watt, 'Experimentelle Beiträge zu einer Theorie des Denkens,' *Archiv. f. d. ges. Psychol.* (1905), 4, 289.

chology to have drawn attention to an important mental process which had almost entirely escaped the notice of the armchair observers. Briefly it consists in the tendency of the mind to carry out a willed or intended act at some appropriate subsequent moment, usually on the occurrence of some predetermined cue, without the necessity of this act being present to consciousness in the interval. It is this ability to dispense with continuous conscious supervision which renders the process so economically valuable. In this respect, of course, it resembles habit, and indeed its relations to habit have not yet been studied with the thoroughness that they deserve. In some ways no doubt it might be regarded as the first stage in the formation of a habit, but it differs from a habit as ordinarily understood in that the element of repetition is not present, or is at any rate less important, whereas the element of intention is far more important. The effect of a determining tendency has often been compared with that of a post-hypnotic suggestion, in which the hypnotized person, in accordance with the suggestion given to him by the hypnotist, carries out an act at an appropriate cue some time after awaking from the hypnotic trance, but without recalling the fact that he has been given the suggestion. This is indeed perhaps merely an extreme case of the unconsciousness of the task or *Aufgabe* (to use the widely used technical term), that is to some extent generally characteristic of determining tendencies, though it is complicated by the influence exercised by the second person, the hypnotist, and by the induction during hypnosis of a specially suggestible state in the subject. In all essentials, however, the process is almost certainly the same, for unless the subject of the experiment accepts or adopts the suggestion (he usually does not do this in the case of what he regards as outrageous commands) the action does not take place.

There is no doubt that determining tendencies play an important part in our everyday life and that in the well-integrated moral character they, like habit, help very considerably in keeping conduct on lines which are approved by the ego, and this with a minimum expenditure of energy. We are constantly making intentions to do certain things or to go to certain places at predetermined times or on the occurrence of predetermined stimuli, and on the whole we succeed pretty well in carrying out our programmes without constantly reminding ourselves that we ought to do so. Lest the very frequency and familiarity of the process should make it difficult for the reader to realize its nature and significance, we may end this chapter by referring to a little experiment which many people have devised for themselves and which, once attempted, is apt to be repeated because of its considerable practical appeal. Suppose we are lying snugly in bed on a cold morning. It is time to get up, but we feel very disinclined to make the effort. Let us now decide that we will get up, not quite immediately, but when we have slowly counted twelve. The decision itself should be short and vigorous, but it is relatively easy in that it involves no immediate action of an unwelcome kind. Then in slow and even rhythm we count twelve, as arranged. It will usually be found that at the word 'twelve' we have risen automatically and without further exercise of will. The dread task has been accomplished without strain or effort—almost, it might seem, without our own complicity.

CHAPTER III

PSYCHO-ANALYSIS AND MORALS

As was indicated in the first chapter, much of our recent knowledge concerning the psychological aspects of morality comes from psycho-analysis. It is now time that we started to examine this psycho-analytic contribution. We find in particular that the psychologists of this school have in recent years had much to say about the factor of moral control which has just been occupying our attention.

From its very beginning, however, psycho-analysis had certain moral implications. It started as a psycho-therapeutic method, the aim of which was to make the unconscious conscious, to render the patient aware of certain thoughts, memories, emotions, and desires which had been, or had become, inaccessible to consciousness. It was found that this process of increasing the scope of the patient's awareness of the contents of his own mind had itself a therapeutic effect; it was as though the mere fact of the inaccessibility to consciousness of certain psychic contents was intimately connected with the occurrence of the mental troubles that had led the patient to the doctor. It was therefore inferred that the increase in awareness of the contents of one's own mind was (at any rate under certain circumstances and for certain purposes) desirable. As a thera-peutic method the procedure of psycho-analysis was thus the exact opposite of that according to which the patient is urged to put aside his troubles, is helped to forget them by the pro-vision of occupations or distractions, or is treated to suggestions (with or without hypnosis) to the effect that these troubles have no real existence and that he himself is feeling well and capable. The method also differs from those straightforward common-sense procedures in which the patient is told to pull himself together and to exercise his will (a procedure which of course also involves some degree of forgetting or pushing out of conscious-ness, and which relies too, as McDougall has emphasized, on an appeal to the self-regarding sentiment). Psycho-analysis shows rather (as has often been pointed out) a certain resemblance, on the one hand to the institution of confession, which bids the penitent review the immoral thoughts and actions of his past, and on the other hand to the various precepts and procedures which emphasize the advantage of fully expressing one's emotions —from Aristotle's theory of tragedy as a process of purging or catharsis through the intense arousal of pity and terror to such homely injunctions as 'Get it off your chest, man', or 'Have a good cry, dearie'.

In all this it is clear that there is a certain opposition also between the psycho-analytic method, with its attempt to face and express (at least in words) all aspects of our nature, and those other methods which adopt the attitude of 'Get thee behind me, Satan', which stress the supreme importance of moral control and which urge us to avoid all thoughts and temptations which might put this control in jeopardy. This contrast between the two methods of approach is enhanced by two further discoveries of psycho-analysis. In the first place it was found that the (apparently pathogenic) contents of the mind that were inaccessible to consciousness were often, either in themselves or through their associations, of an 'immoral' kind, in the sense that they did not accord with the recognized ethical standards of the individual; in particular they were often connected with sexual or aggressive thoughts and desires, of a kind which are not generally tolerated in our culture. In the second place there appeared to be some active (though to a large extent *unconscious*) force in the mind which was opposed to the entry of these thoughts and desires into consciousness. This force had to be overcome before they could be made conscious, and the psycho-analytic technique was indeed a procedure devised to make this possible. The presence of this 'resistance', as it came to be called, gave rise to the whole doctrine of 'repression' and 'conflict' which is so fundamental for all psycho-analytic theory. It seemed clear that, if the repressed contents were 'immoral', the repressing forces were themselves acting, as it were, on behalf of order or morality, and this view found expression in the term 'Censor', which was applied to the 'sum-total of the repressing forces'. Indeed, in the early writings of the school, the repressed tendencies were looked upon very much as though they were outlaws from the moral consciousness, as was indicated in the frequent use of phrases describing them as 'opposed to the patient's ethical principles' or 'out of harmony with his general personality'.

It is easy to see that under these circumstances psycho-analysis became exposed to the charge that it was itself an immoral practice. For did it not consist in an attempt to undo the work of the moral forces and to expose to view immoral tendencies of which it were better to remain ignorant? If these tendencies were recognized by the patient, and freely discussed in the consulting-room, it seemed that it only needed one further step for them to be given free rein in ordinary life —and what would happen to the patient, and ultimately to society, if such things were encouraged? Indeed, were not some psycho-analysts hinting that the conventional inhibitions imposed by our moral standard were more than human nature could comfortably bear? [1] And were not enthusiastic laymen, on the strength of all this, advocating the wholesale overthrow of restraint and discipline—in education, in the relations of the sexes, and in other spheres, so much so that parents were beginning to be afraid of exercising even the most elementary control over their children lest in so doing they became guilty of producing repressions or neurotic symptoms?

As against these charges, the psycho-analyst could reply (though in fact he seldom troubled to do so) that his only concern, as a medical psychologist, was to cure his patients, as a pure scientist, to understand the nature and causes of the psychological problems that confronted him; that he had only reported matters as he found them, that he had no subversive designs against existing moral conventions, and above all that

---

[1] E.g. Freud himself in '"Civilized" Sex Morality and Modern Nervousness,' *Collected Papers*, ii (1924), p. 76. Originally published in 1908.

his discoveries showed that in nervous and mental disease there was already a failure of satisfactory moral control, resulting in much unhappiness, inefficiency, and moral maladjustment, and that his endeavours as psychotherapist aimed at bringing about a new attitude to life which would make the patient into a more reasonable, helpful, and co-operative being. If, on the strength of his discoveries, a few over-enthusiastic—and for the most part ill-informed—supporters had jumped to the conclusion that all repression was bad, and that all conventions should be flouted, this was only an example of the hasty generalization that followed nearly every new advance in knowledge, and he, the psycho-analyst, was no more responsible than any other scientist for the misuse of his discoveries.

While such a line of defence was valid so far as it went, it did not really do justice to the basic fears of those who brought the accusations. Over and above any effects of excessive enthusiasm, misunderstanding, and misuse, psycho-analysis had in fact done something to undermine conventional morality; it had revealed a certain clumsiness and crudity in the operations of man's powers of moral control, and shown with a clarity that had never before been attained that conscience was a factor in the mind that was capable of doing harm as well as good. Neurosis, according to psycho-analytic findings, was due to conflict—conflict between repressed desires and a repressing (moral) force, a conflict which had resulted in a strange and unsatisfactory compromise that made the patient ill. This first discovery showed, of course, that the Censor as the guardian of morality was not always efficient; this much, however, had always been admitted by the moralists, whose efforts were indeed constantly directed towards strengthening man's supposedly all too feeble control over his impulses. The fact, however, that a greater improvement could sometimes be brought about by ventilating the repressed impulses than by attempting to strengthen the repressions strongly suggested that the Censor had in such cases overreached himself. Like a trainer who overstrains the team under his charge and thus leads to breakdowns rather than to the desired increase in fitness, the Censor seemed to have overestimated man's capacity for moral athleticism and to have produced neurosis rather than healthy moral vigour. The possibility—perhaps even the probability—of some such occurrence was indeed implied by the theory of catharsis and the practice of confession, but never before the advent of psycho-analysis had this possibility been made so plain. Moreover, as psycho-analytic knowledge advanced, the trouble caused by over-zealous repression became ever more painfully clear. It was found that a wide gulf often separated the moral standard of the (mostly unconscious) Censor from that of the conscious adult personality, as also from that of contemporary society. Indeed the Censor began to appear as in many respects a rigid, infantile, archaic institution, often lamentably out of touch with the realities of adult life; as in cases where, for instance, it would impede a patient in the exercise of his chosen profession because the work of this profession was unconsciously associated with some repressed childish interest, or where it would make a patient feel guilty about an otherwise suitable marriage because a superficial resemblance of the spouse to a near relative had evoked some echo of an incest taboo from the deeply buried and long-forgotten past. Furthermore the Censor would even fail to preserve the distinction, so important in the eyes of conscious morality and law, between harbouring a desire and giving it expression, so that a mere wish (and an unconscious one at that) would be treated in the same way as an act or a definite intention; as in a certain type of case in which the patient was made to suffer from irrational and guilt-laden anxiety about the health or well-being of a relative (e.g. a child or parent). In such cases it was found that the anxiety in question was connected with unconscious hostile desires against this relative, but that these desires had never been allowed to interfere with a dutiful and friendly attitude, so that the patient was punished for a sin that he had never committed and the possibility of which had not even entered his conscious thoughts.

In fact the difficulties with which the psycho-analyst had to deal in bringing about the cure and readjustment of his patient were, it became apparent, due as much to the stubborn, stupid opposition of unadaptable, repressive moral tendencies as to the clamorous exigency of crude unsocial instincts. In the neurosis some sort of compromise between the two contending forces had been reached, but a compromise pathological and unrealistic in its nature. In bringing the conflict to the surface, the psycho-analyst had not necessarily solved the moral or quasi-moral problems concerned, but he had taken a big step towards rendering a solution possible by bringing to bear upon the conflict the more delicate and discriminative powers of con-

sciousness and reason. The conflict was thus, as it were, handed
over from a lower level at which only crude methods could be
used to a higher level at which finer instruments for dealing
with it were available. The psycho-analyst as a rule refused to
take a hand in the solution at this higher level, e.g. he counselled
neither greater gratification of impulse nor greater submission
to the dictates of moral authority or prudence; contenting
himself with seeing that the field was as far as possible cleared
for the full unhampered operation of the conscious forces. He
refused in fact to give direct advice or admonition, differing in
this respect from most other psychotherapists and spiritual
advisers. Whether and how far he was justified in doing this,
how far his faith in the ability of unhindered consciousness to
deal with mental and moral problems was legitimate, is a matter
that is still discussed in many quarters. The psycho-analyst's
chief reason for stopping where he did was that, if he adopted
a moral rôle, he would from the very start be putting himself
on the side of the repressing forces, and thus rendering more
difficult the task of undoing the repressions and bringing the
unconscious material to light. He therefore limited his aim to
the full discovery of this material in all its ramifications—in
itself a novel, difficult, and, as it appeared to him, sufficient
task. He had ample justification for refusing to proceed further,
and thus could truthfully say that he was no partner to the
advocacy of the flouting of moral authorities or the breaking of
taboos.

But there remained the fact that he had unmasked the pretensions of conscience as the perfect guide, that he had exposed
the primitive crudity of the repressing forces and revealed them
as constituting a serious obstacle to the carrying out of his own
therapeutic task. It was natural that in its later stages psycho-
analysis should devote great attention to the nature and origin
of those forces which in earlier days it had been content to
subsume under the somewhat vague and all-embracing title of
the Censor. It is these later researches which have enabled
psycho-analysis to cast much further light upon the nature of
that factor of moral direction and control with which we were
concerned in the last chapter, and to which we now return.

The period of intensive psycho-analytic study of the moral
factor in man's psychology may be said to have begun with the
appearance of Freud's book *The Ego and the Id* [1] in 1923 (though

---

[1] *The Ego and the Id*, 1927. Originally published in 1923.

of course this work itself owes much to observations and impressions recorded here and there in his earlier writings and those of his followers). In this work Freud attempted a theoretical division of the mind into three main parts or aspects: the Id, which is the primary source of instinctive energy, the most primitive and fundamental aspect of the mind, which supplies the driving force for all our mental life; the Ego, that part which we recognize as most intimately ourselves, the part which is conscious (or mostly so), which interprets and co-ordinates the impressions from the outer world and from our own bodies that reach us through our sense organs, and which controls the voluntary movements that we execute through the agency of our striped muscles; and finally the Super-Ego, the source of our moral control and the part that immediately concerns us here. In what follows in this and the succeeding chapters we shall endeavour to give some account of the super-ego, based on Freud's own formulations in the above-mentioned book and other works, and those of other members of the psycho-analytic school, without concerning ourselves overmuch with details either of chronology or authorship, except in matters of special importance where they seem demanded for clarity of exposition or justice to individual workers in the field. It must, of course, throughout be borne in mind that the super-ego is in great measure an unconscious agency and that the processes that go to its formation (apart from taking place mostly at a very early age) are also to a large extent not of a kind to be directly accessible to introspection.

In its classical form four main elements or sources of the super-ego can be conveniently distinguished. As their relationships make it difficult to consider them in entire independence of one another, we shall first indicate the general nature of these four elements and then return in the following chapters to deal with them in greater detail.

(1) In an earlier paper [1] of great importance in the history of psycho-analytic thought Freud had modified his first and provisional antithesis between libido or the sexual impulse on the one hand (it will be remembered that Freud used this concept in an exceptionally wide sense) and the vaguely conceived ego impulses upon the other. The modification consisted in asserting that not all of the libido was connected

---

[1] 'On Narcissism: An Introduction,' *Collected Papers,* iv (1925)   Originally published in 1914.

with primitive bodily satisfactions or directed on to outer objects, but that some portion of it was, or in the process of development came to be, directed to the self (conceived as an enduring bodily and mental whole). Thus, he maintained, we love ourselves in the same way that we love outer objects, and the portion of the libido so directed to ourselves could be conveniently referred to as the narcissistic libido. In the course of further development this portion of the libido itself undergoes differentiation. A part remains directed to ourselves as we really are, or at least as we conceive ourselves to be, the 'real self'. But this 'real self' does not permanently satisfy our narcissism; as we develop, we become all too painfully aware of its defects and limitations, physical, mental, and moral; and we compensate by building up in imagination a sort of ideal self, which we would like to attain. This is the Ego-Ideal and to this another portion of our narcissistic libido (the so-called 'secondary narcissism') in turn becomes directed. It is as though we refused to stay contented with our real self as a love object, once its deficiencies become apparent, and set out to construct a better and more worthy object, but one that still has some recognizable resemblance to the self. This process of direction of the narcissistic libido to the ego-ideal is the first source from which the super-ego is derived.

(2) The second source is from the process of 'introjection' or incorporation into one's own mind of the precepts and moral attitudes of others, particularly of one's parents or of other persons *in loco parentis* in one's youth. As a result of this process, the attitudes of impressive persons in one's early environment (and to some extent throughout life) become a permanent part of one's own mental structure, become 'second nature', as the popular expression has it. Through this process, too, moral standards and conventions become handed on from one generation to another, thus giving permanence and stability to the codes and traditions of society.

(3) The super-ego is, as we have already noted, no direct copy of the moral standards of the community—in particular, it is apt to be in many respects more severe. This greater severity, in virtue of which the super-ego often seems to behave aggressively and cruelly towards the ego, is traceable to various causes. But in particular it is due to a *recoil against the self of aggression aroused by frustrating objects in the outer world*. The wishes of the young child are frequently and inevitably frustrated

—and frustration of our desires, as all psychologists agree, tends naturally to arouse anger and aggression (the biological purpose of which is no doubt to overcome or remove the obstacles to our desire). But in the young child aggression is very likely to be unsuccessful: first because he is too weak, and secondly because (as he learns a little later) the very persons against whom his aggression is aroused, his parents or others who are tending him, are also persons whom he loves and on whom he is dependent. If he expresses his aggression too freely they punish him, and withdraw their help, love, and approval. Indeed it is man's unique and inevitable tragedy (due to his long period of helpless infancy) that he is compelled to hate those whom also he most loves—a condition which is to some extent continued throughout life in his relations with his own super-ego, which is a centre to which both love and hate are directed and from which both love and hate emanate. But this will become clearer as we proceed. For the moment we are only concerned with the young child who cannot express his aggression towards its natural objects, the frustrating parents. What is he to do with it? He cannot bang the door, kick the cat, behave rudely to some third person, or use any of the other numerous methods of discharge which will be available to him in later life. But he always has himself as a possible object for his anger; and it was one of the remarkable discoveries of psycho-analysis that, among the various lines of displacement along which an impulse can be re-directed, turning inwards or turning against the self occupies an important place. This is what appears to happen in the present case.[1] But the precise form in which the turning against the self here occurs (i.e. that it adds to the forces of the super-ego) is probably determined to a large extent by the occurrence, at or about the same period, of the process of introjection to which we have just referred. The outside, forbidding, commanding persons (the parents) are introjected, i.e. are incorporated in the self in the form of the super-ego, and at the same time the child's aggression against these very persons is also turned against the self. Under these circumstances it seems as though the two processes tend to fuse, with the result that the inward recoiling aggression also becomes attached to the super-ego. The super-ego, which represents the internalized, forbidding parents, is already endowed with the aggression naturally attributed to

[1] For examples of this see Chapter VII.

them as frustrating agents. It is now reinforced by the child's own aggression; and in this way (among others) it becomes more stern, cruel, and aggressive than the actual parents.

(4) The fourth source or element is more uncertain and controversial than the other three. The fierce aggressiveness with which the super-ego can behave to the ego naturally suggests the co-operation of another fundamental human tendency—the tendency to take pleasure in the exercise of mastery and in the infliction of pain for their own sake, over and above such domination and cruelty as may be the inevitable accompaniments of aggression. The true nature of this sado-masochistic tendency, as it is generally called, presents a sinister puzzle to psychologists. In many of its manifestations it has an unmistakably sexual colouring. Indeed, sadism and masochism are among the best recognized and most important sexual 'perversions'; and Freud, in his conception of the libido as made up of a number of originally more or less independent 'component instincts', gave both sadism and masochism a place among these instincts. It was clear, however, that in some respects they presented special problems and were different from most of the other component instincts: first in that they had no particular connection with any organ or part of the body, such as the mouth, the anus, the nose, the eye, the genitals [1]; and secondly in the altogether peculiar way in which they combined the usually distinct and contradictory attitudes to pleasure and pain. Later, when Freud divided the funda-mental human drives into two classes, Eros and Thanatos, the life and death instincts respectively, he supposed that sadism and masochism arose from fusions of these two. McDougall had likewise sought to explain their compound nature as fusions, of sex and self-assertion in the case of sadism, of sex and sub-mission in the case of masochism.

But, however they are constituted, there can be no doubt that, in the infliction of external punishment, sadism and, perhaps to a lesser extent, masochism play a part. It is pretty freely admitted that—before the introduction of 'modern', 'enlightened', or 'humanitarian' methods—the profession of teacher (as to some extent all rôles of authority) presented considerable opportunities for sadistic punishment, while there

---

[1] The former suggestion of a special association with anal erotism is now seldom stressed, at least equally frequent references to oral sadism being found in psycho-analytic literature; and in general it would seem that sadism and masochism can be associated with any other of the component instincts.

is also good evidence that the pupil sometimes experienced a sexually tinged pleasure while being punished. But punishment is (or at least professes to be) itself a moral institution; and it is exercised by just such impressive authoritarian figures—often indeed standing more or less officially *in loco parentis*—as those whose precepts and attitudes we introject to form our super-ego. It would not be altogether surprising then if the sadism of these authorities and the sado-masochistic relation in which we stand to them in our external life were mirrored in the relation between the super-ego and the ego in our internal life; and the element of cruelty so often actually found in the super-ego seems to support the view that the sadism of moral authorities is liable to be introjected along with other characteristic attitudes. As we shall see later, punishment as a social or educational institution also finds an echo in the purely psychological sphere; and Freud went so far as to speak of the 'need for punishment' sometimes experienced by the ego. The super-ego, indeed, often takes over not only the admonishing, prohibiting, and commanding functions, but also the punishing functions of the external authority. To the sadism of the super-ego there would then correspond a masochism of the ego—the rôles being distributed between different aspects or (as Freud is fond of saying) 'institutions' of the mind, instead of between different persons, as in the external world.

It is pretty clear that in many cases this approximates to a true description: the person concerned does seem to inflict suffering on himself and to enjoy both the process of infliction and the actual suffering. (Perhaps we can get a clearer idea of this situation if we imagine ourselves suffering from some pimple, boil, or other sore spot on our body and constantly touching this spot, although we know that it will hurt; in these circumstances we sometimes seem to relish both the process of inflicting pain—the touching, and the pain itself.) But difficulties of interpretation are apt to arise in those numerous cases when this fact of enjoyment is very hard to demonstrate. In so far as enjoyment in general, and sexually tinged enjoyment in particular, are lacking, the boundary between sado-masochism and simple aggression (our third factor) becomes obscured. With these cases in mind, Freud [1] was driven to distinguish a 'moral masochism' from the definitely sexual variety that he had in view when he classified masochism as a 'component

---

[1] 'The Economic Problem of Masochism,' *Collected Papers*, ii (1924), p. 255.

instinct'. Such 'moral masochism' appears to have been shorn of its erotic elements, and indeed is perhaps only a manifestation of Thanatos, the death instinct—or as others, suspicious of such somewhat mystic notions, might prefer to think, is just plain aggression turned against the self.

It was in view of these difficulties, and of the fact that comparatively little progress has been made in our understanding of the sado-masochistic components of the super-ego, that we were induced to say that this fourth element is more uncertain and controversial than the others. Nevertheless, the rôle of sado-masochism in external morality is often so plain, the correspondence between the external and the internal rôles of punishment often so close, and the relation of sado-masochism to general aggression so far from clear, that it would be rash to deny to sado-masochistic tendencies a significant part in the nature and function of the super-ego.

CHAPTER IV

ORIGIN AND FUNCTION OF THE EGO-IDEAL

We must now pursue the theme of the super-ego in somewhat greater detail and wider application.

McDougall's and Baldwin's Contributions

The first two of the four factors mentioned in the last chapter have been well recognized by psychologists and moralists other than those who belong to, or have been considerably affected by, the psycho-analytic school; indeed psycho-analysts have here only consolidated and developed (albeit extensively) positions, as regards the general nature of which there may be said to have existed little dispute. We will, however, confine ourselves to mentioning two authors: W. McDougall, probably that one of modern psychologists who has made the most thoroughgoing attempt to build up a consistent theory of the nature and development of character, and to whose work in connection with our main theme we have already had occasion to refer; and J. M. Baldwin, whose agreement with psycho-analytic doctrines is in some ways even more striking, especially when we bear in mind the fact that his views were given to the world at a time when psycho-analysis was in its earliest infancy.

McDougall's 'sentiment of self-regard' obviously has a very close relation both to the facts ordinarily brought under the heading of 'conscience' and to Freud's doctrine of the super-ego or ego-ideal. This sentiment, as described by McDougall, constitutes a standard or guiding light by which the individual regulates, or at least passes judgment on, his own conduct. If it is absent, or poorly developed, he is not only (as we have seen) incapable, according to McDougall, of an act of will, but lacks the essential corner-stone of moral character, and either falls unduly under the influence of some other sentiment which should properly itself be regulated by the master sentiment of self-regard, or is likely to be tossed about by temporary or conflicting impulses like a ship without a rudder. If it is present but still not in sufficient strength to ensure appropriate conduct in any given case, the individual is liable subsequently, or even at the time of acting, to feel that moral discomfort and dissatisfaction with himself which we term the pangs of conscience.

This sentiment of self-regard is, as McDougall makes clear, a development of the person's realization of the existence and permanence of his own ego. As a child the individual builds up this notion of the ego as differentiated from the other, shifting, objects of his environment. Among such objects, those whom he comes to regard as other *persons* acquire a special interest; and of outstanding importance in the behaviour of these other persons are the kinds of conduct that express approval or disapproval, praise or blame—since these attitudes have such an intimate bearing upon his own weal or woe. In order to win praise and escape blame he must learn to anticipate these moral attitudes of others; and this process of anticipation involves the building up of a standard of behaviour that corresponds to the standards of those about him. It is this standard that gradually gives content to his ideal of self and thus determines the nature of his self-regarding sentiment. At first, of course, the adults in the child's own immediate environment play the chief rôles in this respect, but as he becomes acquainted with literature, history, and art his range and choice of models are vastly increased. Eventually, however, his ideals become to a large extent independent of particular personalities and reflect in greater or less degree the traditional code of the society in which he lives.

McDougall thus recognizes both the existence and great moral influence of the ideal self, together with the fact that it is acquired from models in the environment. He would agree with Freud that people can wholeheartedly approve of themselves only in so far as they live up to the standards incorporated in their self-regarding sentiments—though he would invoke here his twin emotions of positive and negative self-feeling where Freud has recourse to his doctrine of narcissism. He would agree, too, that the content of the ideal is acquired by what Freud would call a process of introjection—of incorporation in the self of qualities (in this case the moral attitudes) of the environment. He also makes it pretty clear that he would in the main agree with certain psycho-analytic writers who have stressed the point that the anticipation of approval or disapproval from the persons around us is only a special case of the process by which we learn generally to secure pleasant stimuli and avoid unpleasant or harmful influences from the outer world. As Alexander has emphasized,[1] the super-ego appears to have become differentiated in order to deal (by anticipation) with the dangers of the social environment, while the ego is chiefly concerned with protection from the dangers and difficulties presented by the physical environment. In ultimate analysis, however, we learn to avoid the displeasure of our fellow human beings in virtue of the same fundamental tendency to self-preservation which teaches the child to avoid an open flame or any other threat to bodily integrity.

Where McDougall differs from Freud, and still more from certain other psycho-analysts, would seem to lie chiefly in four points: (1) the self-regarding sentiment is not brought into relation with the operation of unconscious tendencies, as is the case with the super-ego; (2) less stress is laid upon the importance of early childhood experiences; (3) no attention is drawn to the existence of aggressive elements in the super-ego, such as those which play such an important part in psycho-analytic formulations; (4) the self-regarding sentiment seems to be looked upon as almost or entirely beneficent in its operation, whereas, as we have seen, this is far from being the case with the Freudian super-ego. These points are of course closely interconnected. The very considerable advance that psycho-analysis would seem to have made from the position attained

---

[1] Franz Alexander, 'The Need for Punishment and the Death Instinct,' *Int. J. Psa.* (1929), 10, 256.

by McDougall lies largely in its detailed discoveries under all four heads, and in its success in knitting them together in a way that at least bears some resemblance to a consistent theory.

Baldwin,[1] like McDougall, starts from the child's gradual recognition of those permanent entities in the outer world that we come to call 'persons'. Such entities, which at first perhaps exhibit a bewildering capriciousness in contrast to the mechanical regularity of 'things', themselves appear gradually to acquire a certain orderliness and predictability corresponding to the personality or permanent characteristics of the individual concerned. This achievement on the part of the child in creating order out of chaos as regards a most important part of his experience corresponds to what Baldwin terms the 'projective stage', each distinguishable person being a 'project'. The child later realizes the existence of his own self as a 'project' among others, but one that has unique features—the feelings, sensations, and efforts (pleasant and unpleasant) associated with his own organism. This is the 'subjective' stage, itself to be followed by a third or 'ejective' stage, in which the child's 'subject-sense' goes out by a sort of 'return dialectic' to illumine other persons.[2] 'The "project" of the earlier period is now lighted up, claimed, clothed on with the raiment of selfhood by analogy with the subjective.' Thereafter there occurs a give-and-take between the individual and his fellows which, Baldwin suggests, may be called the 'dialectic of personal growth'.[3] In the course of this the self is largely affected by persons in the outer world by way of imitation. But the copies that the child imitates set certain limits to the freedom of his action and demand obedience to certain norms of conduct. These limitations and norms the child transfers gradually to himself so that there grows up within his own personality a sort of 'copy-for-imitation', which is different from all other aspects of his mind, different, that is, alike from his own personal and selfish desires,

---

[1] J. M. Baldwin, *Social and Ethical Interpretations of Mental Development*, 1st ed., 1897.

[2] Baldwin's 'ejection' would appear to correspond to what in psycho-analysis is termed 'projection'—the attribution to others of one's own qualities; though some psycho-analysts (e.g. S. H. Fuchs, 'On Introjection,' *Int. J. Psa.* (1937), 18, 269) have suggested that it would be desirable to distinguish two stages of projection, which would then in some respects correspond to Baldwin's 'projection' and 'ejection' respectively.

[3] In the third edition of his *Social and Ethical Interpretations of Mental Development* (1902), p. 15, Baldwin claims that this view of the development of the notions of self and others is in essential respects shared by Royce, Stout, Mezes, Ormond, and Avenarius.

from his own mere habits, and even from his dawning capacity for sympathy and altruism.

This is the beginning of conscience, which, as with both McDougall and Freud, is something within the self that demands obedience to its claims and at the same time something the nature of which is determined by social and moral influences from outside. At first this 'dominating other self, this new *alter*', is something for which the child has little understanding, something that is still relatively extraneous to the self of habit and impulse, and still to a large extent dependent on, or copied from, concrete external individuals such as the parents. As development proceeds, however (and this incidentally is to a large extent true of the race as well as of the individual), it becomes at once more intimately a part of the self,[1] more insightfully understood and realized, and increasingly freed from the influence and capriciousness of particular individuals, until in the end it takes on the nature of a general law—a law which applies to others as well as the self. 'Taking up the sense of morality therefore—the sense that we mean when we use the word "ought"—we now have it. Let the child act by the rule of either of his former partial selves—the private habitual self or the accommodating capricious self of impulse or sympathy—and this new ideal of a self, a self that fulfils law, comes up to call him to account. My father, says the child, knows and would say "what" and "how"; and later when the father-self has proved not to know all "whats" and "hows", then my teacher, my book, my inspired writer, my God, knows "what" and "how" still. In so far as I have learned from him, I also know; and this I expect you, my brother, my friend, my *alter*, to know too, for our common life together. And this sense of my self of conformity to what he teaches and would have me do—this is, once for all, my conscience.'[2]

In this statement Baldwin, writing as early as 1897, clearly anticipates many of the psycho-analytic contributions to the psychology of conscience. We may note in particular the

[1] We may note here the agreement with Frenkel's and Weisskopf's results with which we dealt in Chapter II.

[2] *Op. cit.*, p. 56. It is perhaps worth while to compare this with Freud's preliminary statement of the super-ego: 'Now that we have embarked upon the analysis of the ego we can give an answer to all those whose moral sense has been shocked and who have complained that there must surely be a higher nature in man. "Very true", we can say, "and here we have that higher nature, in this ego-ideal or super-ego, the representative of our relation to our parents. When we were little children we knew these higher natures, we admired them and feared them; and later we took them into ourselves,"' *The Ego and the Id.*, p. 47.

following resemblances between the two accounts: (1) the formation early in life of a guiding ideal in the light of which the individual judges his own conduct and which causes him dissatisfaction when he fails to live up to it; (2) the process by which this ideal is formed is of the kind which Freud would call the 'introjection' of external models; (3) among the most important of these models in the early days are the parents, but in later years other persons, teachers and superiors of all kinds, and ultimately God, may come to exercise an important influence; (4) this substitution of later (perhaps superhuman) models for the parents may reflect a growing disappointment in the parents, as these latter inevitably shed the glamour of omnipotence and omniscience with which at first they tend to be invested—a fact which, as psycho-analysts have pointed out, may play a very significant part in the development of religion and in the formation of certain myths (we shall encounter this again when we ourselves come to deal with religion); (5) the projection of the demands of conscience on to others, who may be judged by the same moral standards that we apply to ourselves (with this also we shall have occasion to deal later); (6) that subtle psychological process of give-and-take between the qualities of the self and those of others, which Baldwin calls the 'dialectic of personal growth', exhibits an unmistakable resemblance to a very important aspect of the development of the super-ego that has been much stressed recently by Melanie Klein and other child analysts, i.e. that this development, especially in the very early years, proceeds by a series of introjections and projections—in virtue of which real or imagined aspects of other persons are incorporated in the super-ego, only to be projected back on to these (or other) persons with significant modifications acquired *en route*—a process that may be repeated many times. (To this important matter we shall also have to return.)

Baldwin lays greater stress on the divergent moral standards or attitudes of various adult models than is usually found in Freud or other psycho-analytic writers, and indeed it may well be that, especially as regards the later years of life, psycho-analysts have often paid too little attention to this matter, to which Baldwin is inclined to attribute the fact that conscience ultimately tends to become independent of all concrete models and to find embodiment in the form of abstract rule or law. On the other hand he, like McDougall, fails to appreciate the unconscious and aggressive aspects of the super-ego, which once again we realize therefore to be specially significant contributions from the side of psycho-analysis. Nevertheless it is hoped that this brief consideration of the positions adopted by McDougall and Baldwin will have proved worth while, as indicating that the psycho-analytic views concerning the nature of the super-ego represent in some respects only developments and extensions of what acute students of the mind had already taught, and that they are to that extent less alarming and revolutionary than has sometimes been supposed.

The Ego Ideal

Let us now for the remainder of this chapter confine ourselves (as far as may be possible) to a consideration of the first of the four factors mentioned (in the last chapter) as operative in the super-ego—the existence of an ideal to which our self-love is to some extent directed and with the attainment of which our self-respect and self-approbation are bound up. It has sometimes been complained that, after the first formulation concerning the 'ego-ideal' in his article on *Narcissism*, Freud failed to follow up this aspect of the subject and devoted his attention too exclusively to the introjective and aggressive factors of the super-ego which began to impress themselves so forcibly upon him as his work proceeded. There is indeed some justice in this complaint, though—since even the greatest and most indefatigable of pioneers cannot himself explore fully all the fresh avenues he opens up—we shall surely be very ready to forgive Freud for his apparent loss of interest in this direction, in view of the more novel and startling discoveries he went on to make as regards the other constituents of the super-ego. So absorbing did these new, hitherto for the most part unsuspected, aggressive, elements of the super-ego become that for well over a decade they provided a too exclusive preoccupation, not only to Freud himself but to other members of his school, and it is only in recent years that attention has begun to return to that narcissistic factor which was actually the first to be noticed. Even so, a good many of the contributions to this sphere come from writers who are not actually members of the psycho-analytic school.

Among these writers an important place is occupied by Adler [1]

[1] Alfred Adler, *Study of Organ Inferiority and its Psychical Compensation*, 1917 (first published in 1907); *The Neurotic Constitution*, 1917 (first published in 1912); and many later works.

(whose whole psychology centred round the ego, much as Freud's had, in the earlier years of psycho-analysis, centred around sex). He also enjoys a very definite priority in time, the influence of an ideal development and character being implicit in his writings almost from the start. Indeed it may be claimed for him that, although in general a follower of Freud prior to his secession from the psycho-analytic school in 1912, in this particular matter he was in some respects in advance of Freud, since his own earliest formulations precede Freud's *Narcissism* article of 1914. In all his characteristic works he drew eloquent attention to the way in which our wounded self-esteem is apt to arouse in us a sense of injury and outrage at the limitations of our powers and the frustrations and humiliations that our environment inflicts on us. The most fundamental human urge, according to Adler, is something akin to the 'will to power' of Nietzsche, which bids us to arise, achieve, conquer, dominate, and generally to assert ourselves and prove our superiority. Since it soon becomes all too painfully manifest to us (especially in the impotent years of childhood) that in many respects we are not superior but inferior to others, we erect a 'guiding fiction', an ideal corresponding to that which we are not but which we would like to be. This 'guiding fiction' corresponds in some important ways to Freud's 'ego-ideal'. Nevertheless — apart from the rather far-reaching general divergence of outlook that distinguishes Freudian psycho-analysis from Adler's 'individual psychology'—there are at least two very significant particular differences. In the first place the ego-ideal was to Freud, as we have seen, primarily a moral factor, in virtue of which the individual adopts and makes his own the moral standards of his environment; to Adler, however, it is an outcome of our primary and fundamental egoism, of our selfish need to dominate and be superior. To Adler the psychological source of morality is to be sought rather in the complementary urge of 'social interest'—an urge to which in his later works he attributes great importance but to which he has actually in the course of his researches devoted less attention than to the individualistic will to power,[1] with the result that his contributions to the detailed psychology of moral motivation are not outstanding as are those of Freud. In the second

[1] It may perhaps be said that Adler's treatment of 'social interest' is in this respect somewhat analogous to the treatment accorded to the ego-instincts in the earlier work of Freud.

place Adler's 'guiding fiction' is thought of as itself determined to a large extent by an effort to compensate for inferiority—in the same way that the individual's whole urge to achieve superiority is, according to Adler, constantly strengthened by the realization, or the fear, of inferiority. This emphasis on compensation is indeed another of the most important features of Adler's system, and in the detailed treatment of the various ways in which compensation may be attempted are to be found some of the most valuable additions to psychological knowledge that we owe to him. In some cases (and it is these which are of most importance to us in the present connection) it is found that the guiding fiction may be one which is sufficiently realistic to constitute a real spur to achievement; either by directly overcoming weakness or inferiority (as in the attainment through assiduous exercise of exceptional muscular strength in the case of a man of naturally feeble physique), or by indirectly compensating for it in some other direction (as with one who stakes all on the cultivation of 'brain', in the lack of natural gifts of 'brawn' or beauty). In other cases, however, the guiding fiction may be too unrealistic to constitute an incentive to real endeavour; and the person takes refuge in phantasies, in an attempt to regain in this way his sense of worth. Indeed the various forms of neurosis (which of course often bring a secondary or indirect 'real' gain—though usually of an 'escapist' kind) may from this point of view be regarded as the outcome of such attempts to preserve the patient from the full consequences of his real or supposed inferiority. Far less importance is attributed to compensation and inferiority in the psycho-analysts' accounts of the super-ego. Feelings of inferiority, they admit, are genuine and frequent; but, according to their view, play a lesser rôle in the determination of moral goals, attitudes, and conduct. Such feelings are indeed, most psycho-analysts hold, more likely to be the consequence than the cause of moral ideals, since failure to achieve the goals set by the ideal almost inevitably brings in its train a sense of guilt and unworthiness unless such failure is adequately explained away or camouflaged. Regarding the super-ego as a whole, the psycho-analytic position seems (at least to the present author) to be undoubtedly the more correct, taking into account the full evidence at present available; nevertheless there can be little doubt that Adler's contribution to the particular factor of the super-ego that we are here considering is a very real one.

Among more recent authors who have stressed the importance
of ideals in the sense with which we are at the moment concerned
we may mention Karen Horney [1] and Jennings White.[2]   White
(to whose work we have already drawn attention in Chapter I)
illustrates the great variety and contrasting nature of the 'goals
of life' that may be chosen, as well as the very various and
sometimes devious routes along which an individual may come
to make a given choice—a choice that is often thrust upon him
and which is not necessarily in harmony with his natural
capacities and aspirations.   Both White and Horney also attach
much importance to the influence of parents in determining
these goals, to which—however little real enthusiasm they
arouse—a child must at least pretend to live up, at first in the
eyes of his parents and later in his own eyes as well.   Horney
in particular stresses the necessity for keeping up (moral or
cultural) appearances.   In her criticism of the Freudian doctrine
of the super-ego she suggests that this factor in the mind can
more properly be described as a need than as an agency—and
that the need in question is often a relatively superficial one
which the individual may be glad to cast off as a burden, if only
he feels safe in doing so.   What Freud describes as fear of a
punishing super-ego she would be inclined to interpret as little
more than a fear of being unmasked.   Part of the self revolts
against the necessity of maintaining a façade, and this may be
the source of the sadistic, hostile feelings which according to
Freud have their origin in the super-ego itself.   Horney here
would seem to underestimate the strength of the evidence which
points to an intimate fusion of at least a certain kind and
amount of aggression with the super-ego (our third and fourth
factors in the last chapter).   She is doubtless right, however,
in stressing the constant tendency of a part of the ego to cast
aside the burden of an ideal which is no more than an elaborate
moral bluff.   William James [3] drew attention long ago to the
relief that we experience on giving up pretensions (e.g. the
pretension of a musical self by those who are essentially un-
musical, 'so that they can then without shame let people hear
them call a symphony a nuisance', or the ideal of a fashionably
slim figure by those whose bodies are naturally built on somewhat generous lines).

[1] Karen Horney, *New Ways in Psycho-analysis* (1939), especially ch. 13.
[2] H. D. Jennings White, *op. cit.*
[3] William James, *Principles of Psychology* (1890), i, 311.

What Horney says about the existence of a façade does no doubt often apply very aptly to certain of the superficial levels of the 'ideal' aspects of·the super-ego that we are here considering, but surely fails as an adequate description of the super-ego as a whole; both because she neglects to take account of the degree to which the demands of the super-ego have become an intimate part of ourselves (which makes them much harder to reject than if they were merely imposed upon us from outside), and (here once again, as with the other writers we have mentioned) because she underestimates the elements of aggression associated with super-ego functions which psycho-analysis has brought to light.

Her views, however, may serve conveniently to draw attention to an important point raised by several psycho-analytic writers (though here, too, they have been to some extent anticipated by James), i.e. that much depends on what might be termed the distance between the real self and the ego-ideal. If there is an immense gulf between the ideal and the reality, we shall inevitably feel dissatisfied, guilty, and inferior—but, be it noted, the inferiority is in this case due to the superiority at which we aim. Many people blame themselves for mediocre achievements, when they would not dream of blaming others who achieve no more. These others, they assume, are but ordinary people, of whom not much can be expected. But they find it hard to realize that their own sacred egos are made of ordinary stuff; of themselves they feel that more can rightly be demanded, and if that more is not forthcoming they can, as they think, justifiably upbraid themselves for shortcomings which in others would hardly cause surprise or disapproval. Here we see a vindication of Adler's contention as to the widespread desire for superiority, and at the same time a justification of Freud's theory of 'secondary narcissism', attaching not to the real self but to the ideal one. There is little doubt that a vast amount of psychogenic misery is caused by this setting of too high a standard for one's own self, and the fact that the great majority of those who suffer in this way have never called in question, or indeed explicitly recognized, that they expect more from themselves than they do from others shows both the extent of their primitive narcissism and the degree to which this narcissism has been displaced from the real ego to the ego-ideal. The predominance of shame over satisfaction in their attitude to themselves and their achievements serves as an efficient camouflage of this

D

narcissistic element, so that it is hard to make them realize that they must reduce their aspirations and pretensions if they would enjoy the contentment and complacency which they may envy or admire in others, that they must in short be humbler if they would be happier. Psycho-analysts are in agreement that the successful treatment of practically every case of neurosis involves not only a sacrifice on the part of unrealistic 'id' demands, but a reduction in the often no less unrealistic and unreasonable aspirations and requirements of the super-ego. Here again we meet what might possibly appear as an 'immoral' tendency of psycho-analysis. But once again we must remember also that the setting of too high a goal, either of personal achievement or of moral purity, results not in increased efficiency or higher worth but in unnecessary discontent without compensating helpfulness to others—too often indeed with annoyance and embarrassment to others.

Ideals may of course be too low as well as too exalted. Especially in the absence of strong external incentives (such as the need to satisfy an ambitious parent, to earn a living, or to acquire the wherewithal to marry) those less endowed with emulation or the desire to make a good showing to their fellows may easily become satisfied with achievements that are well below their powers. Some individuals may become like Peter Pan and shirk the toils and responsibilities of adult life—perhaps piloted in this direction by parents who are unwilling that their children should grow up. Others, as Adler has pointed out, may rationalize their lack of endeavour by exaggerating the importance of some obstacle to their advance or some disadvantage under which they suffer (such as poverty, ill health, or lack of opportunity). Still others may appear to be just too lazy or too easily contented to form high ideals. But in this connection it is well to remember that fundamentally there are two ways of diminishing the unhappiness caused by unfulfilled desire—either by making such efforts as may be necessary to bring about a greater measure of fulfilment, or else by reducing our desires so that we are satisfied with less. Although the former course is the one which is characteristic of our present Western culture, there have not been wanting thinkers of eminence in many parts of the world who have taught that wisdom lies rather in the latter. Psychopathology has shown, too, that there may be an obsessive element in our modern urge to be always up and doing and improving. We must avoid, therefore, passing too harsh a judgment on those who do not seem to share this urge. Nevertheless, our present culture being what it is, we may with some reason be a little curious and indeed suspicious of individuals who depart too widely from the norm in this direction, and psycho-analysis has taught us to be chary of simple explanations in terms of mere lack of ambition or of driving power; conditions, it would seem, are often more complicated, involving not mere deficiency of energy but rather an inhibition or displacement of it—and with some of these conditions we shall later have to deal. For the moment we need only note that in our present civilization, with the value it attaches to progress and achievement, ideals that are pitched too far below capacities do not in the majority of cases bring contentment, but rather, in the long run, boredom or dissatisfaction. It is therefore the task of mental hygiene to discover the optimum ideal that is neither too far above nor too far below the level of capacity. With regard to limited specific tasks it has been possible to make the determination of this optimum a matter for experimental study.[1] It has been found not only that there are great individual differences in the 'level of aspiration', but that this level is sometimes very disproportionate (in either direction) to the individual's ability, and that different people react very differently to success or failure. Furthermore a hopelessly high or a needlessly low goal of endeavour tends to reduce both interest and achievement. It has also been found that a succession of intermediate goals, each of which is slightly more ambitious than the preceding one, but each of which we can hope to achieve soon after it comes into operation, is more effective than a single distant higher goal that can be achieved only in a relatively remote future and after long endeavour. It may well be that the lessons learnt from such researches on simple and circumscribed tasks are to some extent applicable to the wider field of ethical, professional, and social aspiration. In so far as this is the case, we may hope in time to develop an experimental science of the 'goals of life'.

[1] Vide e.g. C. A. Mace, 'Incentives: Some Experimental Studies,' *Industrial Health Research Board : Report No. 72*, 1935; F. Hoppe, 'Erfolg und Misserfolg,' *Psychologische Forschung* (1930), 14, 1; J. D. Frank, 'Some Psychological Determinants of the Level of Aspiration,' *Amer. J. Psychol.* (1935), 47, 285; H. A. Murray, *Explorations in Personality* (1938), pp. 461 ff.; R. Gould, 'An Experimental Analysis of "Levels of Aspiration,"' *Genetic Psych. Mon.* (1939), No. 21.

CHAPTER V

SOCIAL APPROVAL AND THE EGO-IDEAL

AT the conclusion of the previous chapter we were considering the ego-ideal as an autonomous and purely endopsychic structure, more or less independent of the outer world. Since such independence is at best only relative, it is time that we corrected our picture by bringing the individual once again into closer relation with his environment, from the moral influence of which he can, of course, never be entirely free. Throughout life the interaction between a person's real ego and his ego-ideal continues to reflect to some extent his relations with the social world about him; more particularly it always corresponds in some measure to the relations between a child and its parent. In childhood we receive the love and approval of our parents in so far as we obey them and live up to the standards that they set us, punishment and disapproval when we fail to do so. We, as children, on our part expect love, praise, help, and protection from our parents when we are 'good', and fear punishment and blame when we are 'naughty'. Precisely these mutual relations are to be found, again, mirrored in the interactions between the ego and the ego-ideal, inasmuch as this latter represents an incorporation or introjection of our parents' moral attitude.

In quite young children the beginning of the introjective process is sometimes clearly manifest in imitative behaviour in which the child loves or punishes himself in the same way as that in which the parents love or punish him. Thus Nunberg [1] reports the case of a child of sixteen months who, after being stroked by his father and showing great happiness thereat, proceeded, when his father stopped, to stroke himself, saying "Ei-ei"—'a sound which to him was always a sign of the greatest tenderness'. I myself have observed a small girl of two years smack herself in exactly the same way as she had been smacked by her mother when the latter was irritated by the child's behaviour, while after a bout of fractiousness or temper she would herself suggest going to stand in a corner to which her mother had previously banished her for a few moments after similar occasions. Children of this age or a little older will

---

[1] H. Nunberg, 'Das Schuldgefuhl,' *Imago* (1934), 20, 257.

sometimes repeat or quote to themselves parental commands when faced with the temptation to disobey them, and may— as Wälder has observed [1]—on such occasions put on a specially deep voice in imitation of their parents. At later ages the manifestations of this self-love or self-punishment are of course likely to be more complex and less easily discernible. This is partly because they are liable to a process of displacement or symbolic distortion—sometimes of the kind that we regard as neurotic; partly also because they may undergo a projection outwards, so that the self-punishment is camouflaged as a penalty that, it is feared, will be inflicted on the culprit by the outside world. As examples of the former (symbolic displacement) we may take the cases reported by Baudouin [2] in which some children studied by him punished themselves for exhibitionist or voyeuristic tendencies by developing eczema or agoraphobia (eczema as an affliction of the skin, the surface of the human body, which the children had desired to show off in themselves or to inspect in others; agoraphobia because one can so easily be *seen* by many people when crossing open spaces). The latter (projection outwards) is illustrated by the cases described by Isaacs [3] in which the imagined punishments for various misdemeanours 'range in severity from being given hard tasks, being scorned, laughed at and reproached, to being put in prison, whipped, deprived of food, starved and done to death in various ways, for instance by drowning'.

While failure to live up to the commands of the ego-ideal gives rise to a sense of dissatisfaction, inferiority, and guilt, comparable to that induced by arousing the displeasure of the parents, the knowledge of having fulfilled them, especially in the face of a longing to do otherwise, fills us with a corresponding pleasure of self-satisfaction. It is as though we then patted ourselves on the back and said 'Good boy!'—much as a parent or teacher might do to a child who had resisted a temptation or carried out some irksome task. The former condition is one in which we seem reduced to a state of weakness, unworthiness, conflict, and self-dissatisfaction; the latter one in which we feel strong, righteous, loveworthy, and in possession of a sense of inner harmony, the union between the ego-ideal and the ego reflecting the relation between a parent who is proud of his

---

[1] R. Wälder, 'The Genesis of Psychical Conflict,' *Int. J. Psa.* (1937), 18, 406.

[2] Charles Baudouin, *The Mind of the Child* (1933), 257 ff.

[3] Susan Isaacs, *Social Development in Young Children* (1933), 370 ff.

child and a child who willingly, obediently, and trustfully follows the precept and example of its parent.

We shall refer to these two conditions again in various connections, but we may note here the extreme and pathological cases presented respectively by melancholia and mania—cases which impressed themselves on Freud [1] relatively early in his work, and the consideration of which indeed first led him to the road along which he made his later discoveries concerning the severity of the super-ego and the importance of what we have called the 'distance' between the real ego and the ego-ideal. In melancholia the patient not only suffers from extreme depression but often accuses himself of many and unpardonable crimes, while the 'voice of conscience' may be heard by him in the form of hallucinated words of reproach or abuse whispered in his ear. Hallucinations of this kind may, moreover, sometimes afflict those suffering from milder pathological conditions, as in the case of a patient who, while carrying out a theft, suddenly *saw* his father looking at him sadly, or of another who *heard* his mother weeping when he visited a brothel. [2] In still other and more normal cases there may be, not hallucinations, but mild delusions, illusions, or semi-fanciful interpretations, as in the notion (a very common one) that the culprit is being watched by the all-seeing eye of God, that this same watchful eye is somehow connected with the droning of hostile aeroplanes overhead during an air raid, [3] or that thunder is the voice of God angrily threatening the transgressor—as amusingly illustrated recently in a comic paper which depicted a small boy, interrupted in the act of stealing sweets by a loud clap of thunder, turning his glance towards the sky as he mutters in defiance 'You big bully!' Even in dreams one may be pursued by conscience in symbolic form, as in a dream reported to me where the dreamer (as he expressed it) 'could not escape the searching glance of a hovering searchlight' which threatened to reveal an intended immoral action, or in that of another recorded by Lowy in which the dreamer encounters spies who correspond to 'deep-seated inner inhibitions which have been established in his psyche as a consequence of parental guidance'. [4] Such phenomena both

---

[1] 'Mourning and Melancholia,' *Collected Papers*, iv (1925), 152. Originally published in 1917. See also *Group Psychology and Analysis of the Ego* (1922), last chapter.

[2] E. Weiss, 'Die Regression und Projektion im Über Ich,' *Int. Zschf. f. Psa.* (1932), 18, 21.

[3] M. Schmideberg, 'Individual Reactions to Air Raids,' *Int. J. Psa.* (1942), 23, 155.   [4] S. Lowy, *Foundations of Dream Interpretation* (1942), 82.

illustrate the reality of projection (in this case of the super-ego, which appears as the accusing voice or eye) and show clearly the line of cleavage between ego and super-ego.

In mania, on the contrary, the patient feels—equally unreasonably—that he is strong and good, that there is nothing too difficult for him to accomplish, that there is no form of excellence that he cannot attain. Here the union of ego and super-ego which brings a sense of power and harmony is no less evident than the dissociation in the previous case; while the more or less regular alternation of the two conditions that is found in 'cyclothymia' or manic-depressive insanity seems to be but a gross exaggeration of the more normal swing between feelings of unworthiness and depression on the one hand, and those of superiority and elation on the other, which is experienced by everyone in some degree.

But however much the super-ego may (through introjection) take over the functions of parents or other moral authorities, we can never—at any rate within the range of normal mental life—become entirely independent of the approval or disapproval of our social environment. As McDougall and others have stressed, even those of us who, relying on our own inner strength or moral conviction, are ready to face the displeasure of the vast majority of our contemporaries (even in extreme cases to the extent of finding ourselves in a minority of one), yet tend to find consolation in the idea that we shall be admired as far-sighted pioneers by generations yet unborn, or that at least we shall be pleasing in the sight of God, whose judgment and rewards are above those of men. Permanent and universal disapproval is a condition that is well-nigh unthinkable and unendurable, and no more appalling calamity can befall a human being than to feel himself utterly outcast and alone. Hence the immense relief of the 'naughty' child when he has been forgiven by his parent (even though at the cost of previous punishment), and of the adult sinner when he has been taken back into the fold of Church or of society. The ecclesiastical threat or penalty of excommunication must have been a terrible one at a time when the Church provided the moral and social foundation of all European society, though of course it lost much of its horror to those (growing increasingly numerous in recent centuries) who could find social approval and support from sources unconnected with the Church.

Our need for the approval of our fellow-beings, for the feeling that we are accepted by society, is indeed probably to a very large extent a continuation into adolescent and adult life of the young child's need for the approval of his parents, while the anxiety and despondency caused by the sense of being outcasts from society corresponds similarly to the infant's distress at losing their love and support. In both adult and infantile situations of this kind it is often not easy to distinguish the moral elements from the more purely ego-centric and self-preservative factors in the situation. Separation of the child from its parents (even on the purely moral or psychological plane) may mean loss of satisfaction and security and thus give rise to anxiety of what we might call a biological or purely realistic order. But in addition to this is the anxiety caused by disapproval, loss of love and praise. The same two sources of anxiety are often found together in later life, as in the refugee (that distressful product of Nazi domination), the worker dismissed from his job, the 'hunted' criminal escaping from justice, or the man who merely cannot find employment (that other sad victim of modern conditions—this time of capitalist society). Several recent writers have endeavoured to illumine and to some extent explain the anxieties—both biological and moral—that spring from these various forms of isolation from society, by regarding them as continuations or renewals of the more primitive fears of loneliness or separation from the parents in childhood. Suttie [1] explicitly connects our dependence on society in later life with our dependence on maternal care in infancy and early youth, and maintains that we suffer from 'separation anxiety' when we feel that we have lost the love of mother or society. Horney [2] also speaks of 'basic anxiety' of infantile origin which can be assuaged only by the establishment of a satisfactory social adjustment, while Fromm,[3] thinking on very similar lines, also emphasizes man's fundamental sense of loneliness, helplessness, and insecurity which leads him to such 'mechanisms of escape' as 'authoritarianism' (the placing of one's life and the conduct thereof unreservedly at the disposal of a dictator), or 'automaton conformity' (the senseless following of fashion, e.g. in dress, that flourishes in democracies). All these writers seem to consider that man's need of social support is due at bottom to an attitude that he inevitably acquires during his long defence-

[1] Ian Suttie, *The Origins of Love and Hate*, 1935.
[2] Karen Horney, *New Ways in Psycho-analysis*, 1939.
[3] Erich Fromm, *The Fear of Freedom*, 1942.

less infancy in which he is dependent on parental love and care.

Other authors, dealing more specifically with later life, have stressed the moral factor (or perhaps we should here say rather the factor of morale) in economic problems. Thus it has repeatedly been pointed out that prolonged enforced unemployment is apt to undermine a person's sense of worth and self-respect by making him feel that he is not wanted and that there is no place for him in society. Von Andics,[1] for instance, in her study of suicide, has shown that the knowledge of having some definite responsibility or of doing some work of importance is a potent safeguard against the temptation to take one's own life, even in situations of grave disappointment or disaster; while the mere sense that one's work or one's existence is of little significance to any one, and is held in small regard, is itself very liable to tip the balance in favour of suicide, should unfavourable circumstances arise. Phillips,[2] in her study of sentiment formation, has also shown the great importance for healthy emotional development of the sense of being wanted and appreciated and of having something useful to contribute. We all possess, she says, a 'need to be needed'. This need is inevitably frustrated by social ostracism, emotional loneliness, or unemployment. As regards the latter condition especially, Schmideberg,[3] approaching the problem definitely from the psycho-analytic point of view, shows how lack of work may produce a feeling of worthlessness comparable to that of a child who finds himself unable to do anything to help his mother or make her love him. What Schmideberg says of the unemployed is true also of the delinquent and the criminal, especially perhaps of the juvenile delinquent. Those who have studied such social misfits are pretty well agreed that the best, perhaps in the last resort the only, way of achieving their rehabilitation lies through their incorporation in a group and the arousal of their interest and enthusiasm in some common task.[4] Finally it would appear that the same rule is likely to apply to criminal and predatory communities, whether these be mere gangs of adolescent ne'er-do-wells or vast and highly organized nation-states. Indeed the very existence of a

[1] Margarethe von Andics, *Vom Sinn und Sinnlosigkeit des Lebens*, 1939.
[2] Margaret Phillips, *The Education of the Emotions*, 1937.
[3] Melitta Schmideberg, 'Zum Verständnis massenpsychologischer Erscheinungen,' *Imago* (1935), 21, 445.
[4] F. M. Thrasher, *The Gang: A Study of 1313 Gangs in Chicago*, 2nd ed., 1936.

criminal community implies that the individuals of which it is composed have found in it relief from the solitude of individual a-sociality—even though they may still be outcasts from the larger society surrounding them. The re-entry of criminal communities themselves into a more all-embracing human commonweal can, as Carr [1] has recently argued in an admittedly important book on the political problems of the nearer future, be achieved only through enlisting the co-operation of such communities in a general scheme of constructive work undertaken with a broader and more inclusive view of human welfare. From all this it is clear that the facts we have been considering are not only of profound significance for individual development, but have an intimate bearing on numerous and most important problems of social, political, and economic life.

CHAPTER VI

CONFLICTS IN THE EGO-IDEAL AND SOME ATTEMPTS AT THEIR SOLUTION

Some Sources of Moral Conflict

From what we have said so far it might appear that the super-ego or ego-ideal is a relatively homogeneous structure, i.e. that the commands and prohibitions which it issues are harmonious and consistent. This of course is a serious over-simplification. Just as the attitudes of individual parents, nurses, teachers, and other authorities *in loco parentis* are not entirely consistent, just as different parents, nurses, and teachers are not consistent with one another, so also the internalized ideals that correspond to different aspects of the same authorities or to the varying aspects of different authorities are never fused into a completely harmonious and consistent whole. Hence there may be conflicts between ideals, conflicts within the ego-ideal itself, as well as conflicts between the ego-ideal and the id. In dealing in Chapter IV with Baldwin's views we referred to the importance he attached to the influence on individual moral development of the different and conflicting attitudes and opinions of the persons with whom the growing individual comes in contact, and we ventured the suggestion that psycho-analysts had

---

[1] E. H. Carr, *The Conditions of Peace* (1941), ch. 9.

perhaps devoted inadequate attention to this factor. It would be far from true, however, to say that it has been entirely neglected by them. Like other psychologists, they have been keenly aware of the importance of differences of attitude between the two parents. If, for instance, the mother is lenient and the father strict, the child will soon adapt himself to the different standards demanded and will acquire a sort of double moral code, a more tolerant one which operates in relation to those persons or aspects of reality that correspond to the mother and a sterner one which is called into play in his relation to father-figures (though naturally this simple pattern may undergo modifications in the course of development). A similar duality may arise in connection with divergent attitudes on the part of parent and nurse, or parent and other relatives. Early in psycho-analytic work particular attention was called to the frequent influence of grandparents as relatively lenient and indulgent figures. Not having the direct responsibility for the upbringing of their children's children, nor being as a rule so much exposed to their constant presence or frequent petty misdemeanours, they can both afford, and feel inclined, to adopt this rôle. At a somewhat later age parent and teacher may present a similar opposition, though here the parent is perhaps more usually (but by no means always) the one to whom the child looks for sympathy, love, tolerance, and under-standing.

But if the contributions of psycho-analysis in this direction are still somewhat meagre, we find that in the related sphere of the varying attitudes or aspects of the same personality it has drawn attention to a number of factors that may be very influential in the production of disharmonies and inconsistencies in the ego-ideal—factors all the more important because they are sometimes of a kind to be easily overlooked in any superficial study. Without attempting an exhaustive treatment, we shall proceed to mention four ways in which, as psycho-analysis has shown, disharmonies within the ego-ideal may arise; and in the first three of these at least the above-mentioned varying attitudes may play a predominant part.

1. In the first place a parent (in the very early days especially the mother, but later the father also) inevitably presents a double aspect to the child, inasmuch as she or he is a source of love, help, and protection on the one hand, of thwarting, frustration, and prohibition on the other. Correspondingly (as

we have to some extent already indicated, though it is a matter that will require further treatment) the super-ego,[1] in so far as it has taken over the rôle of the parent, continues both to love and thwart. The existence of such apparently contradictory qualities in the super-ego necessarily introduces an element of instability into its relations with the ego. As with the real external parent, the individual usually responds to love with love and to thwarting with tendencies to hatred and revolt. It is not surprising that the ego seeks some means of dealing with the ambivalent attitudes and conflicts thus aroused. Often it would seem as though no final solution can be found so long as the super-ego remains merely a part of our own minds. But if we project it on to the outer world it is relatively easy to find, or invent, good and bad figures that correspond respectively to what were originally the loving and thwarting aspects of our parents. This process of 'decomposition' may play an important part in myth, religion, and other fields (e.g. politics); we need only call to mind the good fairy-godmothers and cruel step-mothers of traditional nursery fiction. For the moment, however, it is only incumbent on us to note the potential conflicts connected with the double aspect of the (internal) super-ego itself, conflicts which (like those connected with the actual parents) can be minimized only in so far as the super-ego acquires an attitude which can perhaps best be described as 'good but strict'.[2] Moreover it is important that this good-strict attitude should be as far as possible consistently maintained. Nothing appears to be more confusing or unhelpful to the child than a parental attitude that is capricious and unpredictable, as a result of which behaviour that is condoned, or even encouraged, on one occasion causes reproach, punishment, or irritation on another. In this matter psycho-analysis only confirms the observations and conclusions made by psychologists of several different schools working in several different spheres, who have with surprising regularity found that an upbringing that is sometimes lax and sometimes strict is associated with all sorts of difficulties and maladjustments in childhood, adolescence, and even adult life.

2. In the second place, and rather intimately related to the above, is the circumstance that the harsher and more forbidding

---

[1] We return to the use of the term 'super-ego' here to indicate that we are in this and the immediately succeeding considerations concerned to a large extent with deeper unconscious aspects.

[2] As Susan Isaacs especially has emphasized, *op. cit.*

aspects of the super-ego are derived, not from a true picture of the parents as they are, but rather from the super-egos of the parents. In their attitude to their children parents, perhaps to some extent inevitably, adopt the point of view of their own super-egos. It is as though they said to their children: 'Do as I say, not as I do', and it is this attitude that is, in large measure, introjected by the children. In this way there takes place something in the nature of a direct transmission of the super-ego from one generation to another, comparable perhaps to the continuity of the germ-plasm in its pilgrimage through a succession of individual bodies. There can be little doubt, however, that this aspect of the super-ego, genuine though it is, does not make up its whole essence. Another part of it corresponds rather to the more loving, 'human', tolerant aspects of the 'real' parents, and in the conflict between these two aspects we have another important source of inconsistency within the super-ego itself.

3. Partially, but by no means entirely, overlapping with this distinction between the parent's real ego and his super-ego is a distinction between those aspects of the parent's conduct which it is considered right and proper for the child to imitate and thus incorporate in his ego-ideal, and those which are regarded as the privilege of adults and which the child must therefore not imitate. The child has thus to be in some respects like, and in other respects unlike, his parents; and this inevitably causes some conflict and contradiction in the course of the formation of the ego-ideal. Pre-eminent among those aspects of parental behaviour which must not be imitated are those that fall within the sexual sphere, and the learning of this lesson is rendered all the harder inasmuch as it runs counter to all those desires which form the basis of the Œdipus complex. The little boy is allowed, encouraged, and enjoined to copy his father in many respects, in the ordinary habits of cleanliness and hygiene, in courage and patience in the face of pain or disappointment, in control over emotional expression, in innumerable small skills and habits exhibited in daily life; but any attempt to claim for himself the special intimate privileges of love which the father enjoys with the mother is severely frowned upon, as is any manifestation of jealousy or resentment at his father's possession of these privileges; and similarly with the little girl, who, while expected in many other respects to learn to copy and be like her mother, must limit her claim to the father's affection in a

way that is not incumbent on the mother. Though this is
undoubtedly the chief sphere in which imitation of adults is
taboo, there are a considerable number of minor adult privileges
(e.g. smoking, swearing, staying up late, entering places of
alcoholic refreshment) as regards which the child usually learns
that he is definitely not allowed to copy grown-ups. Indeed it
must often seem to him that he is expected to assimilate the
dull, distasteful, and laborious aspects of adult life, but that
the compensating privileges and pleasures are withheld from
him. Even without the added urge and protest that under
these circumstances almost necessarily arises from the id, the
mere intellectual effort involved in making the required distinctions might be hard enough. In view of the orectic complications, it is not surprising that the enforcement of the restrictions
and prohibitions, alongside of the simultaneously required
imitations and identifications, sometimes calls for so great an
effort of restraint or repression that the taboos in question
become a permanent part of the personality and cannot later
be removed when the time comes to make the readjustments
necessary for entering on adult life. There may then come about
a conflict between the deeper, more infantile, archaic, and unconscious levels of the super-ego, in which these taboos, with
their various and often somewhat grotesque ramifications, have
been preserved, and the more conscious ideals which have been
modified and adapted as life advances; so that a person may
consciously feel it permissible, desirable, and even a matter of
duty to embark on a course of action (e.g. to marry or enter a
profession) which is forbidden by the deeper levels of his
super-ego.

4. This conflict between different levels of the super-ego (or, if
we like to use the terms in what is often a convenient manner,
between the more or less unconscious super-ego and the conscious
ego-ideal) may no doubt also come about in other ways, since—
as was indicated in Chapter III—the earliest layers of the
super-ego tend in any case to become relatively unconscious
and inaccessible to the modifying influence of the experiences
of later life. But in whatever way they may be caused, disharmonies of this kind (i.e. between the prevailing attitudes at
different levels) constitute the fourth type of conflict within
the general sphere of the super-ego to which psycho-analysts
have called attention. In some degree all persons would seem
to be subject to such conflicts, which are indeed among the

most potent, and often also among the most tragic (though sometimes, too, the most absurd), that beset humanity and militate against its happiness and progress. To illustrate briefly from two examples that have come within my own experience: A young woman felt it to be her duty to enter the profession of architecture, not only because this seemed in harmony with her personal interests and ideals but because she came of a family that could boast of a considerable line of successful architects. This conscious ideal was, however, opposed by a deeper level of her super-ego. Her father disapproved of the entry of his daughter into this profession, still a relatively unusual one for women; and this disapproval was connected in her mind with certain forbidden childish interests in the processes of reproduction and creation. The desire to 'create' through architecture was a sublimation of these early interests, so it was not surprising that the paternal disapproval should arouse deep-lying feelings of guilt. These deeper inhibitions seriously interfered with her studies, affecting particularly her ability to pass the examinations required for entry into her profession. The second example is that of a young man who had acquired from his father the ideal of learning and wide reading but at the same time suffered at a deeper level from a moral inhibition of knowing what his father knew, an inhibition dating from an early repression of interest in the sexual sphere. At this level he felt it wicked and presumptuous to pry into matters that were the prerogatives of his elders. The conflict manifested itself in long and obsessive gazing at the contents of bookshops, where he saw books which according to his conscious ideal it was his duty to buy and read, but which a dim feeling of guilt prevented him from purchasing or even looking through (except for brief glances at pages here and there). He was eventually able to solve the conflict by directing his studies to a field as far as possible removed from that of his father's interests.

An Experimental Study

A recent study by Brahmachari [1] has shown that it is possible even without recourse to psycho-analysis to reveal the widespread existence of such conflicts between different levels (though the methods used could not, as psycho-analysis can

---

[1] S. Brahmachari, *Moral Attitudes in relation to Upbringing, Personal Adjustment, and Social Opinion.* Thesis in University of London Library, 1937.

often do, reveal the intimate cause and history of the conflicts). In the course of this study 120 subjects (mostly senior students but including some professional men and women) were presented with 42 questions [1] intended to assess their theoretical attitude towards a corresponding number of moral problems—the measurement being made on an eleven-point scale ranging from +5 (expressing an enthusiastic affirmative answer to the question) through 0 (expressing uncertainty or indifference) to -5 (expressing an emphatic negative answer). At the same time they were asked to indicate on a similar scale their own actual conduct in the matters concerned and also the degree of mental conflict, if any, caused by any discrepancy between attitude and conduct (this last on a six-point scale from 0 to 5). As might be expected in any experiment in which care was taken to get sincere and unbiased replies, there was a fairly large discrepancy between attitude (what the subject thought he ought, to do) and actual conduct, as regards most of the subjects and many of the questions. This is indicated by (among other things) the mere fact that the mean for 'attitude' for all the answers of all the subjects was +2·36 (indicating a moderate tendency to give affirmative answers to the questions as put), whereas the mean for conduct was only +1·08 (showing a tendency to live up only to some extent to the theoretical moral standard indicated by the replies). Actually only 3 of the 120 subjects failed to report appreciable conflict with regard to one or more of the 42 questions, while a considerable number of subjects reported quite a high degree of conflict with regard to many of them, the mean mark for conflict (for all subjects and all questions) being 1·22, while 3 subjects had a mean of over 3·00. Of particular interest in the present connection is the fact that there were many cases of conflict as regards questions where there was no discrepancy between the marks for attitude and conduct, i.e. where the subject apparently considered himself to live up to his ideal. This appears illogical, but the introspections and remarks of the subjects reveal clearly that the conflict in such cases is due to the fact

[1] Two examples of the questions given: 'Ought we always to be careful to avoid all suffering, mental or physical, to others, unless such suffering is unavoidably incidental to preservation of life, health, or absolutely necessary to social discipline?' 'Is it desirable to abstain from alcoholic drink?' The questions were shown to the subjects one at a time on printed cards, and their quantitative answers and comments recorded confidentially by the experimenter under conditions calculated to ensure the utmost spontaneity and sincerity in the replies.

that the recorded attitude of the subject corresponds only to the attitude actually held by one part (usually the more conscious, 'reasonable' part) of his moral self. Another part of the self demands a different, and usually a stricter, attitude, so that there is still a discrepancy between conduct and this more exigent, though less conscious and explicit, ideal; and it is this discrepancy that gives rise to the conflict in such cases—a conflict which, be it noted, is itself detectable in consciousness, even though its causes may be inaccessible to introspection.

Another point of importance to us here is that, where there is discrepancy between attitude and conduct, this discrepancy is not proportionate to the conflict aroused (the correlation between discrepancy and conflict for the 120 subjects is actually no more than $+0.16$ and can scarcely be regarded as significant).[1] In some cases a small discrepancy can be associated with a relatively big conflict, and it may even happen that actual conduct exceeds the demands required by a person's moral attitude and yet there is conflict. In these cases the conflict would seem, as we have just indicated, to be most often caused by a severe (unconscious) super-ego, which (for reasons that the methods employed in this research could not reveal) has not much influenced either attitude or conduct, but which manifests itself indirectly in the discomfort associated with the mental conflict. In other contrasting cases, however, it appears as though this unconscious super-ego had actually influenced both attitude and conduct, but that the more conscious ego-ideal was in revolt and had sided with the id in demanding a more lenient standard for attitude and behaviour, the conflict then arising from the dissatisfaction of the ego-ideal rather than from that of the super-ego. As an example that to some extent illustrates both sources of conflict, we may quote the average figures for the question dealing with 'conventional sex morals'. The question ran: 'Ought we to do our utmost to adhere to the conventional code of sexual morals which condemns all forms of direct sexual satisfaction except in marriage (e.g. extramarital intercourse, homosexuality, masturbation)?' It will be convenient to consider the men's and women's answers separately.

	ATTITUDE	CONDUCT	DISCREPANCY	CONFLICT
Men . . .	$+1.12$	$+1.51$	$+0.39$	1.32
Women . . .	-0.02	-0.38	-0.36	0.92

[1] Here, as with other coefficients of correlation, $+1.00$ indicates complete positive correlation, -1.00 complete negative correlation, 0.00 absence of all correlation.

The fact that the men's attitude agrees more with that implied by the question possibly reflects the 'double moral standard' that current convention still to some extent applies to the two sexes, the women perhaps (in spite of the explanation and examples provided in the question) interpreting the words 'conventional moral code' rather more strictly than the men, but agreeing with it the less. It is to be noted, however, that the men's conduct is actually more in accordance with 'convention' than their attitude indicates as morally desirable, whereas the women's discrepancy is in the opposite direction. In spite of this the men suffer from greater conflict than the women. The comments of the subjects make it fairly clear that this sex difference is due to two different and rather opposite causes. On the one hand the women would seem to suffer from less deep-lying guilt, especially as regards masturbation and homosexuality (i.e. their super-egos were less severe), while on the other hand the men more frequently considered themselves impeded or humiliated by the 'conventional code' and on a superficial plane felt that their masculine prestige demanded a rebellion against it (i.e. their conscious ego-ideals had sided with the id against the super-ego). For both reasons then, stricter super-ego and more rebellious ego-ideal, the men were more liable to suffer conflict than the women; though actually it would seem that the rebellious ego-ideal was in this case the chief source of conflict. This emerges both from the men's comments and from the fact that their 'conduct' approached nearer to 'convention' than did their 'attitude'. Such greater conventionality of conduct is clearly a triumph for the more conservative and unconscious forces of the super-ego and therefore provides the more conscious and rebellious ego-ideal with the greater cause for dissatisfaction.

By way of contrast we may refer to the much simpler picture that is presented by the answers to the question on 'physical courage': 'Do you think it our duty to stand against an aggressor with all our physical might (e.g. if attacked by robbers in superior strength should we oppose them at the risk of grave injury or death?)'?

	ATTITUDE	CONDUCT	DISCREPANCY	CONFLICT
Men . . .	+1·51	+1·23	−0·28	1·39
Women . . .	+0·10	+0·79	+0·69	0·91

Here the answers again—and this time much more clearly—

reflect a difference in the moral conventions affecting the two sexes. The men, as is to be expected, tend to answer the question more definitely in the affirmative, but they do not live up to their higher ideal as well as do the women to their lower one, i.e. relatively to their ideals (and accepting the accuracy of their replies as forecasts of what would really happen) the women are more courageous than the men. Naturally under these circumstances the men have the bigger conflicts—conflicts, however, that are here due not so much to incompatibilities between different moral levels as to simple and direct antagonisms between ego-ideal and id (i.e. between the ideal of courageous resistance and the more instinctive tendency to self-preservation). This last point, however, would seem to apply less to the women, who also have appreciable, though smaller, conflicts—in their case perhaps due to some extent to a disharmony between a more masculine ideal of vigorous self-defence and a more feminine and masochistic ideal of submission and of shrinking from the exercise of physical violence.

In these cases there is considerable conflict with relatively little discrepancy. In the case of some other questions, however, there is a big discrepancy with relatively little conflict, e.g. in three questions suggesting respectively that it is desirable to avoid borrowing, to avoid living on capital, and to engage in work of a public or philanthropic character. The figures here (for both sexes together) are as follows:

	ATTITUDE	CONDUCT	DISCREPANCY	CONFLICT
Avoid borrowing .	+3·26	+0·54	−2·72	1·10
Avoid living on capital . . .	+2·51	+0·10	−2·41	1·22
Engage in public work . . .	+3·86	+1·48	−2·38	1·18

The comparatively small degree of conflict in such cases probably indicates that the mark given for attitude is expressive of a relatively superficial—perhaps almost nominal—ideal, without any deep moral feeling behind it. It perhaps illustrates the distinction that McDougall has sometimes made between an 'ideal', which is little more than an intellectual assent to a moral proposition, and a 'sentiment', which involves a real mobilization of emotions with reference to the aim or object concerned. Anyhow the results show clearly that, just as it is possible to live up to one's consciously formulated ideals and yet have moral conflict, so also we can under certain circumstances [1] fall far behind these ideals and still suffer comparatively little in the way of moral qualms.

The fact that ideals may be influenced from various not necessarily harmonious parts of the personality is also shown in another portion of Brahmachari's research, in which the subjects were asked to name a character from history or fiction which approached nearest to their ideals. The majority of subjects chose a character which seemed to accord pretty well with their own disposition, attitude, and way of life, but a few made choices that seemed distinctly at variance with these. Thus on the one hand the subjects who chose 'scientists' or 'industrialists' were markedly more extravert [2] than those who chose 'thinkers', while those who chose 'religious figures' were socially and politically more conservative than the majority. The few subjects, however, who chose 'adventurers' (e.g. Nansen, Lawrence of Arabia, 'The Three Musketeers') were all very markedly introvert. This last result was probably due to a recognition of the limitations of their own type and an admiration of the opposite qualities in which they were deficient. Reactions of this kind necessarily imply some antagonism between the ideal and the real self (though of course one that can manifest itself more freely in the choice of a phantasy figure than in the adoption of a standard that is seriously intended to influence a person's own conduct). Nevertheless the restrictions imposed by a person's character and mode of life naturally very often cause self-dissatisfaction, which is to some extent mirrored in an increased distance between real ego and ego-ideal. As William James [3] stated in a famous passage, many people only reconcile themselves with regret to the sacrifice of potential 'selves' which inevitably accompanies the development of the actual self in a certain direction and the adoption of some particular career and way of life. Of all the possibilities of early youth only a very few can actually be realized; and the circumstances that prevent the realization of the others are due not merely

---

[1] As Brahmachari points out, the particular results here in question are probably in some measure connected with the population from which the subjects were drawn. Many of them, being students, were as yet removed from the full responsibilities of economic and public life. Though they recognized in the abstract the claims of such responsibilities on the individual citizen, they felt that they themselves were still in some ways exempt from the special duties that such claims entail.

[2] As measured by an adaptation of Freyd's Introversion-Extraversion questionnaire: M. Freyd, 'Introverts and Extraverts,' *Psychol. Rev.* (1924), 31, 74.

[3] *Principles of Psychology* (1890), i, 309 ff.

to the limitations of time, opportunity, and energy, but often also to active incompatibilities between different possible ideals. Hence, if we harbour ambitions at all, some degree of disappointment and disillusion is inevitable and it is natural that our disappointed hopes should seek an outlet in phantasy or through some other means. Here again we see also the value of Adler's point of view, for it was Adler who first clearly drew attention to some of the methods by which we endeavour to compensate for these failures to develop the powers that in other circumstances we might have shown.

Mechanisms of Defence

According to the more recent formulations of Anna Freud [1] compensation should be regarded as only one of the rather numerous ways in which the ego may endeavour to defend itself against attack or humiliation, whether from thwarted impulses, ambitions, or ideals within the mind, or from adverse conditions in the outer world. Here we are directly concerned only with such of these 'mechanisms of defence' as have to do primarily with the tensions created by the existence of the ego-ideal, those which aim in fact at preventing the ego from falling, or appearing to fall, too far below the standard required by the ideal. Those that are concerned chiefly with the more purely restrictive, inhibitory, or punitive aspects of the superego can be more conveniently dealt with in another place—indeed many of them, such as repression, displacement, and sublimation, have from the start been among the most familiar concepts of psycho-analysis and do not therefore fall within our present scope, except for an inevitable reference here and there. There are, however, a few of Anna Freud's 'mechanisms of defence' which are both less well known and more directly relevant to our present theme, and with a brief description of these we may appropriately end our present chapter.

Rather closely connected with compensation and not always easily distinguished from it is 'reaction-formation', i.e. 'the development of a character trait, usually the exact opposite of the original trait, which keeps in check and conceals the original trait'. The classical instances of reaction-formation are: an exaggerated prudery or purity as a defence against sexual interests, an exaggerated brusqueness or petty aggressiveness as a defence against shyness or inferiority feelings, and (the

[1] Anna Freud, *The Ego and the Mechanisms of Defence*, 1937.

opposite of the last) an exaggerated deference or humility (*à la* Uriah Heep) to cover a crude and avaricious egoism. Psychoanalytical work has added two further examples which would seem to be of fairly frequent occurrence: a quasi-obsessive kindliness, friendliness, or humanity overlying aggressiveness, and an excessive concern about some other person's health or welfare to hide unconscious hostility and death wishes against that person. Reaction-formation, in the light of these instances, would seem to differ in two ways from Adler's wider concept of compensation: first, in that it always possesses the character of oppositeness to the tendency against which it is directed (whereas this is only the case with some compensations [1]); secondly, in that it seems to have a more immediate moral and repressive quality. Reaction-formation appears to spring more from the (unconscious) super-ego, compensation more from the relatively superficial layers of the ego-ideal. Reaction-formation restricts and confines the manifestations of the personality, whereas compensation enhances them by surmounting obstacles and limitations, either (as we saw in Chapter IV) directly, by mobilizing energy to overcome them, or indirectly, by finding new channels of expression which are unaffected by the obstacles. Moreover, as soon as we examine its roots, reaction-formation always presents an appearance of spuriousness, hypocrisy, or camouflage. Nevertheless, inasmuch as it substitutes supposedly desirable and ethical qualities for unrespectable or immoral ones, it does often serve the purposes of the ego-ideal and therefore has a claim to be considered here.

Yet another of Anna Freud's 'mechanisms of defence' closely resembles behaviour of a kind to which Adler had already drawn attention, i.e. what she terms 'restriction of the ego'. If we refuse to employ our powers seriously, we are likely to achieve little; but inasmuch as we have not tried, we are saved from the bitterer humiliations of failure and defeat; it is as though we could then at least console ourselves with the thought, 'If I had really exerted myself I could have succeeded'. Such an attitude, as Anna Freud reminds us, may play an important rôle in some cases of educational failure and may enter subtly into many activities of later life. So long as we regard ourselves as dabblers, amateurs, dilettanti, or beginners we feel that we cannot seriously

---

[1] Unless perhaps we consider the relation of 'oppositeness' in a very wide sense, e.g. strength, efficiency, superiority, as against weakness, ineffectiveness, humiliation.

be blamed or despised, that we cannot even blame or despise ourselves, for inferior performances.

Though cramping, and even ridiculous when carried to excess, this attitude has nevertheless a certain sphere of usefulness and justifiability. In a general way it has a bearing on the whole level of aspiration that we considered in Chapter IV. If we are to aim consistently at the highest of which we are capable, we must continually exert ourselves to the utmost. But in so far as we pitch our aspirations to a lower key, we may legitimately and quite realistically console ourselves for the little showing we have made by the thought that we could have done more had we chosen to make the necessary effort. We are here up against a problem of the ultimate philosophy of life, as regards which— as we have already reminded ourselves—the wisest thinkers have held different views. It is safe to say, however, that few if any men or women can struggle consistently to maintain their highest level, and in so far as we more or less deliberately decide to achieve something less than our best, it would be foolish and pedantic to refuse to avail ourselves of the advantages that accrue from this restriction of our egos. Moreover, however high we may aspire towards our chosen ideal, our chosen way of life, our chosen self, there are always, as James has so eloquently told us, those other potentialities, those other selves (as he would put it) that we have had to jettison. It would be absurdly unrealistic, did we fail to bear in mind that there are vast and attractive fields of endeavour in which we are necessarily but the merest amateurs. There is much to be said for the cultivation of high ideals in a particular direction even at the cost of chagrin when we find ourselves outrivalled here, but this very cultivation of a particular field inevitably implies that we have neglected others in themselves no less important; and as regards these others we very sensibly recognize that little, if anything, can be expected of us. As James puts it, speaking of himself: 'I, who for the time have staked my all on being a psychologist, am mortified if others know much more psychology than I. But I am contented to wallow in the grossest ignorance of Greek. My deficiencies there give me no sense of personal humiliation at all. Had I pretensions to be a linguist, it would have been just the reverse'.[1] Here we have an everyday example of the application of the principle of 'restriction of the ego' in its legitimate and useful form.

[1] *Loc. cit.*

Another mechanism, of narrower scope, but one which is sometimes effectively used in dealing with a threatening situation, is what Anna Freud calls 'identification with the aggressor'. It is really no more than a particular kind of introjection. In forming our super-egos we introject our mothers, our fathers, or the other authorities about us; we become like them (at least in so far as our super-egos are concerned), and in so doing we avert the threat of punishment and censure. In 'identification with the aggressor' we meet danger in much the same way, by becoming like the person or agency from which injury or destruction is anticipated. The chief difference is that the threatening external being in this case is not so much a moral figure; it tends to be characterized by simple aggressiveness without the moral qualities we attribute to our parents. Correspondingly the introjection seems to affect the ego rather than the super-ego. We simply become (as it seems to us) like the feared agent, endowed with the same power and aggressiveness, and thus have no longer any need to fear it. In its simplest form this 'mechanism' is due perhaps to what McDougall calls primitive passive sympathy—the fact that the perception of the physical manifestations of emotions in others (in this case anger or any other sign of threat or hostility) tends to arouse the same emotions in ourselves—probably in virtue of an innate mechanism. It is perhaps due also in some degree to the natural oscillation between fear and aggression in the face of danger; for fear and anger are alternative reactions to any kind of threat, and when we see that the danger is not overwhelming an initial alarm may give place to fierce retaliation— as we can often observe in a startled man or dog. But in its further development it soon becomes freed from dependence on perception, so that the mere thought of the threatening object can lead us to feel that we are like that object and thus capable of giving as much as we are likely to get, indeed in some cases of giving more than we can get, thus turning the tables on the aggressor, mastering it, and rendering it innocuous. Such a process has moreover pretty clearly some relation to the motive of revenge on the one hand, and on the other to the manner in which, as Freud has suggested, children achieve a sense of mastery of their environment by doing actively in play what they may in reality have had to suffer passively at the hands of adults. But it would take us too far afield to follow these ramifications here. Among the examples of this mechanism in children mentioned by Anna Freud is the case of a child who said: 'You don't need to be afraid of ghosts now; you just have to pretend you're the ghost you might meet'; and the other more pathological (because unconscious) case reported by Aichhorn of a boy who made strange grimaces which, it was discovered, were an unwitting imitation or caricature of a dreaded schoolmaster. An amusing instance from adult life is to be found in the words of *The Bomber Parade*, a dance tune played in London during the height of the 1940–41 Blitz:

> 'When the sirens are sounding
> We are never afraid.
> We just keep on dancing
> The Bomber Parade.
> We don't hurry away
> When the Dorniers zoom,
> We just make a noise like this:
> Whoooooo........... Boom!'

Accompanying these words there are movements expressing, first the flight of an aircraft, then the fall of a bomb.

This teaches us that, when effective action against an impending danger is impossible, imitation may be the next best thing, and that regression to childish make-believe may have its uses when we are reduced to childish impotence. In spite of its unrealistic and often utterly phantastic character, it can nevertheless help us to overcome fears that might otherwise be paralysing, and thus give us time, courage, and the power of thought to adapt ourselves to a situation to which we might otherwise utterly succumb. And this may serve to remind us that wishful thinking, dangerous as it may often be, is not necessarily without biological value—a consideration to which we shall return in a later chapter.

The last of Anna Freud's 'mechanisms of defence' to which we need refer here is the one which she terms 'altruistic surrender'. It consists in a vicarious satisfaction of one's own needs, desires, and ambitions, pleasure being taken in the successes of others as though they were our own. Here, instead of introjection, there is projection or empathy—an ascription of our own orectic life to others, rather than an incorporation of others' qualities into ourselves. Here too, once again, William James anticipated more recent findings—in his doctrine of the enlargement of our 'self' to include our relatives, our friends, the things we love, our home, our country.[1] There can be little doubt that in this

[1] *Loc. cit.*

process men have found one of the most helpful and beneficent means of dealing with the trials, limitations, and humiliations of the human lot. It is of course capable of exaggeration and misapplication, as in the instance given by Anna Freud of the girl who, confronted with the sexual rivalry of a sister, gave up all her personal ambitions and became interested henceforth only in the triumphs of this sister, and through her of other women. Cyrano de Bergerac, who became a vicarious suitor for other men, is a famous literary instance of the same sort. In such cases there is probably to be found a very large admixture either of guilt or of masochism—probably of both. It is also true, as Anna Freud points out, that this mechanism may on occasion also serve to gratify a person's own aggression under a camouflage of altruism, the most shameless begging or bullying (e.g. for charitable purposes or out of patriotic fervour) appearing permissible if only it is done on behalf of others and not for purely selfish ends. Nevertheless life presents us with innumerable occasions in which this same 'altruistic surrender' can serve at once as a noble form of resignation and renunciation and as a means of transcending the pettiness and narrowness of merely personal concerns. Children take pride and pleasure in the superior power and knowledge of their parents, while these latter in turn can delight in the progress and achievements of their offspring. The athlete can enjoy something of the quiet indoor satisfactions of the scholar, the recluse can taste the triumphs of the man of action. Women can gratify their often unfulfilled desire for physical adventure in contemplation of the exploits of men, while men can satisfy their exhibitionism through their delight in the physical beauty and the more decorative raiment which under our present conventions are considered the prerogatives of women. As von Hartmann long ago pointed out, with the progress of culture, the desire that we should ourselves enjoy personal immortal bliss tends to be superseded by the hope of a happier future for the race, and although there is no doubt (as he and other more recent authors have emphasized) a large element of illusion in this Utopianism of the future, it is yet at once more realistic and more altruistic than the longing for personal experience of heaven. The desire for a better future for mankind is indeed one of the most exalted sources of contemplation and endeavour that men have yet achieved. Without this power there would perhaps be reasonable ground for complaining that the human mind, in virtue of its capacity for looking into the future, had done little more than make us painfully aware of the brief span and narrow limitation of our individual lives; with it, we become not merely spectators of, but to some extent even participators in, the drama of 'all time and all existence'.

CHAPTER VII

NEMESISM (AGGRESSION TURNED AGAINST THE SELF)

Some Varieties and Examples

In the last three chapters we have been dealing chiefly with the first two of the four factors which we distinguished in the super-ego,[1] i.e. with the creation and influence of an ideal and with the introjection of external moral authorities. We must now turn to the consideration of the third and fourth factors, i.e. those aspects of the super-ego in which aggression predominates. Here as elsewhere, however, as the reader has been warned, it is hardly possible to maintain consistently our somewhat artificial division, and it will be found that in pursuit of our present aim we shall also be able (especially in Chapters VIII and IX) to throw some further light upon other aspects of the super-ego, including those connected with its origin and early development. At the same time, in turning to these aggressive elements, we shall become aware of certain correlative changes which the super-ego appears to undergo when we look at it from this new point of view. These changes may be noted briefly at once, though their full nature and implications will, it is hoped, become clearer as we proceed. In the first place, of course, is the element of harshness or cruelty itself. Whereas in the elements we have been considering the super-ego appeared to operate largely (though of course by no means exclusively) by holding before us a moral ideal, failure to attain which arouses shame and guilt, the aspects with which we are now concerned rely on punishment and goading rather than on exhortation and appeal. Secondly, these new aspects are more negative and restrictive in character; they are concerned with prohibitions rather than with positive goals or ideals. In virtue of this they

---

[1] In Chapter III.

offer little inducement to the expansion of the ego or the development of its powers by way of sublimation or otherwise.　In the third place, the relations between the ego and these aspects of the super-ego are characterized by hate rather than by love; this part of the super-ego corresponds to the child's picture of the parent as a harsh, forbidding, terrifying, and punishing being rather than as a loving, helping, and protecting one.　The parent, in virtue of these aspects, is no high—perhaps unattainably high —'copy for imitation' (to use Baldwin's term), but rather a cruel, sadistic taskmaster and tyrant, who seems to take delight in placing taboos on many potential sources of joy and satisfaction and in inflicting punishment at the slightest hint that these taboos may be infringed.　Fourthly and lastly, these aspects of the super-ego are more characteristically and completely unconscious in their operation.　In place of an ideal of which we are at any rate in some degree aware, there are restrictions and inhibitions, of the meaning and source of which we have often little, if any, understanding, and in the place of more or less conscious feelings of guilt for moral failures which we realize, punishment is often inflicted on us for crimes we do not recognize by a force of which we have little comprehension.　Corresponding to this greater unconsciousness there is also a lesser capacity to undergo modification in the light of experience, so that this part of the super-ego is liable to remain particularly archaic, unadaptable, and out of touch with adult reality.

The differences that we have noted are of course only differences of degree and of general tendency, and it would be an easy matter to point to individual instances that seem to belie them; nevertheless, if we attempt to draw distinctions of a general kind between the aspects of the super-ego with which we have been dealing and those which we are now about to consider, we believe that the distinctions will be of the kind indicated.[1]

----

[1] In view of these differences (and especially the last) it has sometimes been proposed to give different names to the two parts of the super-ego in question. The more aggressive, unconscious parts of the super-ego have seemed to a few writers to be specially in need of a new designation—perhaps because the word 'super' is generally associated with a more conscious (as opposed to a 'subconscious') level in psychology and with a 'higher' rather than a 'lower' value in ethics, and therefore tends to be understood in ways different from, and indeed to a large extent contrary to, those intended by Freud in this connection. Thus Odier (Charles Odier, 'Vom Über Ich. Ein Beitrag zur Terminologie,' *Zschf. f. Psa.* (1926), 12, 275) would call this part of the super-ego the 'super-id', to emphasize especially the characteristic of being unconscious which it shares with the Freudian id. Jekels and Bergler (Ludwig Jekels and Edmund Bergler, 'Übertragung und Liebe,' *Imago* (1934), 20, 5) suggest that it be called the

In the last three chapters we have of course already had occasion to deal pretty often with aggression. But this aggression had an external source in the behaviour of the parents or other moral authorities, and it only became internalized and attached to the super-ego as a result of the introjection of these external authorities. The aggression with which we are now concerned has a different origin; it springs from the person's own anger and revolt against the frustrating parent figures. As we have already indicated (in Chapter III), the arousal of such aggression is inevitable, inasmuch as parents are bound to frustrate their children in some degree, and it is likewise inevitable that a child's aggression cannot be fully and freely expressed, and this for two reasons: because the child is too weak to stand up to the opposition of the parents, and because at the same time it loves them and is dependent on them. Unable therefore to direct this aggression against its natural object, the child must deal with it in some way: by repression, displacement, or by turning it against himself. In the very young child the capacities for both repression and displacement are probably less than at a later age; there is therefore a special likelihood of recourse being made to the remaining alternative. But throughout life there is a tendency for frustrated or inhibited aggression to recoil against the would-be aggressor—a fact well recognized by Marlowe when, in the parade of the Seven Deadly Sins before Dr. Faustus, he makes Wrath say: 'I have run up and down the world with this case of rapiers, wounding myself when I had nobody to fight withal'. This tendency would seem to be of such fundamental importance as to merit a special name by which it can conveniently be designated. We propose here to

'daimon', since in their view it corresponds in some striking respects to what the Greeks understood by this term. Alexander (Franz Alexander, *Psychoanalyse der Gesamtpersönlichkeit*, 1927) prefers to use the 'super-ego' for the more unconscious and irrational elements, and the 'ego-ideal' for the more conscious and adaptable ones. Without deliberately setting out to do so, we have ourselves fallen into a similar usage, which is perhaps, all things considered, the most convenient. It should be noted, however, (1) that there is no general sanction for this usage, (2) that it is not intended to imply that the ego-ideal and the super-ego in this sense can be simply and easily distinguished. Indeed it has to be admitted that the distinction, though sometimes helpful, is largely artificial, and should be used, if at all, in relation to cases or aspects where there is a fairly clear predominance of one or other set of characteristics. Nevertheless we shall continue to make the distinction where it seems useful and appropriate, although we shall also continue to use the term 'super-ego' in those cases where no such distinction is intended and where the whole entity covered by the four factors of Chapter III is under discussion. It is hoped that the context will indicate with sufficient clearness whether the wider or the narrower meaning is intended.

adopt Rosenzweig's suggestion [1] and to use the term 'nemesism' as an alternative and technical term for 'aggression turned against the self'.   Such a term has the advantage of being easily compared and contrasted with the already familiar 'narcissism', which designates the comparable process of love directed to the self.

The tendency, however, in spite of its importance, has, at any rate until quite recently, received but little notice from psychologists other than psycho-analysts, so that it is perhaps worth while to familiarize ourselves with it by means of a few simple examples. We may begin with some which illustrate the common case (particularly important for us here) where a person's aggression against himself takes the form of actually reinforcing the opposition or frustration due to a parent.   Since in such cases the parents' commands and the child's aggression manifest themselves in the same direction, it is rather easy for the existence of the second factor to be overlooked, but when we study the child's behaviour from the quantitative rather than the qualitative point of view we see that it exhibits a certain characteristic exaggeration or over-intensification which distinguishes it from the conduct that would result from a simple copying or introjection of the parents' attitude; in other words, there is over-obedience rather than a simple straightforward compliance.

The other day I was watching a mother feed her little girl of two.   The child resisted the soup that was being offered her in a spoon and endeavoured to push away the mother's hand with considerable show of force and displeasure.   After a while, however, the mother still persisting, the child suddenly altered her behaviour, seized the spoon herself and, without changing in any other way her combative expression, pushed it into her own mouth with quite unnecessary violence and poured the contents down her throat.   There occurred indeed a quite unmistakable reversal in the direction of the child's aggression; from being directed against the mother, it was turned against

---

[1] Saul Rosenzweig, in H. A. Murray *et al.*: *Explorations in Personality* (1938), 588, footnote.   Alternative terms sometimes used in this connection are 'auto-aggression' and 'destrudo' (E. Weiss, 'Todestrieb und Masochismus,' *Imago* (1935), 21, 393).   The former however suggests the opposite of 'auto-erotism', which as generally used in psycho-analysis indicates the more or less independent operation of a 'component instinct' not closely connected with an integrated 'self' or permanent object in the outer world (whereas 'narcissism' implies love directed to the 'self'); while 'destrudo' does not differentiate between outwardly or inwardly directed aggression or 'death instinct'.

the child's own self, in a way that fulfilled the mother's wishes, but with a kind of savage energy that was quite foreign to the mother's attitude. Here there was no mere copying of the mother, no simple adoption of her rôle, but an addition to it of a new element derived from the child's own aggressiveness, suddenly directed against herself instead of against the outer world. In this little incident we see an example of the way in which the nemesistic element of autogenous aggression complicates and distorts the picture that would result from mere adoption and introjection of the parents' moral attitude.

A girl of fourteen had considerable conflict with the older members of her family over matters of dress. Compelled by adult pressure to abandon the style which she herself approved, she made herself, whenever possible, into something resembling a caricature of what her elders wanted, and regarded it as a triumph when her schoolmates considered her 'a perfect fright'. Here the wish to put her elders in the wrong was clearly manifest; nevertheless her method of achieving it involved, as she herself put it, 'an assault against her own dignity'—an assault committed by herself.

An amusing instance of a somewhat similar exaggeration is to be found in the autobiographical novel *Merrily I go to Hell* by Mary Cameron. The heroine had contrived to get herself expelled from school. Her father, who took a very serious view of the situation, gravely informed her that of course nobody would want to know or have any association with a girl who had suffered such a deep disgrace. Whereupon the culprit seized a small bell that stood near by and, ringing it loudly, left the room, uttering as she went the warning cry, 'Unclean, unclean!'

In other instances a similar attitude of exaggerated or caricatured obedience, resulting in impediment, harm, or humiliation to the self, may persist when the parental source of the attitude has become forgotten or inaccessible to consciousness. This is to be found both in hysterical cases, where there is either a fear of some forbidden object or action (often disguised in symbolic form), or an anæsthesia or paralysis of some sense organ or part of the body which might be used for forbidden purposes, and in obsessional cases, where a compulsive action (itself perhaps a gross caricature of some moral injunction) serves to prevent the patient from infringing a taboo. Quite often, however, the exaggerated obedience takes on a form that would not usually be recognized as pathological. A young woman undergoing psycho-analysis in London complained to her analyst that whenever she was in a hurry some slow and clumsy person would get in her way, blocking her progress, for instance on the escalator of a Tube or on the approach of an omnibus. After discussion of various recent instances that she remembered, it began to dawn upon her that the truth was, not so much that a slow-moving person got in her way, as that she on her own initiative, though without noticing it, tended often quite unnecessarily to take up her position just behind such a person. Further consideration reminded her of the fact that she had for many years been irritated at the slow and clumsy movements of her mother, who, she said, was always getting in her way. She usually controlled her outward behaviour, but her irritation had recoiled against herself and caused her gratuitously to seek situations of a similar kind even when her mother was not present. Such a symptom is an example of the self-imposed obstacles and handicaps which are found so frequently in the careers of those who in recent years have often been called 'neurotic characters', i.e. persons who present no obvious or easily recognizable pathological symptoms, but who throughout their lives suffer from disabilities or disasters, sometimes of a much graver kind than that in the instance just described, unconsciously contrived by themselves as though in response to some hidden demand for self-punishment and self-humiliation. Such persons will eagerly embrace any opportunities for suffering they happen to encounter and will spontaneously add to any pain or distress occasioned by outer circumstances or by their fellows. Except for the implied clear conscious recognition of the tendency (a recognition which is, of course, really due to the psychological insight of a great writer) the following account of himself by Arkad in Dostoevsky's *A Raw Youth* brilliantly describes the condition: 'Strange to say, I always had, perhaps from my earliest childhood, one characteristic: if I were ill treated, absolutely wronged and insulted to the last degree, I always showed at once an irresistible desire to submit passively to the insult, and even to accept more than my assailant wanted to inflict on me, as though I would say: "All right, you have humiliated me, so I will humiliate myself even more; look and enjoy it"'.

In all the cases so far considered there appears to be what we might call a collaboration between the aggression from outside (or from the corresponding introjected moral authority) and the recoil of the person's own aggressiveness (our factors 2 and 3 respectively). In other instances, however, this latter element may operate in relative or complete purity, and it then becomes more easily and unmistakably recognizable for what it is. Nunberg reports a very clear case from a child as young as fifteen months.[1] A little boy was indulging with obvious signs of pleasure in an attempt to pull other people's hair and scratch their faces. When told 'No, no!', and prevented from continuing his attacks, he said: 'Hi(t) B(obb)y', and began to pull his own hair and scratch his own face with such energy that he had to be protected from himself.

Turning to older people, an undergraduate of my acquaintance at one of our ancient universities had for some time been suffering from suppressed fury at the behaviour of a fellow-student who, he considered, had treated him unfairly in a number of matters, ranging from love affairs to the borrowing of text-books and tobacco jars. On learning suddenly of some fresh outrage on the part of this student, the undergraduate systematically smashed every easily breakable article, pictures, crockery, and several pieces of light furniture, in his own room. The fury that he had not the courage to express face to face with the culprit was vented on completely innocent objects at his own expense.

Nor is the infliction of bodily pain or injury on the self by any means excluded. A mother, upset by her son's scrapes and vagaries, would bang her head repeatedly against the wall while complaining of his lack of decorum and sense of responsibility. A somewhat nervous schoolboy, tormented by a fellow-pupil, bigger, stronger, and more extravert in character than himself, broke off a half-hearted effort to assert his own rights and, leaping on his bicycle, rode down a short steep hill and deliberately crashed into a hedge at the bottom, damaging himself and his bicycle considerably.

In a few cases resort may be made to the extreme expedient of suicide, or at least the semblance of attempted suicide. Psycho-analysts have sometimes told us that suicide may be a substitute for murder, and the relative frequency of suicide pacts or suicide plus murder shows pretty clearly that these two acts of violence are related.[2] This last fact serves to remind us also that in nearly all cases of aggression turned against the self

[1] H. Nunberg, 'Das Schuldgefühl,' Imago (1934), 20, 261.
[2] There are of course other important aspects of suicide and of 'dying together' with which we cannot deal here. Cf. Ernest Jones, Essays in Applied Psycho analysis (1923), chapters 2 and 3.

F

a channel is left open along which the original object of aggression can be made to suffer. The suicide or would-be suicide thinks, 'Now they will be sorry' (just as do those who in their own less drastic fashion indulge in the 'tyranny of tears'), while those who commit minor aggressions on themselves can practically always count on causing shame, embarrassment, irritation, sympathy, or at the very least inconvenience, to the individual to whom their anger is, or was originally, directed. Thus the person who is regarded (by the self-tormenter) as the culprit seldom really escapes his punishment, though it may be less in degree and different in kind from what it would be without the turning of the outraged party's ire against himself. This latter however on his part enjoys, at the cost of his own suffering, a relative freedom from the fear and guilt that a direct and straightforward indulgence in his aggression might entail. In addition he may enjoy something in the nature of a triumph over his adversary—one which would seem to have two main sources, either of which may predominate in any given case. In the first place he may succeed in making this adversary feel guilty, whereas if he had expressed his aggression through its natural channel it would have been he who felt the guilt. In the second place he may deprive the adversary of the opportunity of himself expressing his aggression. This may be felt keenly in certain circumstances, as when a criminal condemned to death forestalls his execution by committing suicide. He is then sometimes said to have 'escaped justice', and indignation may be felt against him (or admiration for him, if we take his side), much as though he had escaped from prison and avoided punishment altogether; whereas in reality he has only brought about the result that official justice sought to achieve, and in so doing has saved his captors trouble. Nevertheless the fact that he has exercised aggression on himself instead of allowing them to punish him has made them feel that he has deprived them of a legitimate satisfaction.

The process of turning aggression against the self sometimes takes on a socialized or institutionalized form, and when this is the case, the intention of influencing, through guilt or otherwise, the persons who were responsible for arousing the aggression is as a rule extremely clear. Miners who stay down in their mines, shop assistants or industrial workers who stage a 'sit down' strike in their stores or factories bring discomfort, loss, and inconvenience primarily on themselves, but they hope in this way indirectly to bring pressure on their employers—largely of course by influencing public opinion. Practically all forms of 'passive resistance' and 'non-violence', including the hunger-striking of prisoners or political captives, fall into the same general category.[1] In some schools the experiment has been tried of punishing the staff (e.g. by not allowing them to leave the school premises) for the misdemeanours of the pupils. Here the teachers have to turn upon themselves the aggression which under older and more conventional régimes they would have freely vented on their charges. Cases of this kind form a transition to what might be called collective self-punishment.[2]

Experimental Approach

Recently there have been certain attempts to throw light by experimental methods upon the phenomena of nemesism.[3] In experiments in which students were asked to solve very difficult puzzles S. Rosenzweig, on the basis of the results obtained, classed his subjects into two main groups: the 'extrapunitives', who on the whole refused to admit that their failure to solve the puzzles was due to any deficiency in themselves and who either guessed at a solution or declared that no solution was possible; and the 'intropunitives',[4] who tended to admit that they were not able to find a solution (i.e. that failure was due to their own deficiencies). Various character qualities were at the same time estimated by other methods, and significant correlations were found between some of these and the subject's degree of extrapunitiveness. Among the most important were the following:

Extrapunitiveness and	Aggressiveness	.	.	. +·67
„	„ Dominance	.	.	. +·51
„	„ Exocathection [5]	.	.	. +·60
„	„ Super-ego Conflict	.	.	. −·53

---

[1] An interesting study of this subject is to be found in Richard B. Gregg, *The Power of Non-Violence*, 1935.

[2] Of course not all collective punishment is self-punishment. When collective punishment is inflicted by a higher authority, as usually in war, it falls into a different category, since those who suffer are not of their own initiative turning their aggression against themselves, nor need the offence for which the punishment is given be one in which their own aggressive impulses are in any way involved.

[3] The most convenient account of these experiments is to be found in H. A. Murray *et al.*: *Explorations in Personality*, 1938.

[4] A problem arises as to how, if at all, we should distinguish between nemesism and intropunitiveness. It would probably be best to apply the term 'nemesism' to the wider concept embracing all forms of aggression turned against the self, and to use 'intropunitiveness' only where there is clear evidence of guilt as well as of aggression (since 'punishment' is usually taken to imply guilt).

[5] A term corresponding more or less to the better-known 'extraversion'.

Thus it would seem likely that extrapunitiveness measured by reaction to the puzzles is an aspect of a more general quality of aggression, dominance, and extraversion freely shown in ordinary life, the puzzle situation indicating in some considerable degree the extent to which a person is generally liable to vent his aggression against the outer world or against himself.[1]

An interesting experiment on the tendency of extrapunitives to find fault with their environment rather than with themselves, in fact to deal with their own faults by projecting them on to others and thus failing to recognize that they possess them themselves, was carried out by R. R. Sears. Members of three college fraternities rated themselves and one another for 'stinginess', 'obstinacy', 'disorderliness', and 'bashfulness'. Those who were, according to the pooled marks, rated for more than the average of these traits were divided into two groups: those who recognized their own excess and those who did not. The latter group with astonishing regularity tended to rate their fellows higher in these very traits than did the former group. Thus we find some statistical justification for William James's statement [2] that 'it is one of the strangest laws of our nature that many things which we are well satisfied with in ourselves disgust us when seen in others'. But this statement, it would now appear, is not true of all. The intropunitives fall into a different category; they are not able to become blind to their own faults by projecting them on others. Indeed, as we

[1] Based upon some results of this and other experiments Rosenzweig distinguished a third type, the 'impunitive', characterized by a rather marked tendency to forget the occasion of frustration and in this way to reconcile themselves—and perhaps others too—to a disagreeable situation. It is, he suggests, as though they adopted the motto 'Forgive and forget', whereas in the two other types there is relatively little forgiving and forgetting, their aggression being preserved, to be expressed against outer objects in the case of extrapunitives, against themselves in the case of intropunitives. It is interesting to note that the impunitives tend to provide one of the exceptions to the general rule (established by Zeigarnik and since corroborated by others) that uncompleted tasks are remembered better than completed ones, whereas both extrapunitives and intropunitives tend to follow this rule; probably the impunitives' facility for forgetting the unpleasant or troublesome triumphs over the general psychological tendencies underlying the rule—tendencies into the nature of which we cannot enter here; whereas it is easy to imagine that the extrapunitives and intropunitives may both in their different ways have additional motives for following the rule. There is some evidence that impunitives are relatively easily hypnotizable persons, so that Rosenzweig has tentatively erected what he calls a triadic hypothesis, according to which impunitives are characterized by three traits: (1) impunitiveness (i.e. lack of aggressiveness either outwardly or inwardly directed) as the immediate reaction to frustration; (2) repression as the preferred 'mechanism of defence'; (3) easy hypnotizability.

[2] Itself based, as James points out, on Horwicz. W. James, op. cit., 314, 326 ff.

have already seen, there are cases with regard to which the opposite of James's statement might approximate much more nearly to the truth.

Further light on what Rosenzweig has called extrapunitiveness and intropunitiveness is thrown by an interesting experiment carried out by D. W. MacKinnon. Here, as in Rosenzweig's work, the subjects (in this case ninety-three college graduates) were asked to attempt to solve a series of difficult puzzles. The answers to the puzzles were conveniently accessible to the subjects, who, according to the instructions given them, were allowed to consult these answers in the case of some puzzles but not in that of others. By means of special techniques the subjects were studied during their work, both as to whether they 'violated' the instructions by looking up answers where this was forbidden, and as to their general emotional behaviour, expressed verbally or otherwise. It was found that 46 per cent. of the subjects were 'violators', 54 per cent. 'non-violators'. The verbal reactions of the subjects were classified under three heads: (1) simple non-directed, e.g. such exclamations as 'Oh, Gosh!', 'Oh, what the Hell!': (2) directed against an outer object (usually but not always the puzzle itself), e.g. 'You bastard', 'You crazy bitch', 'These are the God-damnedest things I ever saw'; (3) directed against the self, e.g. 'Jesus Christ, I must be dumb', 'You fool, you', 'Idiot', 'God, I must be a nit-wit'.

Violators and non-violators were more or less equally expressive, about 65 per cent. of both groups actually speaking in one or other of the above ways during the experiment. But the proportions of those falling under classes 2 and 3 above were very different in the two cases. The figures can be most strikingly conveyed in the form of a fourfold table:

	EXTRAPUNITIVE VERBAL REACTIONS	INTROPUNITIVE VERBAL REACTIONS
Violators	31 per cent.	0 per cent.
Non-violators	0 ,,	10 ,,

Here the two zero figures are particularly impressive. It seems that the non-violators never indulged in extrapunitive verbal reactions and the violators never in intropunitive ones. Remembering that 'violation' is itself an aggressive or 'immoral' act (inasmuch as it involves infringing a prohibition, or in plain words 'cheating'), we have once again reason to suppose that extrapunitiveness and intropunitiveness as thus experimentally determined have some very significant relation to the person's general tendency to express his aggressiveness outwardly against the world or inwardly against himself.

The same picture emerges when we consider non-verbal behaviour. This was also classified into three groups: neutral, extrapunitive, and intropunitive respectively. Into the first group fall the examples of behaviour described as 'non-aggressive restlessness': 39 per cent. of the violators and 26 per cent. of the non-violators exhibited behaviour of this kind. As marks of extrapunitive aggressiveness were taken such actions as pounding the table, stamping, kicking, etc.: 31 per cent. of the violators and 4 per cent. of the non-violators manifested behaviour of this kind. As marks of intropunitiveness were taken any actions which seemed to be directed against the subject's own body. These fall into three chief classes which are listed separately, together with the proportions of violators and non-violators indulging in them:

	VIOLATORS	NON-VIOLATORS
Oral activities	48 per cent.	83 per cent.
Nasal activities	14 ,,	28 ,,
Hirsutal activities	5 ,,	11 ,,

Under all three heads the percentage is much greater among the non-violators than among the violators, this seeming to corroborate the experimenter's suggestion that these activities can be regarded as intropunitive.

Various questions were put to the subjects at the time of the experiment. With the complete answers we cannot deal here, though they are often full of interest. Asked 'Do you often feel guilty in ordinary life?', the answer 'Yes' was given by 29 per cent. of the violators and 75 per cent. of the non-violators. Here we see what appears to be an experimental corroboration of the psycho-analytic finding, perhaps first clearly expressed in *The Ego and the Id*, that the more we repress our aggression the more likely is this aggression to turn against ourselves and (in harmony with the principles we have endeavoured to expound in Chapter III and in the present chapter) to ally itself with moral tendencies. Another item of evidence reinforcing this conclusion is to be found in the fact that the violators had more often experienced bodily chastisement in their youth and had often reacted aggressively to it, whereas the non-violators had more often been subjected to psychological discipline— apparently resulting in the growth of a more tender conscience.

The results show again an inverse relation between outwardly directed aggression and the inner feeling of guilt. They illustrate also the important fact often noted in clinical practice that the severity of the super-ego may be altogether out of proportion to that of the real parental authority. When the parental régime is really harsh, children often feel that they can justifiably express some measure of their own aggression in return. When, however, parents are on the surface always loving, tender, or at most reproachful, never severe, bad-tempered, or unreasonable, but when they are at the same time in reality frustrating, children are much more liable to feel that it would be wicked to express their own aggression against those who on their part ostensibly display only mildness, consideration, and solicitude. Under such circumstances, the channel for the discharge of the children's aggressiveness towards the natural outer objects being blocked, there may be no alternative for them but to become nemesistic and intropunitive. With the further moral and practical corollaries of this we cannot here concern ourselves, but what we should be well advised to note is that work of this kind does seem to have opened up a profitable experimental approach to the rather bizarre and much neglected phenomena with which we are concerned in the present chapter.

Asceticism

The development of the capacity to turn one's own aggressiveness inwards and then to put it in the service of morality represents—as Glover [1] has pointed out—a very ingenious device of Nature for rendering man fit for social life, and it may have played a very significant part in making him a gregarious animal capable of participating in an elaborate and hierarchical society in which both assertion and submission are required. The process might perhaps be compared in some respects to those *tours de force* of phylogenesis whereby an organ acquires new functions in the course of evolution, as when the pineal gland, originally a cyclopean eye, became endowed with the power of manufacturing a secretion which appears to have the function of retarding the onset of maturity (itself an extremely important characteristic of humanity).

Nevertheless it is clear that this ability to turn aggression against the self is liable to be very seriously misused and over-used. It would indeed appear that such exaggeration or misuse

---

[1] Edward Glover, *War, Sadism, and Pacifism*, 1933.

of what, when employed with moderation, may be a very
valuable function, is responsible for some of the strangest
oddities and extravagances of human behaviour (including some
we have already noticed and others to which we shall have to
refer on later pages). These varieties of conduct are all concerned with what in the widest sense might be termed asceticism
—that apparently wilful and perverse forgoing of the possibilities
of pleasure that presents such a hard problem to the doctrine of
psychological hedonism, the simple and naïve view, so popular
in the nineteenth century, according to which man always seeks
to achieve pleasure and avoid pain.[1]   On closer inspection, cases
of apparently ascetic behaviour can be grouped into a number
of classes, each of which has its distinctive features.   Not all of
them concern us intimately here; nevertheless a brief review of
the chief kinds of asceticism may help to make still clearer the
all too insufficiently recognized rôle of aggression in morality,
and as the subject is in any case of considerable interest to the
student of the psychological aspects of moral conduct it may
afford a fitting conclusion to this chapter.[2]

The first type might be called **Utilitarian Asceticism.**   All
mental and cultural development implies the ability to postpone
some immediate satisfaction or to undergo some immediate
hardship in order to achieve some eventual greater gain.   As
soon as we are able to foresee the probable outcome of various
lines of action we must, therefore, if we are reasonable beings,
forgo certain pleasures that are at the moment within our
grasp, since we realize that by so doing we shall be able either
to enjoy still greater pleasure in the future or (what is, alas, more
frequent) to avoid certain future pains which outweigh the
present pleasures.   Since reason is at best but a relatively
feeble power when confronted with some strong instinctive
impulse, we have developed that capacity which we term 'will'
to reinforce our reason, and those persons who are endowed with
a high degree of Webb's 'w' factor (as described in Chapter II)
are no doubt distinguished by a relatively great ability to
control immediate impulse in order to achieve remoter goals.

---

[1] Not that asceticism constitutes by any means the only objection to psychological hedonism.   For a fuller discussion of this doctrine, see the present
author's paper on 'Feeling and the Hormic Theory,' *Character and Personality*
(1939), 7, 211.

[2] In the remaining part of this chapter I have followed fairly closely the first
part of an address on 'Asceticism and Education' given for the King Alfred
School Society at the 23rd Annual Conference of Education Associations, London,
1935.   See the *Report* of this Conference.

So far, behaviour of this kind is both perfectly rational and perfectly compatible with psychological hedonism. This temporary 'asceticism' is no more than a means to an end. In the language of ethics, it is an 'instrumental' and not an 'intrinsic' value. When, however, the goal is distant, general, or indefinite, rather than near and specific, and when the preliminary period of painful effort or renunciation is very prolonged, it acquires a rather special character which might tempt us to give it a new name and to call it **Disciplinary** rather than Utilitarian **Asceticism.** Into this category might fall the training of the soldier, the athlete, or the religious devotee, who usually hope to acquire capacities of body or mind that will be generally useful to them in their avocations rather than to achieve some relatively near and well-defined goal. In the same class too is the 'formal training' of educationists, as when the study of Greek and Latin grammar or mathematics is advocated (usually on insufficient evidence), not for their own usefulness, but as fostering a capacity for 'logical thinking' or 'mental application'.

Strictly speaking, the difference between Utilitarian and Disciplinary Asceticism is one of degree rather than of kind. In the case of prolonged training, however, a complication is apt to arise, inasmuch as through association or 'conditioning' we very easily come to attribute an absolute rather than a relative value to what was originally but a means. Because renunciation, patience, and endurance are so often essential to the attainment of our more ambitious goals, we are only too liable to consider that they possess a moral value in themselves, just as we are prone to think that money has an economic value of its own apart from the satisfactions to which it is the means. In his famous experiments on the conditioned reflex Pavlov taught his dogs to salivate when they were given a stimulus that was artificially associated with food; he even succeeded in producing a salivary response to a strong electric shock (such as would normally produce violent attempts at escape). The dogs, however, ceased to respond in this way when the shock (or other stimulus) was experienced a number of times without being followed by the food; these animals had not confused the painful or neutral stimuli with the intrinsically desired stimulus.[1] In human beings, however, a confusion of this kind seems much

---

[1] Though dogs do seem liable to acquire phobias or other enduring neurotic disturbances as a result of a single 'traumatic' experience that has produced a violent emotional upset—much as in the case of human beings.

more likely to occur, probably to a large extent through the influence of precept and tradition (themselves perhaps to some extent based upon, and in turn reinforcing, the general tendency to nemesism with which we have been dealing). It is as though human beings sometimes considered that pain had a value in its own right, quite apart from the question whether it leads to an intrinsically desirable result or not. In this way rational or utilitarian asceticism passes almost imperceptibly into one or other of the varieties of more genuine, or as we might perhaps call it 'intrinsic', asceticism, to which all the other classes to be mentioned belong, and to which we must now turn.

The type which is nearest to Utilitarian Asceticism is that which might appropriately be called **Epicurean Asceticism**; it might perhaps in some respects even be considered a variety of the former. The chief difference is that with Utilitarian Asceticism the suffering or renunciation involved is in itself purely incidental and in other circumstances might be avoided, whereas in Epicurean Asceticism the previous suffering is essential to the subsequent satisfaction. If we want to enjoy the view from a mountain-top we must undertake the laborious business of climbing the mountain, unless it happens to be, for instance, Snowdon or the Jungfrau, in which case we can ascend by railway and enjoy the view without exertion. Where there are mountain railways there is no need for the purely Utilitarian Asceticism that exists in other cases. Nevertheless there are, as every mountaineer knows, certain satisfactions to be gained by climbing the mountain which are lost when the ascent is made without exertion—and similarly with regard to many other fields of achievement and creation (e.g. sport, art, science, literary work) in which quite generally we tend to place the highest value upon that which has cost us the most effort. Even in the purely sensory sphere, if we want to relish the fullest satisfactions to be obtained from drinking, eating, rest, a cooling swim, or a warm fire, we must first undergo, at least in some degree, the corresponding pains of thirst, hunger, exertion, heat, or cold; we must in fact submit ourselves to some degree of Epicurean Asceticism.

The psychology of this form of asceticism is, however, apt to be complicated and leads us to some deep questions of motivation which can only be roughly indicated here. In the first place there is of course the fact, stressed by many psychologists of different schools but especially by McDougall, that pleasure accompanies the satisfaction of a desire or need. The more urgent the need, the greater the resulting pleasure when it is satisfied, but an urgent need is by its very nature a condition of unpleasure, so that the enjoyment of great pleasures, so far as they really depend upon antecedent needs,[1] inevitably implies preceding pains. In the second place there is the joy, very real and positive, that is undoubtedly to be found in effort, strain, tension, and even in danger. To some extent this may be accounted for by saying that all our capacities need exercise and that this exercise gives pleasure. But when, as is so often the case, the exercise is pursued even when it has ceased to be agreeable and has become definitely painful, when moreover, as again often happens, it takes the form of renunciation rather than activity, it would seem that a more subtle explanation is required. Such an explanation is perhaps to be found in the fact that in some minds the satisfaction of desire has become intimately and permanently dependent on the existence of inner inhibitions or outer obstacles—so much so that a straightforward and direct satisfaction without difficulties and complications is well-nigh impossible, appearing either shocking or pointless as the case may be. In such minds what I have elsewhere called the principle of 'the increase of satisfaction through inhibition' has come to play a most important part.[2] The indulgence in a high degree of apparently Epicurean Asceticism in accordance with this principle in all probability implies some admixture with one or more of the three remaining types.

In **Masochistic Asceticism** there is enjoyment of suffering or renunciation for its own sake, not for any ulterior end as in the utilitarian, disciplinarian, or epicurean varieties. As already mentioned (Chapter III), Freud distinguishes sexual from moral

---

[1] For a discussion of the question how far all pleasures and unpleasures are thus related to antecedent needs, a question on which there has been much difference of opinion, see the above-mentioned paper in *Character and Personality* (1939), 7, 211.

[2] Such minds present a very striking contrast to certain others of an opposite type, which enable their possessors to proceed towards their goals with a directness that may seem to border on childishness and naiveté, scorning all unnecessary sophistication and complexity. The French novelist Maurice Bedel has portrayed two extreme examples of these types in his *Jerome or the Latitude of Love*, and thus stated a problem of ethics and psychology which perhaps deserves more attention than it has yet received from either discipline. For a preliminary discussion see the present author's 'Maurice Bedel's Jerome: A Study of Contrasting Types,' in *The Psychoanalytic Quarterly*, 1932, i, reprinted in *Men and Their Motives*, 1934, in which the above-mentioned principle of the increase of satisfaction through inhibition is formulated and illustrated.

masochism (he also distinguishes a third kind, feminine masochism, to which we shall refer in our next chapter). In moral
masochism, as the very name implies, the suffering is undergone
in response to a demand of conscience. The super-ego takes
over the punishing aspects of the outer moral authorities and
demands that the ego should suffer in atonement for its guilt.
Doubtless often enough there are also elements of pure internally
directed aggression. But in either case there is here added the
essential (for this kind of asceticism) complicating factor of
pleasure in one's own pain. Our view of the precise nature of
this complicating factor will of course depend upon our theory
of masochism itself; but in any case we can say that the
masochistic impulse, whatever its ultimate nature, has taken
advantage of the morally-toned self-inflicted suffering to gain
satisfaction on its own account. In the apparently simpler form
of sexual masochism this tendency to seek and find enjoyment
in suffering may be an all-sufficient explanation (if we admit,
as we surely must, that there is a peculiarly intimate relation
between this impulse and the sexual instinct). Nevertheless it
seems likely that even here some elements of moral punishment or
of simple aggression turned against the self may also be present,
so that it is only in rare cases, if in any, that we get masochistic
asceticism in quite a simple and uncomplicated form.

In **Punitive Asceticism** the element of self-inflicted punishment for guilt is the sole or the predominant factor, the element
of pleasure contributed by masochism being totally or relatively
lacking. Into this category fall a great number of more or less
institutionalized religious practices, such as fasting and penitence, and many individual neurotic forms of suffering—the
latter probably to some extent taking the place of the former
when religious belief tends to decay. In the neurotic cases the
element of punishment is for the most part not consciously
recognized, and even in the institutionalized forms it may often
be camouflaged as training or discipline, though in other cases
it may be openly imposed as a penance—either self-decreed by
the penitent himself or as directed by some higher authority.
Thus punitive asceticism may be characterized by all degrees of
consciousness of the punitive purpose. It permeates extensively
religious practice and neurotic symptoms. It merges into pure
discipline at one end of the scale, while at the other it is sometimes hard to distinguish from simple punishment, provided that
the culprit willingly submits to the punishment and is himself

a party to its execution. Finally, where the punishment takes the form of self-imposed deprivation of some means to comfort or well-being rather than any more direct and active infliction of suffering, it has obvious affinities to the widespread institution of sacrifice. Punitive asceticism is indeed the most important of all forms of asceticism from our present point of view, and we shall have frequent occasion to touch on it again in one aspect or another in the later chapters of this book.

Our final category might be termed **Aggressive Asceticism.** Here the simple recoil of aggression against the self is the predominating element, there being neither the pleasure in suffering that is characteristic of masochism, nor the moral element that plays the chief rôle in punitive asceticism. There is even more doubt than in the previous cases whether aggressive asceticism ever occurs in a pure form. Single acts of self-inflicted violence, or conduct of this kind enduring only for a brief period, may indeed be dictated wholly, or very nearly so, by simple inward-turning aggression, but the term 'asceticism' is usually understood as referring to behaviour of appreciably longer duration. We have, moreover, to take into account the fact—illustrated by our examples of a few pages back—that very often the turning of aggression against oneself does not prevent the indirect expression of hostility towards our enemies. Though we suffer most ourselves, they are also made to suffer—or such at least is our intention. The satisfaction thus derived may greatly reinforce the motive for aggression against the self and may be capable of making us persist in our self-inflicted pain. It doubtless plays a great part in such manifestations as the hunger-striking of political prisoners. But where this element of outwardly directed aggression is absent, and the self-torment is nevertheless prolonged, there is almost certainly present some other of the motives that belong to asceticism proper—probably those characteristic of the masochistic and punitive varieties.

Asceticism in its various forms and ramifications permeates our social life. It has indeed become to a large extent an integral part of our educational and religious systems, and it exercises a very considerable influence on our legal, political, and even medical and economic thinking. To some extent the renunciation of immediate satisfaction and the endurance of pain, effort, and distress are essential means to mental and social progress. But, under the influence of the various motives we have been considering, man would appear so far to have forgotten that this renunciation and endurance are from the biological standpoint no more than means, so far to have elevated deprivation and suffering into self-sufficient ends, that it would often seem that he might just as truthfully be called a pain-seeking as a pleasure-seeking animal.

CHAPTER VIII

AGGRESSION AND SADO-MASOCHISM

Freud's Discovery of the Aggressive Element in Morals

In Chapter IV we devoted some consideration to the way in which the super-ego comes into existence, and we noted the satisfactory resemblances in many respects between the accounts given by Baldwin, McDougall, and Freud. But we also noted that neither Baldwin nor McDougall had considered the aggressive aspects of the super-ego. Nor, indeed, have we ourselves as yet had anything substantial to add to the brief account of the origin of these aggressive elements that we gave in Chapter III. The treatment of aggression in the last chapter was mainly descriptive, though it is to be hoped that the reader has received some enlightenment both as to the fact of nemesism, i.e. of the turning of aggression against the self (together with its utilization in this form for moral ends), and of the ways and circumstances in which such a process of recoil is liable to occur. But having dealt, at any rate provisionally, with the phenomena (we shall return to them in Chapter XI), it is our duty to see how far psycho-analysis has anything further to suggest as to the origin and ultimate nature of these important aggressive elements of human morality. To this task the present and the following chapter are devoted.

The realization of the existence and significance of these elements would seem to date from Freud's paper on 'Instincts and their Vicissitudes' (1915),[1] in which he pointed out that among the important transformations of instinct was the process of 'turning round upon the subject', as when a person instead of desiring to exercise mastery desires himself to be mastered, or instead of desiring to look at a love object desires himself to be looked at (as illustrated in the complementary tendencies of

---

[1] *Collected Papers*, iv, 60.

sadism-masochism and scopophilia-exhibitionism respectively). This was followed by a very important paper on 'Mourning and Melancholia' (1917), to which we have already referred (in Chapter V). Freud there drew attention to the fact that the accusations which the melancholic patient would (usually with little apparent justification) bring against himself often seemed to apply, with small modifications, to some important person in his environment—a person indeed whom the patient had lost as a love object (perhaps for a physical reason, such as death, desertion, or separation; perhaps for a psychological one, such as a reduction in the person's apparent loveworthiness). In this fact of loss, Freud suggested, melancholia resembled mourning. The melancholic had solved his problem by introjecting the lost object; when this object had thus become a part of himself, love was replaced by hate, and this hate was turned upon the object as introjected, i.e. upon the self. Thus three distinguishable processes were involved: loss of the object, its introjection, the substitution of hate for love. In this paper Freud hardly attempted an explanation of the last-named process, which indeed would necessitate a discussion of the whole complex relationship of love and hate. As he makes clear elsewhere, all love relationships involve some degree of ambivalence, inasmuch as all love objects (like their maternal prototype) both satisfy and—at any rate in some degree—frustrate. In melancholia the circumstances connected with the loss of the object have greatly intensified the elements of hatred; hence the aggressiveness, scorn, and contempt with which the object is treated after introjection, though of course the patient no longer distinguishes between this introjected object and his own self, which latter for this reason appears to him so blameworthy and vile. Aggression from this source is also manifested in the suicidal attempts which frequently occur in this condition, for it is the hated object in the patient's self against which such attempts are in the last resort directed. Nevertheless, as Freud noted, the patient's conduct (in accordance with what we ourselves saw in the last chapter to be a pretty general rule) still exhibits some externally directed aggression: he does not behave with the humility and submission that would be appropriate if his accusations against himself were true, but on the contrary gives a great deal of trouble, easily taking offence or considering himself unjustly treated.

A few years later Freud realized that this process of introjection of a lost object was a very common one; indeed he was inclined to think that it occurred to some extent in every case of the loss of a love object, the character of an individual being thus in considerable measure determined by his past history of abandoned love objects. Be that as it may (the sceptical reader will probably be tempted to dismiss it as one of Freud's wilder flights of imagination), there is at least one case in which such introjection plays a supremely important rôle, and that is the case of the parents. The individual only frees himself from the more infantile dependence on the parents and from the attitudes and emotions associated with it (i.e., in short, the Œdipus Complex) by introjecting their image—and this introjection has unique consequences inasmuch as it results in the super-ego. Earlier, in his 'Narcissism' paper (1912), Freud had seen that the ego-ideal corresponds to some extent to the critical attitude of the parents; it was in connection with melancholia (1917) that he realized the importance of introjection; and in *The Ego and the Id* he brought the two ideas together (1923). But the example of melancholia was of course specially suited to bring into prominence the element of aggression—an aggression reflected back from an object in the outer world, put in the service of the super-ego, and directed against the self; and that is its particular importance to us here. It is this discovery of Freud's in 1917 which seems first to have opened the eyes of psycho-analysts to the significance of aggression in the super-ego, though its full import was not clear till Freud had more completely formulated the theory of the super-ego six years later.

Sadism and Masochism : General Considerations

In this same paper on melancholia Freud also drew attention to another co-operating aggressive factor—sado-masochism, our fourth factor of Chapter III. He tells us that 'the self-torments of melancholiacs are without doubt pleasurable' and that they signify a gratification of sadistic tendencies as well as of simple hate—both of course being turned against the self.

It is time that we considered a little more clearly the fascinating problem of sado-masochism or 'algolagnia', not that we must expect to emerge with clear-cut and final conceptions, for it is fairly well agreed among all investigators that much remains to be understood concerning the origin and functions of this queer tendency to experience pleasure in pain.

Apart from psycho-analytic approaches, attempts to explain

algolagnia have usually proceeded on one or other of two main
lines, stressing either the inevitable *biological* connection of
pain with sexual behaviour or the existence of a *psycho-physical*
attunement or connection between pain and sexual feeling. As
regards the first of these, it is clear that aggression is involved
as an element in many aspects of sexual life, both with human
beings and other animals. Courtship and the act of copulation
present quite a number of opportunities for aggression. Some
degree of violence characterizes the mating procedures of most
animals, which may sometimes be carried to the extremest
limits, as in insects like the praying mantis in which the female
eats the male while the latter is engaged in the performance of
his rôle. Added to this is the aggression associated with sexual
rivalry or jealousy, in itself, as some writers think, one of the
greatest biological sources of violence, and which, as Zuckerman
has shown in a well-known study,[1] plays a prominent part in
the lives of some monkeys and apes; while in man the same
motives perhaps find expression in the partly serious and partly
playful practices of 'marriage by capture' that are, or were till
recently, to be found in so many parts of the world. Connected
with sex again perhaps, though more remotely, is the aggression
called out for the protection and care of the young, which may
lead on occasion to offensive action even on the part of otherwise
peaceful and timid animals. There is therefore ample biological
reason for a close association of sexual function with the use of
violence and the inevitably correlated infliction and suffering of
pain.

The psycho-physical argument is perhaps less clear and
convincing. The general view would seem to be that pain, in
virtue of being an intense form of stimulation (indeed as being
'prepotent' over other stimulations, as Sherrington might say),
is somehow peculiarly liable to be associated with that other
intense form of stimulation that corresponds to sex. There is, it
is true, good evidence that high intensity of stimulation of any
kind may itself be pleasant, provided we adopt a suitable attitude
to it, i.e. provided either that we 'feel equal to it' and welcome
the rough-and-tumble it involves (as in the cases of bright sun-
light, a loud thunder-clap, a fortissimo passage on the orchestra,
the heat of a Turkish bath, or the blast of a bitter winter wind),
or that we willingly submit to it and expose ourselves passively
and unresistingly to the strong stimulus. In the first case we feel

[1] S. Zuckerman, *The Social Life of Monkeys and Apes*, 1932.

'braced' or 'excited' by the stimulus, made vividly alive by its impact, while in the second we find it agreeable to submit ourselves without opposition to an overwhelming outside force. In so far as we can adopt similar attitudes to it, pain may be no exception to the general rule, and it may be possible to enjoy the intensity of pain in the same way as the intensity of any other strong stimulus. But whether we enjoy pain in virtue of its intensity, or in any other way (e.g. in virtue of its biological conditioning as described above), the enjoyment is dependent on our attitude and not on any peculiar quality of pain itself. It is indeed fairly certain that pain as such is never pleasant, except perhaps at quite low intensities; it is rather the general situation that may under certain circumstances be pleasant—a general situation that may include pain as an essential element but that is pleasant *in spite of* the disagreeable quality of pain itself. McDougall has made this pretty clear in his considera- tion of the general relation between feeling and conation.[1] The normal effect of pain (as of other unpleasant sensations) is to make us endeavour to remove the stimulus, to escape from the pain-causing situation. If for any reason we do not make this usual reaction, if we do not seek to escape but on the contrary seek to experience the sensation fully and 'enjoy' it, the gener- ally disagreeable character of the experience at once disappears, or becomes at least considerably reduced. This has been amply demonstrated by experiment and is doubtless what occurs in the masochist, who through association or conditioning has learnt to welcome and relish the painful experience (e.g. flagel- lation), just as Pavlov's dogs learnt to welcome, rather than to escape from, the electric shock when it had come to mean that they were to be fed. McDougall has suggested that some martyrs, just because they 'embraced' martyrdom instead of trying to escape from it, may have actually enjoyed the torments under which they died. Groddeck has insisted (in spite of the protests of some incredulous women) that mothers really enjoy their labour 'pains', not only because of the satisfaction con- nected with carrying out a supremely significant biological function, but also because of the zest produced by a quite unusually intense sensation (he here draws attention to the enormously high degree of vaginal stimulation in parturition as compared with that in coitus). Neither martyrdom nor child-

---

[1] For a more detailed consideration of this whole matter see the present author's article on 'Feeling and the Hormic Theory' already referred to.

birth lends itself conveniently to careful introspective study, but in so far as the results of laboratory experiments, working for the most part with far feebler stimuli, are at all comparable, it would seem indeed that neither statement need be entirely untrue. The total situation, if it is sought as the means to a highly important end and has even acquired in this way an appeal of its own (as may be the case with both martyrs and mothers), may be one that contains a definite element of pleasure or may even be generally pleasant, in spite of the devastatingly unpleasant quality of the pain itself.[1] And the total situation depends upon one's general attitude.

The clue to sadism and masochism must be sought therefore, not in any special qualities or connections of sensory experience, but rather in a particular conative attitude. What are the motives to be found in such an attitude? McDougall (as already mentioned in Chapter III) gives a very simple answer—one which seems to bring out well the explanatory, or at the very least the descriptive, virtues of his psychological system. He says that sadism and masochism are both compound attitudes or emotions, in this respect like contempt, shame, reproach, or (within the sexual sphere) coquetry. Just as contempt is a fusion of the more primary tendencies of disgust and positive self-feeling (the emotion corresponding to self-assertion), so sadism is also a fusion—of sex and positive self-feeling; while masochism is a fusion of sex and negative self-feeling (or submission). Granted the existence of sex, assertion, and submission as three primary instincts, this explanation is not only delightfully simple but perfectly natural so far as it goes. Any theoretical difficulties that arise are concerned: (*a*) with the rôle of pain as a sensation; these can probably be overcome by a reference to the biological and conative factors already referred to; (*b*) with what Freud termed moral masochism. For McDougall this latter would probably not be regarded as a problem, as he would refuse to admit that the term masochism is properly applied in this sense, though he would doubtless

---

[1] In some respects (but not of course in all) the situation here is similar to the one implied in the widely recognized distinction between happiness and pleasure. Happiness and unhappiness are relatively enduring conditions dependent on the satisfaction or non-satisfaction of deep-lying conations; pleasure and unpleasure are more transient conditions dependent on temporary circumstances or stimulations. Thus we may be happy because in general life is going well, even though at the moment we may be very tired or have a headache; or unhappy because of some great loss or serious anxiety, even though we are laughing at a good joke or enjoying some choice dish.

consent that such emotions as shame and negative self-feeling were involved. Masochism, however, he would probably have considered, is a word that should be used only when the sexual component is clearly manifest.

Sadism and Masochism : Psycho-analytic Contributions

In the development of Freud's thought on this matter three stages can conveniently be distinguished. In the *Three Contributions to the Theory of Sex* (1905) sadism and masochism were looked upon as more or less independent members of a fairly long list of 'component instincts'. Describing this stage at a later date, he says the view was 'that sexual excitation arises as an accessory effect of a large series of internal processes . . . indeed that perhaps nothing very important takes place within the organism without contributing a component to the excitation of the sexual instinct. According to this, an excitation of physical pain and feelings of distress would surely also have this effect'.[1] This accounted for masochism. Sadism on its part was thought to be connected principally with the function of the muscles and thus eventually with the exercise of power. Nineteen years after its formulation, in 1924, Freud complained that this earlier theory of the independent origin of sadism and masochism gave no satisfactory account of their undoubted connection, easy convertibility, and complementary nature.

It might seem, however, that the source of this connection could easily be found in the experience that the use of violent muscular force is very liable to arouse pain in the person against whom it is directed, and it is this view which Freud seems to have adopted as a part of what we might call his second theory, expounded in his article on 'Instincts and their Vicissitudes' of 1915. According to this, masochism has its origin in the connection between sex and pain, sadism in the connection between sex and force or dominance, and, since the use of force and the suffering of pain so often go together, the two tendencies inevitably become associated. As a further part of this theory, however, Freud considered that sadism was the primary member of the pair and that masochism is only sadism turned against the self, the external partner taking over the active rôle of sadist. Here the earlier view is enriched by the dawning realization of the importance of aggression turned against the self. As a

---

[1] 'The Economic Problem of Masochism' (1924), *Collected Papers*, ii, 259.

corollary of the view that sadism is the primary tendency, it would appear that mastery (or submission) rather than the infliction (or suffering) of pain is the fundamental motive in sado-masochism.

Freud's third theory, as developed in the 'Economic Problem of Masochism' (1924), is rather more complicated. This time both sadism and masochism are brought into relation with the concept of the 'death instinct' which he had meantime developed and which has caused so much puzzlement to psychologists ever since. In virtue of the death instinct (Thanatos) all living matter tends, not abruptly and catastrophically but ultimately and so-to-speak in its own appointed way, to return to the non-living state. This tendency is impeded or opposed by the 'life instinct' (Eros or the libido), a concept which had developed out of Freud's always very wide view of sex. Neither of these two fundamental opposing instincts is easily, or perhaps ever, to be observed in its full purity, actual behaviour usually corresponding to some fusion or interaction of the two. Sadism and masochism both represent such fusions. Masochism is the simpler and more primitive form, inasmuch as it represents the death instinct employed in its original direction, i.e. against the self. The admixture of an element of Eros, however, reduces its primitive destructiveness and makes it relatively harmless. But the danger inherent in the death instinct is still further averted by the device of turning it outwards against others, and this is what happens in the case of sadism, though of course here too an admixture of Eros can effectively reduce the element of destructiveness. Sadism and masochism, Freud thinks, are distinguished from the more straightforward aggression of the super-ego against the self which he calls the 'need for punishment' by the fact that in the case of the latter there has been a defusion of Eros and Thanatos, i.e. a desexualization. From this point of view it would appear that the sexual element in sadism and masochism has a helpful and protective function— one however that is liable to be abolished by the process of defusion, which allows the death instinct to carry on its dread work without the saving grace of love. There are indeed, it would thus seem, two main ways in which the danger inherent in the death instinct can be neutralized: (1) by turning it outwards as aggression towards others (this of course averts the danger from the particular individual only, and at the same time illustrates again the inverse relation between intropunitiveness and extrapunitiveness that we considered in the last chapter), (2) by diluting it with Eros.

As already implied, few psychologists (even of the psycho-analytic school) have found themselves at home with the death instinct, which as a scientific concept seems to many both unattractive and lacking in precision. If we deprive it of its more fundamental (or, as we might be tempted to think, more mystic) implications it becomes very like simple aggression—so long as we remember that aggression can be turned against the self as well as against the outer world. But the valuable concept of fusion still remains, and it is clear that Freud's views in this respect are not so very different from McDougall's, though he has given them a greater power, (a) by emphasizing the comple-mentarity and convertibility of sadism and masochism, (b) by considering the quantitative aspects of the fusions involved (with the possibility of complete defusion as a limiting case). As regards this last matter, the tendency among psycho-analysts in considering the difference between (eroticized) sado-masochism and simple nemesism is to think in terms of regression rather than of defusion. As Ernest Jones first put it in an early discussion of the problems of the super-ego,[1] the more purely aggressive and destructive tendencies manifested in the 'need for punishment' seem to depend on a regression to a level at which erotic and aggressive elements are more intimately related and fused than at later more developed stages. The secret of nemesism would thus lie in fusion (of aggression and sex) rather than in defusion (of Thanatos and Eros) as Freud maintained. This is a view which has undergone considerable elaboration in some of the later developments of psycho-analytic thought, as we shall see in the next chapter.

In the article to which we have been referring, Freud dis-tinguishes three kinds of masochism, the erotogenic, the feminine, and the moral kind. The erotogenic represents the more obvious kind of fusion between Eros and Thanatos (or, if we prefer to deal with the simpler concepts, between sex and aggression), about which nothing more need be said here. As regards feminine masochism Freud rather paradoxically (but, as some might think, characteristically) makes his approach through the study of its manifestations in the male sex, and in defence of his procedure we shall perhaps be ready to admit that any

[1] Ernest Jones, 'The Origin and Structure of the Super-Ego,' *Int. J. Psa.* (1926), 7, 303.

special 'feminine' aspects of masochism are likely to emerge more clearly and strikingly when exhibited by men. Such manifestations are, he thinks, largely confined to phantasy and, even if given some real expression, 'the real situations are only a kind of make-believe performance of the phantasies'. The phantasied situations, such as those of being pinioned, bound, beaten, mishandled, forced to obey unconditionally, defiled or degraded, show, Freud believes, that the masochist 'wants to be treated like a little helpless, dependent child, but especially like a naughty child'. Moreover he goes on to say that, when the phantasies are sufficiently detailed and elaborated, one easily discovers that in them the subject is placed in a situation characteristic of womanhood, i.e. they mean that 'he is being castrated, is playing the passive part in coitus, or is giving birth'. It would seem, however—and Freud himself appears to be aware of it—that such phantasies have as much right to be described as either childish or moral (because the suffering is regarded as a punishment) as they have to be called feminine, and although in the general literature of sexual psychopathology there has been a tendency to consider that masochism is somehow specifically feminine, the concept of a special variety of feminine masochism is one that seems to have aroused considerable misgivings in recent writers. There are of course, it is admitted, biological factors (e.g. the weaker average physical strength, the possibility of rape, the physiological details of coitus, the pain associated with menstruation, defloration, and childbirth) [1] that may serve to gratify masochism in women or even predispose them to it, but, it is argued, any more special connection between masochism and femininity is in the main sociologically determined, and to regard masochism in general and any type of masochism in particular as specifically feminine is no more justified than is the long-since discarded theory that hysteria is a specifically feminine disease.

As regards moral masochism there is the question, to which we have already referred, whether it can properly be regarded as sexual at all. Freud, after a somewhat detailed discussion,[2] concludes that it does in fact contain a germ of sexuality and that this is derived by way of regression from a sort of resuscitation of the Œdipus complex: 'In moral masochism morality becomes sexualized afresh, the Œdipus complex is reactivated,

---

[1] Cf. Karen Horney, 'The Problem of Feminine Masochism,' *Psa. Review* (1935), 22, 241.　　[2] 'A Child is Being Beaten' (1919), *Collected Papers*, ii, 172.

a regression from morality to the Œdipus complex is under way'. In such cases the super-ego largely plays the part of sadist, the ego that of masochist. How far we are to follow Freud in regarding moral masochism as sexual (and therefore perhaps correctly described as masochism at all) depends of course to some extent upon our willingness to follow him also in adopting a wide view of the 'sexual' and also upon our agreement with him as regards the existence and importance of unconscious factors. But he is surely correct in supposing that many people do really in a sense enjoy the sufferings and misfortunes to which they are exposed (largely, it would seem, through their own complicity), and the relation he has established between moral masochism and such forms of physical punishment as beating— which are so often unmistakably sexual in tone—would seem to provide a strong argument in favour of the fundamental correct- ness of his view.

Besides the three *kinds* of masochism just enumerated, Freud also distinguishes various *phases* or stages of masochism. The actual manifestations of masochism, he tells us, depend to a large extent upon the nature of the sexual 'component instinct' that preponderates at the stage or level at which the masochism is operating. At the most primitive or oral stage, masochism will show itself in the fear of being devoured by some fierce beast, ogre, or monster—ultimately a father figure. We need only think of the innumerable children's stories (e.g. *Red Riding Hood*) and the considerable number of myths (e.g. that of Cronos eating his children) of this description to realize the im- portance of this stage. Developmentally later, and largely characteristic of the anal stage, are the phantasies of being beaten or defiled; later still and connected with the 'phallic stage'[1] is the fear of castration and other forms of mutilation, while 'from the final genital stage are derived of course the situations characteristic of womanhood, namely the passive part in coitus and the act of giving birth'. The various forms of masochistic phantasy thus give an indication of the develop- mental levels with which they are connected, from which they spring, or to which the mental life of the masochist (so far as his phantasies are concerned) has regressed. The same of course is true, *mutatis mutandis*, of the corresponding sadistic phantasies and practices.

---

[1] Cf. S. Freud, 'The Infantile Genital Organization of the Libido' (1922), *Collected Papers*, ii, 244.

In a recent book Reik [1] has made some interesting comments on, and additions to, the discussion of masochism as it was thus left by Freud. He agrees with Freud as to the enormous importance of phantasy. A masochistic perversion, he says with Freud, is little more than an 'acted' phantasy. He returns, however, to Freud's earlier (second) view that sadism rather than masochism is primary and that masochism is only inverted sadism and not really a separate tendency existing in its own right; nor does he fully accept Freud's death instinct. In accordance with a good many other psycho-analysts in recent years he stresses the intrinsically aggressive nature of much infantile conation. This aggression necessarily meets with a good deal of frustration, which in turn gives rise to an attempt to find gratification in imagination rather than reality. But since the would-be sadist is vividly conscious of the penalties he would incur did he attempt to translate his phantasies into reality, he adds to his imaginative picture the suffering of punishment. Finally gratification and punishment become fused in a more or less inseparable phantasy, both rôles—that of culprit and of punisher—being played of course within the self, though when the phantasy is 'acted' in reality they are distributed again.

Reik considers that there is an inverse relation between sexual and moral (or, as he prefers to call it, social) masochism. It is very rare, he says, for a sexual masochist to be unhappy or a failure in everyday life, while on the other hand the person who is haunted by misfortune and lives a life of social misery very seldom has a tendency to sexual masochism.[2] The relative predominance of sexuality and aggression in a person's make-up decides which form of masochism he is likely to adopt.

In addition to the importance he attaches to phantasy, Reik thinks there are two other distinctive characteristics of the masochist: what he calls 'the demonstrative factor', the wish to make a show of his suffering; and the 'factor of suspense', the tendency to indulge in long-drawn-out tension, with a constant fluctuation between anxiety and pleasure. At first sight this last seems somewhat to resemble what in the previous chapter we called epicurean asceticism, but Reik suggests that the aim is rather to avoid the final or culminating pleasure than

---

[1] Th. Reik, *Aus Leiden Freuden*, 1940.
[2] In so far as this is a true account, we have here an exception to Freud's rule of 'psycho-sexual parallelism'. It is rather a manifestation of 'compensation'.

to prolong the preliminary pleasures (and accompanying pains) of anticipation. In other words, the emphasis is on the anxiety accompanying fulfilment rather than on any pleasurable torments of delay.

Reik, like Horney, is suspicious of Freud's special category of feminine masochism. Masochism, he suggests, depends much upon a regression to the mother-child relationship when the mother was sole ruler of the child's body and soul, and he points in this connection to the long line of cruel mythical women, from Salome to Turandot. At very bottom, however, masochism is only sadism turned against the self, and this sadism has its root in the fundamentally aggressive character of infantile love and much of infantile behaviour generally. Reik thus in essence supports the view which, as we have already noted, was suggested by Ernest Jones in one of the first critical appreciations of Freud's super-ego doctrine—i.e. that the ultimate sources of sadism and masochism are to be found in the ambivalence and intimate fusion of love and hate that is characteristic of the very young child and in the very important part played by primitive aggressive tendencies in the earliest days of life.

CHAPTER IX

THE INFANTILE ORIGINS OF AGGRESSION AND THE SUPER-EGO

IT is now our duty to go further into this matter of infantile aggressiveness in relation to our present theme. It is an awkward subject to discuss because it is connected with highly controversial points, so that, in whatever way we attempt to deal with it, we shall inevitably be considered to have distorted, over-emphasized, or under-estimated some of the matters in dispute. Nevertheless the importance of the subject is such that it is necessary to say something about it at this point, however great the dangers and difficulties to be encountered.

Freud, as we have seen, connected the super-ego with the fully developed childish attitudes to the parents that make up what he calls the Œdipus complex; indeed he calls the super-ego 'the heir to the Œdipus complex' and connects it with the 'passing' of this complex.[1] But it seemed unlikely that the super-ego (or for that matter any other important mental function above the instinctive level) should come into existence suddenly and in a more or less final form, as this view of Freud's was sometimes taken to imply. As early as 1916 Abraham,[2] in the course of his studies of the 'pregenital stages of the libido' (in which he was of course, as he himself freely admitted, only mapping out in greater detail the territory already outlined by Freud in his *Three Contributions*), realized that the infant might experience acute anxiety at the earliest oral or 'cannibalistic' stage and considered that something that might be called guilt could occur at the next or anal stage. Ferenczi,[3] writing nine years later, was much more definite on the latter point. He emphasized the fact (already noted by Freud and other psycho-analysts) that some of the earliest and most important aspects of the child's education are concerned with learning to control the processes of excretion so that they shall occur only at what are from the adult point of view convenient times and places. The attempts to meet the parents' demands in this respect constitute indeed, he suggested, the child's earliest moral endeavours. What he wrote in this connection is sufficiently illuminating to deserve quotation: 'The anal and urethral identification . . . with the parents appears to build up in the child's mind a sort of physiological forerunner of the ego-ideal or super-ego. Not only in the sense that the child constantly compares his achievements in these directions with the capacities of his parents, but in that a severe sphincter-morality is set up which can only be contravened at the cost of bitter self-reproaches and punishment by conscience. It is by no means improbable that this as yet semi-physiological morality forms the essential groundwork of later purely mental morality'. Here we find clearly indicated the beginnings of the formation of the super-ego in connection with pre-genital functions that definitely antedate the full flowering, let alone the 'passing', of the Œdipus complex.

The most important of the later developments of psycho-analytic thought along these lines are nearly all connected with a group of investigators who have sometimes been referred to

---

[1] 'The Passing of the Œdipus Complex' (1924), *Collected Papers*, ii, 269.
[2] Karl Abraham, 'The First Pregenital Stages of the Libido,' included in *Selected Papers*, 1927.
[3] Sándor Ferenczi, 'The Analysis of Sexual Habits' (1925), included in *Further Contributions to the Theory and Technique of Psycho-analysis*, 1926.

as the 'English School'. This school centres round the pioneer work of Melanie Klein,[1] who developed a play technique which enabled something resembling psycho-analytic treatment as employed with adults to be adapted to the use of very young children of from 2 to 6 years old. Through this technique the early development and conflicts of the child could be studied in the light of psycho-analytic concepts in a way that was not possible before, and it is therefore far from surprising that the psycho-analytic notions concerning the early stages of development should themselves undergo considerable change as a result of the application of this technique, especially among those who regularly practised it. The boundaries and membership of this school are somewhat ill-defined and have been subject to a good deal of fluctuation. Among those who have closely adopted Klein's point of view should perhaps be counted Susan Isaacs (especially notable for her very important observational studies of young children carried out at the experimental Malting House School), Joan Riviere, M. N. Searl, and D. W. Winnicott. Ernest Jones, the doyen of British psycho-analysts, seems to have been favourably disposed to Klein's approach from the first, and such authors as Róheim and Money-Kyrle, whose studies are concerned for the most part with the apparently remote fields of anthropology and sociology, have also been largely affected by it. Indeed it may be said that few British psycho-analysts have altogether escaped the influence of Klein's work, so much so that just before the outbreak of war in 1939 there were some fairly marked divisions of outlook and opinion between what were sometimes described as the 'English' and the 'Continental' analysts. Since the war, with the virtual cessation of psycho-analysis in continental Europe, these divisions have been to some extent transferred to Great Britain itself, and it is the fact that at the moment of writing many aspects of Klein's work and thought are still the subject of dispute that makes it so extremely hard to deal with them in the short compass which alone is suitable for a book of this description. In what follows we shall endeavour to indicate some of the principal views of this school in as non-controversial a way as may be possible.

According to the findings and interpretations of Klein, and those who follow her, the growth of the super-ego is a relatively

---

[1] Described in *The Psycho-analysis of Children*, 1932, and in various earlier and later papers.

slow process, the beginnings of which can be traced back to the earliest stages of an individual's psychological development. There are two characteristics of these earliest stages that are of special importance from our present point of view. In the first place the very young child has not yet formed any clear distinction between himself and his environment; in the second place his impulses are highly ambivalent, i.e. are compounded of love and aggression to a degree and with an intimacy of fusion that are seldom to be found in later life. This last statement requires however some slight qualification, inasmuch as in Klein's view indeed the baby finds all stimuli painful during the first few weeks of life, and therefore reacts to them with the infantile equivalent of hate. In these early days he had, we must presume, not yet got used to the new and far more varied surroundings to which he has been transferred from the homogeneous and protective environment of the womb. He then gradually learns that some stimuli satisfy his needs and are not mere disturbances of his would-be Nirvana state; such stimuli he comes to love and enjoy. But the very young child, with no more than a minimal appreciation of time, is unable to bear tension; he does not possess the knowledge, so consoling to older human beings, that loss, frustration, pain, and discomfort are usually but temporary and will be followed by relief. Consequently a very small change in the situation (e.g. a less comfortable posture or pressure of his clothes, a less easy grasp of the nipple or a less ready flow of milk) will convert a pleasant satisfying stimulus into an unpleasant dissatisfying one. Thus the child can both love and hate the same objects in rapid succession or alternation, and his love and hate alike tend to work on the all-or-nothing principle—there are not the qualifications and quantitative variations that are found in later life.

At the same time, as we have said, the child has not learnt the distinction—later of such far-reaching import—between the self and the not-self. He does not clearly recognize the difference between a disagreeable outer stimulus and an unpleasant tension in himself (such as that caused by being cold, wet, or hungry). Everything connected with a state of tension, e.g. his own hunger sensations on the one hand and the breast that does not easily supply milk on the other, are regarded as 'bad' in the same way; just as the feeling of satisfied hunger and the satisfying nipple are regarded as 'good' in the same way.

Associated with this fundamental absence of the distinction

between the subjective and the objective, between the self and the not-self, are two further confusions of detail with important consequences. There is no adequate distinction between sensations and their accompanying feelings and impulses, nor—more important still—between these feelings and impulses and the associated outer objects. In other words the child does not distinguish between the cognitive and orectic aspects of his own experience, nor between his own orexis and the outer world. Thus the sensations of hunger are not separated from the distress and anger aroused by these sensations,[1] nor is anger, with its accompanying tendency to suck or bite aggressively, separated from the mother's breast which is failing to satisfy the hunger— and similarly in other situations. When distress is not alleviated and unsatisfied desire persists, the child begins to feel overwhelmed by his own inner tension, and it is this condition which gives rise to what psycho-analysts have sometimes described as fear of the instincts (i.e. of uncontrollable instinctual tension).[2] In the earlier days of psycho-analysis the instincts which were thought of as arousing fear were mainly sexual, but as psychoanalysts began to concern themselves more and more with aggression, the accent in this connection passed from the sexual to the aggressive elements. The 'English School' intensified and hastened this process by drawing attention to the importance of these aggressive elements in very early life. A vivid impression of the way in which the infant can come to feel threatened and overmastered by its own aggressiveness is conveyed, for instance, by Riviere[3]: 'The child is overwhelmed by choking and suffocating; its eyes are blinded with tears, its ears deafened, its throat sore; its bowels gripe, its evacuations burn it'. Thus the child's autogenous aggression, the biological purpose of which, as manifested for instance in crying, is no doubt to get others to relieve its needs, may threaten to destroy its owner, and it is the impotence of the child in face of the mounting

---

[1] To some extent this confusion between sensory states and the orectic (especially conative) tendencies that accompany them persists throughout life, especially as regards the 'lower' sensory modalities, i.e. those other than vision and hearing. Thus the sensations accompanying sex, hunger, nausea, itching, muscular ache, the 'call' to urination or defæcation are often very hard to distinguish from the conations which are so closely associated with them. The experiences in question 'mean' certain tendencies to action—a fact well brought out in Boring's illuminating introspective studies of experiences of this kind. Cf. E. G. Boring, 'The Processes referred to the Alimentary Tract,' *Psychol. Rev.* (1915), 22, 306.

[2] Cf. S. Freud, *Inhibitions, Symptoms and Anxiety*, 1926.

[3] Joan Riviere, 'On the Genesis of Psychical Conflict in Earliest Infancy,' *Int. J. Psa.* (1936), 17, 402.

tension which makes uncontrolled and unrelieved aggression appear as a situation of acute danger. If at these earliest stages there is at the same time no clear distinction between such distressful and alarming inner conditions and the associated outer objects or circumstances, it is easy to see that the first step has been taken towards the creation of an outer 'bogy' of ill-defined but intense and almost unimaginable evilness.

A later and more definite step in the same direction occurs as soon as the mechanism of projection comes into play. The origins of this mechanism—of such immense importance to mental development and, especially in later life, to psycho-pathology—are perhaps to be found in the primal lack of distinction between the self and the not-self. In any case, however, when the distinction does actually begin to be drawn, the line of demarcation is not logical or consistent and the not-self will include many elements (both of 'badness' and 'goodness') which a more experienced and sophisticated mind would un-hesitatingly consider to be subjective and to belong to the person's own inner orectic life.[1] Soon, however, other tendencies (our understanding of which admittedly still leaves much to be desired) begin to exercise a more selective influence in leading the child to ascribe some of his own experiences to the outer world and thus to cause projection. The most important factor in this selective influence (and here psycho-analysts are in pretty general agreement) is the attempt to identify pleasure with the self and unpleasure with the not-self. Many harmful and painful stimuli come from the outer world; the satisfactory way of dealing with them, as the child gradually learns, is to remove the stimuli or to remove himself from them. A 'bad' thing that falls into the not-self category can very often be dealt with in this way; hence there arises a very natural endeavour to place it in this category and thus to establish a correspondence on the one hand of the 'good' and pleasant with the self, and on the other of the 'bad' and unpleasant with the not-self. Unfortu-nately not all 'good' or 'bad' things really fall into these

---

[1] Throughout life, however, it would seem to be easy to regress to some extent to the primal condition in which the customary distinction between the subjective and the objective becomes blurred or even non-existent. Indeed with a little practice an attitude conducive to this can be voluntarily adopted and then studied introspectively. (Cf. the chapter on 'Experiments in Objectivating' in C. Spearman, *The Nature of Intelligence and the Principles of Cognition*, 1923.) In the last resort, too, it can be maintained that all so-called objective values are ultimately subjective in origin, inasmuch as things in the outer world are good or bad only in virtue of our attitude to them.

respective categories, so that the attempt necessarily predisposes to delusions and unrealism; it is in fact a manifestation of Freud's 'pleasure principle'. Nevertheless the impulse to divide the universe of 'good' and 'bad' along these lines is so strong that it is only corrected slowly and with difficulty, and throughout life the tendency to project the evil in ourselves is a constant menace to our true appreciation of reality. Anyhow, in the early stages of his life the child has in his desire to achieve this correspondence a strong motive for projecting his own painful feelings and the accompanying aggressive desires upon the outer world—and most naturally of course upon the outer objects or persons that are, in virtue of temporal and spatial contiguity, associated with these feelings. In this way the outer bogies become natural recipients, representatives, or incarnations of the infant's own distressful states and hostile tendencies, and reality becomes distorted in a way that is at once both pessimistic and grotesque.[1]

The qualities projected on to the bogies depend upon the stage of development at which projection occurs, in much the same way as the manifestations of sado-masochism depend upon the level concerned. Thus at the earliest or oral stage the projected figures suck, bite, tear, or rend; at the anal or urethral levels they are liable to flood the world with filth or water, or indulge in other forms of widespread and fierce destructiveness; while at the phallic level they castrate, mutilate, and maim— all of these stages finding expression not only in individual childish phantasy but in frequently recurring themes of fairy tale and myth. Projections of this type are responsible for the weirder forms of childish phobias, which people the world with strange and sinister figures liable, as it seems to the child, to attack him in queer, malignant, and terrifying ways.

At the stage at which the earliest projections occur there is, according to Klein, as yet no full and clear appreciation of persons as such. The child has not yet learnt to recognize his mother as a permanent complex organic unity; at first it will for instance only distinguish the nipple and then the breast as an 'object' of the outer world, even this being moreover an object that is intimately connected with, and therefore still to some extent confused with, his own weal or woe. It is thus at

[1] In its tendency to confuse the self and outer world and to make immoderate use of projection the young child resembles the adult psychotic, and it is no doubt this resemblance that has led at least one well-known psycho-analyst to say 'we are born mad'.

first the breast or other parts of the body, rather than whole and complete persons, upon which the infant's own aggressive tendencies are projected.

Early and primitive as this stage is, it yet leaves some very significant impress upon the human mind and even upon human culture. Money-Kyrle,[1] at any rate, is inclined to believe that the magical instruments, substances, and fluids (e.g. the famous quartz crystal of the aboriginal Australian wizard) are institutionalized relics of this stage; indeed he has ingeniously suggested that the curiously vague but very widespread notion of 'mana', a magical force or power inherent in certain objects, is ultimately derived from the same source. Freud in his *Totem and Taboo* had already used child psychology to illumine anthropological problems, the phenomena of totemism and exogamy being considered in the light of the Œdipus complex. Money-Kyrle (if we accept his view) has made a further important step in correlating an earlier stage of mental development in the child with a more primitive and pre-totemic phase of culture, the at-first-sight entirely remote and unconnected work of Melanie Klein, the child analyst, and R. R. Marett,[2] the anthropologist, being thus brought together in most suggestive fashion. Money-Kyrle's valuable contributions are themselves based to a considerable extent upon the earlier work of Róheim, who was the first psycho-analytically trained anthropologist to attempt actual field-work on a large scale. Among Róheim's more important findings [3] was the discovery of a pre-totemic layer of culture among the primitive tribes of Central Australia, surviving (chiefly among women and children) as a background to the more official totemism, in much the same way as pagan beliefs and practices often continue to lurk behind official Christianity in Europe. This 'primal religion' takes the form of belief in demonic or spiritual entities of queer shapes and qualities, and often of cannibalistic tendencies, corresponding, it would appear, in many respects to the early 'objects' which

[1] R. Money-Kyrle, *Superstition and Society*, 1938.

[2] To whom we owe both the introduction into general anthropological usage of the term 'mana' itself and a realization of the importance in savage life of the concept denoted by it.

[3] Géza Róheim, *The Riddle of the Sphinx*, 1934. It is only fair to add that there are some important differences of emphasis between Róheim and Klein. The former attaches a good deal more significance to early traumatic experiences ('the primal scene') than does the latter. Róheim indeed regards such experiences as among the important factors that are responsible for the differences between one form of primitive culture and another. It is possible, however, that the differences between Róheim and Klein are themselves largely due to the still bigger differences between the respective cultures in which they worked.

Klein first discovered to be of such importance in the mental development of the young child.

At the age of two to three months, when, according to Klein, the child begins to perceive its mother as a person, his impulses are still at the aggressive-ambivalent stage. He wants ('cannibalistically') to incorporate the nipple and the breast, and later to consume the contents of the mother's body (this last being perhaps one of the most startling of Klein's discoveries). The attitudes characteristic of this stage, carrying over to later periods with fuller understanding, give rise to the notions of sucking out, biting, tearing, or otherwise destroying these contents—which may be regarded in some aspects as 'good' (e.g. as milk) but in other aspects as 'bad' (e.g. faeces, or an undesired and hated rival in the form of an unborn baby). These impulses, crude in form and often intensely hostile in nature, are projected on to the mother as a person, so that there arises the notion of a fierce mother-figure who is in her turn prepared to bite, tear, rend, destroy, and eviscerate. Thus the projection of the child's own aggressiveness may create a quite phantastic notion of the cruelty and severity of the parents, in comparison with which their real tendencies to express anger or impatience or to administer punishment sink into insignificance. Some writers, e.g. Ernest Jones,[1] have been so impressed with this element of aggression that is projected on to the parents that they have been tempted to think that the parents' real aggressiveness is a comparatively negligible factor and that, such as it is, it is often 'exploited' by the child, as affording a convenient 'rationalization' of his own phantastic fears, themselves due to a projection of his own aggression. They have thus come to attribute much less importance to the factor of external disapproval to which Freud (together with such predecessors as Baldwin and McDougall) had given first place; in other words, the emphasis they would lay on our third factor (of Chapter III) has become greater, while that on our second factor has diminished. On the whole, however, the general view would still seem to be that both factors are genuinely operative, even though later work would show that the third factor—that of nemesistic autogenous aggression (here in its projected form) —is a great deal more important than had been at first supposed.

---

[1] Ernest Jones, 'The Early Development of Female Sexuality,' *Int. J. Psa.* (1927), 8, 463. Cf. also Susan Isaacs, 'Privation and Guilt,' *Int. J. Psa.* (1929), 10, 335.

In connection with the child's own primitive desires and aggressions Ernest Jones has also developed the concept of 'aphanisis',[1] corresponding to the child's fear that all sources of satisfaction and relief of tension may be—or perhaps have been—permanently and totally removed (though it is of course to be understood that such ideas as 'permanently' and 'totally' involve a translation into adult terms of the child's feeling of utter and overwhelming deprivation). It is largely to guard against this sort of psychic annihilation, this sense of terrifying frustration, rather than to protect against external punishment and withdrawal of love that, in this view, the super-ego is built up.

What fresh light indeed is thrown upon the development of the super-ego from this new standpoint? We have seen that the child carries out a series of projections, characterized by two main features: (1) in the early stages the projections are on to 'objects' rather than on to (complete) persons, (2) the projected impulses are of a crude, ambivalent, and very aggressive kind, related to 'pre-genital' (and largely oral) tendencies. We have now to note that, corresponding to this series of projections, there is an equivalent series of introjections. The hostile and primitive impulses originally displaced outwards on to objects or persons are turned inwards again, once more incorporated into the self; in fact it is these objects or persons, phantastically and unrealistically endowed with the child's own impulses, that are now incorporated, so that the child feels that he possesses them within himself. And it is just these introjected objects or persons that constitute the beginnings of the super-ego.

It is clear that the parent-figure (or at earlier stages the 'object') thus introjected is a figure very different from the real parent, inasmuch as it is endowed with all the crude and primitive aggressiveness of the young child himself. In this way then, it would appear, does the super-ego acquire its more alarming and barbaric features. Here we have the true origin of the harshness and severity of the super-ego which, from the start of its investigations in this direction, had been among the most astonishing and disconcerting discoveries of psycho-analysis. As we have already said, the formation of the super-ego, according to Klein and her school, is very far from being a single process connected with a particular stage or event of psychological history (e.g. the passing of the Œdipus complex). It

[1] Ernest Jones, *loc. cit.*, 461 ff.

results rather from a long series of introjections carried on through a long period of time, and thus bears the marks of many different developmental levels. And between each process of introjection there occurs a corresponding process of projection, so that the complete series of alternating introjections and projections presents a striking resemblance to that 'Dialectic of Personal Growth' of which Baldwin had written some thirty years before.

Nevertheless, it may well be asked, why this long series? Partly no doubt it is connected with the cyclic nature of the physiological prototypes of introjection and projection. These, according to most psycho-analysts, are to be found respectively in the processes of feeding and elimination. Just as we incorporate or eliminate physical substances, so also do we introject or project aspects of the mind, and it may be that the mental alternation of introjection and projection is built up on analogy with the corresponding physiological rhythm, with which indeed it is, to begin with, in some measure identified and confused. Partly, however, the mental cycle is the result of psychological attempts at adaptation. Feeling that he has incorporated a 'bad' object (or one that is to some extent 'bad'), the child is impelled to deal with the unpleasant and dangerous situation thus created. He does so by projecting the 'bad' object upon the parent and thus attempting to re-establish the equations good = self, bad = outer world. This is followed in turn by a new introjection.[1] But although the projected object is, as we have seen, a grossly distorted one, it is nevertheless to

---

[1] At the more developed stages, when introjection and projection have lost their intimate connection with their physiological prototypes, it is perhaps not so easy to see the *immediate* reason for introjection as that for projection (the *ultimate* very important result of diminishing the primitiveness and aggressiveness of the super-ego by making it more realistic is indicated in the text). Through projection the child endeavours to get rid of unpleasant feelings and conations by ascribing them to the outer world. What does he gain by introjection? It may be that he somehow guards against the attack of the fearsome outer objects he has created, that he attempts to master them, much in the way we have already described in dealing with 'identification with the aggressor' (Chapter VI). In other words, he only feels capable of dealing with them when he has their power and aggressiveness *within* him. Or it may be that he attempts to guard against the feared attack from without by erecting within himself a copy of the attacker which will ensure that he will be 'good', i.e. that his behaviour will be such as to assuage the wrath that threatens from without, as in the erection of the internal parental authority on the lines we have previously described (Chapter IV). It would seem that in the former case the introjected aggression would be more ready to express itself 'extrapunitively', in the latter case 'intropunitively'. It seems likely, too, that introjections of the latter kind form the deeper and more fundamental layers of the super-ego. But this at present is no more than speculation.

some extent modified by the real qualities of the outer object, which in the vast majority of cases are, of course, far less alarming than the imagined qualities derived from the child's own crude aggressiveness; real parents, though they may sometimes express anger and impatience, may slap and scold, may be preoccupied or negligent, do not bite, tear, devour, or otherwise destroy. To the extent that the distorted idea of the parent has been affected by these real qualities, the re-introjected image will be less terrifying than it was before its projection. In this way a benign cycle of events may be established and the introjected parent that is the primitive super-ego gradually grows less savage and grotesque and more adapted to reality.[1]

This process of what might perhaps be called the taming or civilizing of the primitive super-ego is aided and complicated by two further factors, which for the sake of simplicity we have hitherto left out of account, but which make the picture we are asked to form of the growth of the super-ego rather less fearsome and macabre than it might so far have appeared. In the first place there tends to come about a fusion of the originally in-compatible and contradictory notions of good and bad objects. We have seen that the child, with little or no appreciation of time and of the inevitable periodic recurrence of needs and satisfactions, tends to experience feelings on the all-or-nothing principle. In moments of satisfaction everything is well, and the breast—and later the mother—is an entirely good object, the prototype perhaps of the fairy-godmother or genie who fulfils all wishes completely and instantaneously. At moments of dissatisfaction the child feels that all is lost, that he is over-whelmed by his distress, and that the object or parent is entirely bad, hostile, and frustrating. Thus the child builds up two opposite but equally distorted pictures of the parents. Gradu-ally, however, the two pictures begin to fuse and interpenetrate. The bad parent is seen as not utterly hostile or vindictive. The good parent does not gratify every wish immediately; on the contrary, by imposing restraints upon the child's own aggressive-ness, he (or, more often, she) can afford some measure of re-assurance and protection even in the very act of frustration. Thus there gradually arises the notion, to which we have already referred, of what Isaacs calls the 'good-strict' parent, one on

---

[1] In certain unfavourable cases, where something that happens during the projective phase serves to reinforce rather than allay the fears connected with the projected bogy figure, the cycle may be a malignant rather than a benign one.

whose superior strength and power of control the child can rely when he feels the danger of being overwhelmed by his own instincts. Since frustration may thus also give protection, it may in certain cases bring a welcome feeling of security and relief rather than an increased sense of overpowering and devastating need. In so far as this attitude of the parent is itself introjected in the growing super-ego, the super-ego begins to be welcomed as a source of strength within the individual which shields him from the consequences of his own unbridled passions. In Riviere's words, 'the feeling that "I am an un-controlled bundle of unpleasant and dangerous impulses towards myself and others" leads to "I have somebody like my good helping mother inside me, who will watch over me and never allow me to go too far, who will save me and herself from serious danger"'.[1] Here then we get some further light upon the more beneficent aspects of the super-ego, aspects of which in our later considerations we have perhaps tended to lose sight.

The second complicating factor is one on which Klein in particular has laid much stress. The young child not only possesses extremely aggressive impulses but has no clear idea of the limitations of his own powers. On the contrary, in virtue of what Freud in quite early days of psycho-analysis had called the 'omnipotence of thought', he feels that his destructive impulses are only too liable to achieve their aim[2] and that the breast or the loving, helping mother has probably been destroyed beyond repair. Any external real withdrawal of love, help, or presence is apt to be interpreted in this sense.[3] With the loss of the good external object, the child feels that he

---

[1] Joan Riviere, 'The Genesis of Psychical Conflict in Earliest Infancy,' *Int. Psa.* (1936), 17, 412.

[2] There is an apparent contradiction here between the doctrine of infantile omnipotence which so many Freudians have stressed and the other view, especially emphasized by Adler, according to which the child is vividly and painfully conscious of the limitations of his own power. No doubt both views are true of particular situations, aspects, or stages of development, and probably on the whole the Adlerian view applies to later rather than to earlier stages. But the detailed confrontation of the two views, their limitations, and fields of application present interesting problems to the child psychologist which have not as yet received the attention they deserve. (An indication of a field in which Adler's view seems to be admitted to apply even by Freudian writers is contained in the suggestion of Isaacs referred to below.)

[3] It may be that the disturbances in conduct and development apparently due to prolonged separation from the mother at an early age may to some extent be due to this cause. At any rate there seems very little doubt of the reality of these disturbances. Cf. John Bowlby, 'The Influence of Early Environment in the Development of Neurosis and Neurotic Character,' *Int. J. Psa.* (1940), 21, 154; Dorothy Burlingham and Anna Freud, *Annual Report of a Residential War Nursery* (1942), pp. 32 ff.

has also lost the corresponding good internal object that he had acquired, or can acquire, through introjection. Confronted with a catastrophic situation of this kind, the child resorts to attempts at reparation or restitution; he tries to make good the damage he has done. For the most part he can only do this in more or less symbolic form, and indeed in the play techniques devised by Klein and others such attempts at reparation are often to be observed. Moreover the impulse of reparation thus started is one that tends to persist throughout life. It is seen at work in many obsessional symptoms (in which indeed there may be an alternation of symbolically destructive and symbolically restitutive thoughts and actions, as in the very clear case reported by Fenichel [1] of a boy who constantly muttered a prayer for his mother's return to health and then slapped his mouth to annul the effect of what he had just said). Above all it enters as an important element into many of the phenomena usually classified as sublimations, and in this way contributes very greatly to human culture.[2] In the ability to carry out creative and constructive work men find the most satisfactory means of reassurance and of assuaging guilt. It is, Isaacs suggests, one of the greatest tragedies of early life that just when the child's need to make good is so urgent, his powers of doing something creative are so limited and his capacity for causing destruction and disorder so relatively great.[3] But in so far as the need for reparation is a genuine and persistent one, it is clearly of the greatest moral, educational, and sociological importance; perhaps the greatest injury that we can do a child or man is to make him feel that he is quite incapable of helping and of doing useful work. Here we have arrived by another route at the 'need to be needed' that we considered in an earlier chapter (Chapter V). We can now see something of the infantile roots of this need and realize more acutely the great psychological harm that may be occasioned by pedagogic, penal, or economic systems that frustrate this need.

We may conclude this chapter by drawing attention to the way in which, according to Klein,[4] certain of her fundamental theses, including that of reparation, are illustrated by a work

[1] Otto Fenichel, *Outline of Clinical Psychoanalysis* (1934), 138.
[2] Cf. the present author's paper on 'Sublimation: its Nature and Conditions,' *Brit. J. Educ. Psychol.*, 1942, 12—especially Section 7 (pp. 100 ff.).
[3] Susan Isaacs, *Social Development in Young Children* (1933), 318.
[4] M. Klein, 'Infantile Anxiety Situations Reflected in a Work of Art and in the Creative Impulse,' *Int. J. Psa.* (1929), 10, 436.

of art, which at the same time indicates the rich symbolism which we must learn to read if we would understand the manifestations of the unconscious in this, as in most other, of its aspects. The work in question is Ravel's opera *L'Enfant et les Sortilèges*, with libretto by Colette. The opening scene shows a boy supposed to be doing his home-work but thoroughly fed up with it. He doesn't want to do his lessons but to go for a walk in the park. He would like best of all, he says, to eat up all the cake in the world, pull the cat's tail, pull out the parrot's feathrse, scold everyone, and put mama in the corner. Here we see the signs of his primitive infantile aggression, including oral elements (eating up all the cake) and aggression directed against his mother. At this moment his mother appears, or at least her presence is indicated by a skirt, an apron, and a hand. Everything on the stage is very large, as though to indicate the way things look to the young child. The mother, whose affectionate inquiries as to the progress of the home-work are angrily rebuffed, retires with the words: 'You shall have dry bread and no sugar in your tea'—a talion punishment for the boy's aggressive oral wishes. The boy on his part flies into a rage and proceeds to smash the contents of the room. He breaks the tea-cups, furiously pokes the fire, and hurls away the kettle amid a cloud of steam and ashes. With the tongs he begins to tear the wallpaper. He attacks the squirrel in its cage, pours the ink upon the table, opens the grandfather clock and snatches out the pendulum.

Then the things he has maltreated come to life. The pieces of furniture lift up their arms in protest. The fire spits out a shower of sparks. The clock appears to be in pain and begins furiously to strike the hours. The torn wallpaper, on which are depected shepherds and shepherdesses, emits a sad lament through the shepherd's pipe. The rent separates Corydon from his Amaryllis, but to the child's imagination it now seems like a rent in the fabric of the world. Finally a little man emerges; he is the spirit of mathematics and proceeds to put the boy through a long phantastic examination that only ends when the wretched little examinee faints from exhaustion and anxiety.

Here the child's acts of violence correspond to his primitive pregenital aggression. The ink and steam represent the childish method of attack by soiling with his excrement, while the smashing and tearing correspond to the use of muscles, teeth, nails, and other weapons at the disposal of his infantile sadism.

The various objects attacked (including the furniture, which consists largely of things to lie or sit on) represent the mother, while the assault on the squirrel in its cage and the pendulum in the clock are just such attempts to destroy things in the mother's body as Klein had discovered in the phantasies of young children. The rent in the wallpaper which parts Corydon from Amaryllis is an attempt to separate the father and the mother, of a kind that has long been familiar to psycho-analysts.[1] Finally the tormenting little examiner is at once a phallic representation of the father and a symbol of the boy's own super-ego calling him to account for the damage he has done.

In another scene the boy takes refuge in the park around the house. But here again there is at first an atmosphere of terror, and the place seems full of wounded or hostile animals and things. A dispute arises as to who shall bite the child, and a squirrel that has itself been bitten in the fray falls screaming to the ground. Touched at last by pity, the boy takes off his scarf and binds up the little creature's paw. As he does so he whispers the word 'Mama', apparently a magic word (which gave the opera the title under which it was played in German-speaking countries—*Das Zauberwort*). The child immediately begins to feel that he is restored to the sane human world of helping and of 'being good'. In the finale the animals sing, 'That's a good child, a very well-behaved child', as they leave the stage. Some of them cannot themselves refrain from calling out 'Mama'.

The park in this scene represents Nature. Like the room, it is a mother symbol, but on a larger scale. The wounded animals and things represent the harm that the boy has done his mother. Here again, however, he is threatened with punishment for his own aggression. But an opportunity for reparation presents itself, and the magic word 'Mama' makes clear who it is that has been endangered by the child's violence and has been restored to him by his act of reparation. The genius of Ravel and Colette would seem to have given a very striking artistic portrayal of some of the findings of Melanie Klein and her school, which when described in forthright scientific language are apt sometimes to appear so far-fetched, weird, and sinister as to be scarcely credible.

[1] And is represented also in such myths as those of Atlas, who keeps Heaven (the father) apart from Earth (the mother).

CHAPTER X

TABOO AND ITS EQUIVALENTS

Functions and Psychological Nature of Taboo

We have now concluded our examination of the nature and growth of the super-ego. In the last chapter in particular we traced it to its sources, so far as our present meagre and uncertain knowledge would permit. We have still much to do by way of illustrating its effects in the various fields of human thought and action, and there is still something further of importance to be said with regard to its relations to the other aspects of the mind. This we shall attempt in later chapters. For the moment let us leave the individual, with the problem of whose early moral development we have just been struggling, and turn to what is in some way the corresponding social problem—the problem of taboo.

The institution of taboo [1] in human society corresponds in three main ways to the super-ego in the individual. In the first place it is the basic factor in moral control. Secondly it is primitive and archaic. Thirdly it is orectic and intuitive and is divorced from reason. Like the super-ego it may have useful, perhaps indeed essential, functions. But this usefulness is at best the result of dim and clumsy attempts at adaptation; it depends on feeling rather than cognition and is devoid of any clear insight into means and ends. At its worst and most phantastic it involves mankind in unnecessary and quite unrealistic fears, and imposes curious and often crippling restrictions on its liberty of thought and action. Nevertheless, in spite of these similarities between the purely psychological super-ego and the social institution of taboo, the reader may perhaps experience some relief in turning for a short while at this point from the primitive moral elements in the individual to the corresponding feature in the race. Taboos primarily affect, and are upheld by, adult social human beings, and even the strangest and most bizarre conduct on the part of the grown-up members of a community is likely to appear less

---

[1] As is the case with almost all who write upon this subject, I am greatly indebted to Sir J. G. Frazer, whose works constitute such a vast treasure-house of information. I refer here particularly to *The Golden Bough, Totemism and Exogamy*, and *Folk Lore in the Old Testament*.

remote, incomprehensible, and perhaps repellent, than the queer and somewhat uncanny aspects of infantile development with which we were concerned in the last chapter. We are ourselves adult social beings; we ourselves observe taboos; and we may very well feel that we are separated by a smaller gulf from the attitudes, however strange, of other taboo observers than from mental events of our own childish pre-history of which we have long ceased to have even the dimmest personal remembrance.

A taboo is a prohibition that carries a supernatural or a social sanction. It differs from restrictions dictated by individual conscience or by sympathy on the one hand, and from those enforced by legal penalties upon the other. Taboo is the characteristic method of ensuring conformity and obedience to social custom in primitive societies. Notions concerning the actual nature of the sanctions involved are often vague and fluctuating; but it is possible to distinguish between what appear to be various developmental stages. At the most primitive level the sanction is supposed to follow automatically from the operation of 'mana', a dangerous force which somehow inheres in tabooed objects and which can be relied upon to punish or destroy those who infringe taboos relating to these objects—much in the same way as those who touch a live electric wire will inevitably receive a shock, a fatal one if the current happens to be strong enough. At this stage there is a certain physical inexorability about the process, of the same kind as that supposed to be involved in magical procedures; there is no question of motive, extenuating circumstances, or degrees of guilt. A classical example is to be found in the Biblical story of Uzzah, who stretched out his hand to save the Ark of the Covenant from falling. His action may have been little more than a natural reflex, or may have been dictated by a pious desire to protect the holy object; this did not prevent him from being immediately struck dead. Except perhaps in the extreme suddenness of his calamity, there is nothing to surprise us here, for there are numerous reports of persons in primitive societies who have died within a very short time of learning that they had quite innocently and unwittingly infringed some grave taboo, e.g. by eating some forbidden food, such as that left over by a chief. The only means of escaping the effects of breaking a taboo is by special ceremonies of purification, in which washing usually plays a prominent part. The use of this symbolism, which throughout the world applies so often not only to material but to moral decontamination, points to the existence of guilt and moral feeling even at this level, in spite of the fact that the sanctions are still regarded as predominently physical in nature.

At a somewhat higher level magic gives place to animism, and the sanction attaching to taboo is supposed to be enforced by spirits or demons, who will be angry whenever a taboo is broken. At a still higher level these spirits or demons (for the most part malignant beings) give place to gods, and the infringement of a taboo becomes the occasion of divine displeasure and divinely administered punishment. Inasmuch as such beings, whether demonic or divine, are psychological rather than physical in nature, something of the rigidity and inflexibility of the sanctions attaching to taboos is usually lost at these higher stages, and the sanctions themselves can to some extent be avoided or mitigated by means calculated to appeal to spiritual agencies—measures such as intercession, penitence and sacrifice, which gradually come to play so large a part in the practices connected with the higher religions.

At still higher or more sophisticated levels even the religious sanctions disappear and the punishment for breaking a taboo lies solely in the disapproval or active interference of society. At these levels the equivalents of primitive taboo are to be found in a number of different beliefs, attitudes, and practices—such as superstitions, conventions and good manners, and these themselves merge into individual conscience on the one hand and codified law upon the other, so that taboo may be said to become differentiated till it embraces the whole gamut of moral categories as found in civilized societies. Rarely, however, do the primitive attributes of taboo, particularly its lack of reasonable basis and its vague and sinister implications of evil and danger, altogether disappear; some element of mana usually remains to remind us of the primitive social origins of the long list of what is or is not done in any particular society, including that in which we live.

Taboos in Primitive Peoples

Primitive taboos themselves are of many kinds and can be classified in various ways. Some taboos relate primarily to acts, such as dealings with strangers, eating or drinking at forbidden times or places, watching secret ceremonies or enjoying illicit sexual intercourse. Others are concerned with persons, such as chiefs, kings, priests, medicine-men, relatives, warriors, hunters, fishermen, murderers, adolescents, menstruating women or women during or after childbirth. Others again relate to things, such as blood, weapons, rings, knots, thresholds, foods, utensils, or substances and objects that were formerly parts of the human body, such as blood, spittle, excrement, nail-parings and hair-clippings. Still others apply to words and names, such as the names of gods, certain personal names, the names of tabooed relatives, or words for certain common things.

Amid this welter of prohibitions it is difficult to find any trace of guiding principle. Freud in his *Totem and Taboo* was the first to throw any really satisfactory light upon the psychological processes involved, but in doing so he built upon a distinction that had been made by earlier observers, notably Wundt, i.e. that there is a sort of double attitude towards many objects of taboo. These objects are at once holy and sacred on the one hand, unclean and polluted on the other, though these two strangely contradictory qualities combine in making the object dangerous and a source of fear. Freud, by a characteristic stroke of genius, saw a resemblance between this double attitude involved in taboo and the double attitude or compromise that from the start of psycho-analytic work had become apparent in so many products of the mind: in dreams, in wit, and above all in neurotic symptoms. The neurotic symptom, Freud had shown, was very often of the nature of a compromise between two conflicting and incompatible tendencies, between a desire that had suffered inhibition or repression and a repressing moral or quasi-moral force opposed to the desire. The taboo, he suggested, was only a social or institutionalized form of the same compromise, and had its origin in the same fundamental type of conflict. Taboos therefore are the socialized expressions of conflicts, they are in their very nature ambivalent and imply a double attitude of desire and fear, of attraction and repulsion. It is true that the negative or prohibitory elements preponderate. But underneath each prohibition is a real or potential desire, for people do not trouble to prohibit things that no one wants to do. In its predominance of the negative aspects, taboo exhibits a special resemblance to one particular form of neurosis, the obsessional or compulsion neurosis, and Freud worked out in some detail the parallelism between these two manifestations of mental conflict, the one social and primitive, the other individual and, as we are accustomed to regard it, pathological.

Neither in the one case nor in the other is there any adequate rational motivation, though in both cases there is compulsion by an urgent sense of inner necessity, with a corresponding fear, guilt, or at the very least discomfort, if the prescriptions of the obsession or taboo are in any way infringed. Another very important similarity (in this case not only with obsessions but with most forms of neurosis, especially hysteria) is that the original object of desire, and therefore also of prohibition, tends to be replaced by other objects associated with it or symbolic of it—this in virtue of the mental process of displacement, which according to psycho-analytic findings plays so large a part in psychopathology, as indeed also in healthy mental development. It is this process which (together, of course, with the resistance due to the continued action of repression) makes it so difficult to discover the true meaning, alike of dreams, symbols, neurotic symptoms and taboos, while at the same time it is responsible for the great number and variety of symbols, of symptoms, and of things tabooed. Here we have, it would seem, at least a partial explanation of the welter of prohibitions to which we just now referred. Finally, both taboos and obsessional neurosis tend to give rise to ceremonial procedures by way of purification, expiation, or 'undoing' (in view of Melanie Klein's contributions, we may perhaps add 'reparation'). As already mentioned, the effects of infringing a taboo can under certain circumstances be made good by appropriate sacrifices, abstinences, lustrations, or decontaminations, as when the victors in a battle in Logea (an island near New Guinea) must live apart for a time, avoid encountering their wives or friends, must eat only vegetable foods and must not touch even these with their own hands. Similarly as regards the individualistic rituals that the obsessional neurotic imposes on himself—as when he must follow a strict sequence in washing, dressing or undressing, and in the event of any suspected departure from this sequence must start again from the beginning—it has been shown that they have the purpose of undoing the effects of evil actions which he fears unconsciously that he may have committed or been tempted to commit (for here also no clear distinction is made between criminal thoughts and the corresponding actions).

If we accept Freud's view as fundamentally correct, the main task in the psychological study of particular taboos must be to discover the nature of the underlying desires against which the prohibitions are directed and the ways in which the prohibitions and ceremonials are related to these desires. In cases where the mechanism of displacement has been operative this may involve the further task of following the sometimes complicated associations or symbolizations which have determined the course of the displacement. Finally we may sometimes have to take into account the rationalizations or secondary justifications by which the prohibitions may have been buttressed (in the absence of any insight into their primary purpose of combating unconscious wishes). All this is very like the process involved in the psychoanalytic investigation of cases of individual neurosis, though with the one important difference that, whereas in neurosis a full understanding of the symptoms may involve some considerable investigation of the past history of the individual, in taboo it is the relevant social history, with its background of beliefs, superstitions, and conventions, that has to be examined.

Freud and other psycho-analysts have endeavoured to interpret along these lines a number of taboos of primitive peoples, and we may indicate here in brief outline some of their conclusions. Among the most common of such taboos are those connected with kings and chiefs. The king is regarded as a source of danger, so that for unauthorized persons to touch him or anything that belongs to him or is connected with him, such as his clothes, his personal utensils, or his food, involves the direst risks. At the same time the conduct of the king himself is hedged round with taboos. He has to observe a strict routine and almost everything he does must be carried out with proper ceremonial; he may not be allowed to see the sun or sea or touch the earth; his diet may be rigorously circumscribed and supervised; he may have to sit immobile upon his throne for certain periods; he may have to submit to sexual restraints (and yet his reign, or even his life, may be in danger at any hint of sexual incompetence). The ostensible purpose of all these taboos is to protect and honour him and to prevent the mana in him from doing harm to lesser people. But concealed under these respectable motives is to be found an underlying attitude of hostility and envy and a desire to curtail his power. These latter tendencies find expression in the taboos affecting the king's own day-to-day existence, which are well calculated both to set limits to his effective action and to make his life a burden, beneath the mask of ceremony, honour, and obedience. The desire to hurt the king is, however, in its turn controlled in its more active manifestations by the taboo on any kind of contact with him; but occasionally even this desire will break through openly, as in one celebrated case in Sierra Leone where, according to tradition, the king had to submit to a sound beating before his coronation.

The last instance is strongly reminiscent of the practices accompanying another set of taboos—those affecting adolescents at or before initiation. Here again there is a double attitude. Ostensibly the purpose of initiation ceremonies and the period of preparation that precedes them is to fit the younger generation for assuming the privileges and responsibilities of adult life and to usher them into this life with due pomp, ceremony, and rejoicing. Actually initiation ceremonies are nearly always irksome, arduous, or disagreeable, usually in quite unnecessary degree, and beneath the apparent friendliness and helpfulness of the elders who carry out the ceremonies there stands revealed an element of hostility based on envy of the younger generation.[1] Those who hold the adult privileges—whether these be of a kind that applies to all grown-up members of the community or to some smaller specialized group—are willing to grant them to their younger rivals only on condition that these latter undergo a certain amount of anxiety and suffering. Initiation ceremonies are of course widespread, not only in primitive but in civilized communities. Among the very numerous ceremonies of the kind to be found in our own society the examination is perhaps the most important; it is of course an institution for which it is easy to find a perfectly rational justification, but this does not prevent it from possessing a psychological significance of the kind that attaches to other less reasonable forms of initiation. If we trace back the origins of modern examinations to the practices of mediæval universities this becomes clearly apparent.[2] Among such practices are to be found traces even of physical violence, though these would sometimes find expression not towards the initiate himself, but (in virtue of a process of displacement) towards a substitute. Thus in Cambridge it was sometimes the custom for 'a shrewd boy' to be hired to receive a whipping destined originally for the actual candidate for graduation. When we remember that young princes also sometimes had whipping boys, to act as vicarious recipients of the punishments that the royal pupils had themselves deserved, we

---

[1] See Th. Reik, 'The Puberty Rites of Savages' (1915), contained in *Ritual*, 1931.

[2] See the present author's paper on 'The Examination as Initiation Rite and Anxiety Situation,' *Int. J. Psa.* (1939), 20, 275.

can see that the motives underlying the initiation of graduates were probably not very different from those connected with the coronation ceremonies of the kings of Sierra Leone.

Other very numerous taboos relate to the dead and all who are connected with them, both warriors and murderers on the one hand and relatives and mourners on the other. At first sight these taboos might seem adequately explained if we bear in mind that death is usually considered the worst calamity that can befall a man and that the condition of the dead is looked upon by primitive people as an unhappy one. The dead in fact are thought to be envious of the living, and are often imagined to haunt the earth in the shape of malevolent spirits. But Freud has raised the question whether this malevolence can be accounted for solely in terms of the supposed unhappy conditions of life beyond the grave. Why should even loved and helpful people become demons after death? It is, he says, in virtue of projection. Those who are still living had an ambivalent attitude towards those who are now dead; they loved them and respected them, but at the same time envied and feared them and resented the restrictions they imposed. These more hostile feelings were to a large extent repressed, but at the death of the ambivalently loved person they none the less gave rise to feelings of guilt in the survivors. This guilt was dealt with by projecting it upon the dead, and this in turn aroused the fear that the dead would recognize the latent hostility and would seek revenge. In fact the primitive attitude towards the dead is much the same as the child's attitude towards its parents, as revealed by the studies that we dealt with in the last chapter. The demons are endowed with sinister powers and qualities very reminiscent of those attributed to what we called the bogies created by the child's imagination, and in both cases these qualities are derived by projection from the autogenous aggression of those who fear the demons or bogies. This parallelism between the two cases both illustrates the value of the comparative method in psychology, as revealing similarities between the child mind and the mind of the savage, and affords some considerable corroboration of the correctness of Melanie Klein's findings with young children.

Not only the deceased themselves, and those connected with them, but their names are often subject to taboo, and if the name of a dead person happens to be the same as that denoting an object or animal this may also have to be avoided, and a

I

new name substituted. Similarly the names of gods and sacred or unclean objects may be taboo. This prohibition of the use of names is, of course, in many ways similar to the existence of tabooed names and words among ourselves.

Among the taboos the origin of which has aroused the greatest interest and controversy, especially since Freud's attempt at interpretation, are those connected with totemism. All the taboos coming under this head seem ultimately reducible to two main classes: those that forbid killing and eating the totem animal and those that prohibit certain (but very varying) forms of endogamous marriage. As many anthropologists had noted, totemism seemed to be culturally connected with exogamy, the two institutions being found together in many different parts of the world, though the actual relation between totem clans and the classes within which marriage was forbidden differed greatly from one place or tribe to another. Freud's theory endeavoured to explain at one step both the nature of the desires underlying the two main classes of totemic taboo and the reason for their co-existence. He maintained that these two main classes of taboo were at bottom only the negative aspects of the tendencies which he had already discovered as operative in the Œdipus complex. This complex arises from the boy's desire to get rid of his father (i.e. to kill him) and to take the father's place with the mother (i.e. to marry her). Granted that the totem animal is a symbolic representative of the father or ancestor (a connection which was first suggested to Freud by his analysis of a child's animal phobia, but for which there is ample anthropological evidence), the first part of the totem taboo represents a prohibition of the first aspect of the Œdipus complex, the killing of the father, while the second part of the taboo (i.e. the insistence on exogamy) corresponds to the prohibition of incest, ultimately with the mother. This is not the place in which to enter into the discussions and criticisms to which Freud's theory has given rise. It must suffice to point out here that the theory, in so far as it is generally acceptable, does satisfactorily explain the two great totemic taboos in terms of repressed wishes of a widespread or universal kind, though of course in dealing with the particular form of the taboos in any given primitive culture we have to take into account a number of important sociological and historical factors that are peculiar to that culture, and may not be found in others (e.g., as has often been pointed out, the conditions in matrilineal societies are in some very significant respects different from those prevailing in our own patrilineal civilization).

Another and in some ways stranger set of taboos, again of widespread incidence, are those connected with the custom of Couvade. The taboos and compensatory ceremonials here apply to the father of a new-born child. In fully developed forms of the Couvade the father pretends during the mother's labour that he too is suffering the pangs of childbirth, while after delivery he has to lie-in for a while and must keep away from the baby. Primitives themselves, if pressed for an explanation of this practice, usually assert that it lightens the labour of the mother and prevents harm coming to the child. The first part of this statement is easy to understand if we allow for the belief in the possibility of the magical transference of pain, so that the father bears part of the mother's burden. It is less easy to see why such steps should be beneficial to the child. Reik [1] however has shown that the purpose of the whole custom becomes clearer if we assume that underneath the alleged motives (to help the mother and the child) there exist unconscious motives of exactly the opposite kind. The dangerous situation of the mother calls out all the latent hostility towards her (just as the possibility of death for anyone who is important to us, e.g. a parent, seems to arouse thoughts of what we have to gain—as well as lose—by his decease; thoughts which in the case of a loved person are likely to undergo strong repression and denial). This hostility, moreover, is not only that which is, so to speak, due to her in her own right, but is increased by the fact that she is bringing into the world a rival and successor. The desire to help her by magically participating in her labour is therefore in the nature of an obsessional reaction formation against the desire that she should die or suffer. It is also probably (among other things) a self-inflicted punishment for the guilt aroused by the existence of the hostile desires; in other words it is an example of nemesism, of aggression turned against the self. But here again, as in other cases, the hostility towards the original object of aggression often finds an outlet, and is manifested in the many alarming and disagreeable things that may be done to the parturient mother among those who practise the Couvade; as when she is subjected to the ordeal of sword-play over her body, of the firing of guns in her vicinity, of being smothered by smoke, roasted by fire, or beaten with sticks—all carried out nominally

---

[1] Th. Reik, 'The Couvade,' *op. cit.*

with the best intentions, in order to drive away the demons who are supposedly assailing her. After the birth, the father's feelings of hostility are largely transferred to the child, and it is then that the enforced inactivity connected with his lying-in keeps him from temptation. Thus the explanation that the practice prevents harm coming to the child is a true one, if we allow for the unconscious hostile motives.

A last example of primitive taboo may be mentioned, in this case one that depends entirely upon the symbolic meaning of the thing tabooed. In many parts of the world certain taboos apply to thresholds,[1] especially the thresholds of important or sacred buildings, such as a chief's hut, a king's palace, or a temple (the reader will perhaps recall the Old Testament reference to the curious crime of leaping on the threshold of the Temple at Jerusalem. He may also remember that superstitions concerning thresholds still exist among ourselves, e.g. that the bride must be carried across the threshold, or that good or bad luck may be brought by the first person who crosses the threshold on New Year's Day). Psycho-analytical studies of the individual use of symbolism and anthropological evidence from many different places make it abundantly clear that the significance of the threshold is derived from the fact that it stands symbolically for the entrance to the womb. Just as a church, temple, or palace may represent the mother (or a woman who is in some sense a mother substitute), so the entrance to such a building represents the approach to the mother's womb, i.e. the vagina, and any liberties taken with the threshold are liable to be regarded unconsciously as sexual liberties, ultimately with the mother, but in any case with some forbidden woman. Here once again a taboo is revealed as a prohibition of a desire; and it seems probable that many other objects (we are likely to think at once of such objects as nails, rings, and knots) have acquired their taboos owing to some symbolic value, in virtue of which they stand for something else that is more naturally liable to prohibition.

Taboo in Civilized Societies

As already indicated, the equivalents of primitive taboo must be sought in various directions. In the first place, taboo as a primitive **social** institution limiting the freedom of action, often

[1] See Th. Reik, 'Die Türhüter' (*Imago* (1919), 5, 344); G. Róheim, 'Die Bedeutung des Überschreitens,' *Zschf. f. Psa.* (1920), 6, 242.

in irrational ways, tends to lose some of its importance as civilization advances, because its functions are to a considerable extent taken over by the **individual super-ego.** This in turn is no doubt largely the result of the fact that civilized society is far less homogeneous than primitive society, exhibiting as it does a far greater variation in aims, ideals, habits, and traditions. This diversity, as some anthropologists, sociologists, and psychologists have emphasized,[1] almost inevitably subjects the growing individual to conflicting influences from which the younger members of primitive communities are free; hence the greater tendency to mental conflict and consequent neurosis among the civilized. We may indeed say that individual neurosis is the price that society has to pay for the greater diversity of thought and outlook that is a characteristic of civilization. **Individual neurosis in general** and (as Freud showed) **obsessional neurosis in particular** can be regarded as among the equivalents of taboo in our society; for repression of desire is an essential factor in neurosis, and with us individual repression has largely taken over the rôle played by taboo in primitive cultures. But even if the individual is not neurotic, even if he does not distort reality and submit himself to unnecessary and irrational restrictions, or to cumbersome expiatory ceremonials of the kind associated with taboo and obsessional neurosis (and few of us consistently attain this degree of realism), he must yet rely on his own conscience to restrain him from many anti-social actions to which his instincts and desires would naturally prompt him. What we might call **rational restraint** on the part of the individual is therefore another substitute for taboo.

Since the need for many of such rational restraints is common to all members of a civilized community, and since the power of exercising them on purely personal initiative is only too often deficient, society has codified some of them, incorporated them in the body of its **laws,** and has furthermore provided sanctions for the enforcement of these laws. Law, as Ranyard West has recently urged in an illuminating book,[2] can indeed be looked upon as a social institution the purpose of which is to reinforce our individual consciences and compel us to live up to those standards which in our ethically more enlightened moments we recognize as binding on us. Such a view is true, at least in

---

[1] E.g. Margaret Mead, *Coming of Age in Samoa*, 1928; K. Mannheim, *The Diagnosis of Our Time*, 1943 (ch. 5); K. Horney, *The Neurotic Personality of Our Time*, 1937.

[2] Ranyard West, *Conscience and Society*, 1942.

theory, of a democratic society, though we have to recognize that even under the most satisfactory constitutions yet devised, and in the most educated and progressive communities, law has a certain inertia and may therefore fail, at any rate as regards many points of detail, to be in harmony with what the more advanced thinkers of these communities would regard as truly ethical and reasonable. On the whole the laws in this country against dangerous driving, against murder, theft, fraud, and all forms of violence, would be recognized as reasonable and as embodying the individual conscience. Other laws however, such as those concerned with divorce and those that deal with blasphemy, are at present giving rise to serious misgiving among the more progressive and left-wing sections of our population; to such people these laws appear far from reasonable and seem to bear all too obvious signs of origin from a distant and outmoded past, in fact to be tainted with an element of primitive taboo. But whether any particular law appears rational or irrational, law in general must be reckoned as a most important social institution that takes over the function of taboo, with on the whole a great increase in rationality.

There are in every civilized society a number of other equivalents of taboo which are less easy to classify. Perhaps the most satisfactory method of dealing with them is to distinguish four classes: divine law, superstitions, conventions, and good manners, though there are borderline cases which make these distinctions somewhat arbitrary. In each class, moreover, we could distinguish behavioural and linguistic prohibitions, i.e. restrictions on conduct and on words. We could, of course, also attempt to classify taboos according to the nature of the objects, acts, or intentions to which they relate, though when we have exhausted certain obvious themes, such as the social, the sexual, and the religious, there might remain a residue which would be difficult to place.

Divine law differs from human law, first in that it applies only to those who believe and practise a particular religion (except in so far as the injunctions of this religion have been incorporated in state law, as in our own still existent but little used laws against blasphemy or breaking the Sabbath), secondly in that the sanctions are those of heavenly displeasure or ecclesiastical censure rather than those of state-administered justice. Until a decade or two ago the religious taboos against Sunday work and play nevertheless imposed great restrictions on the carrying out of all sorts of useful and enjoyable activities on the one day of the week when most people were free to undertake them, and even to-day these restrictions still make Sunday an occasion of quite unnecessary boredom to many. This is not to say that good secular reasons cannot be found for a day of rest from ordinary work, and even for a period devoted to meditation on problems of a higher order than those that preoccupy us in our daily avocations. But as long as an atmosphere of religious taboo invests the question of 'Lord's Day Observance' it remains very difficult to treat the matter impartially, and to see where conditions ensuring reasonable rest and relaxation merge into those that enforce restrictions which the majority no longer think it necessary or reasonable to observe.

As examples of other taboos of a religious order may be taken the restrictions on food involved in the practice of fasting, and the prohibition—recently removed—against women entering a church without a covering (if no more than a handkerchief) upon their heads. The former represent a very widespread type of asceticism practised in many climes and at almost every stage of culture; it seems likely that they take their origin from the first of the two great totemic taboos, that on killing and eating the totem animal. The latter, in itself a trivial matter, has aroused some feeling and interest because it was generally taken to imply that the sight of a woman's head (as indeed the rest of her body if too much of it were visible) was in some way displeasing to the deity; this latter view in turn being merely an instance of the numerous special taboos affecting women that have been operative since the earliest times. There has been a constant tendency to look upon women either as paragons of purity or as dangerous sources of contamination, and they have been placed in one category or the other according to position, circumstances, and occasion; but it is noteworthy that among primitives, and to some extent among civilized peoples, severe taboos have attached to women at the time of the specifically feminine physiological functions of menstruation [1] and childbirth, both of which often necessitated a subsequent ritual purification. With ourselves menstruation taboos have for the most part been degraded into superstitions (often rationalized in the name of

---

[1] For suggestions concerning the great psychological importance of menstruation taboos, see C. D. Daly, 'The Rôle of Menstruation in Human Phylogenesis and Ontogenesis,' *Int. J. Psa.* (1944), 24, 151, and various earlier papers.

hygiene), but the Christian religion still bears witness to the need for purification and thanks-offering after childbirth by its ceremony of the 'Churching of Women', which was in fact originally called the 'Purification of Women'.

In our **superstitions** [1] we seem for the most part to have regressed from the state of animism and religion to that of magic and mana. It is not God's disapproval that we fear but those vague, usually unnamed, but sinister, forces that bring 'bad luck'. In so far as spiritual agencies are supposed to be at work, these are devilish or demonic rather than divine—as in the present cult of 'gremlins'. Many of our superstitions are of hoary antiquity, though new ones are constantly arising, especially among those exposed to great and incalculable risks, such as sailors, airmen, gamblers. Superstitions differ from the other equivalents of taboo in that defiance of them meets with comparatively little social condemnation, being regarded as dangerous rather than immoral. As in the case of other infringements of taboo, however, this danger can sometimes be averted by appropriate magical procedures, as in those numerous devices used to counteract the 'Evil Eye', in the familiar process of 'touching wood' or (in German-speaking countries) of saying 'Unberufen'—the first and last of these indicating an origin in animistic beliefs which in the Western world have themselves almost disappeared, leaving behind only a faint aura of magic. The fact, however, that many people who would not confess to any serious belief in superstitions yet feel some spiritual discomfort when these magical procedures are omitted, illustrates both the power of the psychological forces underlying taboo, even in this, one of its last strongholds, and (once more) the essential psychological resemblance between taboo and obsessional neurosis, in which the patient also feels strain and worry whenever the compulsive ceremonial is not carried out.

Our two remaining classes of taboo equivalents, **conventions** and **good manners,** are less easy to distinguish from one another than are the other categories. In both, however, the sanction is provided by social disapproval or contempt. In this they differ rather strikingly from superstitions. But the social disapproval is not codified as in the case of law, and connected

---

[1] As regards what follows in this chapter I would refer the reader to two short but very stimulating books in the 'To-day and To-morrow' series: *Lars Porsena*, by Robert Graves (1927), and *It Isn't Done*, by Archibald Lyall (1930).

with this is the fact that conventions and good manners are more variable than superstitions both in time and space. The modification of human law is a cumbrous process requiring decisions by legislative bodies, while divine law can be altered only by reinterpretation of God's will by his ministers on earth. It is true that in both cases there can be modification of the importance attached to a law and in the strictness with which it is enforced, so that in extreme cases it may become a 'dead letter', i.e. is little thought about and seldom if ever enforced. Nevertheless there is a certain rigidity and fixity about law that is absent from conventions and manners. Law can be neglected or ignored but cannot be altered, except by a deliberate decision, whereas conventions and manners are essentially more fluid and elastic, especially in communities in which social conditions are undergoing rapid change. Law, moreover, is the same (except for minor modifications in its application) for all the members of a state in the case of human law and all the adherents of a religion in the case of divine law, whereas conventions and manners often differ considerably from one place to another or one social stratum to another within the same country. In their social, temporal, and (to a lesser extent) spatial aspects conventions and manners present certain interesting resemblances to fashions.[1] The main difference, perhaps, between conventions and manners on the one hand and fashions on the other is that there is a greater element of moral disapproval in the former case, of social emulation in the latter.

Even at times and places where definite conventions and manners are at the moment in force they are in any case seldom entirely rigid. There is, as Harding has rightly emphasized,[2] a limit of permissible action, opinion, and language [3] (not only as regards phraseology but accent), and those who stray beyond this limit are regarded as outsiders so far as concerns the group within which the conventions hold. The limits themselves vary greatly, in some cases being fairly wide and in others so narrowly determined as almost to approach to a prescribed ritual, e.g. in the case of procedure at official gatherings or ceremonies, or in

---

[1] For consideration of the motive forces underlying fashions in dress see the relevant chapters of E. R. Hurlock's *Psychology of Dress*, 1929, and of the present author's *Psychology of Clothes*, 1930.

[2] D. W. Harding, *The Impulse to Dominate* (1941), 45 ff.

[3] The great social importance of local and class distinctions with regard to language has been stressed by T. H. Pear in several of his recent writings, e.g. *Voice and Personality*, 1931; 'Psychological Aspects of English Social Stratification,' *Bulletin of the John Rylands Library* (1942), 26, No. 2.

the more or less uniform apparel that constitutes male civilian dress for formal occasions.

Convention would seem to possess two main real advantages, one primarily individual, the other social. The first lies in the fact that, in prescribing within narrow limits what has to be done, said, or worn, it saves us from the mental effort of thinking or deciding for ourselves and provides us, so to speak, with a number of formulæ (which may, as Pear suggests, have value as social lubricants) for use on suitable occasions. In this it is like habit, but of course it shares with habit the disadvantage that it may lead us to behave in ways that, with changing circumstances, may have ceased to be appropriate. The second, social, advantage of convention consists in helping to preserve the solidarity of the groups or classes concerned. Our judgment as to its value in this last respect will largely depend upon how far we consider the retention of such groups and classes is desirable. Those who demand a classless society will rightly look upon many of our conventions with a certain suspicion.

In any case, however, conventions imply rules and restrictions (we can indeed without serious inaccuracy call them taboos) which are usually arbitrary and often in themselves absurd. The frequently pilloried convention of New York men to change from one kind of hat to another on a certain date, regardless of the weather, falls into this category. It is likewise not easy to find a satisfactory reason why men should be expected to remove their hats on entering a house (as distinct from a shop—in this country at least) while women are supposed to await an invitation from their hostess before doing so; though the origin of this distinction may have something to do with a religious differentiation between the implications of men's and women's headgear. The taboo in this country on dickies, loose cuffs, and made-up ties could perhaps be rationalized as an objection to an element of pretence and spuriousness (since cuffs and dickies suggest that they are integral parts of a shirt, and ties suggest that they have actually been tied for the occasion), but this does not hold of waistcoats, which, though highly respectable, reveal themselves, if the coat be removed, as no less spurious behind than a dicky is in front. The speed with which fashions in clothes can change and the ease with which we adapt ourselves to them (even, to take an extreme example, to doing without clothes altogether, as in a nudist camp) would seem to show that particular conventions and taboos of this sort do not depend to any large extent on any intrinsic factor of usefulness, beauty, or convenience, or even on any deeper symbolic significance, but that social approval and desire for conformity are the chief influences at work. Nevertheless there can be no doubt about the very real feelings of guilty discomfort that failure to conform can produce in most people—and these feelings are very similar to those aroused by the infringement of more primitive and permanent taboos.[1]

Little need be said about good manners; indeed, as already indicated, the boundary between them and conventions is difficult to draw. Perhaps the chief difference is that manners apply to relatively intimate and personal contacts and relationships. It would be a breach of convention to appear in bathing costume in a city street, but a breach of manners to attend a private party thus attired. Good manners, moreover, to a higher degree than conventions and superstitions, often have a sound rational and ethical basis, inasmuch as they may save our fellows from reasonably grounded inconvenience, discomfort, and embarrassment. It is good manners, for instance, to refrain from talking or quoting a foreign language which some of those listening would not understand; in fact, quite generally, good manners imply behaviour that puts people at their ease. The trouble with manners is that they often tend to outlive their usefulness and to degenerate into mere conventions. It is usually thought that the custom of allowing a woman to walk on the inside of the pavement dates from the period when the contents of household utensils were thrown from upper windows into the central gutter of the street with no more ceremony than a warning cry, and that the gentleman by taking the outer position gallantly exposed himself in greater degree to the danger that threatened from above. But in modern towns slops are not emptied through the windows, and the convention may involve an amount of unnecessary dodging and shifting of a kind that to a psychiatrist unconversant with the practice might easily suggest that the gentleman was suffering from a phobia or an obsession.

---

[1] It might prove a fascinating task to try to assess the relative importance of intrinsic meaning (rational or irrational, i.e. symbolic) and social approval in the various forms of taboo equivalents, and the reason why this relative importance varies (if it does vary) from one case or class of taboo to another; also how far and in what ways there are differences of attitude and behaviour in the taboo observer and taboo breaker from one case to another. These, however, are largely matters for future research, and to speculate upon them with our present insufficient knowledge is beyond the limits of the present work.

Certain manifestations of what are often considered to be good manners appear, moreover, to be based psychologically on reaction formations, and are to that extent excessive, cumbersome, and at bottom insincere.   The rule of 'women and children first' in an emergency may have a sound moral justification, and it is at once an act of kindness and good manners to offer one's seat in a bus to a woman laden with shopping baskets (this is written in war-time!) or carrying a baby.   But it is (or was— for it is seldom practised now) surely an excessive and embarrassing politeness that compelled a man to rise from his seat, perhaps some distance away, to open the door for a perfectly healthy and unencumbered woman.   Practices of the latter kind abounded in the nineteenth century, when women were still suffering from many real social and legal disabilities— disabilities, however, of which society was becoming conscious; and it is probable that over-compensations in trivial matters served to conceal or mollify nascent feelings of guilt at the realization of injustice as regards more important things.   At any rate there can be no doubt that as women's social position has improved the amount of *petty* deference and politeness shown to her has considerably decreased—often to the relief of all concerned.   Nevertheless some rules that were perhaps originally reaction formations may have a really appreciable secondary value.   That it is considered polite to let a woman pass through a doorway before a man is instrumental in saving us considerable time and embarrassment, as we can realize when we witness the rather fussy hesitations and protestations that sometimes accompany the passage of a group of men across a threshold.

We have so far limited ourselves to actions, and have said little about the linguistic aspects of taboo equivalents.   Nevertheless these aspects are psychologically very interesting and socially often of considerable importance.   Thought itself to a large extent depends on language, and the communication of complicated thought does so almost entirely.   If certain words or topics are 'unmentionable', it means that these topics cannot be freely communicated or discussed—sometimes with disastrous results.   The taboo on the mention of venereal disease (now in process of being lifted) is probably the most striking instance of this, but the whole sphere of sex is, of course, still the most taboo-ridden of all subjects in the modern world, in spite of the very considerable advances that have been made in the last half-century or so as regards the liberty of both speech and action. With regard to speech especially, we are in a period of rapid change, and it looks as though many cumbrous circumlocutions such as 'an interesting condition', 'a certain operation', 'a woman of a certain class' will soon have vanished. Nevertheless an immense amount of feeling still attaches to certain words, and to refer in ordinary talk to the external genitalia of either sex even in their Latin anatomical terms is only possible in 'advanced' circles. What Lyall calls the 'twelve unprintable monosyllables', all with sexual or excremental associations, but most of them respectable enough philologically, seem unlikely to come back into general usage because of the offence they arouse even in more or less enlightened quarters, and the present writer well remembers the embarrassed confusion into which a drawing-room was thrown when a guest suddenly pronounced one in the midst of an otherwise impeccable conversation. As Ernest Jones has pointed out,[1] the English language is in some respects peculiar in that it has a double vocabulary, Anglo-Saxon and Latin-French respectively, for many common objects, acts, and situations. The Anglo-Saxon words almost invariably carry a higher degree of feeling and for that reason are far more often subject to taboo. The fact that two modes of expression—one less charged with feeling than the other— were so often available may, as Jones suggests, have had something to do with the development of British reticence in the expression of emotion and love of understatement (which of course—along the lines of irony though with less accent on aggression—has come to possess a peculiar affective significance of its own).

Particularly interesting from the psychological point of view is the deliberate breaking of verbal taboos involved in the practice of swearing. 'Bad language' is as a rule sexual, lavatorial, or blasphemous, sometimes a combination of all three, and the satisfaction that it gives in situations of pain, annoyance, and frustration is clearly derived very largely from the fact that it is possible to 'relieve one's feelings' by the process of infringing the taboo (the other element lying in mere verbal emphasis and explosiveness which affords a motor outlet for the aggression aroused).[2] This in itself indicates again—if

[1] Ernest Jones, 'A Linguistic Factor in English Characterology' (1920), included in *Essays in Applied Psycho-analysis*, 1928.
[2] There seems little doubt that a 'displacement from below upwards', from the anal to the oral zone, is often involved here. Further evidence for the

further evidence were necessary—that taboo involves the prohibition or inhibition of a desire. When we are angered, we find a channel for our aggression by directing it against the moral authority embodied in the taboo, in showing our defiance of it—even though the actual meaning of the words employed may have no relevance to the situation that has aroused our anger. Verbal taboos which can be broken thus play in a sense the rôle of scapegoats on which we can displace our hostile feelings, and fulfil much the same function as that intended for the small porcelain figures that an enterprising American firm has recently put on the market in order that we may smash them when we get into a temper.

Fairly early in the history of psycho-analysis Ferenczi drew attention [1] to the great affective significance of obscene words and the rôle which resistance against saying them might play in actual psycho-analytic treatment. Basing his views on what Freud had already said about 'smutty' jokes in *Wit and its Relation to the Unconscious* (1905), he came to the conclusion that such words had retained to a greater extent than others their original close connection with the things or actions they denoted. They were in most cases the first words heard that bore these meanings, the politer and more scientific terms (what Lyall calls 'their degenerate sesquipedalian supplanters') being learnt much later. But they had very early come under the influence of taboo, and owing to their disuse, or use only in pornographic contexts, had failed to undergo the processes whereby other words had become sharply differentiated from, and of lesser emotional value than, the things they signified. They were in fact nearer to action than other words, and possessed a remnant of that primitive regressive hallucinatory power that shows itself in the tendency to substitute visual hallucinations for language as we become drowsy and begin to fall asleep—a power that other words have lost. There has unfortunately, in the long interval since Ferenczi wrote, been little attempt to test the truth of this view by more systematic observation and experiment. The study of profanity by experimental and introspective methods might throw some further very interesting light upon the satisfactions and inhibitions connected with the use of tabooed words, and through them

connection between 'bad language' and excretory functions is to be found in the widespread practice of covering the walls of public lavatories with obscene remarks or drawings.

[1] S. Ferenczi, 'Über Obszöne Worte,' *Zentralblatt f. Psa.* (1911), 1, 390.

upon the mental aspects of taboo in general. In any case, however, there seems no doubt that our peculiar attitude of mixed attraction and aversion towards certain words exhibits the same ambivalence that Freud discovered in the taboos of primitives, and that when we swear we enjoy a 'sudden glory' that is derived from a temporary overthrow and defiance of our super-ego, and of the social authorities from which our super-ego is derived. From the pleasure and the sense of power this gives us we can form some estimate, both of the severity with which the super-ego rules us, and of the strain which obedience to its rule imposes on the still relatively crude and primitive fundaments of our orectic life.

CHAPTER XI

THE NEED FOR PUNISHMENT AND THE POLYCRATES COMPLEX

The Origin of Punishment

We have seen in the last chapter how great are the restrictions that man's morality places on his thought and actions. But the facts we have considered in earlier chapters have already made us realize that the influence of the super-ego cannot be described in terms of restriction alone; there are in the super-ego active and aggressive elements which are not content with the mere renunciation of desire and the erection of stern prohibitions, but which would seem rather to urge mankind irresistibly towards the infliction of positive suffering. With some aspects of this suffering we have already dealt, but we are still far from having done justice to this nemesistic urge, which in its curious and widespread ramifications is liable to affect the most varied fields of social and individual life. In this chapter and the next we must therefore return to the more direct study of the super-ego, in order to follow up and illustrate some of the remoter consequences and implications of the existence of this moral factor— with special (though not exclusive) emphasis on its more aggressive aspects.

Undoubtedly one of the most important results of the formation of the super-ego is the development of that peculiar mental condition which we often describe as guilt or sense of sin—a condition that is perhaps peculiar to the human race, though

we may sometimes be tempted to ascribe it, at least in a rudi-
mentary form, to some gregarious or domesticated animals, and
more especially to that one animal, the dog, with which we seém
to have such a strange psychological affinity.[1] Guilt no doubt
is grounded in fear, which is a very primitive emotion shown
throughout the animal scale,[2] and in the human race guilt is at
first hardly distinguishable from it, though later the differentiation becomes very clear. Guilt (unlike fear) undoubtedly
implies the existence of at least some budding moral 'sentiments',
some notion of how we ought and ought not to behave, and the
fear from which it seems to arise, and which perhaps always
remains an integral part of it, is a fear of the unpleasant consequences of not acting in accordance with these sentiments.
Such consequences may vary in kind from physical chastisement,
through censure and the withdrawal of love, to a purely internal
sense of sin, unworthiness, or self-dissatisfaction; and in degree
from a mother's slap or mild reproof to a death sentence
delivered by a judge, from a gentle prick of conscience to suicide
or lifelong shame.

Like other emotional or quasi-emotional conditions, guilt is
a state of tension, and gives rise to a need for the removal of
this tension, but unlike the simpler emotions, such as fear and
anger, it does not at first sight appear to be associated with any
obvious and biologically determined kind of behaviour that will
satisfy this need. It might seem that, just as guilt is itself a
morally and socially determined emotion, so also the methods
of dealing with it arise through moral and social influences.
Nevertheless here too, perhaps, we can detect at least a biological
core. Guilt implies wrongdoing (or at least the presence of a
temptation to wrongdoing) and wrongdoing is in the last resort
a kind of behaviour that hurts other people (physically, mentally,
or socially). Now men, like many other animals, grow angry
and retaliate when they are hurt, i.e. they react aggressively to
those who hurt them, in this case to the wrongdoer. Such
retaliation, when it is not immediate and spontaneous but
implies some degree of deliberation, is what we often speak of

---

[1] As Buytendijk suggests (F. J. J. Buytendijk, *The Mind of the Dog*, 1935),
the dog seems to have given up his dependence on the herd and replaced it by
an attachment to, and dependence on, man—often where possible some individual
man. The relations between a dog and his master seem in many respects to
mirror those of a child to its parent or of the ego to the super-ego.

[2] For a discussion of the more intimate details of the complex relation between
guilt and fear see Ernest Jones, 'La Crainte, la Culpabilité, la Haine,' *Rev.
Française de Psa.* (1931), 4, 454.

as revenge; and when it is itself moralized, that is directed against a person who is regarded as guilty, we call it 'punishment'. External punishment thus springs ultimately from the natural impulse of retaliation. Actions that arouse guilt, being actions that hurt others, are therefore also actions that tend to involve us in punishment, and by an inevitable process of conditioning we learn to expect punishment when we feel guilty.[1]

Now the infliction of punishment, inasmuch as it implies the natural reaction of aggression, tends to relieve the outraged feelings of those who have been hurt; after its infliction their anger abates, and they tend to regard the incident as closed. This applies perhaps especially to adults when children are the culprits, and more particularly to the attitude of parents towards their children. But it is just this latter attitude that we introject when we form our super-ego. It is hardly surprising, therefore, that we learn not only (in virtue of conditioning) to expect punishment when we are guilty, but also (in virtue of introjection) to experience relief when we have been punished. Just as the anger of our parents or other moral authorities in our youth abated when they had retaliated by administering punishment, so also our super-ego (which corresponds to these authorities) is satisfied when punishment has been inflicted. Here, as in other matters, the relations between the ego and the super-ego mirror those between the child and parent (though, as we have seen, the mirror image may often be distorted in the direction of increased severity through the operation of nemesism and sadism). Guilt implies a condition of tension between the ego and the super-ego, which in turn corresponds to tension between child and parent, and in both cases punishment is the

---

[1] In this way punishment may become indissolubly associated with the satisfaction of 'guilty' wishes, and men may come to accept punishment as a natural or unavoidable accompaniment of many forms of pleasure (in much the same way as Pavlov's dogs came to accept an electric shock as an accompaniment of feeding). This, Alexander suggests (*Psychoanalyse der Gesamtpersönlichkeit* (1927), p. 138), may be the ultimate foundation of the association of pain with satisfaction, and here also there is a parallelism between our relations to the social and the physical environment of the kind to which, again following Alexander, we drew attention in Chapter IV; just as certain forms of satisfaction, which we might classify as 'dangerous', often bring us pain from non-human sources, so also certain other satisfactions, which we might call 'wicked' or 'guilty', bring us pain that is inflicted by our fellow human beings. Alexander may be right in regarding this as a (perhaps *the*) ultimate biological foundation of punishment. Nevertheless punishment seems to have acquired (even, and indeed especially, on Alexander's own showing) to such a high degree an independent value of its own that it seems clear that any explanation in terms of mere conditioning carries us only a little way, and that other factors must be invoked, such as that of introjection, as indicated immediately below in the text.

K

natural method of relief. Thus the suffering of punishment comes to play much the same rôle in relation to guilt as does escape from danger in the case of fear or aggressive action in the case of anger, and just as there is an instinctive need to carry out the biological reactions to fear and anger (in their simple or modified form), so also there arises a conditioned need (based originally on the instinctive aggression of the punisher and then introjected) to carry out the corresponding reaction to guilt, i.e. to submit to punishment.

Small wonder then that when psycho-analysts began to investigate the super-ego they should discover that guilt was associated with a 'need for punishment'. Startling as this result at first appeared (especially perhaps in view of the rather crude assumption of psychological hedonism with which psycho-analysis began), it ceases to be astonishing when we take into consideration the way in which the super-ego is formed and the energies with which it operates. Indeed, in this intimate psychological relation between guilt and punishment we must probably seek the origin both of the social institution of punishment and of the closely related concept of justice, which, in its application to the individual, involves the notion of some sort of equilibrium between crime and punishment, virtue and reward. Punishment and justice are no mere inventions of later educational and legal thought but have their deep foundations in the mental constitution of mankind.[1]

Equivalents of Punishment

We must shortly set about the task of examining a little further some of the devious ways in which this 'need for punishment' may find expression. But before we do so we may pause for a moment to consider a complicating circumstance. The endurance of punishment would appear to be at once the most primitive, most natural, and most important way of dealing with guilt; but it is not the only way. There are several other methods by which at least some degree of relief from guilt can be obtained.

[1] A more detailed treatment of the consideration we have so briefly dealt with here will be found in Th. Reik, *Geständniszwang und Strafbedürfnis*, 1925; Franz Alexander, *Psychoanalyse der Gesamtpersönlichkeit*, 1927; René Allendy, *La Justice Intérieure*, 1931; F. Alexander and Hugo Staub, *The Criminal, the Judge, and the Public*, 1930; A. Hesnard and R. Laforgue, 'Les Processus d'Auto-punition,' *Rev. Française de Psa.* (1930), 4, 2 (also published separately). These works also form the basis of much that is to follow in this and the two succeeding chapters.

The first of these is **reparation.** The infliction of punishment may satisfy the outraged feeling of an aggrieved person; it may also relieve the guilt of the culprit. But in both cases it is a purely psychological satisfaction, and any material damage that may have been caused by the guilty act remains. Hence there arises a further desire that this damage should itself be made good, a desire for reparation, restitution, compensation, which is of course not satisfied by the fact that the transgressor is made to suffer. If a thief steals my dinner, I may get some satisfaction by knocking him down or handing him over to the police, but this does not appease my hunger. From this point of view it would be better for me if I could make him provide me with another dinner. Rationally indeed, reparation, where it is possible, is more satisfactory than punishment, both for soothing the outraged feelings of the transgressee and for removing the guilt of the transgressor, though emotionally it may be less satisfactory for the former purpose inasmuch as it affords a less direct and instinctive outlet for the transgressee's aggression. It is in fact a more sophisticated method than is punishment, for at least three reasons: because a real wrong is righted, because it implies a quantitative and qualitative adjustment of behaviour to the wrong committed, and because it involves a renunciation of the primitive motive of crude revenge (unless of course, as is sometimes the case, both punishment *and* reparation are demanded, the former for dealing with the psychological, the latter with the material, consequences of the crime). It is therefore not surprising that, according to the careful studies of children's moral development carried out by Piaget [1] and those who have followed in his train, reparation as a method of dealing with guilt appears at a later age than does that of simple punishment. Nevertheless, the work of Melanie Klein and her school seems to show that at least some crude notions of reparation are to be found at a very early age, and that therefore the principle of 'making good' has its roots in the deepest layers of our moral life. It would indeed seem likely that it is only the predominance of aggressive elements in the super-ego, and in our moral standards generally, that to some extent conceals and overlays the motive of reparation and prevents it from manifesting itself more clearly at earlier and more primitive levels—a consideration that of course lends great support to the view that, in educational and legal practice,

[1] Jean Piaget, *The Moral Development of the Child*, 1932.

opportunity and encouragement should, wherever possible, be given for reparation rather than for simple punishment.

Reparation may of course itself be arduous and painful and thus have something in common with punishment, inasmuch as both may involve suffering. Indeed a distinction between the two may not always be easy, especially when the punishment takes the form of renunciation rather than of active suffering. In the institution of sacrifice particularly, the motive of reparation is predominant. The savage may throw back a portion of the food or water he has gathered, in order to appease the appropriate guardian spirits. In the higher religions the worshipper may make offerings to his gods to stave off or mitigate the misfortunes of drought, earthquake, or tempest, which he tends to regard as divine punishments. Our own thanksgiving services or harvest festivals have sprung from practices with similar intent; while in purely secular affairs the minor offender makes good his injury to society by payment of a fine.

A second alternative to punishment is **confession,** in which the culprit avows his guilty thoughts or acts, suffering in the process self-reproach or reproach from the moral authorities to whom he confesses. Almost all of us can testify from personal experience to the relief of guilt that may follow confession, and our criminal procedure shows that we regard confession as in some degree a substitute for punishment, by passing a lighter sentence on those who have freely acknowledged their guilt or who have spontaneously delivered themselves into the hands of justice. Confession is indeed the mildest way of satisfying the need for punishment, and increasing weight is attached to it both by the individual and by society as moral development proceeds. Reik,[1] who has made a special study of confession from the psycho-analytic point of view, suggests that four stages in its evolution can be conveniently distinguished. In the first, punishment is inflicted without opportunity being given for confession or significance being attached to it. In the second, punishment and confession are intimately blended, as in torture, where confession is as a rule nominally the end, but often in reality little more than an excuse or accompaniment. In the third, punishment is reduced for those who confess, and confession is itself regarded as important; while in the last stage, confession may be considered a sufficient substitute for punishment.

[1] *Op. cit.*

The increasing weight laid on confession is itself an accompaniment of the increasing importance attributed to the motive of an immoral act as distinguished from the act itself—a process which, as it occurs in the individual mind of the growing child, has also been studied in detail by Piaget.[1] At the earliest stage, which Piaget calls that of 'moral realism', the guilt is considered to be entirely proportionate to the material consequences, a greater injury brought about by accident being regarded as more blameworthy than a smaller one deliberately contrived. At this stage the attitude of the child is clearly similar in many respects to that implied in taboo, in which punishment follows automatically without respect to motive; but, as development proceeds, the proportion of 'realistic' moral judgments steadily decreases, while considerations of motive take an ever-larger place.

There is such a thing as an indirect and involuntary form of confession as well as a direct and deliberate form. The indirect form may be said to be practised by all those who 'give themselves away', as with those criminals who unnecessarily provide clues pointing to their guilt. A recent very interesting case reported in the British newspapers of January 27, 1943, was that of a man who, accused of murder and imprisoned, wrote a story in his cell in which he described the murder with correct place-names and certain details which were not known to the police at the time, but which could easily be verified, thus providing a much better case for the prosecution.

A third alternative of punishment as a method of dealing with guilt is **repression.** Here guilt is lost to consciousness and forgotten, in much the same way as guilty desires themselves may be repressed. Indeed there is, of course, a close connection between the repression of the feeling of guilt and that of the guilty thoughts and actions; and it is an interesting point whether, and how far, guilt can be repressed apart from the thoughts and actions that are associated with it or have given rise to it. According to the general principle of the 'displacement of affect' it should be possible, and on the question of fact it is very clear that the affective tone of the memories of our past deeds and thoughts can change without any corresponding alteration in these memories themselves, and that among such changes there may be a loss of the shame and guilt attaching to them. The same is true of contemplated actions, among

[1] *Op. cit.*

which there are some that may at first arouse qualms of conscience but that later we can carry out with little or no moral conflict.[1] But it is often difficult to say whether this diminution of guilt is due to repression or to some other cause. If Rosenzweig is right in considering that the important characteristics of his 'impunitive' type are due to repression of aggression, either inwardly or outwardly directed (see Chapter VII), it would seem likely that the 'forgiving' and 'forgetting' tendencies of this type are to some extent dependent on repression of shame and guilt, as well as of humiliation and frustration. But, whether or not guilt suffers repression independently of the memories of the causes and occasions of guilt, there can be little doubt that repression does often affect a guilty experience as a whole, so that in any case we are justified in regarding repression as one of the methods by which guilt can be dealt with otherwise than by punishment.[2]

Another such method is to be found in the process of **rationalization,** in which we endeavour to assuage our guilt by finding a secondary justification for the guilty action, as when we persuade ourselves that some borderline case of sharp practice or deception in business is permissible because it is within the letter of the law (and who are we that we should try to improve upon the law?), or that some infliction of suffering upon a child or animal is essential for its training (and do we not all in the last resort learn through suffering?). Rationalization may, of course, vary in rational or ethical justifiability from the most flimsy and transparent pretexts to cases where there may be a very genuine moral conflict, as in the stock example of the otherwise honest man who steals food for his starving wife and children.

The last alternative to punishment that we need mention consists in **projection** of guilt on to some other party, who is then regarded as responsible, so that we ourselves feel innocent. This could perhaps be considered as merely a rather extreme kind of rationalization, but it differs from most forms of the latter in that it involves a definite element of delusion. This last is particularly clear in the 'delusions of persecution' so

---

[1] I know, for instance, of people who, when they receive an embarrassing appeal for help in the form of cash or service, find themselves unable to refuse it at once without incurring feelings of guilt, but who after a few days can do so without hesitation or discomfort. It would seem that during the interval the guilt had somehow been dealt with, usually without conscious intervention.

[2] A further reference to this subject will be found in Chapter XIV.

characteristic of the disease of paranoia. In these delusions the patient feels that he is the victim of a conspiracy, that people (it may be some particular person, or some group or organization, such as the Post Office or the Salvation Army) are constantly and deliberately subjecting him to annoyance, humiliation, or frustration, or are constantly spying on him and commenting unfavourably upon his doings. It is one of the triumphs of psycho-analysis that it was able to show that in these cases the patient's aggressive and guilty impulses (among which those of a homosexual kind are apt to play a prominent part) were projected on to the supposed persecutors. Projection does not necessarily, or perhaps even usually, do away with punishment, but the punishment is diverted to the supposed culprit on whom our guilt is projected, who becomes in fact a scapegoat. For this reason, and also because of its very great importance for our subject, we shall (in the next chapter) have more to say about projection in connection with punishment, to which latter we must now return.

The Polycrates Complex

In dealing with punishment and its equivalents as methods of assuaging guilt we are, of course, considering to a large extent the same phenomena with which we were concerned in Chapter VII under the heading of nemesism or aggression turned against the self. A realization of the rôle of guilt in this process affords us, however, some slight further insight into the reason why this process is of such frequent occurrence and such fundamental importance. We are all at least dimly (many of us acutely) conscious of failing in numerous respects to live up to the standards of our super-ego; hence we all feel guilt, and in turn experience in some measure the 'need for punishment' which is the basic method of dealing with guilt. We are all 'miserable sinners', as the Prayer Book has it. If man is, as we ventured to suggest, a pain-seeking as well as a pleasure-seeking animal, it is because only through the pain of punishment can he get rid of the burden of his guilt. If we do not experience sufficient pain, if things go too well with us and we have too much luck, we begin to feel uneasy because our need for punishment has not been met. Hence at bottom the fear of Hubris, of arrogance or 'uppishness', which the ancient Greeks, themselves a relatively guilt-free people, were yet able to discern as a fundamental human trait.

The influence of this fear in retarding human progress is difficult to estimate but has certainly been very great.[1]   Any striking advance that man has made in the control of his environment, in securing better conditions of life, even in the free exercise of thought and the acquiring of knowledge, has been liable to arouse a feeling that he was somehow behaving in a presumptuous manner, ill befitting one living in a universe whose immense power—in contrast to his own feebleness—he could dimly realize, of whose working he could understand little, but whose malignancy he had, he thought, good reason to suspect.   In this it is easy to see a reflection of the child's attitude towards its parents.   For the child also there is much that is taboo, many desirable things which, if pursued, will only lead to punishment, much knowledge (e.g. that concerning sex and other interesting matters that are 'for adults only') that is not permitted.   The parents, too, possess overwhelming power in comparison with that of the child, and it is dangerous to provoke a hostile usage of this power.   Man's attitude to Nature thus mirrors his attitude to his own super-ego, and this in turn is built up on the basis of the child's moral and physical dependence on its parents, magnified and distorted by the influence of nemesism.   It is not surprising then that throughout history those who have sought to increase human power and understanding should have aroused a degree of suspicion and distrust that has often led to martyrdom, for at bottom it is felt that such pioneers are guilty of Hubris, and that if they had their way they would involve all mankind in the penalties incurred by those who presume 'above their station'.   It is only in so far as this fear of Hubris is diminished that rapid human progress becomes possible, and there is good reason to suppose that the periods which have seen the greatest adventures of the human spirit have also been periods of relative freedom from the more primitive forms of fear and guilt.   It will be a fascinating task for the future historian of culture to trace the influences that have led at certain times and places to a loosening of these shackles on human thought and action and the effects of this loosening upon civilization, but this (even if we had the necessary knowledge) is far beyond our present theme.

[1] It is, of course, not suggested here that this is the only cause of unreasonable conservatism.   Mental laziness (unwillingness to abandon old habits of thought and to make the effort necessary for the assimilation of new ideas) and vested interests (reputational as well as material) have certainly also played a large part.

Just as there have been differences between cultures as regards the fear of Hubris and the need for punishment, so also of course there are differences between individuals within a given culture. In our own civilization all of us probably experience this need in some degree; we all tend to be suspicious or 'superstitious' about good fortune and successful enterprise, but some far more than others. In this respect we would appear to be the victims of a complex comparable to certain other complexes of widespread (perhaps universal) incidence but varying intensity, such as the Œdipus complex, the castration complex, and some others with which psycho-analysis has made us familiar. I would suggest that it be called the Polycrates complex, after Polycrates the tyrant of Samos (whose story is told by Herodotus and who is the subject of a well-known poem by Schiller). The unprecedented run of success enjoyed by this potentate aroused ever-increasing alarm among his friends and allies, who began to think that his balance of ill-luck must be accumulating at a most alarming rate (much perhaps as we in England, during a spell of unusually fine weather, are apt to shake our heads and mutter 'we shall have to pay for this'). It was suggested that it might help to avert disaster if he were to make some voluntary sacrifice. Moved by these representations, he threw a valuable ring into the sea. The ring, however, was swallowed by a fish, which was caught by a fisherman and, being an exceptionally fine specimen, was served up at the tyrant's table. To the consternation of all the ring was duly found inside; it was clear that the sacrifice had not been accepted and that the gods were unwilling to mitigate the penalties they had in view. In fear of an approaching catastrophe, his ally, Amasis of Egypt, left the doomed man's presence with unseemly haste.

Methods of satisfying the Need for Punishment

Among those who suffer appreciably from the Polycrates complex the need for punishment can be met in a variety of ways. Four sets of alternatives can perhaps be conveniently distinguished. In the first type of case, 'punishment' in the shape of some kind of disaster, frustration, or harsh treatment is provided by the environment, physical or social, without the complicity of the 'culprit' (as we may conveniently call the person who experiences the need for punishment—though without necessarily implying that he is guilty according to standards other than his own). This satisfies his 'need', and it is only when for some reason the external hardship is removed that he begins to experience the necessity for discovering a substitute (which is the second alternative in such a case). In the course of his work, Freud [1] noticed that certain patients succumbed to a neurotic disorder only when some external obstacle to their success had been removed. This type of case presented a striking contrast to the more usual type in which neurosis seemed to be due to frustration and lack of opportunity for self-expression; but, viewed in the light of psycho-analytic theory, it need hardly cause surprise. All neuroses, according to this theory, are due to conflict, but in most (especially those of the hysterical type) it is the dissatisfaction of (partially repressed) id impulses that appears most prominently in the picture. But the super-ego on its part is making itself felt through the repression, and the consequent neurosis is itself a 'punishment' through the restrictions and sufferings it entails. In those other cases to which Freud now drew attention the punishment had previously been supplied by the outer world, and it was only when the external difficulties ceased that the super-ego resorted to intropunitive measures, in the form of increased repression, which gave rise to a neurosis. Subsequent work has shown that the number of cases of this kind is by no means inconsiderable. As long as the external obstacle persists (be it poverty, an uncongenial occupation, an unhappy marriage, or even a physical disability or illness), the 'culprit' remains mentally healthy, though he may of course complain of the difficulties that beset his life. But as soon as his way is smoothed, instead of enjoying happiness and success as we might expect, he falls a victim to mental disease. In other cases the converse may be observed: a person is neurotic or inhibited as long as external circumstances are favourable, but suddenly acquires a new freedom when difficulties or disasters are encountered. This is perhaps particularly true as regards the expression of aggression. We have already noted how a mild parental régime may render difficult the external direction of aggression in children and thus encourage nemesism. Favourable circumstances in later life may have a similar influence, and a disaster may be looked upon in the same way as a sudden increase in parental harshness. Indeed it may sometimes

[1] S. Freud, 'Einige Charaktertypen aus der psychoanalytischen Arbeit,' *Imago* (1915), 4, 317.

actually release long-pent-up aggression against the parents themselves, as in the instance reported by Alexander [1] where a man who had met with a severe accident exclaimed: 'Now I have suffered enough. I have paid for everything. Now at last I can tell my father my mind'. This is no doubt a somewhat exceptional case, but if we may assume that the same attitude, even in a very minor degree, is at all prevalent, it is obvious that the social implications are important, inasmuch as improvement in the conditions of life may, under certain circumstances, lead to an increase of inhibition or neurosis to set against the increased happiness and efficiency and the reduction in crime that we might reasonably hope for.

If external hardship spontaneously forthcoming can satisfy the need for punishment, it is not surprising to find that some persons themselves provoke such hardship if it is not otherwise available, thus behaving like Polycrates, though for the most part more or less unconsciously. Among these are the so-called 'neurotic characters', to which we have already alluded (Chapter VII), who will often land themselves in troubles (financial, professional, matrimonial, hygienic, etc.) which their knowledge and experience should have enabled them quite easily to avoid. Here the alternative (the second of the four sets that we mentioned above) is usually between the satisfaction of the need for punishment through *provoked* outer disasters or through real neurosis with the development of some specific symptom. Needless to say, however, as already indicated in Chapter VII, such persons often involve others (and thus indirectly express aggression extrapunitively) in the disasters that they bring upon themselves.

The third set of alternatives is that between suffering in body or in mind. Within the sphere of neurosis proper it is manifested very clearly in the contrast between 'conversion hysteria' (in which the symptoms are of a bodily or sensory character, almost any bodily disease being simulated, though there are also a number of symptoms, especially certain paralyses or anæsthesias, peculiar to hysteria itself) and 'anxiety hysteria' (in which the patient develops more or less specific phobias or fears and worries of a more general kind). A very neurotic but highly gifted man whom I once knew suffered for the greater part of several years *either* from severe neuralgia *or* profound depression. Like some other 'culprits' of this kind he possessed

[1] *Op. cit.*, 53.

the capacity to exchange one symptom for another, almost it would seem by an act of will; but one or other of these burdens he was compelled to bear. For a few months only in each year was he free from them, and these months followed immediately upon his annual holiday, during which he always contrived to have some surgical operation performed upon some part of his body, preferably with a local anæsthetic (better still, a rather inadequate one), so that he could watch the proceedings, which he followed with the greatest interest. It would seem that the operation freed him for a time from the need for further punishment, though its cathartic effect was of short duration, so that the need soon returned, to be satisfied in one or other of the two customary ways. In this case we see not only an alternation between bodily and mental punishment (neuralgia and depression) but a yearly rhythm centring round a temporary satisfaction through a major punishment (the operation). We may compare this case with that described in detail by Morgenstern,[1] of a boy who from the start exhibited externally as well as internally directed aggression, fits of violence alternating with depression and threats of suicide. Both of these disappeared when he broke his leg, which, as revealed by psycho-analytic treatment (in this instance with the help of the boy's drawings and the explanations that he gave of them), was a symbolic castration. Such instances throw a fascinating light upon the undoubtedly very numerous cases where a patient suffering from a mental disease (including those of a definitely psychotic order) undergoes marked improvement, even to the point of apparent complete recovery, during severe bodily illness. They naturally suggest that this same alternative of bodily or mental trouble may play a part in some modern treatments of mental disease that have proved surprisingly effective, though their working either on the physiological or psychological side is as yet far from being fully understood (e.g. the malarial treatment of general paralysis or the various forms of 'shock' treatment—by means of electricity, insulin, cardiazol, triazol, etc.—in schizophrenia).[2]

[1] Sophie Morgenstern, *Psychanalyse Infantile*, 1937.
[2] Though Silbermann, on reviewing his own and some other work from the psychological point of view (Isidor Silbermann, 'Psychical Experiences in Shock Therapy,' *Int. J. Psa.* (1940), 22, 179), considers that complete regression rather than the alleviation of guilt is the principal factor. Nevertheless his reports show signs of guilt as well as of other emotions, such as fear of death and religious and sexual excitement before an induced fit, as witnessed by such words as those uttered by one patient: 'Lord! Where is the Lord? Lord, forgive me! I will

The fourth set of alternatives is of a rather different character from the other three. It is concerned with the relative intimacy between the elements of punishment and of gratification respectively in neurotic symptoms. In hysteria the degree of fusion between the two elements is usually very close, the symptom when fully understood revealing itself clearly as a compromise between the repressed and the repressing forces. Thus, to take one of Freud's instances, blushing (or the fear of blushing, 'erythrophobia') is on the one hand a punishment, in that it is a sign of shame and embarrassment, and on the other a gratification of exhibitionistic tendencies, in that it obviously calls attention to the blusher. Similarly the fear of falling is at once a threat of physical disaster and a promise of mental gratification (through the symbolic expression of a moral fall, as when we speak of a 'fallen' woman). A very interesting case, for instance (one that I had opportunity to study myself), was that of a clergyman whose fear of falling when walking in the street was greatly intensified if he found himself alone in the neighbourhood of Piccadilly but diminished when he was in respectable company and almost disappeared if he was accompanied by his wife (though he was totally unaware of the meaning of his fear till it was revealed by psycho-analysis).[1] In obsessional neurosis the two elements tend to fall apart, being exhibited in different

never do that again! Do not punish me, Lord! Come on, Lord! I will have you. Lord, come near to me! Lord, come and make love to me!' This sequence, if it has any general significance, would seem to intimate an overcoming of fear and guilt by love.

[1] The compromise involved in such symptoms is, of course, an example of the mechanism of 'over-determination', which is itself of wide application and not confined to the sphere of neurosis. Even over-determination in the particular sense of satisfying through one action both gratification of an id impulse and the need for punishment is sometimes to be found outside neurosis—for instance in the practice of confession, which is itself, as we have seen, a sort of equivalent of punishment. This is exemplified in the story of the Polish peasant woman who scandalized her father confessor by the frequent accounts of her extra-marital amours. When these persisted even into a relatively advanced age the priest's suspicions began to be aroused. Questioned on the subject, the woman admitted that all the sins of this description of which she had more recently accused herself were pure fabrications, but added: 'Father, it's so nice to have one's memories' (Allendy, *op. cit.*, 216). Others, including children in particular, are liable to self-accusations of this kind, in which the main purpose is to glory in misdeeds which they would like, but do not dare, to commit. This, of course, is only a special form of that wider kind of childish lying which is little more than verbalized phantasy. In this connection we may call to mind that Burlingham (D. T. Burlingham, 'Mitteilungsdrang und Geständniszwang,' *Imago* (1934), 20, 129) considers that in some forms of confession the main purpose is to obtain a confederate and thus to gratify exhibitionistic tendencies, although it may also relieve conscience by the sharing of a guilty secret. This, she thinks, is to be distinguished from those other forms of confession which serve as equivalents of punishment (though there are surely borderline cases where the distinction is difficult to draw).

aspects of the compulsive behaviour, as in the already mentioned case of the boy who was alternately compelled to pray
for his mother's recovery and to annul the effect of the prayer
by slapping himself on the mouth. Obsessions may take the
form of compulsive thoughts or compulsive actions, and, in the
opinion of Alexander, the former more usually correspond to
the expression of guilty desires, while the latter represent the
punishing tendencies, often in the shape of reparations or
reaction formations. Finally, in cyclothymia, gratification and
punishment occur in altogether separate phases, and each predominates entirely for a time, the former in the manic, the latter
in the melancholic, phase.

Alliance between Id and Super-Ego

The peculiar relations of interdependence that obtain in
many cases between the satisfaction and the punishment of
guilty desires have suggested to Alexander a situation that can
best be likened to a sort of pact or alliance between the id and
the super-ego. By the terms of this pact the super-ego permits
a certain amount of gratification of desires of which it does not
approve, on condition that tribute is paid in the form of suffering
or punishment. The super-ego, Alexander maintains, is—in
spite of its severity—frequently open to this kind of bribery or
corruption, in much the same way as a harsh judge might be.
This corruptibility seriously interferes with the efficient function
of the super-ego as the guardian of its own strict standard; it
also opens the way for all sorts of abuses, even as judged by the
more lenient and realistic standard of the conscious ego-ideal,
for it means that many crimes and cruelties can be committed
on condition that they are adequately paid for in the peculiar
currency that the super-ego recognizes. The existence of this
pact is therefore very definitely a source of weakness in man's
moral constitution. It may also be an obstacle in the way of
therapeutic treatment, for the alliance between the id and the
super-ego may give rise to a very stable compound. Both the
id and the super-ego have something to lose by a breakdown of
the alliance; the super-ego anticipates loss of power, control,
and sadistic gratification, the id fears that it may lose the
opportunities it has enjoyed for its forbidden satisfactions.
The analyst who seeks to dissolve the alliance may therefore
encounter opposition from both sides. If we allow a social
parallel, we may perhaps find one in the curious and unofficial,

but nevertheless effective, co-operation of the churches and the bootleggers in America, who, each of them for their own reasons (morals and financial gain respectively), were violently opposed to the removal of Prohibition.

The whole notion of an alliance between id and super-ego has been attacked in some quarters, notably by Reich,[1] who indeed is also opposed to the idea of the 'need for punishment'. Reich goes so far as to suggest that there are no facts to prove that the human mind has a tendency to wipe out guilt by punishment, and, it appears, would himself seek to interpret all the relevant phenomena in terms of simple (i.e. unmoralized) nemesism; the ego (in his opinion), infuriated by its inability to satisfy its fundamental desires in the face of innumerable social taboos and inner prohibitions, turns back its aggression on itself. But Alexander's reply to Reich's objections seems sufficiently convincing. He is able to point to whole categories of phenomena which seem to imply that guilt is atoned for by suffering: our methods of training children, primitive penal codes, religious sacrifice, confession, and ascetic self-torture; and from this it is only one small step to assume that, guilt having been removed and the super-ego satisfied by suffering, the ego is free to turn a favourable ear to the solicitations of the id towards forms of gratification that would be unacceptable as long as guilt remained. Indeed introspection and observation from ordinary life seem to provide ample evidence in favour of Alexander's view. Do we not most of us feel that we can enjoy relaxation 'with a good conscience' after a hard spell of work—a condition very different from that in which an attempt at enjoyment is spoilt by a nagging thought of some distasteful duty that we have left undone? Do we not all tend to feel that a painful illness, an accident, a disaster, or unusual handicap entitles us to some recompense or privilege in return? Are there not, too, people who compensate for an unusual laxity of practice or opinion in one sphere by insistence on an unusual severity in another? Of three advocates of sexual reform, for instance, that I happen to call to mind, one is an ardent anti-alcoholist, another an equally fervent anti-tobacconist, while the third is never tired of stressing the virtues of bodily cleanliness. And cases of the opposite kind are probably much more frequent, for it is a characteristic of Puritan ethics that strictness in the

---

[1] W. Reich and F. Alexander, 'Discussion on the Need for Punishment and the Neurotic Process,' *Int. J. Psa.* (1928), 9, 227.

sexual code relieves the sense of guilt connected with the infringement of Christian morality in other respects, not excluding 'envy, hatred and malice, and all uncharitableness'. With still others a strict observance of religious ritual may atone for numerous backslidings in purely secular affairs. Reich himself indeed, in a later work,[1] says of certain 'neurotic characters' with which he had to deal in mental clinics that 'their moral inhibitions were—as a result of their economic misery—reduced to such a minimum that their perverse and criminal impulses came near forcing their way into behaviour'. Does this not imply that the hardships of poverty had led to a relaxation of the super-ego, which is an illustration of Alexander's principle? Indeed the whole of the evidence, both social and psychological, concerning 'punishment' and 'justice' that we have dealt with in this chapter would seem to point almost irresistibly in the same direction. We seem justified, in fact, in agreeing with Alexander that in this matter 'the intrapsychic penal system of the neurotic reflects the basis of the primitive social organization of mankind'.

Guilt and Punishment

Nevertheless Reich in his criticism raises one very pertinent question. If Alexander is right, he suggests, the longer and severer the neurosis, the more the sense of guilt should be assuaged. Why is not this relief from guilt more frequently apparent? The question leads on to a wider one, to which Freud and others had in various connections already drawn attention: why do punishments, and disasters generally, sometimes lead to a decreased sense of guilt, sometimes to the opposite? The mere fact that such a question can be posed shows that we have so far dealt with only one aspect of the relation between crime and punishment, and that Reik's and Alexander's formulations concerning the need for punishment and the pact between the id and the super-ego, extremely important as they are, do not cover all aspects of this relation. If punishment only produced a freedom from guilt it would have no deterrent effect at all, which is clearly contrary to the facts; if lack of satisfaction of the need for punishment were the only cause of neurosis, how are we to account for the more frequent cases of neurotic disturbance in which frustration of

---

[1] W. Reich, *The Function of the Orgasm* (1942), 54.

id impulses rather than absence of 'punishment' appears to be the principal causative factor?

Although this question has several times been broached, there has, so far as I am aware, nowhere in psycho-analytical literature been any attempt to deal with it fully and systematically. Here then there is at present an obvious and grave lacuna, and it would be idle to pretend that the knowledge we as yet possess enables us to fill it. The most that we can say is that the answer seems to depend on highly complex interrelations of fear, guilt, and aggression, on the relative strength of the super-ego and the id impulses, of the different layers of the super-ego, and of the different impulses (including Freud's 'component instincts') within the id. At bottom the factors that produce the one reaction or the other are probably much the same as those underlying Rosenzweig's 'extrapunitive' and 'intropunitive' qualities, and these are clearly compounded of different admixtures of fear, aggression, guilt, and various other factors. All that psycho-analysis has done up to the present is to cast a few side-lights on the operation of these factors here and there, and we may conclude this chapter with a brief reference to some of the more important of them.

Punishment by parent-figures, by the internal parent representative, the super-ego, and by those more shadowy external influences, Nature, fate, and luck, that we at bottom also tend to identify with the parents, will cause us fear in so far as we feel ourselves weak and dependent on these figures. When fate delivers us a blow, we may feel that parental love and care have been withdrawn (as opposed to 'basking' in the approval of the parents, being 'the darling of the gods', etc., when fate 'smiles' upon us), and, if we feel ourselves as little children, we may be overcome by the same sense of loneliness and helplessness that we experienced in early years if we imagined our parents had forsaken us. We then inevitably feel both guilty and alarmed, and as long as this attitude continues, the greater the punishment, the greater will be our humiliation and the more earnest our attempts at reconciliation; we shall then freely admit our guilt and submit ourselves, if necessary, to still further punishment in order to prove our contrition. If, however, we feel strong enough to stand by ourselves, to defy our parents and our fate, the greater the blow, the more we are freed from any sense of obligation and the less we are impeded in retaliating with our aggression.

L

Further on the side of fear, it is also relevant that punishment and frustration tend naturally to cause regression; if we cannot satisfy our present impulses, we are liable to fall back upon earlier and more primitive developmental stages (in particular illustration of this, it has of course frequently been shown that sexual frustration at the genital level may occasion regression to the pregenital anal, and oral levels). This regression may lead on the one hand to a restimulation of the affects connected with early traumata, including the various aspects of castration and mutilation, and ultimately of what Ernest Jones has called aphanisis. This in turn may intensify our fears and make us more humble, guilty, and obedient.

On the other hand the process of regression (apart from the influence of such traumata) may also lead to greater aggressiveness, inasmuch as the pregenital levels are essentially more aggressive than the genital one. This aggressiveness in itself would no doubt lead to a greater rebelliousness in the face of frustration or disaster, but it may happen that its arousal leads in turn to a greater counter-effort on the part of the super-ego, and therefore to the opposite reaction of greater guilt and submission. It is to this, according to Schmideberg,[1] that punishment often owes its efficacy; either directly or because of the regression to aggressive levels, punishment rouses such an intensity of hate that (perhaps to avoid aphanisis in the way indicated in Chapter IX) the super-ego is spurred into activity and we become 'good' and amenable to discipline. Punishment acts, according to this view, as a sort of *agent provocateur*; it stirs up sedition in the mind and then proceeds to combat this by more vigorous and repressive police activity. These considerations suggest that one important factor in deciding a person's reaction to punishment or frustration may depend on whether or not there is regression. If regression does not occur, the aggression and guilt aroused by the punishment may be more manageable in quantity and quality, the super-ego may not be stimulated to increased activity, and the 'culprit' may react outwardly with rebellious behaviour and enjoy inwardly a greater freedom from guilt; while if regression occurs he will be more likely to react with increased submissiveness and guilt.

Another factor of importance in deciding the issue may be one which we have already touched upon in Chapter IX. In

[1] Melitta Schmideberg, 'Zur Psychologie des Strafens,' *Zschf. f. Psa., Pädagogik* (1931), 5, 308.

view of the terrible picture of the 'bogy' parent-figures conjured up in the child's imagination as a result of the projection of its own primitive aggressiveness, any actual punishments received or disasters encountered may seem relatively insignificant in comparison with the vaguer but more catastrophic events that had been anticipated. In such cases the threat of punishment is apt to appear far more menacing than punishment itself, and when actual punishment or disaster has been incurred there may be a sense of relief that it has proved so relatively mild. Here then, again, there is likely to be an increased freedom from fear and guilt as the result of punishment.

But the same result may also be brought about if the punishment really is experienced as overwhelming. If our position is so desperate that we have practically nothing more to lose, when we are, in a famous phrase, 'with our backs to the wall' so that further retreat is impossible, then we lose our fears and are free to fight with the courage of despair.

Again, a good deal may depend upon the strength and solidity of the repressions at the deeper levels. If the controls governing the deep layers of our moral life are relatively secure, we can often allow ourselves a fair amount of latitude as regards the expression of id impulses at more superficial levels, without arousing any considerable guilt. We may then have little need for punishment and are free to react to frustration vigorously and aggressively. If our controls are more precarious, we may be liable to feel guilty whenever we enjoy ourselves or express aggression, unless our guilt has been temporarily assuaged by punishment; we can be happy or assertive only when we have paid for it (the typical Polycrates attitude). At still greater degrees of moral insecurity, any expression of impulse, or even temptation to such expression, may arouse overwhelming guilt, and we feel safe only when we suffer; in this case the need for punishment may be almost insatiable (the attitude of punitive asceticism).

This in turn is clearly connected with moral masochism. And the mention of masochism reminds us that there may be a libidinal satisfaction in the process of suffering itself. The principle of 'the increase of satisfaction through inhibition' (as manifested in Epicurean asceticism) must also not be lost sight of. All these last-named factors may tend to make us experience some measure of relief or benefit when we suffer punishment, frustration, inhibition, or disaster, whereas the factors that we mentioned earlier tended on the whole in the opposite direction.

These somewhat incidental, and as yet for the most part unco-ordinated, observations made by psycho-analysts suffice at any rate to show how extremely complicated are the forces that determine our individual reactions to punishment and adversity, how little we at present know about their interrelations, and how difficult it is either to account fully for any reaction that has been made or to predict with certainty what a person's reaction is liable to be in any given circumstances.

All that we can safely say is that, as often happens at a certain stage in the progress of scientific thought, improved insight has revealed a somewhat bewildering confusion of factors at work behind familiar phenomena. But we may add that some of these factors have already shown themselves to be of far-reaching importance. The notions of punishment and justice are, it is now obvious, very deeply seated in the mind of man, which in its moral endeavours seeks to establish and maintain a kind of equilibrium between suffering and satisfaction. In the maintenance of this equilibrium the need for punishment plays a significant and hitherto largely unsuspected rôle, and in the chapters that follow we shall be concerned with it again in certain of its further manifestations.

CHAPTER XII

VICARIOUS PUNISHMENT AND THE PROJECTION OF GUILT

In the last chapter we mentioned projection as one of the methods by which guilt could be dealt with. We also said that projection does not necessarily do away with punishment, but only diverts it, together with the guilt, away from ourselves on to the scapegoat or supposed new culprit. This is clearly a most convenient method for the individual, who by its aid is able to relieve his sense of sin without having to suffer in person the expiatory punishment. Indeed the infliction of vicarious punishment can become a very pleasant process. With each blow that we inflict upon the guilty party we feel that our own conscience is lightened; in our 'righteous indignation' we satisfy

at one and the same time our primitive aggressiveness, the disapproval of our super-ego (now, however, no longer directed against
ourselves), and our sadism (which finds itself free in this situation
to indulge in its peculiar satisfaction without incurring censure).

With all these advantages we need hardly wonder that the
punishment of scapegoats is such a constantly recurring theme
in human history. But admirable as this process of the projection of guilt would seem to be from the point of view of purely
individual happiness, its social implications are distinctly
sinister. A society in which people are all bent on punishing
each other for their own sins is not likely to be harmonious or
co-operative. Since man is a gregarious animal, dependent on
the care and help of others from his birth onwards, it would
seem likely that natural selection would set very definite limits
to the use of this comfort-bringing device, in which we might
otherwise be tempted to over-indulge. Men have, however,
discovered a partial solution of the dilemma as to whether they
should accept their own guilt and the corresponding disagreeable
punishment, or should project it, with the consequence of social
disruption. This solution lies in projecting the guilt on to
another human group, which is regarded as distinct from their
own group. In so far as all the members of a given group thus
project their guilt outside the group boundaries, disruption
through this cause within the group is prevented—though of
course at the cost of antagonism between groups. The same
process can be, and often is, conveniently combined with a
similar extra-group projection of aggressive tendencies that are
not connected with guilt. In this combined projection lies one
of the main psychological causes of war and other forms of
inter-group conflict—a subject to which we shall return in a
later chapter. For the moment let us confine ourselves to the
projection of guilt.

For the purposes of this projection 'our own' group and the
'other' ('guilty') group may be of very varying kinds and have
very varying relations one with the other, all the very diverse
factors, geographical, cultural, economic, etc., that make for
group feeling being operative on one occasion or another. Sometimes it is the inhabitants of a neighbouring village who are
made to play the part of scapegoat, sometimes the members of
a different tribe, country, or race, sometimes again those who
belong to a different clan or who worship other gods, or the same
god in a different way, sometimes those who differ from us in

their political views, their occupations, their social status, or even in their age or sex. Recent grandiose examples of this kind, in which the mechanism of projection has been deliberately exploited for political purposes, are so painfully familiar that it should be quite unnecessary at the present time to dwell upon this aspect. All we need is to remember that when Hitler created scapegoat classes such as the Jews, the Communists, or the Pluto-democrats, he was only making use for his own ends of a psychological tendency which has doubtless been at work from the beginning of human history. Did not Adam say, 'the woman tempted me'? And did not Eve in her turn succumb to the lures of the serpent? The symbolic significance of the latter as a representation of the male genital organ has long been known to us, so that we can safely say that the alleged progenitors of mankind endeavoured to escape the consequences of their first sin by projecting their guilt one upon the other; and we have not been slow to follow the example that they set. Adam and Eve did not escape punishment in their own persons, but that has not prevented their successors from attempting to put blame on others, and often succeeding in escaping punishment themselves. They have felt satisfied if there was punishment, and if someone else was punished so much the better for themselves.

Apart from its manifestations in war and politics there have been innumerable variations on the scapegoat theme,[1] the influence of which can be seen in almost every important sphere of human life. In what follows we will briefly call to mind a few examples from some varied fields.

We should hardly need to be reminded that this theme constitutes the central *motif* of the Christian religion. Christ died in order that men might be redeemed from sin. In the doctrine of the Atonement we have the supreme example of the religious treatment of the scapegoat theme and of vicarious punishment. True, in the sphere of religion we customarily speak in this connection of sacrifice rather than of punishment: and the motives of sacrifice may be highly over-determined.[2] But the fundamental fact about it is the suffering of destruction, aggression, or deprivation by the sacrificed person, animal, or object, for the benefit of others, and it is that which Christ exemplifies

---

[1] A classic study of the subject in the anthropological sphere is of course to be found in Sir J. G. Frazer's volume on *The Scapegoat* in *The Golden Bough*.
[2] See R. Money-Kyrle, *The Meaning of Sacrifice*, 1930.

in the highest degree. Moreover the benefit to others in this case (as fundamentally also in so many other instances) was the removal of their guilt; the followers of Christ are rendered safe and guilt-free by the cruel death of their leader.

The fact that guilt can be removed by a brutal act of aggression is so paradoxical, so contrary to our other ethical notions, that it might appear utterly incomprehensible but for the existence of the 'need for punishment' and the possibility of this punishment being suffered vicariously by a scapegoat. The peculiarity of moral redemption by the sacrifice of a divine victim is that the victim's guilt has been lost sight of (though of course Christ was guilty—and guilty of Hubris—in the eyes of most of those who were actively concerned with his death). This quality is possessed by Christ in common with many less-known sacrificed divinities. In religious sacrifice generally the excellence, indeed the perfection, of the victim is often stressed, though in the case of Christ this perfection is regarded as a moral one, which makes the problem even more perplexing. How can morally imperfect humanity achieve salvation by the sacrifice of a morally perfect being? By all the ordinary canons of logic and ethics men should only have succeeded in enormously increasing the degree of their moral imperfection. The most essential clue to the solution of the problem (into the intricacies of which we cannot enter here) lies almost certainly in the ambivalent attitude towards God, who in turn represents our parents and our super-ego. By the act of violence the aggressive elements in this ambivalent attitude have been appeased, the elements of love and respect are left in sole possession,[1] and in virtue of these elements the victim appears perfect. It is in this feature of marked ambivalence that the attitude towards the divine scapegoat differs from that to other victims who play the same rôle. The divine scapegoat to some extent represents both our ego and our super-ego, our ego inasmuch as he is sacrificed, our super-ego inasmuch as he is perfect. But it is

---

[1] As may be the case also with ambivalently loved persons who are purely human. After a quarrel with parent, child, or spouse, when our anger has been duly expressed, we may experience for a time an exceptionally 'pure' love—pure in the sense that it is freed from the usual admixture of hate or irritation. And if, in our anger, we have done harm to the person concerned we may be bitterly remorseful. *King Lear* of course affords a classic example of this. As between lovers and spouses some couples are reputed to like quarrelling for the sake of the joy of subsequent reconciliation. In the religious sphere Freud stressed the same change of attitude in his theory of totemism; after the murder of the primal father (for whom the totem stands) the sons were overcome with love, respect, and regret.

predominantly in virtue of the former rôle (as representative of our guilty ego) that his sacrifice serves to remove our guilt, and in this respect he is (again paradoxically enough) comparable to those other victims who serve as the very incarnations of all evil (e.g. those sacrificial victims on whom the guilt of the community has been deliberately projected by a magical or religious rite, or, to take a modern instance, the Jews, who, according to the Nazi view, are by their very nature the supreme example of almost every human vice).

Passing, as it might seem, from the sublime to the ridiculous, let us turn for a moment from mighty religious or political events to take a glance at the small world of the nursery (in view of a well-known injunction of Christ concerning 'little children', the transition may perhaps not be so very inappropriate). One of the curious features of children's play that has attracted the attention of psychologists [1] is the 'imaginary companion'—a fictitious child in whose doings and adventures the real child takes a lively interest. It is evident indeed that the real child to some extent lives vicariously and expresses certain of his desires through this imaginary figure. Among the rôles played by this figure is that of scapegoat, inasmuch as it is not infrequently 'naughty' and indulges in various petty misdemeanours for which the child himself may have previously been punished or admonished. The imaginary culprit then often incurs punishment in his turn. This time the real child plays the rôle of parent or super-ego, while he projects his guilty thoughts and wishes on this *alter ego* whom he has himself invented.

A somewhat comparable phenomenon (in the respects which are here of interest to us) is the delight that adults experience in gossip and scandal, in which they gloat over the peccadillos and moral frailties of their neighbours and acquaintances. Like the child with his imaginary companion, they are indulging their own guilty desires vicariously, preserving their own virtue intact (the implication is that they themselves would never partake in such scandalous proceedings as those under discussion) and expressing their disapproval through appropriate inflections of the voice and shakings of the head.

From these relatively harmless manifestations of the projection of guilt let us return to more serious matters. Much the same attitude as that we have just noticed is apt to be displayed towards the criminal. Like the imaginary companion whose

---

[1] E.g. George H. Green, *The Daydream* (1923), ch. ii.

naughtiness fascinates the child, or like the neighbours who scandalize the gossip-mongers, the criminal is a person whom we envy and admire but at the same time condemn. We envy and admire him (especially if his crimes are on a bold and striking scale) because he has dared to do what, if our own crude impulses had their way, we should also like to do. He has, in fact, defied his super-ego. But we cannot allow our approval to express itself unchecked. He also, like the imaginary companion and the subjects of our gossip, merits punishment, and of course in larger measure, as befits the greater enormity of his offence.

Psycho-analysts have drawn attention to three main motives in our attitude towards law-breakers and criminals that operate in addition to the conscious reasons that are more readily recognized and more frequently discussed. These motives are really the same as in the two last-mentioned cases, but reveal themselves a little more clearly, perhaps because (unlike the imaginary companion) the criminal has committed crimes in the real world instead of crimes in phantasy, and (unlike the subjects of our gossip) has definitely broken the law instead of merely outraging our sense of the proprieties. All three motives, moreover, are closely interrelated. In the first place, the criminal provides an outlet for our (moralized) aggression. In this respect he plays the same rôle as do our enemies in war and our political scapegoats in time of peace. That some very real satisfaction is to be found in this way is shown by the vast crowds that attended public executions when this form of enter- tainment was available and the still not inconsiderable numbers who go to prison doors to be rewarded with nothing more exciting than an official notice indicating that a prisoner has been executed. In the second place, the criminal by his flouting of law and moral rule constitutes a temptation to the id; it is as though we said to ourselves, 'if he does it, why should not we?' This stirring of criminal impulses within ourselves calls for an answering effort on the part of the super-ego, which can best achieve its object by showing that 'crime doesn't pay'. This in turn can be done most conveniently and completely by a demonstration on the person of the criminal. By punishing him we are not only showing him that he can't 'get away with it' but holding him up as a terrifying example to our own tempted and rebellious selves. Thirdly, and closely connected with this, perhaps little more than a generalization of it, is the danger with which our whole notion of justice is threatened when we observe that a criminal has gone unpunished. The primitive foundation of this notion, as we saw in the last chapter, lies in an equilibrium of pleasures and pains, of indulgence and punishment. This equilibrium is disturbed, either if the moral rewards of good conduct are not forthcoming (as may be the case in periods of insecurity, economic maladjustment, disaster, and upheaval), or if the normal punishments of crime are absent or uncertain (as may also happen in the above-mentioned circumstances or in unsettled, thinly populated regions of the 'wild west' type). It is to prevent disturbance of the latter kind that we insist that those who have broken the law shall be duly punished. Through their punishment the equilibrium is re-established, without it (so we dimly feel) the whole psychological and social structure on which morality depends is imperilled.

It is easy from these considerations to see what strong forces are enlisted on the side of punishment, and what real psychological demands we may be making when we ask (as humanitarians have done and are still doing, and as others have begun to do in the name of 'the scientific treatment of delinquency') that punishment should in many cases be mitigated, or abolished altogether, for the sake of the criminal himself and through him of society in general. Not that these humanitarians or scientists are wrong; on the contrary they are often justified, alike from the points of view of logic, realism, and enlightened morals. From each of these points of view we should seek, not the gratification of primitive emotions or the maintenance of primitive standards, but the best way of ensuring that as little crime as possible occurs—and as we have seen in the last chapter (and as people are beginning to realize, quite apart from psycho-analysis) punishment can by no means be relied upon to do this; it may indeed in many cases have the opposite effect. Nevertheless, in dealing with the often very reasonable suggestions of the humanitarians and criminologists, it is well to remember that punishment not only affects the person who receives it but also those who (directly, or indirectly through the law) administer it, and that, while remission of punishment may be a relief and a benefit to the one, it may involve for the other some degree of sacrifice and some effort of psychological readjustment. Naturally this necessity for sacrifice and readjustment is likely to engender considerable opposition (the motives of which will not be fully conscious) to any far-reaching proposals for penal reform.

Still another field in which the need for punishment can be satisfied vicariously through projection is that of education. It is easy, natural, and indeed inevitable, that those in charge of the young should feel themselves *in loco parentis* and should adopt the rôle of the super-ego, including its punishing aspects. One of the advantages and at the same time one of the pitfalls of the educational profession is that it is so easy to feel virtuous and self-satisfied and to project one's own guilt and inferiority upon one's pupils. Modern methods and the modern outlook have, however, to a great extent reduced the opportunities in this direction, and it would be interesting to study in detail the modifications in the attitude and satisfactions of the teacher (perhaps also any alteration in the character of those who are attracted to the profession) that these changes from the old to the newer educational régimes may have entailed. In this respect the readjustment required must have been much the same as that in the case of parents, who have also been rendered less sure of being always right than they were in the time of *The Barretts of Wimpole Street*. However, it is still true that some super-ego qualities remain with both parents and teachers and make themselves felt in our educational attitudes and institutions generally. Hence the need for punishment in its vicarious form is often rationalized as what in Chapter VII we called 'disciplinary asceticism', and revealed in an insistence on a certain amount of irrational and unnecessary harshness. In our older educational establishments, such as the British Public Schools, this carries with it all the prestige of an ancient tradition, though punishment and other forms of suffering are often inflicted not so much by the authorities on the pupils in general as by the older pupils on the younger ones. The authorities nevertheless connive at this, as J. Langdon-Davies [1] has well brought out, though in stronger terms than most would care to use. 'There are', he says, 'two parts of education—the civilized, or at least the conventional, controlled by the faculty, and the savage, controlled by the students themselves. . . . Torture is not so much as mentioned in any school syllabus, but subconsciously most adults believe it to be valuable and provide for its practice in secret. Thus they avoid responsibility without having to give up methods on which they rely'. In so doing the authorities are obviously adopting a compromise between conflicting standards;

---

[1] Quoted in the *Report of the Annual Conference of Educational Associations*, 1935, p. 315.

the compromise marks the process of transition from the open avowal of the desirability of suffering characteristic of the old régime to the more lenient views that distinguish the 'new education'. Nevertheless an attitude that condones, and indeed indirectly encourages, a certain brutal aggressiveness among the pupils contrasts strangely with the very different attitude adopted towards certain other instinctive manifestations, e.g. those connected with sex, as regards which the sternest measures of suppression and disapproval are considered quite in order.

Our reluctance to do away with suffering altogether is shown also in the retention of a good many minor asceticisms, such as hard beds, unpalatable food, and underheated rooms. In America, where these particular forms of hardship are less cherished (in accordance with a generally less suspicious attitude towards material domestic comforts), there is a much greater development of initiation ceremonies, usually of an unpleasant kind, while on the continent of Europe unhappiness is, or was until recently, more closely associated with the purely academic side of education, the demands of which have not so very infrequently driven pupils to suicide because of failure, or fear of failure, in examinations (a very rare occurrence in this country).[1] Though this form of disciplinary asceticism has in its turn been abolished by the Nazis, other and cruder forms have been substituted, in harmony with the generally regressive tendencies of their 'new order'.[2] All this seems to point to a general unwillingness to do away with punishment in education—ultimately of the same kind as that which is manifested in the legal sphere.

The uneasiness caused by the prospect of the abolition of pain was shown with quite exceptional clarity in the case of anæsthetics, which on their first introduction were greeted with a chorus of disapproval and alarm from clerical, lay, and even medical quarters. It was evidently felt that the attempt to abolish bodily suffering smacked disconcertingly of Hubris, and that men (and still more women) by evading the pains that nature had decreed would assuredly call down upon humanity some manifestation of divine displeasure. Thus a clergyman described the use of anæsthetics in childbirth as 'a decoy of Satan, apparently opening itself to bless women, but

---

[1] The austerities of education in Germany formed one of the major themes in Wedekind's well-known play *Frühlings Erwachen*.
[2] Cf. A. Ziemer, *Education for Death*.

in the end hardening and robbing God of the deep earnest cries that should rise to him in time of trouble'.[1]

This last instance brings us to the sphere of sex, which, being particularly associated with sin, is also particularly likely to arouse anxiety when the need for punishment has not been met. Hence the unusual degree of reluctance to remove sufferings and punishments whether inflicted by nature or by man. Birth-control has been violently opposed because it tends to remove the responsibilities attaching to sexual indulgence; divorce is looked upon as sinful for the same reason, the implication being that a certain number of unhappy marriages removes some of the general guilt attaching to humanity through sex. Abortion, though secretly practised on a large scale, is often condemned by religion and sometimes by the law, even in cases where the continuance of the pregnancy constitutes a grave danger to the mother's life.[2] The unmarried mother and the prostitute have at various times and places been subjected to almost every kind of persecution and indignity, and the virtue of respectable women has been sharply contrasted with the disgrace of their 'fallen' sisters. In venereal disease men have almost welcomed what has seemed to be a natural punishment, and, in contrast to their attitude in the case of other diseases, have displayed a great unwillingness to spread the knowledge of how it can be prevented otherwise than by the avoidance of all possibility of infection; so much so that in this country an important society founded for reducing the incidence of venereal disease was split in two over this very question. Even at the moment of writing, in the face of a marked increase in the disease and of a national emergency of the very gravest kind, there is surprisingly little change in this attitude, and such change (in the direction of greater publicity) as appeared unavoidable has been undertaken most reluctantly. There is still on the part of many a readiness to attack venereal disease only by the method of advocating chastity, not by the supplementary method of providing and popularizing prophylaxis, although there is ample evidence that the first method by itself is insufficient. It is as though we were to insist that the only method of avoiding tropical diseases is to keep away from the tropics. The actual difference in the two cases is, of course, due to the fact that living in the tropics

---

[1] Quoted by Margaret Morris in *Health and Efficiency*, January, 1938.

[2] It is, of course, not suggested that the above-mentioned motives are the only ones operative in such cases. For a fuller discussion of the subject see J. C. Flugel, 'The Psychology of Birth Control,' in *Men and their Motives*, 1934.

is not in itself considered wicked, whereas so much guilt attaches
to sex that it is thought dangerous to remove a natural punishment, even though, as is generally recognized, the innocent (as
in so-called *syphilis insontium*) may suffer with the guilty.[1]

These instances, to which others could easily be added,[2] must
here suffice. It is evident that the need for punishment and the
Polycrates complex can be dealt with by the punishment of
others. Men are not merely concerned themselves to undergo
the penalties of guilt; their super-egos can be satisfied and their
sins atoned for by the sufferings of their fellow-men and women.
Hence any alleviation of 'the martyrdom of man' is likely to
arouse misgiving, in so far as it promises to reduce the opportunities for vicarious punishment, to upset our moral equilibrium,
and to increase our private sense of guilt and the anxiety attaching to it. No wonder again that man is a pain-seeking animal,
though in this connection it is the pain of his fellow-creatures
that he seeks, in order to ensure a more comfortable conscience
for himself.

CHAPTER XIII

PROJECTION OF THE SUPER-EGO

WE saw in Chapter V that, although the development of the
super-ego provides us with the power of self-regulation in a
moral sense, it does not render us entirely independent of social
support, approval, and control. Except perhaps in the case of
a few rare individuals whose super-egos are so strong and independent that they have become a moral law unto themselves,
we remain morally sensitive to our environment, are rendered
happy by the approval and admiration of those about us,
and to that extent are willing that their approbation should
reinforce, supplement, or even replace, the approval of our
own ego-ideal. There can be little doubt that, just as external
moral control is more primitive and earlier in its development
than internal control by the super-ego, so also it is in some
respects easier and involves less strain and a lesser expenditure of energy. There is therefore a constant temptation to

---

[1] As I write, however, the Archbishop of York has indicated a change of
attitude, in telling us that 'It is unchristian for us simply to say a man is suffering
the due penalty of his sin'.

[2] Some further instances will be mentioned later.

project the super-ego and to find fresh super-ego representatives in the outer world, provided only we can discover external figures that sufficiently resemble the pattern of our super-ego as it has been formed by early introjections. Obedience is easier than self-control, and admiration of another easier than the actual attainment of such qualities as will allow us freely to admire ourselves; hence our liability to find in the outer world masters who will guide our conduct and heroes who will exemplify our ideals, thus affording us some relief from the greater effort of self-regulation in the light of these ideals. In this chapter we propose to consider some of the manifestations and consequences of the projections of our super-ego that from time to time occur in later life.

One of the most interesting problems raised by the tendency to project the super-ego is connected with the fact that the actual figures on to whom the projection takes place are much more varied than might perhaps at first have been expected, and it has to be confessed that at present we are still considerably ignorant concerning the ultimate psychological differences in the projective processes that correspond to these different sorts of figures. To some extent they would seem to depend on different layers or aspects of the super-ego or ego-ideal. As we have seen before, the external super-ego figures may represent sometimes a further and higher development of those aims which we have actually pursued, sometimes rather those different or opposite aims and ideals which we ourselves have left undeveloped. Again, the figures may correspond predominantly to the positive and helping, or to the negative and prohibiting, aspects of the super-ego. In other cases the process of projection would seem to be the result of an attempt to find new and better super-ego figures to replace old ones that have been lost.

This last type of choice is perhaps the most obvious and the easiest to recognize. We have already (in Chapter IV) drawn attention to the way in which our primitive belief in the unbounded power, knowledge, and (in their 'good' aspects) moral perfection of the parents is gradually undermined by a realization of their human limitations. This realization is a painful one, and is apt to give rise to a sense of physical and moral insecurity; the strong support on which, as little children, we felt we could utterly rely, reveals itself to be far less solid and unshakable than we had thought. It is only natural that under these circumstances we should look round for substitutes. Such a substitute can sometimes be found in a teacher, priest, or any other superior whom we know personally; in a writer, artist, film star, scientist, discoverer, politician, or military leader, whom we know only from his portrait and repute (though under modern conditions, thanks to the radio and sound track, we may also be familiar with his voice); or even in a fictitious person, such as a character in literature.

The doctor is also a person who is peculiarly fitted to play the rôle of super-ego, inasmuch as we turn to him in times of emergency when we ourselves feel ignorant, impotent, and unable to rely on our own efforts, times at which the balance of life and death itself may depend upon his skill and knowledge. Although this tendency to projection of the super-ego applies to all medical practice, it is perhaps particularly clear in the case of psychotherapy. It is true that with regard to psycho-analysis this might at first appear paradoxical, for in psycho-analysis, as we have more than once indicated, the super-ego is required to undergo changes which result in a weakening in the power of at any rate its deeper layers. But this modification of the super-ego, as was discovered early in the history of psycho-analysis, can be brought about only when the parent-regarding attitudes are temporarily directed to the analyst—the process technically described as 'transference'. In this transference there are, as was also early found, both positive and negative elements; the analyst represents both the helpful loving parent and the stern frustrating one, corresponding to the ambivalent attitude of the child towards his original parents and his own super-ego. Though the negative phase of the transference is unavoidable and also essential for a 'deep analysis', it is the positive phase which is the ultimate stepping-stone to therapeutic success, for it is only by means of the projection of the more positive aspects of the super-ego on to the analyst that the patient can face the task of becoming aware of his own repressed impulses and inner conflicts. He needs the help, understanding, and security afforded by the analyst before he can venture to relax the control exercised by his own super-ego.[1] The fact that the analyst does not side with the super-ego, does not directly play the part of moral mentor, in no way prevents him from becoming a figure on

---

[1] This, together with its theoretical and practical implications, is well brought out by W. R. D. Fairbairn, 'The Repression and the Return of Bad Objects,' *Brit. J. Med. Psychol.* (1943), 19, 327.

whom the patient's super-ego is projected (which is a second paradoxical feature in the situation). Eventually however, in the course of psycho-analytical treatment, the transference is as far as possible itself resolved, so that the patient loses his dependence on the analyst; that is, he reintrojects his super-ego.

In those other forms of psychotherapy in which suggestion rather than exploration or analysis plays the chief part, the rôle of the physician as super-ego representative is much more immediately evident; since from the start he puts himself in a position of command, actively impresses the patient with his power and knowledge, and lays less stress upon the latter's co-operation. Nearly all psychologists who have written on suggestion have emphasized that success along these lines depends largely or entirely on the prestige of the suggester on the one hand, and on the submissiveness and lack of criticism of the person who accepts the suggestion on the other. As regards hypnotic suggestion in particular, Ernest Jones [1] considers that the peculiarly high degree of suggestibility characteristic of hypnosis is due to the full projection of the super-ego upon the person of the hypnotist. This view, while it does not, of course, exclude the operation of other conditions such as dissociation,[2] has the merit of easily explaining three facts which might otherwise be puzzling. First, the fact of *rapport* or special relationship between the hypnotist and the person in hypnotic trance, who is as a rule suggestible towards the hypnotist only, and may even appear to be hardly aware of the presence of others; secondly, the fact that criminal or immoral suggestions given in hypnosis seldom succeed; and thirdly, the undoubted similarity in certain respects between ordinary or hetero-suggestion (as given for instance by a psychotherapist in hypnotic treatment) and the rarer process of auto-suggestion (as advocated for instance by Émile Coué). The first of these facts, according to this theory, is accounted for by the unique position that the hypnotist acquires for the patient in virtue of the projection upon him of the latter's super-ego. The explanation of the second fact is that when the hypnotist gives an 'immoral' suggestion he forfeits his rôle of super-ego repre-

---

[1] Ernest Jones, 'The Nature of Auto-Suggestion,' *Int. J. Psa.* (1923), 4, 293.

[2] Dissociation, as manifested for instance in the failure to exercise the usual degree of criticism in the face of any suggestions that are made, may quite well be a direct consequence of the adoption of a childlike, trustful, and dependent attitude, though it may perhaps also (as McDougall for instance has maintained) come about for other reasons.

sentative, and therefore also the patient's uncritical obedience; the projection is withdrawn and the patient usually 'wakes up', his reintrojected super-ego at once beginning to assert itself.[1] The similarity between hetero- and auto-suggestion is explained by the operation in a similar sense of the super-ego in both cases; in its projected form in the case of hetero-suggestion, in its usual (internal) form in auto-suggestion.

In both cases, however, it is, as Jones rightly insists, not quite sufficient to say that the super-ego is at work. There is clearly some special attitude of trust, faith, and obedience, probably depending on a regression to a relatively infantile level, on which the ego abandons itself in complete confidence, as a child might to its parent. In this process the usual boundaries and distinctions between the ego and the super-ego are at the same time blurred or abolished, so that the super-ego can work upon the ego without criticism or opposition. It would perhaps be correct to say that the ego identifies itself with the super-ego. This condition, or something like it, is also, as we shall see, to be found in certain other special states, all of which seem to involve some obliteration of the frontiers between the ego and the super-ego (and often also some projection of the super-ego). For the moment we need only note the justification of the injunction given by Coué,[2] Baudouin,[3] and other advocates of auto-suggestion (sometimes under the heading of the 'law of reversed effort') to avoid anything in the nature of an effort of will in attempting to use the method, for an act of will, as usually understood in this connection, far from obliterating the boundaries between ego and super-ego, renders them more distinct, and relies for its efficacy upon a strengthening of the super-ego against resisting impulses which are seeking to control the ego. This difference between the psychic state in carrying out an act of will in which the ego is, as it were, overpowered by the super-ego, and the other relatively effortless and conflict-free state that is involved in suggestion, auto-suggestion, and certain related conditions, raises problems

[1] As in the classical instance, recorded by Janet, of the female patient who immediately woke up when a student suggested to her that she should undress before a class. Had she been a member of a modern nudist society the suggestion might have seemed less outrageous and might not have had the same effect. It is interesting to note that suggestions of a silly and childish, as distinct from those of an 'immoral', kind are not usually resisted—probably because the regression to a childlike condition makes them seem less absurd than they would do in the normal state.

[2] Émile Coué and J. Louis Orton, *Conscious Auto-Suggestion*, 1924.

[3] Charles Baudouin, *Suggestion and Auto-Suggestion*, 1921.

of the greatest interest, the full solution of which would no doubt carry us far towards a greater understanding of much that is still obscure in psychopathology, psychotherapy, mysticism, and perhaps even social psychology. Unfortunately in the almost complete absence of relevant further knowledge, we must content ourselves here with doing little more than noting the existence of the problem.

Freud,[1] in his characteristic way of seeing resemblances between apparently distinct phenomena, drew attention to the similarity between hypnosis and the state of being in love, which also, according to him, involves a projection of the super-ego upon the loved person, who is looked upon as little short of perfect. Compared with the excellences of the loved object, the lover is apt to feel humble and unworthy, a condition which Freud describes as 'impoverishment of the ego'. While this state of humility is undoubtedly characteristic of many cases, it is in itself obviously very far from implying the kind of misery, dejection, and self-reproach that is found, for instance, in melancholia and depressive states generally. On the contrary, the lover usually experiences an intense glow of satisfaction, even if he worships from afar. There is something in his attitude that is reminiscent of that process of 'altruistic surrender' of which we spoke at the end of Chapter VI. But, as with many other instances of this kind (as also perhaps *mutatis mutandis* with hypnosis and certain other conditions), the surrender is a joyful and satisfying one, in which the lover seems to experience an expansion rather than a contraction of his personality. Indeed, even in his humility, he feels a certain exaltation in the presence, or at the mere thought, of his beloved; without ceasing to worship, he may lose his humility altogether (at any rate towards all but his loved object) and feel himself endowed with a joy and power that are in some ways (though not in all) even reminiscent of the manic condition. This strength seems to emanate from the loved object, and he may feel that there is nothing that he cannot accomplish so long as she approves. Here again, then, the super-ego, in its projected form and working through the loved object (as in the previous instance through the hypnotist), seems, as we might be inclined to say, to embrace, attract, and elevate the ego, thus giving it unusual powers which it does not possess as long as there is a sharp distinction between the ego and the super-ego.

[1] *Group Psychology and the Analysis of the Ego*, 1922. First published 1921.

We may remember that in mania also the distinction between the ego and the super-ego seems in some way to be obliterated, and here too there is a feeling of power, though the condition differs from that in hypnosis and love in that there is no projection of the super-ego, but rather perhaps an engulfing of the super-ego by the ego.

Passing to the opposite condition of melancholia and comparing it in turn with hypnosis and love, we may note that, although there may be some degree of (delusional) projection of the super-ego in the former state, there is at the same time: (1) a very sharp distinction, a great 'distance', between the ego and the super-ego; (2) an aggressive (persecuting, accusing, humiliating) element in the super-ego, which is largely or entirely lacking in its projected condition in hypnosis or in love. We may therefore perhaps tentatively conclude that the beneficent features of hypnosis and love lie: (a) in the power of the projected super-ego to exercise a sthenic and elevating effect upon the ego, to raise the ego to its own level and there to undergo in some respects a fusion with it, and (b) in the predominance of the good, loving, and helpful aspects, as distinct from the aggressive aspects, of the super-ego. In virtue of both these conditions there is probably an absence of conflict and a reduction of usually existing inhibitions, and the resulting greater freedom and availability of mental energy perhaps underlie the peculiar powers and special features associated with love, hypnosis, and certain other states. Here, too, further tasks of great interest await the psychologist who attempts to distinguish the finer differences between these various conditions; for our part we must be content here to point out the resemblances.

The process of auto-suggestion, with its resemblance to hetero-suggestion, seems to indicate, however, that projection of the super-ego is not an absolutely essential condition of this beneficent *rapprochement* between the ego and the super-ego. Here the super-ego seems to exercise the same influence without projection (though, as several psychologists have pointed out, the image, the memory, or the ideal of M. Coué, or some other impressive figure, may very well be operative behind the scenes —in much the same way as the image of the loved person in the lover's mind).

Another rather similar case, according to Freud,[1] is presented

---

[1] 'Humour,' *Int. J. Psa.* (1928), 9, 1.

by humour, in which, if we follow his interpretation, the ego adopts the point of view of the super-ego and from this height looks down upon itself like a kindly parent smiling at the petty concerns and quaint behaviour of a little child. Freud takes as an instance the well-known story of the prisoner who, being led out to execution on a Monday morning, remarked: 'Well, here's another week beginning nicely!' A more recent and in some respects comparable instance is provided by the survivor from a ship, torpedoed in mid-ocean, who, sitting precariously on a raft, accosted a passing vessel with the words, 'Say, are you fellows going my way?' [1] In both cases there is an implied indifference to life, a deliberate overlooking of the seriousness of the situation, and a half-playful assumption that things are much as usual and that normal values therefore still obtain; all of which contribute to the peculiar quality of humour—as we might feel inclined to say here again, a quality of exaltation. From the point of view of the super-ego the ego sees its own unimportance, with a consequent indifference to its own extinction, but at the same time presents a bold, united (we might say heroic) front towards a hostile and menacing reality.

In other perhaps less extreme cases, where the individual is not in immediate peril but has encountered a severe disaster, humour again comes to the rescue, in enabling us to surmount the disaster and assert ourselves in spite of it. Thus many Londoners, during the days of the Blitz, felt heartened and uplifted by the sturdy signs of resistance and defiance chalked up on some of the bombed buildings, inscriptions such as: 'Blast!'; 'Bombed out, blown out, burnt out, but not sold out'; 'Still open'; and then after a further visitation: 'More open than ever'; and again (in front of a very humble establishment): 'Don't be alarmed at this; you should see our Berlin branch!' [2]

---

[1] *The Listener*, April 8, 1943.

[2] In the light of these cases of humour we perhaps obtain a hint as to what brings about the predominance of the kindly aspects of the super-ego that we have already noticed also in auto-suggestion, love, and hypnosis. It would seem likely that the super-ego, having so to speak sided with the ego and adopted the rôle of its protector, proceeds to direct its aggressive elements towards the outer world, much as a parent might endeavour at once to protect his child and to ward off an attacker.

The aggressive elements in humour have been emphasized by certain other psycho-analytic writers (e.g. Ludwig Jekels and Edmond Bergler, 'Übertragung und Liebe,' *Imago* (1934), 20, 5, and Th. Reik, 'Zur Psychoanalyse des jüdischen Witzes,' *Imago* (1929), 15, 65) who—in contrast to Freud's view—have even seen in certain forms of humour an attack by the ego on the super-ego and the external authorities that correspond to it, rather than an adoption by the ego of the standpoint of the super-ego. I believe, however, it would be possible to show that the differences in question are quantitative rather than qualitative.

Humour here appears as 'a very present help in time of trouble', reminding us in this way of the religious aspects of the projection of the super-ego, to which we will turn in a few moments. As I have pointed out elsewhere,[1] the attitude implied in humour is also in many respects like that which we adopt in war, when we consider that the sacrifice of our own lives is a small matter if it is made in the service of our country. Here also our ego is somehow lost in the higher corporate entity on to which we have projected our super-ego. The call of our country is in this case also the call of our super-ego, and in such a mood we can joyfully exclaim with Kipling, 'Who dies if England lives? '

This last consideration brings us to the social aspects of the projection of the super-ego. When our country or nation takes the place of the super-ego we are projecting the latter not upon an individual, but upon a group. We abandon the moral control of ourselves through our (internal) super-ego in favour of control by the standards of the group. Here we have the explanation, in terms of our present concepts, of that loss of individual critical power and moral sensibility which so many social psychologists, from Le Bon [2] onwards, have noticed and deplored. The early writers on this subject dwelt, however, too exclusively on the dark side of the picture.[3] Actually, as McDougall has pointed out,[4] the abrogation of individual conscience in favour of control by a group does not of itself necessarily imply a deterioration of morality. The issue depends on the nature, organization, and motives of the group. If the group is a more or less fortuitous and unorganized crowd, it is capable of behaving with a ferocity, brutality, and total lack of decency or sympathy of which hardly any individual in the crowd would be capable by himself—as is shown in panics, lynchings, pogroms, and sundry other unedifying group phenomena. If, on the other hand, the group is organized, and

and that there is a continuous transition: (*a*) as regards the relative proportions of the protective and aggressive elements (just as a parent in the above-mentioned analogy might be more concerned with protecting his child or retaliating on an attacker); (*b*) as regards the direction of aggressiveness towards the ego, the outer world, or even the super-ego itself (or at least the values which in the past the super-ego has adopted).

[1] 'The Moral Paradox of Peace and War,' *Conway Memorial Lecture*, 1941.

[2] G. le Bon, *The Crowd*, 1895.

[3] Though there are not wanting modern writers who continue to be extremely pessimistic in this matter. *Cf.* Reinhold Niebuhr, *Moral Man and Immoral Society*, 1941.

[4] W. McDougall, *The Group Mind*, 1920.

inspired by high ideals, the level of ethical behaviour may be raised above that of the average individual standard, since it is capable of being determined by the highest intelligences and characters to be found in the group, and is kept in this path by the fact that in such a group every man is to some extent his brother's keeper, so that any individual backslider is at once exposed to the scorn and disapproval of the other members. Neither organization nor the presence of ideals is, however, by itself sufficient for this purpose. Without organization (which incidentally may be greatly helped by the existence of suitable traditions) there is, except perhaps in the very smallest groups, no means by which the higher characters and more able minds can consistently influence the group. Without the requisite ideals the organized power of the group may be used only for immoral ends, perhaps under the influence of one of those master criminals to whose existence we made a passing reference in Chapter II.

The moral danger inherent in handing over the individual conscience to the group is, of course, that we are placed at the mercy of the emotions and ideals that govern the group, and, with our sense of individual responsibility abolished, may easily acquiesce in conduct of a crude and primitive type of which we should be heartily ashamed were we judging by the standards of our own super-ego,[1] and in so far as the projection of our super-ego on the group may be a relatively enduring condition (such as is aimed at in totalitarian states), the lowering of moral sensibility may be permanent. Under the influence of grossly perverted standards and ideals, those who introject these standards and ideals acquire what has sometimes been called a 'criminal super-ego', i.e. a super-ego that urges its possessor in a direction which, judged by the standards of other individuals or communities, is highly blameworthy, much as it might do in the case of those who had been brought up by parents who were criminals or gangsters. Even if the group standards are in themselves respectable enough, the mere relaxation of individual responsibility that is implied in group action is not

---

[1] This seems to indicate that the projection of our super-ego on the group is of a more thoroughgoing and enduring kind than the corresponding projection on to the person of the hypnotist. This is probably connected with the immensely impressive power of numbers, of an all-pervading atmosphere (and in the case of nations, or other long-standing groups, also of traditions) which is not operative in the case of the hypnotist, who is after all but a single person. But, whatever the reason, there can be no doubt that the individual all too seldom 'wakes up' when subjected to immoral suggestions from the group.

without its dangers; hence the genuine grain of truth in the otherwise far too sweeping statement that 'corporations have no conscience'. For this reason, too, small committees are often more satisfactory than large ones, the lesser amount of collective wisdom available being more than compensated by the greater sense of individual responsibility among the members.

It is abundantly clear (as we have already implied) that the character of groups is intimately dependent on that of their leaders. A leader is indeed especially important to us here, as he is *par excellence* the figure on whom our super-ego is projected. Freud [1] went so far as to suggest that the essential factor in the cohesion of the group, and in group psychology generally, is to be found in the projection by all the members of the group of their super-ego on to one single figure, that of the leader. This, viewed in the light of the work of other social psychologists, would seem to be an exaggeration; we may have potent sentiments for groups, even large national groups, apart from their leaders. But it remains true that sentiments for concrete persons or objects are easier to form than sentiments for abstractions (and the national group that we refer to when we speak for instance of Britain, the United States, or Germany is an abstraction). To consolidate and help our loyalty to such an abstract group we seek at least for some concrete symbol. This may be a flag, a motto, a tune, a colour, but more satisfactory in some respects than all these is a human figure; and, except perhaps for allegorical figures like John Bull or Uncle Sam, which may have a certain importance in virtue of their relative permanence, the leader of the group for the time being is himself the most natural figure to select. A successful leader does indeed inevitably become to a large extent the object of super-ego projection on the part of his followers; and in totalitarian countries this projection is of course deliberately fostered. He is idolized and endowed with superhuman attributes of impeccability, as when the Italian youth was told that 'Mussolini is always right'.

Nevertheless, societies which depend largely, or principally, upon a common projection of the super-ego upon the figure of the leader suffer from certain weaknesses. In the first place, if the leader is lost through death or otherwise, the group also loses the common bond that keeps it in being. The consequence of this is often to be observed in the rapid dissolution of groups

[1] *Group Psychology and Analysis of the Ego*, 1922.

(ranging from small schools or societies to mighty empires) which have crystallized around a single dominant figure. If the individual leader is to have supreme importance and the group is yet to be capable of surviving him, he must acquire much of his significance not merely from his personal qualities, but from the prestige attaching to his office. This prestige he can at least hand on to a successor. In the second place, the attitude to a leader is almost inevitably to some extent an ambivalent one, as we saw when dealing with the taboos attaching to kings and rulers (Chapter X). In this respect it is the same as that of the child to its parent or the ego to the super-ego. The hostile elements may be repressed, but are always liable to break out if the leader's success or prestige should decline. We then have the conditions for a revolution, which may end in the deposition of the leader, and perhaps also the dissolution, or at any rate the disorganization, of the group. Here we see the advantage from the point of view of stability (though of course not necessarily in other respects) of prestige attaching to office rather than person. A still further advantage is to be gained from the institution, which is to be found in many parts of the world, of a double leadership, one leader being in active control of practical affairs, the other being more in the nature of a spiritual head, standing somewhat in the background and in a certain sense *au dessus de la mêlée*. This is exemplified in constitutional monarchy. As Eder pointed out,[1] the great value of such a monarch is that he serves as a unifying symbol that rides serenely above the political conflicts and emotions of the moment. The prime minister can then lose both favour and office without loyalty to the state being imperilled. The king also serves as a common figure for the projection of the super-ego of his subjects, even of those with the most diverse attitudes and opinions. [2] But in order that he may carry out these functions he must as far as possible keep aloof from controversy, and embody only those ideals which constitute the common denominator of the ideals of all his subjects. His personal activities and his capacity for serving the state through his own initiative and powers of leadership are thus rigorously circumscribed. Nevertheless, in this way he continues to stand for the loved and respected parent, while the attitude towards

[1] M. D. Eder, 'Psycho-analysis in Politics,' ch. 4 in *Social Aspects of Psychoanalysis*, ed. by Ernest Jones, 1924.

[2] It is hardly necessary to point out the particular significance of the Crown as a unifying factor in the British Empire.

successive ministers undergoes the inevitable alternations of popularity and disfavour.

The king, spiritual leader, or head of the state is the highest earthly figure on whom we can project our super-ego. But beyond this is the sphere of the superhuman and divine. With all human representatives of the super-ego we are liable in some degree to a repetition of the disappointment that we suffered when we realized the limitations of our own original parents. As a final refuge we can turn to God, and here we are at least relatively safe; the ways of God being inscrutable, and his presence and manifestations being only indirectly perceptible to the senses, he is not subject to those imperfections which are sooner or later discernible in all human figures. God then is in some ways the most suitable of all figures for projection of the super-ego. In his relations with his God, the religious man can to a large extent find relief from the burden of self-direction and moral conflict, and, like a little child, turn trustfully for help and guidance—this time to a divine parent of whose power and infallibility he feels assured. Indeed in the more ecstatic kinds of religious experience (which, however, seem to be enjoyed by relatively few) is to be found possibly the most perfect of all forms of 'altruistic surrender', in which the ego seems to have lost its petty individuality, with all the trifling fears, worries, and concerns of personal existence, and to have become an integral part of a larger, more embracing, indeed universal, whole, to be 'in tune with the infinite', and to enjoy a sense of bliss and harmony that is unattainable by any other means. To writers like Suttie this condition would mean the complete alleviation of that 'separation anxiety' with which man is plagued from birth onwards, while according to the concepts of another school of thought it may exemplify that kind of activity in rest which is sometimes implied to be a characteristic of the Nirvana state, which, it is insisted, is not synonymous with mere changelessness or annihilation.

Short, however, of the attainment of this mystic blissful state, one difficulty remains, even when we project our super-ego on to a divine figure: that same problem of ambivalence that we encounter in our attitude to our parents and our earthly rulers. God, too, represents both the loving, protecting and the frustrating, punishing aspects of parents and rulers. We can attempt to solve the problem in the same way as is often done in the earthly sphere, viz. by the method of 'decomposition', whereby the contrasting aspects are projected on to different figures. Hence the prevalence at certain stages of religious development of two deities or divine principles, such as the Zoroastrian Ormuzd and Ahriman, or in Christianity God and the Devil.[1] At more primitive levels this problem is less acute; the savage is content to regard his gods as punishing, malignant beings as well as helpful ones (though the malignant aspects are actually as a rule more prominent)—in much the same way as the child looks upon its parent as sources both of protection and frustration. Even the ancient Hebrews, who played such an important rôle in the religious sphere by their development of monotheism, were for the most part satisfied that Jahveh should, on the one hand regard them as his own privileged people, and on the other should administer the harshest and most arbitrary punishments. But with the further advance of religious and ethical thought there comes about a need to free the conception of the divinity from the cruel and frustrating elements and to equate God with the perfect loving parent; and many of the efforts of the great religious reformers have been directed to this end. Christianity (at least so far as it follows the actual teaching of Christ) and Judaism represent a particularly striking contrast in this respect. But even in so far as such efforts are successful, two problems still remain. One is the intellectual difficulty connected with the actual existence of evil, which is hard to reconcile with the all-powerfulness and all-lovingness of God and which has exercised the minds of theologians and philosophers throughout the centuries. The other (which is more germane to our present theme) arises from the emotional 'need for punishment', which is opposed to the above-mentioned other need for the solution of the problem of ambivalence, and which is not satisfied by a purely loving and merciful God. Hence a constant tendency to regress, in the sense of attributing fierce, cruel, and jealous qualities to the Deity. Apart from the difficulties associated with the problem of evil, it seems to require a greater freedom from guilt and the need for punishment than humanity usually possesses before men can regard God as consistently benevolent. It is owing to this guilt and need for punishment, to the Polycrates complex and the fear of Hubris, that, time after time, men tend to return to the primitive notion that their God is a jealous God, that he

[1] For a detailed psychological study of the Devil, see the relevant sections of Ernest Jones, *On the Nightmare*, 1931.

is angered by the sight of human success or happiness and is appeased by human suffering.

How very deeply rooted is this tendency can be realized when we see that even if the metaphysical aspects of religion are abandoned, as by confessed atheists, the dim fear of divine displeasure still remains. To cast off the intellectual belief in a Deity who imposes prohibitions and taboos, and who punishes those who transgress them, does not necessarily mean that we can throw aside these prohibitions and taboos themselves. When we can no longer project our super-ego on to our God we are compelled to reintroject it, and are to that extent more completely dependent on our own individual moral structure. In some respects our individual super-ego, when internalized, may be more stringent in its prohibitions than when we could project it on to God, and rely on the divine mercy. To lose our God may thus in some ways be comparable to losing our earthly parents. When they were alive, we could persuade and cajole them, we could beg them for forgiveness and atone for our misdemeanours by little acts of penance and obedience. When they are dead, this is no longer possible, their attitude can no longer be modified, but remains fixed and rigid as it was when they were last alive; and what psycho-analysts have sometimes called 'postponed obedience' to dead parents may be a harder discipline than obedience to a living parent. Hence the inflexible code that may often govern the lives of those who are in theory freethinkers, atheists, or even hedonists—a code which (as is well indicated in Bernard Shaw's *Too True to be Good*) may sometimes drive their children into what seems to them the lighter burden to be found in the service of God. If we seek, therefore, to achieve a morality that is free as regards feeling and behaviour as well as free from metaphysical constraints, it is not sufficient to abandon what we may consider outworn superstitions and beliefs as regards the external aspects of the Universe. We have also to free ourselves from the archaic aspects of our own internal super-ego.

CHAPTER XIV

OVERCOMING AND EVADING THE SUPER-EGO

Introduction

In a very significant phrase Freud once suggested that psychoanalysis had shown that man was not only far more immoral than he believed but also far more moral than he had any idea of. The former quality was due to those crude, 'shocking', primitive, and egoistic impulses that have their source in the id; the latter to those arising from the super-ego. It is with the super-ego that the present volume is primarily concerned; it does not aim at any consistent treatment of the id. Nevertheless we have, of course, been compelled to take cognizance of those impulses emanating ultimately from the id which it is the business of the super-ego to control, and we have seen that these impulses in their struggle with the super-ego are by no means always unsuccessful. In spite of the great power of the super-ego, which we have by now had ample opportunity to realize, it is capable of being outflanked, outwitted, and even overcome. In the present chapter it is proposed to review further and rather more systematically some of the methods by which the id asserts itself against the super-ego, some of the ways in which, notwithstanding their possession of so strong a moral mechanism as the super-ego, men can yet contrive so frequently and obviously to behave immorally. It is evident that we are here touching on a vast and complex subject—none other than 'man's first disobedience and the fruit', from the minor peccadillos of our earliest years (which, incidentally, are minor only because our power is small [1]) onwards to the more serious offences that we classify as delinquency and crime, and even those ferocious forms of collective misbehaviour of which we are wont to accuse our enemies in war.

Without taking into account minor misdemeanours, there is now a vast literature on criminology alone and a considerable number of able and important contributions to the narrower field of the psychology of crime. As regards the more general aspects of the latter subject we must refer the reader to these

[1] On this subject, see for instance, M. Klein, 'Criminal Tendencies in Norma Children,' *Brit. J. Med. Psychol.* (1927), **7**, 177.

books, some of which contain admirable theoretical treatments and ample illustrative case material.[1] All that we can do here is to indicate briefly, and perhaps for that reason in what may seem a bald and abstract manner, some of the ways in which the super-ego is liable to be vanquished or evaded. In so doing we shall unavoidably to some extent be traversing ground that is already familiar, but in surveying it from a rather different point of view we shall also, it may be hoped, supplement the knowledge we have gained concerning the nature, power, and mode of working of the super-ego by a further realization of its shortcomings and limitations as a means of moral direction and control.

In dealing with immorality and criminality it is well to bear in mind that, as several writers have stressed, we are all of us born criminals in the sense that we are extensively endowed with impulses which, if unchecked, lead to anti-social conduct. This is no doubt the element of truth in the doctrine of original sin. We have only to be put in charge for a short time of a young child of, say, from two to four years old to realize that if left to itself it would soon make havoc of any civilized environment, probably ending in its own destruction, or at least in considerable self-injury. It is only in so far as the restraints imposed by adults find an echo in its own mind (i.e. have been incorporated in its own developing super-ego) that it can be left alone with safety to itself and others. In fact the primal liability to criminal behaviour is dependent on the ratio between the strength of anti-social impulses and that of the restraining tendencies, external or internal. It is only in so far as the super-ego itself and the relations between the super-ego and the id become complex (in some of the ways we have already studied) that this simple quantitative picture becomes inadequate, and the need for more delicate qualitative evaluation becomes apparent. In what follows we shall endeavour, as far as possible, to consider first the simpler quantitative aspects of

[1] In addition to the works by Reik, Alexander, and Alexander and Staub, already mentioned, we may refer especially to: W. Healy, The Individual Delinquent, 1915; Cyril Burt, The Young Delinquent, 1925; The Subnormal Mind, 1935; F. Alexander and W. Healy, Roots of Crime, 1931; A. Aichhorn, Wayward Youth, 1935; A. S. Neill, The Problem Child, 1930; The Problem Parent, 1932; Th. Reik, The Unknown Murderer, 1935; W. Norwood East and W. H. de B. Hubert, The Psychological Treatment of Crime (H.M. Stationery Office), 1939. Also the following symposia in the British Journal of Medical Psychology: 'Delinquency and Mental Defect' (1923), 3, 153; 'The Definition and Diagnosis of Moral Imbecility' (1926), 6, 1; 'The Psychology of Crime' (1932), 12, 234.

anti-social behaviour, and afterwards to deal with some of the more complicated conditions, though, inasmuch as the operations of the human mind are nearly always involved and over-determined, we shall inevitably be introducing some distortion and over-simplification in so doing.

Bearing in mind that we are in reality always concerned not with the super-ego or the id alone, but with the ratio of one to the other, we can treat the problem of criminality in its simpler quantitative aspects by dealing first with those factors which tend to produce over-strong id impulses, and then with those which tend to bring about a deficiency or weakening of the super-ego.

Excessive Strength of Impulse

Approaching the phenomena of delinquency from the point of view of McDougall's psychology rather than from that of Freud, Burt has consistently pointed out that criminal actions are in the last resort only the natural unimpeded manifestations of instinctive drives. The various kinds of delinquency, stealing, assault, sexual offences, etc., perhaps even vagrancy, can, he suggested, be regarded as to a large extent the expressions of particular instincts in McDougall's sense. In virtue, however, of his finding [1] that there is a general factor of emotionality or strength of instinct, comparable on the side of orexis to that of general intelligence on the side of cognition (the 'g' of Spearman's Factor School), Burt is inclined to attach greater importance to the strength of this general factor (which he suggests should be called 'e') than to that of any particular instinct. An individual in whom 'e' is strong will, other things being equal, be more prone to delinquency than one in whom it is weak; he will require a greater measure of control (internal or external) if his generally more powerful instinctive drives are to be prevented from finding expression in anti-social ways. Burt further suggests that the kind of emotion most frequently or strongly experienced is also of importance, and that persons more liable to the positive or sthenic emotions, such as anger, gregariousness, sex, and self-assertion, are, other things again being equal, more likely to be criminal, while those in whom the negative or

[1] Cyril Burt, 'The Analysis of Temperament,' *Brit. J. Med. Psychol.* (1938), 17, 158; 'The Factorial Analysis of Emotional Traits,' *Character and Personality* (1939), 7, 238, 285; *The Factors of the Mind*, 1940. Burt's first publication on the subject is, however, to be found in 'General and Specific Factors underlying the Primary Emotions,' *Brit. Assoc. Ad. Sc. Ann. Rep.*, 1915.

asthenic emotions, such as fear, disgust, and submission, pre-ponderate, are more likely to become neurotic. This suggestion gains in strength by his subsequent discovery by the methods of factor analysis of a second factor (this time a 'bipolar' one) in virtue of which individuals tend (in addition to their varying endowment with 'e') to incline to one or other of these two forms of emotional expression. The detailed application to criminological and psychopathological data of the new knowledge gained through this discovery has, however, yet to be made.

These variations in instinctive equipment are, of course, regarded as hereditary in nature, a view which agrees with that of Freud and most other psycho-analysts, who have always attributed some considerable importance to innate instinctive differences between individuals, though—like other psycholo-gists—they have admitted the great difficulty of distinguishing between the basic qualities of orexis that are due to nature and to nurture respectively. It is pretty generally agreed, however, that all the further factors that we shall mention in connection with the strength of id impulses are due, not so much to innate endowment, as to environmental and developmental influences which modify the original instinctive tendencies and direct their expression into particular channels.

The first and simplest of these influences from the point of view of classification is the effect of 'spoiling' or undue indulgence. In essence this would appear to mean that an individual is allowed to express his impulses in anti-social ways with profit to himself, i.e. to attain his object at the cost of others, and without incurring in the process any considerable degree of frustration, punishment, or withdrawal of love. In popular parlance he 'gets away with it', and thus learns that crime does in fact pay. Just as the neurotic who enjoys an 'epinosic gain', i.e. who has learnt to extract a social profit from his symptoms (such as winning sympathy or being excused from irksome tasks), has little inducement to get rid of them, so also the 'spoilt' child can see little point in improving his behaviour, and has little motive to develop those restraints on impulse that are embodied in the super-ego. In the language of the behaviourists, the child (and thus later the adolescent and the adult into which he develops) is 'conditioned' to react to every need by the crude expression of impulse; crime in fact becomes a habit. There is in consequence a failure also to develop that balance of restraints and rewards, of pains and pleasures, that corresponds to the notion of 'inner justice' that we considered in Chapter XI. It is clear that, in broadest terms, the rehabilitation of delinquents of this type can only be achieved through teaching them the hard lesson that in the long run, in the social sphere, renunciation of immediate gratification is often a necessary preliminary to approval or reward. But the process of 'deconditioning' may be a long one. Fortunately it is extremely doubtful whether any pure examples of this class exist; even the most indulgent parents are compelled to draw the line somewhere, thus forcing on their children some restraint on the free exercise of egoistic desires—and this in turn usually brings about some degree of super-ego formation and some development of guilt. In so far, however, as approximations to this type exist, especially when they are in addition burdened by an unfortunate hereditary equipment, orectic and intellectual, they are probably members of that class of 'moral imbeciles' defined in the British Mental Deficiency Act of 1913 as 'persons who from an early age display strong vicious or criminal propensities on which punishment has little or no deterrent effect'.

A different class of delinquents is composed of those whose development of the sense of 'inner justice' has been impaired in the opposite way, i.e. by a lack of love and reward in return for 'good' conduct and an over-emphasis on severity, guilt, and punishment. In distinction to the 'spoilt', these might be called the 'over-punished'. With them there is no inducement to restrain their impulses, because restraint brings them no answering recompense or approval; they naturally tend to develop the attitude that, if nothing they can do will procure them the love they require, they may as well obtain whatever satisfaction they can through primitive and egoistic self-assertion. They are like those in a 'desperate position' whom we referred to at the end of Chapter XI; of them, at least in their own view, it can be truly said that they have nothing to lose but their inhibitions.[1] The appropriate treatment here is also of the opposite kind to that suited to the previous type of case. Further punishment would be useless; they have already had their fill, and more, of this. What they require is love,

---

[1] As Kris has recently pointed out, this attitude may have a potent social influence in producing cohesion among outlawed individuals or groups (including nations) whose outrages against society are such that they cannot hope for forgiveness (Ernst Kris, 'The Covenant of the Gangsters,' *J. Criminal Psychopathology* (1943), 4, 445).

tolerance, and absence of the customary disapproval. The treatment of such cases, who make up a large proportion of the inmates of institutions for difficult youths and children (and probably in later life of prisons also), is undoubtedly far from easy. Love and tolerance are not at once requited by good conduct; on the contrary they are at first regarded as signs of weakness, so that behaviour is apt to become even more outrageous than before. But (if we are to trust skilled exponents of 'new' educational methods, such as Neill or Aichhorn) if sufficient patience is shown, there arrives a point at which aggression turns to breakdown and to tears, and the culprit openly admits his need for love and the helping hand of a guide who will protect him from his own hate and destructiveness. When this stage has been reached, it may be possible to re-educate him by rewarding with approval his efforts at restraint and co-operation, and providing him with a sense of having useful work to do for the community, thus satisfying his 'need to be needed' and removing the feeling that he is an outlaw from society, with all men as his enemies. It is perhaps with cases of this kind that the more modern and lenient methods of dealing with delinquency have had their greatest success, though it must be admitted that the practice of these methods places very considerable strain on those who employ them, and demands a much higher and rarer degree of skill, insight, and tolerance than is needed by those who rely only on the old-fashioned but mostly futile procedures based purely on severity and discipline.

In some respects midway between these two classes are those who 'don't know where they stand', who suffer from inconsistency of treatment, having encountered sometimes harshness and unjust punishment, sometimes leniency and 'spoiling'. Cases of this kind have already been referred to in a previous chapter. The treatment indicated here lies in making good the lack of consistency on the part of the moral authorities, in showing clearly where the line is drawn, in a regular reward of good behaviour, and a no less regular disapproval or punishment of conduct that falls short of the required standard.

In the course of ascertaining just how far he may go in the expression of aggressive or anti-social tendencies, a child almost inevitably resorts to experiment. He wants to see whether he will still be loved when he has transgressed, thus submitting his elders to a sort of 'testing' process. With some individuals this testing may become a permanent habit of obsessive character, leading to repeated commission of minor acts of aggression or disobedience, in order that the culprit may be reassured that he has still not forfeited the love of those about him. Sometimes the crimes actually paraded may be committed in phantasy only, and may be clearly of a symbolic or substitutive character, as in the boy described by Burt [1] who at bedtime pestered his mother with an interminable catechism of imaginary sins, stating with regard to each that he had not committed it that day but asking, 'If I had, you would forgive me, Mummy, wouldn't you?' More often, perhaps, real crimes are committed and then forgiveness asked, as in Morgenstern's case already referred to (Chapter XI) in another of its aspects, where a boy wanted his mother to give him twice as many kisses as he had given her blows. In the case of an adult studied by myself, a man occupying a teaching post in an important school, on returning home each evening immediately looked around for something to grumble at, and having found it 'let off steam'; after which, if the members of his household stood the test and remained friendly, he was prepared to be an agreeable companion. [2] In all such cases there is a great amount of underlying guilt. In Burt's instance the boy was really worrying about auto-erotic activities after going to bed; it was for these that he really wished forgiveness. In Morgenstern's case there had been, as we have learnt, fits of violence and threats of suicide; while the teacher had genuine reasons for feeling guilty towards his wife. In circumstances like these it may be necessary for the subject to understand the deeper sources of his guilt before the testing and the need for reassurance that give rise to it can be removed. Failing this, a kindly tolerant attitude in which the aggression is treated lightly as a childish prank rather than taken seriously is, judging from my own experience, the most satisfactory way of dealing with the symptom. This gives reassurance at the deeper levels and, by causing some degree of superficial shame or disappointment, reduces any 'epinosic gain'.

Real or imagined lack of love, together as a rule with guilt feelings, is at the bottom of many other forms of unsocial behaviour which are not of the 'testing' variety but which express a relatively simple aggressiveness towards the parents

[1] Cyril Burt, *The Subnormal Mind*, 278.
[2] Numerous other cases in children will be found in Susan Isaacs, *Social Development in Young Children*, e.g. pp. 310, 417.

or others who have, as it seems to the culprit, refused to provide the desired affection. Anti-social expressions of this kind often do not follow any easily recognizable withdrawal of love on the part of the environment: they are indeed frequently based on simple jealousy or envy, as when a child is jealous of his father or a sibling. This matter has been so amply discussed in earlier psycho-analytic literature that there is no need to dwell upon it here.[1] We should perhaps only remind ourselves that, as several recent writers have stressed, we are apt (rather unreasonably) to be more unsympathetic and intolerant towards the expressions of jealousy in children than we are with adults; a somewhat greater sensibility to children's feelings would often be in order—though an increasing knowledge of psycho-analytic findings has undoubtedly already produced considerable improvement, especially among the more educated classes.

When love has to be repressed, either because it is not returned or because it is associated with guilt (as in the Œdipus complex), it may easily give place to hate, much in the same way as with those we have called the 'over-punished', or as is often to be seen in jealousy. Only a frank conscious recognition of the existence of jealousy and guilt and of the need for love, an understanding of their origins in infantile situations, and a 'reality' appreciation of the limits within which love can in effect be given, are able perhaps to produce a permanent improvement in difficult cases of this kind. Fortunately most of us outlive or overcome the inevitable jealousies of infancy, largely, it would appear, through displacement on to other persons or situations of the affects concerned.[2]

When anti-social conduct occurs in spite of guilt and the disapproval of moral authorities, there is often present something in the nature of a definite rebellion against these authorities, or against their internal representative, the super-ego. Rebellion, as usually understood, means more than a mere assertion of crude instinct; it implies that there is at least a dim awareness of the authorities as permanently existing tyrannous powers against whom revolt is justified, this in turn involving in some degree a split in the super-ego itself, part (usually the more superficial and conscious part) of the super-ego siding with the id in the manner indicated in Chapter VI. To this we will

[1] A discussion of jealousy by the present writer is contained in 'Some Problems of Jealousy' in Men and Their Motives, 1934.
[2] An attempt at a short comprehensive survey of such displacements will be found in J. C. Flugel, The Psycho-analytic Study of the Family, 1921.

return shortly in dealing with the more complex conditions underlying crime. For the moment let us be content to note three frequently recurring and important accompaniments of rebellion against authority, which link on to other factors that we have already mentioned in earlier chapters.

The first is the peculiar attraction of the forbidden: just because an action is forbidden there arises in many people a desire to do it, though apart from this it might not appear particularly attractive. There is little doubt that the determinants of this attitude (which might be called 'moral contrasuggestibility') may be various and complicated. The most obvious motive is rebellion for rebellion's sake, i.e. the mere existence of the prohibition arouses in some persons the latent hostility to authority; the ego sees, as it were, a fresh threat from authority and seizes the opportunity to assert itself. In some cases the desire may take on an absolutely compulsive quality, indicating that here again some part of the super-ego is siding with the id. Apart from this (though not necessarily unconnected with it) various other factors have been noted by psycho-analysts,[1] e.g. the need for punishment, the satisfaction of masochism, the lure of anxiety and danger (the infringement of a prohibition is often less attractive if there is no chance of being found out), and, as Eidelberg in particular has maintained, the re-establishment in some measure of the lost feeling of infantile omnipotence. With regard to this last, he suggests that our original frustrations (e.g. not being given the breast or bottle when we wanted it) caused the first wound to this feeling of omnipotence. Every subsequent prohibition may reopen it by painfully reminding us of the obstacles to our desires. The feeling can be restored only if we satisfy ourselves in spite of a continuing prohibition, the mere removal of which would not produce this satisfaction.

The second accompaniment of rebellion to which we would draw attention is connected with the subject of our last chapter, though we barely touched upon it there. Like the punishment of our own guilt, rebellion against our own super-ego is sometimes easier if we project it on to another person or group of persons, whom we can then look upon as the embodiment of tyrannous authority. There can be little doubt that internal conflict plays a large part in rebellions and revolutions of all kinds and degrees,

---

[1] E.g. Th. Reik, *Geständniszwang und Strafbedürfnis*, 207 ff.; Ludwig Eidelberg, 'Das Verbotene lockt,' *Imago* (1935), 21, 352.

from minor fits of insubordination in the nursery up to, and including, major political upheavals. As Ernest Jones has pointed out in a recent study of the subject,[1] where there is internal mental harmony people may often remain surprisingly content with defective environmental conditions, but where there is conflict there is also very often outward discontent and aggression, sometimes leading to revolution and the overthrow of existing authorities (who, in virtue of projection, represent the super-ego). Here again, however, when the revolution is something more than an unorganized rebellion or temporary mutiny, it would appear that there is often a split in the super-ego, some part of which takes the side of the revolutionaries, who may indeed feel an intensely righteous indignation against the authorities who have oppressed them.[2]

The third accompaniment of rebellion to which we would refer is liable to come into operation when the rebellious tendencies though present are partially repressed. The ego may then, without being clearly conscious of the cause, feel itself hampered and enslaved, and may be envious of those who apparently suffer from fewer inhibitions. This may manifest itself in intolerance and persecution of those who enjoy a greater freedom, whether in the sphere of morals (as with the notorious Anthony Comstock,[3] or many others in all ages who have embarked on 'purity campaigns'), in that of religion (as in many of the wars of religion of past centuries), or that of politics (as in the totalitarian states of to-day). This intolerance is clearly connected with the notion of 'inner justice' and the attitude towards the criminal that we have previously discussed. The existence of those whose super-egos are less burdensome is an outrage to our sense of justice (why should we bear this burden and they be free from it?) and a menace to our own obedience to our super-ego. For both these reasons we resent the heretic, the freethinker (religious or political), and the moral

---

[1] Ernest Jones, 'Evolution and Revolution,' *Int. J. Psa.* (1941), 22, 193. See also E. F. M. Durbin and John Bowlby, *Personal Aggressiveness and War*, 1939.

[2] The situation is often further complicated by the projection upon the authorities of the revolutionaries' own guilt in the manner indicated in Chapter XII. The solution of the apparent paradox involved in the simultaneous projection of the super-ego and of guilt upon the same 'authorities' is probably to be found in the fact that guilt is almost from the start bound up with the aggressive and nemesistic qualities that have been incorporated in the super-ego and then projected on to the external authorities, who thus correspond to the 'bogy' figures we described in Chapter IX.

[3] See H. Broun and M. Leech, *Anthony Comstock, Roundsman of the Lord*, 1928.

nonconformist, and in consequence we persecute them and turn them into scapegoats.   Here again tolerance is dependent on some degree of inner contentment and absence of conflict and guilt.

Even though repression be normally operative, there are liable to occur temporary manifestations of rebellion.   Children who are usually 'good' may occasionally suffer from tantrums, and even in later life normally stable people may sometimes experience an uprush of feeling which may tempt them to behave in a rude, violent, or aggressive manner that is quite at variance with their usual behaviour.   It seems as though at such times the super-ego were suddenly and for a brief spell overpowered by the rebellious forces of the id.   When action ensues under such circumstances we speak of impulsive anti-sociality or crime, and of the person being 'carried away' by his emotion. The occasions for such outbursts may vary greatly from one individual to another and may sometimes in themselves seem trivial and absurd.   One man of my acquaintance is liable to be stung to fury by his rare and generally unsuccessful efforts to cope with the intricacies of evening dress, another when a fellow-traveller attempts to lean across and read his newspaper in train or bus, still another by a split infinitive;   while several American studies [1] of occasions of anger and 'annoyances' have revealed many further cases of a similar kind, some of which may actually lead to unsocial behaviour.   Analytic investigation of such cases would doubtless show that most of them arise from the fact that the apparently trivial occasion had stirred some deep-lying complex, in much the same way as may happen with irrational fears.   When impulsive actions follow in such instances, as perhaps also sometimes in more easily understandable situations, there is generally a predominance of unconscious motivation, which for the moment renders the conscious will relatively or absolutely powerless.   This is still more the case with genuinely compulsive (as distinguished from the relatively less uncontrollable 'impulsive') actions of a definitely criminal kind, such as those involved in kleptomania or arson (to mention two examples of such behaviour that are often quoted in the literature).   Hadfield,[2] as perhaps a good many other authors, would regard all such actions as coming under the head of

---

[1] E.g. Hulsey Cason, 'Common Annoyances: A Psychological Study of Everyday Aversions and Irritations,' *Psychol. Mon.* (1930), No. 182; and several subsequent papers.

[2] J. A. Hadfield, *Psychology and Morals.* 1923.

'moral disease', whereas more permanent and deliberate kinds of unsocial conduct would qualify as 'sin'. The former, he says, are due to morbid complexes, the latter to wrong sentiments. But on the grounds both of psycho-analytic investigation (which shows the widespread influence of unconscious factors even in apparently 'normal' behaviour) and of the experimental studies of the will process, to which we referred in Chapter II (which reveal a continuous transition from a deliberate act of will, through relatively passive 'consent', to sudden impulse), it would seem hard to maintain any clear-cut distinction, though no doubt extreme cases present little difficulty. All that concerns us here, however, is to note that a sudden and apparently uncontrollable impulse may lead to a temporary overpowering of the super-ego and consequent unsocial action.

Weakening of the Super-Ego

We may now pass to the other quantitative factor concerned in immorality and consider the influences which may lead to a weakening of the power of the super-ego (as contrasted with those that lead to a strengthening of the id). Here again in the first place the question of heredity confronts us. Many older psychologists would have stated with little hesitation that there existed an innate moral sense or power of moral inhibition in which the habitual criminal is deficient; and the fact that there are some persons with a persistently bad moral record from early years onwards, in spite of an apparently favourable environment, might seem to justify their views. But more recent evidence from psychology, psychopathology, physiology, and anthropology has led most modern writers to consider that the inherited elements in character, though undoubtedly present, are of a simpler kind than that suggested by such a term as 'moral sense', and that moral or immoral behaviour is due rather to the way in which these relatively simple inherited elements have been conditioned to interact by the experience and training of the individual.[1] The primary instincts concerned (e.g. love, fear, submission, the need for protection and approval), the capacity for introjection and projection, the general tendencies to narcissism and nemesism—these and the other factors that we have seen to operate in the formation of the super-ego are surely of so fundamental a nature as to be present in all human

---

[1] The most convenient short discussion of this problem is perhaps to be found in Burt, *The Subnormal Mind*, pp. 65 ff.

beings. Moral defect can therefore scarcely be due to the simple absence of the basic mechanisms of morality. On the other hand, quantitative weakness or excess in one or more of them, or a lack of proper balance between them, may make the formation of an efficient super-ego more difficult than in other cases where their relative strength is more favourable. Even this, however, will not of itself necessarily lead to immorality, since an unfortunate hereditary endowment may be compensated by good environmental influences. The ultimate factors in morality are certainly more elementary than anything we should naturally understand by 'moral sense', but whatever they are we know as yet very little as to how far they are innately determined.

To this last statement, however, there is one exception. We do at present know of one factor concerning which there is a good deal of evidence both that it can play an important part (though here again not necessarily a decisive part) in moral development and that it is innate (i.e. is within wide limits not affected by environmental influences). This is not an orectic factor at all, but the factor of intelligence ('g'), to which in this work we have made no more than a passing reference. In Chapter II, however, we did point out that intelligence, knowledge, and understanding of moral issues, though they do not of themselves ensure moral conduct, may yet help towards this end by allowing their possessors to foresee more clearly the distant outcome of immoral behaviour and to realize that in the long run 'crime doesn't pay'. As Burt has emphasized on the basis of his own extensive work with young delinquents, intelligence is particularly important, from the present point of view, in those who possess strong native impulses. An individual highly endowed with 'e' is likely to experience a very powerful urge towards the satisfaction of his desires, and with him it may require a higher degree of intelligence to maintain moral control than would be the case with a person in whom 'e' is weaker. So far as intelligence is concerned then, moral behaviour is largely a question of the ratio between 'e' and 'g'.

As regards the question of heredity in general in relation to the super-ego, all we can say on the basis of our present evidence is that there would seem to be no such thing as simple innate weakness of the whole super-ego as such—of the kind that the (now admittedly inconvenient and misleading) term 'moral imbecility' might suggest; though innate factors (of which 'g' is for the moment the one concerning which we have most knowledge) may quite well have an important indirect influence on super-ego development by affecting the quantitative relationships between the various forces and tendencies involved.

Passing now to definitely environmental factors liable to produce a weakness in the super-ego, the first and most obvious is a weakness in the moral (parental) authorities whose introjection gives the super-ego its first content. Corresponding to the 'spoilt' child are the over-indulgent 'spoiling' parents, who fail to teach the child the necessary lessons of restraint or give the necessary moral guidance. Even here, however, the situation is not always simple. Complete absence of restraint, as we have already said, is never possible; hence there is always, it would seem, some development of the super-ego. And, as Klein, Isaacs, and others have shown, the child does not always (even immediately) experience complete absence of restraint as an unmitigated benefit. He appears to have some real need for control and even for protection against his own aggressive and anti-social impulses, and the necessity for pure self-guidance may be felt as a burden from which he seeks relief.[1] Hence the tendency manifested by some children to provoke their parents and teachers into exercising control by a gratuitous display of 'naughtiness'.

At the opposite end of the scale, corresponding to the 'over-punished' child is the over-severe tyrannous parental authority, which invites rebellion by its very harshness. Here the super-ego, if it has not been overcome by the strength of the rebellious tendencies, has been 'corrupted' by the suffering endured; guilt has been wiped out by punishment. Between these two extremes is the inconsistent and unreliable authority which is sometimes strict and sometimes lenient. This inconsistency may derive from the variable behaviour of a single person, or from the conflicting standards or examples set by two or more different persons who occupy positions of authority. Almost certainly connected with this last are the behaviour difficulties that seem so often to follow on a change of authority, such as occurs in the case of stepchildren, foster-children, or (in recent years) young evacuees. The same sort of difficulties may (as was noted earlier) arise from prolonged or frequent separation from the mother in early years. It would seem, indeed, as though a mere change of moral authority in itself (apart from

---

[1] As indicated in the often-quoted case from *Punch* of the child who asks his mother, 'Mummy, must I *always* do what I want?'

any striking variation of standards) tended to interfere with the smooth development of the processes of identification and introjection on which satisfactory super-ego formation depends.

A curious, and as yet insufficiently understood, type of case apparently exhibiting deficient or distorted super-ego development is presented by what have sometimes been called 'neurotic characters' (or 'psychopathic personalities', to use a term perhaps more generally used in psychiatric literature). Such characters, in Glover's words, display 'a character grouping in which the whole personality is permeated with reactions which, if localized and concentrated, would irresistibly remind us of neurotic symptoms'.[1] In our previous references to them we were concerned chiefly with their nemesistic and self-punishing proclivities. This was the aspect of these characters that was chiefly stressed in the earlier work of Alexander,[2] who is perhaps more than any other responsible for regarding them as forming a distinct class among the varied patients who seek psychotherapeutic treatment. Reich,[3] however (under the term 'impulsive characters'), drew attention rather to their liability to criminal or anti-social conduct,[4] and there has been a certain amount of as yet rather inconclusive discussion as to how such characters arise, by what processes of development they come to differ from neurotics on the one hand and psychotics on the other, and whether we are justified in regarding the self-punishing and anti-social groups as belonging fundamentally to the same category. Very possibly this latter difference merely depends upon a predominance of intropunitive or extrapunitive tendencies determined in some of the ways we have already discussed. It would be inappropriate, however, to enter here into vexed questions of this kind. All we can do is to point out that characters of this class, however they arise, represent a failure of healthy super-ego development and may thus contribute more than their fair share of human immorality.[5]

The conditions so far enumerated correspond to a more or less permanent lowering in the efficacy of super-ego control.

[1] E. Glover, 'The Neurotic Character,' *Brit. J. Med. Psychol.* (1925) 5, 20.

[2] F. Alexander, 'The Castration Complex in the Formation of Character,' *Int. J. Psa.* (1923), 4, 11.

[3] Wilhelm Reich, *Der Triebhafte Charakter*, 1925.

[4] In his later work, *The Function of the Orgasm*, 1942, Reich seems to give the term 'neurotic character' a different meaning, connecting it more specifically with sexual inhibition and contrasting it with a freer, more spontaneous, and healthier type, which he calls the 'genital character'.

[5] For a general discussion of these types of character see 'Character Diseases and the Neuroses,' ed. D. Feigenbaum, *Medical Review of Reviews*, March 1930.

Such control may also be diminished temporarily through alcohol or drugs, which, taken in suitable doses, may reduce for a time the higher-level inhibitions without interfering very appreciably with the function of the instinctive and motor mechanisms. The euphoria, the sense of freedom and relief experienced by many people in mildly alcoholic states, is almost certainly due to a temporary partial paralysis of the super-ego; and it would be interesting to study how far, and in what ways, these euphoric effects of alcohol are correlated with various kinds and degrees of control normally exercised by the super-ego. It might prove, for instance, that such effects are greater with intropunitive than with extrapunitive persons, though no doubt, as with other investigations on the effects of alcohol or drugs, there are complicating factors which might make the obtaining of clear-cut results by no means easy.

The super-ego is, of course, also impaired in many, or perhaps all, of the graver forms of mental disease; and indeed more permanently and often progressively. A decline in the customary politeness or consideration for others is, for instance, very often among the earlier symptoms of schizophrenia and general paralysis of the insane, while a very marked increase in anti-social behaviour is one of the most striking consequences of that strange and relatively new disease now usually known as endemic encephalitis.

Returning to more definitely psychological factors, an interesting question arises as to whether the super-ego can suffer from that active process of dissociation and exclusion from consciousness that in psycho-analytic literature is called repression. In all earlier psycho-analytic work stress was laid, in accordance with the actual clinical findings in the cases examined, on the repression of what appeared to be immoral or unsocial tendencies by, or on behalf of, the moral aspects of the patient's personality, and in his later works Freud spoke of repression being carried out at the behest of the super-ego. This view seemed to preclude the possibility of the super-ego itself succumbing to repression. Yet it would sometimes appear, even from the findings of psycho-analytic writers, that a kind of dissociation or exclusion, at least analogous to that brought about by repression, can affect the super-ego. In the case of the 'over-punished' for instance, which we considered a few pages back, there seems often to be superficially little if any sense of guilt; the more ethical feelings would appear to have somehow disappeared from consciousness in much the same way as may happen with forbidden anti-social desires in the better-studied types of repression. But when, through appropriate treatment, psycho-analytical or educational,[1] certain resistances and hostile attitudes have been overcome, social feelings and guilt that might before have been thought non-existent begin to manifest themselves, often in a way strongly suggesting that they are not new but had formerly been repressed. Evidence pointing in a similar direction is forthcoming from certain cases of religious conversion and of multiple personality, in both of which there may be a sudden change from a carefree, amoral, or even immoral, state to one in which there is very a powerful consciousness of guilt, or *vice versa*. Ordinary introspection moreover shows that, just as there is a conscious process of suppression of importunate primitive desires that seems to correspond on the conscious level to the unconscious process of repression of such desires, so also there can be a suppression, a deliberate brushing aside, of moral qualms. In so far as there is a continuous transition from conscious to unconscious inhibition in both cases, this provides an additional argument for the existence of repression of tendencies emanating from the super-ego as well as of those whose source is in the id. There is little doubt, too, that certain compulsions of an immoral kind (ranging from the utterance of blasphemous or obscene words, through such minor misdemeanours as those involved in petty theft, to serious crimes such as arson or perhaps even murder) may involve a temporary overcoming or dissociation of the super-ego.

Criminalization and Corruption of the Super-Ego

That repression of the super-ego tendencies has possibly received inadequate attention from psycho-analysts is perhaps largely due to the circumstance that those who seek psycho-analytic treatment are drawn from the ranks of neurotics rather than from those of criminals. Nevertheless the evidence at present available seems to indicate that simple repression of this sort, if it does occur, is relatively rare, and that the super-ego is more often evaded, cajoled, bribed, or even in part enlisted on behalf of the immoral action, rather than dealt with by the

[1] For examples of analytic and educational treatment respectively, see for instance the cases described by Alexander and Healy, 'Ein Opfer der Verbrecher-moral und eine nicht entdeckte Diebin,' *Imago* (1935), 21, 5 and 158, and Aichhorn, *op. cit.*, ch. 8.

method of repression. Even in the sort of compulsions to which we have just referred there would often seem to be some degree of super-ego operation, or at least complicity. Reik,[1] for instance, shows how there may be a continuous transition from compulsions of what seem to be a purely immoral kind to those in which a super-ego element is clearly at work, even though the compulsive action still falls in the immoral class. An example of the latter kind would be a vow to do something that is known to be forbidden, e.g. (in the case of a small girl he studied) to cock a snook at the next person who entered the room—a vow comparable in its ethical force and bindingness with vows to *abstain* from an instinctive or immoral action. (He suggestively compares this vow to that of Jephthah in the Book of Judges to offer up the first being he sees on his return, which actually happened to be his own daughter.) Compulsive actions of this immoral kind may indeed sometimes become institutionalized, and it then becomes the duty of everyone to participate in certain actions that are otherwise forbidden, as in the obligation of all present to partake of the totem meal or communion (which represents the killing and eating of the god or ancestor) or to indulge in the liberties and licences characteristic of festivals of the Saturnalian type. Even among ourselves, those who are unwilling to 'celebrate' on suitable occasions are frowned upon as 'spoil sports' and in this way considerable pressure may be brought upon them to break the ordinary rules.

Examples of this nature lead us to conflicts within the super-ego itself, a subject that we dealt with in Chapter VI. Quite often a crime or delinquent action may be performed in order to live up to some (perhaps unrealistic and distorted) aspect of the ego-ideal; for instance, in the case of young people, to assert their grown-upness or manliness (which may easily lead to smoking, drinking, burglary, or aggressive behaviour by boys) or one's attractiveness (which may cause the pilfering of clothes or ornaments by girls). Actions of this kind merge at the one end of the scale into mere egoistic over-compensation for deficiencies or inferiorities (of the sort so much emphasized by Adler), at the other into very genuine and serious conflicts between the more progressive, enlightened aims of the more conscious levels of the ego-ideal and the more conservative taboo-like standards of the primitive levels of the super-ego.

---

[1] Th. Reik, *Geständniszwang und Strbedafürfnis*, 207 ff.

As Stärcke especially has emphasized,[1] nearly all progress, individual and social, involves some infringement of the moral rules of the past. As they grow up, men and women have to do, not merely as privileges but even as duties, many things that were forbidden in their childhood, while the advancing culture of society implies a frequent break with the values and traditions of the past—a break which, judged by conservative standards, is a wicked one. Hence, as we have already observed, many of the pioneers whom we now revere as benefactors of mankind were in their own day looked upon as dangerous and subversive revolutionaries.

From crimes due to conflicts in the super-ego we pass again by a natural transition to those that spring from a super-ego that is itself criminal as a whole, i.e. is based upon ideals and introjections which are at variance with those which are current in society and which seem to make for social harmony. A child who grows up under the influence of parents and neighbours who are themselves grossly immoral, or who is early subjected to the influence of a criminal or anti-social gang, necessarily to some extent forms his super-ego by introjection of the same anti-social standards. He may thus come to regard the ordinary standards as contemptible, will hold that 'wide boys never work' or that only 'mugs' are honest; and is likely in due course to develop the ideology of the crook, thug, or gangster. Hence, as is generally recognized by criminologists, the very sinister influence of a 'bad environment'. It is indeed perhaps surprising that the criminal super-ego is not more prevalent in our society. That we actually seem to encounter it so rarely is probably due to a variety of circumstances, all depending, however, on the fact that it is practically impossible to be consistently immoral or unsocial. There must be, as the proverb indicates, some degree of 'honour among thieves' for any form of social life to be possible (and man cannot help but be a social animal). As the results of the American 'Character Education Inquiry' showed (Chapter II), even the most dishonest are honest sometimes. Moreover both the natural need for love and approval and the pervading traditions of decent behaviour (to which at least lip-service must usually be paid) ensure that, however demoralizing the immediate environment, however anti-social the behaviour of those who are taken as

[1] August Stärcke, 'Conscience and the Rôle of Repetition,' *Int. J. Psa.* (1929), 10, 103.

ideals, there are always tendencies opposed to the continuous successful operation of a criminal super-ego. Indeed we should probably be justified in assuming that criminal action resulting purely and solely from the influence of a criminal super-ego is relatively rare, and should be regarded as something in the nature of a limiting case. It is nearly always complicated by one or more of the other conditions we have mentioned or to which we have still to refer.

Among these latter some of the most curious are those connected with what have been called 'crimes from conscience'. These are more complex in origin than those that spring from a criminal super-ego, and differ radically from these latter in that they are usually committed (paradoxically enough) in an endeavour to assuage a sense of guilt. It would indeed perhaps be better to call them 'crimes from guilt'. Judging from the recorded instances and the theoretical considerations in the psycho-analytical literature (and it is a special merit of psychoanalysis to have drawn attention to the existence of such crimes) there would seem to be two main ways in which the attempt may be made to relieve guilt for (real or imagined) past crimes by commission of a new crime. The first and simpler operates through the punishment which (it is hoped and expected—though of course not in clearly conscious fashion) the new crime will bring in its train. In such cases the crime is usually committed in such a way that detection is easy or inevitable, and the culprit appears quite willing to give evidence against himself. The whole procedure, in fact, constitutes one of the methods of dealing with the need for punishment that we considered in Chapter XI, accent (at least in the unconscious) being laid on the punishment rather than the crime.[1]

In the other type of case relief is sought for guilt (the origin of which is usually unconscious) by attaching it to some new action—or perhaps to some real one, if the original crime is imaginary. The attempt to obtain relief in this way may be successful, either because the new crime is regarded as less serious than the old or imaginary one (which is very often connected with the Œdipus complex), or because, by arousing retaliatory measures (perhaps again 'punishment'), it seems to provide some excuse for the aggressive impulses that the criminal dimly feels to be at work within himself: it is then as

---

[1] A simple and very transparent example of this will be found in A. S. Neill, *The Problem Parent*, 212.

though he said to himself, 'I am justified in my anti-social attitude; just see how badly society treats me!' This differs from the more usual form of 'need for punishment' in that what is required is justification for present aggression rather than atonement for a past crime.

Of course the original unconscious source of guilt and aggression remains untouched by such criminal actions. Although conscious guilt may be relieved for a time, the need which prompts the crime is likely to recur, and thus lead to recidivism; indeed something like a vicious circle may be established, in which aggression begets retaliation and this in turn encourages further and fiercer aggression from the culprit. It is clear that only a fundamental readjustment, probably involving some fuller realization of the culprit's deeper hostile impulses and the nature of their origin, is likely to be of lasting benefit here. Not punishment but psychotherapy is called for in such cases.

Differing, again, in certain important respects from these so-called crimes from conscience (or from guilt) are other crimes which to the unconscious represent punishment inflicted on a scapegoat on whom the criminal's own guilt has been projected. The whole of our Chapter XII was really an essay on this subject. Here we need only say that in addition to the more usual cases (often deeply based on our whole social attitude and tradition) which we there considered, there sometimes occur crimes of a more exceptional and startling character which spring from the same fundamental causes. A well-known literary example is afforded by Hamlet, who, as Ernest Jones has, I think, convincingly shown,[1] projected his own guilt on to his stepfather. Hamlet, however, differs from certain other unusual cases of crime in which punishment is carried out upon a scapegoat. Hamlet suffered acutely from conflicts connected with his own guilt; but in certain related crimes, such as one that has been studied in detail by Marie Bonaparte,[2] the aggressor may appear to be quite remarkably free from guilt, may indeed feel that he has carried out a highly meritorious action. In these cases a special important factor seems to be the adoption by the criminal of the standpoint of his own super-ego; not only does the victim of the crime represent his id, but he (the

[1] Ernest Jones, 'A Psycho-analytic Study of Hamlet,' in *Essays in Applied Psycho-analysis*, 1923.
[2] Marie Bonaparte, 'Der Fall Lefebvre,' *Imago* (1929), 15, 15. A detailed account of another similar case (that of 'Karl') will be found in Alexander and Staub, *op. cit.*

criminal, as external justice sees him) self-righteously plays the rôle of his own avenging super-ego. As we saw in Chapter XII, freedom from a sense of guilt and a resultant feeling of increased approximation to the demands of the super-ego are the great advantages of the whole process of projection on a scapegoat, but in certain cases it would seem that there is not merely an approximation to the super-ego standard, but a taking over of the super-ego rôle, and that this last may lead to what might perhaps be considered a temporary criminal super-ego for the purpose of carrying out some specific action.

In still other cases, the projection of guilt is of a more permanent and systematized character, as in the delusions of persecution so often found in paranoia. As is generally recognized, such delusions will often lead to crime; the culprit (in this case one should rather say the patient) feels so outraged by the continuous insults, suspicions, or torments to which he thinks he is subjected that finally 'his patience is exhausted' and he commits some violent retaliatory act, which, in his view, those who suffer from it have brought upon themselves.

. As we saw in Chapter XI, rationalization is another method by which the super-ego can be evaded. In its moral aspects it might be described as an opiate applied to the super-ego, with the help of which we can lull it into a relative insensibility. Men are very ingenious in discovering reasons for carrying out their wishes rather than their duties, and it is indeed often easy enough to find some secondary ethical justification either for doing that which at bottom they feel should not be done or for leaving undone that to which their duty points. As regards the former, the cleverer kinds of rationalization nearly always evoke, or make use of, some conflict in the super-ego itself, while as regards the latter, rationalization is greatly facilitated by the fact that (as we pointed out in Chapters IV and VI) there are in any case so many good things that we must leave undone.

From general considerations, and from what has been said in earlier chapters, it should be clear that in a great many of the mechanisms of evading or overcoming the super-ego to which we have referred in the last few pages social influences play a great part, both in the sense that the general social, cultural, and economic background affects the whole mentality of the individual culprits, and in the further sense that whole groups of people (even whole nations) may display the same psychological mechanisms as these latter. As we showed in the last chapter, submission to group prestige and the projection of the individual super-ego upon the group may lead to a great and tragic lowering of moral standards. All the individuals concerned may in fact acquire what, according to the standards of other times and other groups, might be called a criminal super-ego; they regard as right and praiseworthy what in the light of these other standards would be considered callous, treacherous, cruel, intolerant, or unjust. This is exhibited on the one hand by war, or in religious, political, or racial persecutions, when wholesale murder and destruction (to say nothing of mental torture) may be inflicted by one group on another, not only without guilt but with a supreme sense of moral rightness; and on the other by the changing standards of successive generations. In the past many highly moral people have, without any qualms of conscience, kept slaves; burnt heretics and witches, or passed sentence of death on those who have committed petty thefts— all carried out under the influence of moral standards that we now deplore. It may well be that the complacent attitude of the nineteenth and early twentieth centuries towards the exist- ence of widespread poverty and unemployment (an attitude largely helped by the 'scientific' rationalizations of *laissez-faire* and the invocation of 'iron' economic laws) will soon be looked upon as no less shocking. Our view of what constitutes a criminal super-ego is therefore dependent on circumstances of time, place, and contemporary tradition.

In such cases the adoption by the group as a whole, and by the members of the group who follow its traditions, of a 'criminal' super-ego is usually accompanied by some degree of projection of guilt upon the victims. Slaves are lazy, inferior, and incompetent, heretics wilfully reject the word of God, witches have dealings with the Devil, the poor are thriftless, the unemployed are 'unemployable', and petty thieves have no respect for the rights and property of others. In war too, of course, our enemies exhibit almost every form of wickedness.

It is quite probable that not only the projection of guilt and the adoption of a criminal super-ego but also such motives as the need for punishment and the provocation of retaliatory aggression affect groups as well as individuals. The rise of highly aggressive totalitarian régimes in Italy and Germany followed a period of acute social demoralization which must un- doubtedly have introduced shame and guilt into the sentiments that many of their citizens held with reference to these countries. The principle of 'World Conquest or Downfall' adopted by Germany in both world wars in itself contains a suggestion at once of crime and punishment on a megalomanic scale, as does also perhaps the institution (tricked out with every attribute of pomp and circumstance) of official days of mourning following defeats (such as that of Stalingrad); while Hitler's startling technique of broadcasting to the world the aggressions that he proposes shortly to commit is reminiscent of the procedures sometimes adopted by relatively humble criminals, as in the case of McMahon's curious attack on Edward VIII, which was announced to the Home Secretary by letter and by telephone beforehand.[1] Incidentally, neither in the one case nor in the other was any serious notice taken of the warnings.

One final group of cases of evasion or overcoming of the super-ego should be mentioned here. They are all connected with the upsetting of the sense of 'inner justice' to which we have referred both in this and in earlier chapters. In these cases the ego revolts against the super-ego, corrupts or overcomes it, when the rewards of morality are denied or when excessive punishment is suffered. Crimes from this source imply, not so much a criminalization of the super-ego, as its defeat by rebellious impulses which, following on the 'injustice', have been allowed to take possession of the ego. In some instances of this kind the upset of justice is due ultimately to biological causes, such as deformity, chronic illness, or infirmity. The individual may then feel that he starts life at such a disadvantage that the ordinary rules of morality do not apply to him. As Freud pointed out in first drawing attention to this type,[2] Richard III affords an example of the kind, as is indicated in the words that Shakespeare makes him utter:

> Cheated of feature by dissembling nature,
> Deformed, unfinished, . . .
> Therefore since I cannot prove a lover . . .
> I am determined to prove a villain.

As Freud also emphasized in another connection, many of us tend to approximate temporarily and in some degree to this

[1] The final words of McMahon's letter might have been written by Hitler with regard to his more grandiose demands, did he possess sufficient insight into his own condition: 'In the event of failure [of his petition to the King regarding supposed police persecutions], I will exercise my own prerogative and obtain the necessary satisfaction which I, in my tortured mind, consider adequate' (*The Times*, July 25, 1936).

[2] 'Some Character Types met with in Psycho-analytic Work. II. The "Exceptions"' (1915), *Collected Papers*, iv, 318.

type when we are ill. Then, too, we can to some extent regard ourselves as 'exceptions' who can claim special privileges and exemptions. In terms of inner justice we have been 'over-punished' and have a balance of pleasure due to us which, if not spontaneously provided, we take steps to procure, if necessary at the expense of others. The permanent 'exceptions' are those who, because of their abiding handicap, are chronically in this condition.

In the great majority of cases, however, the upset of the sense of inner justice comes from social or economic influences. We have already in effect considered in Chapter XII the circumstances under which such an upset can occur and we need do little more than re-enumerate them here. They can perhaps be adequately classified under six main heads: (1) when our own virtue is unrewarded, (2) when we have suffered undeservedly, (3) when our guilt has been wiped out—or perhaps more than wiped out—by suffering (both these last categories can be regarded as varieties of 'over-punishment'), (4) when others have received unmerited rewards, (5) when others who have transgressed are seen to have escaped punishment (both these last constituting a 'temptation' to ourselves), (6) as a final all-inclusive category, when all the usual social sanctions and rewards are to some extent suspended—as in war, revolution, or any other condition producing social disorganization. With regard to this last, we may note that the general relaxation of moral and conventional standards in ways not directly connected with the war is largely consequent upon the feeling that some recompense is due for the increased hardships, efforts, and dangers to which war exposes us. If so much of life is 'grim', we are justified in being 'gay' when we have the opportunity; and the guilt that we might otherwise feel in overthrowing customary restraints and venerable taboos is cancelled by the 'blood, toil, tears, and sweat' that we must in any case endure.

As the reader was warned at the beginning of the chapter, this review of the chief methods by which the super-ego is overcome, evaded, or otherwise rendered of no account, has been somewhat bald and abstract. Deprived of the flesh and blood of detailed concrete instances, any account of the mentality of sinners is likely to be almost as dull as are the customary stories of the lives of saints. Still, theory and classification have their proper place, alike in ethics, psychology, and criminology, and for the purpose of our exposition of the mental aspects of morality it was necessary to examine how the undoubted prevalence of crime and immorality could be reconciled with the picture of the stern super-ego as it has emerged from psycho-analytic findings. We have seen that, even within the realm of present psycho-analytic theory, there is a considerable diversity of routes along which, notwithstanding the super-ego, we may succeed in becoming sinners. But, intricate as the pattern of delinquency that we have tried to outline may appear, there can be no doubt that it does less than justice to the actual facts, both in that some important routes have been left uncharted altogether and that in many individual cases simultaneous use is made of more than one approach. In delinquency, as in psychopathology and human conduct generally, 'over-determination' would seem to be the rule rather than the exception; few if any actual cases fit neatly into any simple framework that theory can provide. Here we must be satisfied if we have drawn no more than the roughest sketch-plan to fill out an obvious gap in our picture (itself no doubt still lamentably inaccurate and incomplete) of the deeper levels of man's moral nature.

CHAPTER XV

WISHFUL THINKING, AUTISM, AND UNREALISM

Unrealism—Pleasant and Unpleasant

During the last few years we have heard much of 'wishful thinking'—a useful term which has served especially to put us on our guard against the exaggerations, omissions, and optimistic distortions of war communiqués, from whatever source they come. It is a remarkable and perhaps encouraging fact that in the present war popular feeling has in this respect often shown itself more realistic than the official mind, which has invented so many euphemistic circumlocutions to camouflage setbacks and retreats. Wishful thinking (it is popularly implied) is dangerous, as indicating an unwillingness to face unpleasant stern realities. This distinction between 'wishful thinking' and 'realistic thinking' (a term less often used, perhaps because of its opposition in another sense to 'idealistic' thinking or thinking in terms of ethical principles) seems in some important respects to mirror the distinction made by Freud between the 'pleasure principle' and the 'reality principle',[1] which itself corresponds largely to that drawn about the same time by Jung between 'phantasying' and 'directed thinking'[2] (later called—though, it would seem, with some modification in meaning—'passive' or 'intuitive' thinking and 'active' thinking[3]) and by Bleuler between 'autistic'[4] (in his later works called 'dereistic'[5]) and 'realistic' thinking. As the contrast between Freud's terms implied, thinking according to the pleasure principle represented an attempt at a short-cut to obtain pleasure or avoid unpleasure by ignoring the less agreeable aspects of reality. In Freud's view one of the characteristics of mental development was the replacement of the pleasure principle by the reality principle (though of course this replacement was never complete), and in so far as psycho-analysis corrected faulty development by providing insight into the nature of unconscious pathogenic processes it also helped to facilitate this replacement. The transition from the one principle to the other implied no fundamental difference of aim, which remained the satisfaction of man's basic desires (in hedonistic terms, the pursuit of pleasure and avoidance of unpleasure), but whereas the pleasure principle made use of the short-circuit through imagination whenever satisfaction in reality was difficult, the reality principle implied the seeking of satisfaction in reality itself. According to a later but useful distinction made by some psycho-analysts, this latter could be achieved either 'autoplastically', by adapting the self to the environment, or 'alloplastically', by so modifying the environment that, instead of frustrating, it satisfied the needs of the self.

In our own study we have already had ample occasion to observe that there is a strong element of unrealism, not only in the attempted satisfaction of desires along the lines of wishful thinking, but also in many of our morally determined actions, feelings and ideas, especially those that spring from the more archaic and unconscious levels of the super-ego, e.g., to take a par-

---

[1] 'Formulations regarding the Two Principles of Mental Functioning' (1911), *Collected Papers*, iv, 13.

[2] C. G. Jung, 'Wandlungen und Symbole der Libido,' *Jahrbuch für Psychoanalytische und Psychopathologische Forschungen* (1911), 3, 120. Later translated with the somewhat misleadingly broad title *Psychology of the Unconscious*, 1919.

[3] *Psychological Types*, 1920.

[4] E. Bleuler, 'Das Autistische Denken,' *Jahrbuch für Psychoanalytische und Psychopathologische Forschungen* (1912), 4, 14.

[5] *Textbook of Psychiatry*, 1923.

ticularly crass example, the creation of the 'bogy' parent-figures
discussed in Chapter IX. It is plain, however, that unrealism of
this latter sort is often very far from being of the kind that we
would naturally consider 'wishful thinking' or thinking according to the 'pleasure principle'. A great deal of it seems rather
to aim at a curtailment of our pleasures, even those that are
open to us in reality (as in the case of many taboos or the
manifestations of the need for punishment and the Polycrates
complex). As Bleuler pointed out in his first contribution to
the subject, not all unrealistic thinking is pleasure thinking, and
it would seem that we must either regard the 'pleasure principle'
as something that is, at any rate in some directions, narrower in
scope than unrealism in general, or else use the term in a very
strained and inconvenient way. The fact that Freud and many
other psycho-analysts have continued to use it in what would
seem to be a misleadingly wide sense is no doubt chiefly due to
two circumstances: first that Freud never subjected the concept
of the ' pleasure principle', first formulated in 1911, to a thoroughgoing revision in the light of later findings,[1] and secondly that
(as we have noticed before) psycho-analysis started from the
rather naïve assumptions of psychological hedonism. It seems
therefore much more convenient to use one of the other terms
proposed, and we shall here employ the older, shorter, and more
widely used of Bleuler's expressions, 'autism' and 'autistic
thinking', while keeping 'wishful thinking' for the more conscious
pleasure-seeking manifestations of autism.

The reason why autistic thinking does not always aim at
pleasure is probably due to two facts: first that it is determined
not only by desires but also by fears, and secondly that it
serves as a medium of expression, not only for impulses emanating directly from the id, but also for those connected with the
super-ego. In the degree in which desires and the more positive
id impulses preponderate, we get an approximation to a distortion of reality that seeks to 're-mould it nearer to the heart's
desire'. But inasmuch as fear often inhibits our desires, and
the super-ego often disapproves of them, these desires are in
turn modified and distorted so that various compromises are
reached, of the kind that (e.g. in dreams and neurotic symptoms)
were detected and studied from the early days of psycho-

---

[1] It is true that in *Beyond the Pleasure Principle*, 1922 (first published 1920),
he suggested a wider philosophical interpretation of all vital activity, but this
left the more proximate distinction between the 'pleasure principle' and the
'reality principle' comparatively untouched.

analysis onward. These distortions usually reduce the pleasure or turn it into pain. They do not, however, of necessity imply that the compromise formations arrived at are any more in accordance with reality than simple manifestations of the id would be. This in turn is probably due to the fact that the lower levels of the super-ego are themselves unconscious; and unrealism seems to be a characteristic of the unconscious as such rather than of the id in particular. Unconscious morality is no more realistic than is unconscious impulse; it is only in its higher and more conscious levels that the ego-ideal often sides with reality against the demands of short-cut pleasure seeking—as illustrated in our customary condemnation of wishful thinking.

Generalizing perhaps from this latter higher-level association between morality and realism, Freud, in his earliest formulations, was inclined to ascribe to the super-ego the function of 'reality testing'. Later, however, in *The Ego and the Id*, he corrected this and considered that it was the business of the ego to apprehend external reality and to control action in accordance with it. Not, however, its only business. The ego, he maintained, is in the unenviable position of having to deal with three hard taskmasters—external reality, the id, and the super-ego—and of having to do the best it can to satisfy their often conflicting demands. When it concedes too much either to the id or to the super-ego (especially the more primitive aspects of the latter) reality appreciation is likely to suffer. If, when this happens, the more positive desires of the id preponderate, there tends to be pure pleasure thinking; when fear or the super-ego plays a larger part, our phantasies become less pleasant—often less pleasant than reality itself. But in either case there is autistic thinking with consequent distortion of reality. This at least seems to be the general implication of psycho-analytic findings, though in the literature we seldom if ever find it stated as a general principle—largely perhaps owing to the misleading nature of the term 'pleasure principle' when it is applied to autistic thinking as a whole.

Fields of Unrealism

The degree of simple pleasure seeking (as distinguished from the unpleasant distortions due to fear or super-ego influence) varies greatly from one instance of autistic thinking to another. It varies also in the different general spheres or kinds of autistic thinking that can be conveniently distinguished—often for reasons that we do not yet fully understand. It is, of course, very high in **wishful thinking** of the kind that is usually implied in the everyday use of the term, e.g. in relation to the war, perhaps because the super-ego raises no objection to the wishes concerned. Not only do we earnestly desire victory for ourselves in war, but we consider such victory to have the highest moral justification. In wishful thinking of a more personal kind, in which there is a similar optimistic under-estimation of adverse reality factors, there is also perhaps as a rule little super-ego opposition; we feel that we deserve to achieve the ends we have in view. In all such cases it may be that the super-ego stands, as it were, aloof, and allows the id to triumph over the 'reality-testing' functions of the ego—though perhaps at other times the super-ego is evaded, corrupted, or overcome in ways similar to those that we studied in the last and earlier chapters. Similar considerations apply to many **parapraxes** and momentary illusions—slips of the tongue, pen, hand, eye, or ear—which imply a fleeting distortion of reality in a sense favourable to id gratification (though we may in some cases have to pay dearly for this neglect of reality later on). Another and still more important field in which pure pleasure thinking predominates is that of **day-dreaming.** Here no doubt the well-preserved distinction between reality and phantasy serves in some way to keep this reserved field free from super-ego interference—for quite a number of our phantasies would probably incur lively super-ego opposition if we attempted to put them into practice.[1] Again there are certain **psychotic conditions** in which id impulses, often of a crude and megalomanic kind, appear to triumph completely over the appreciation of reality, within at least a certain field. Thus in delusions of grandeur the patients may believe themselves to be kings, emperors, millionaires, strong men, or religious saviours, sometimes combining various hardly compatible forms of greatness in ways that remind us of William James's regrets concerning the inevitable sacrifice of 'potential selves' in the passage quoted in an earlier chapter. A patient known to me, for instance, insisted that he was 'Jesus Christ, Duke of Argyll', and that he was the owner of 'fifty thousand diamond motor-cars'. Bleuler

---

[1] Though (as we saw in connection with sado-masochism) there may also be certain actions that are in the nature of acted phantasies, their main significance being derived from elements of phantasy rather than from real features of the situation.

and Jung,[1] in their epoch-making studies of schizophrenia, have shown, too, that many of the apparently nonsensical actions or phrases of patients suffering from this disease can be interpreted as crude wishfulfilments. Thus one patient who was intensively studied described herself as 'Socrates' Representative' (a symbolic expression of wisdom), 'Double Polytechnic' (indicating knowledge), 'The Cranes of Ibycus' (indicating guiltlessness), and 'Threefold World Proprietress' (indicating power and riches). In such severe pathological conditions it would seem that both the ego (with its power of reality appreciation) and the super-ego (with its restraints on crude self-exaltation) have been impaired, so that primitive egoistic tendencies find expression in unimpeded but grotesque fashion.

More numerous however, on the whole, would seem to be the cases where autistic thinking reveals the influence of the super-ego as well as of the id, and where in consequence reality is distorted in a more complex way than by that of simple disregard of its less pleasant aspects. Schizophrenia affords examples of this kind also; as in another of Jung's cases, that of an archæologist who during his two attacks imagined himself to be fighting battles on a cosmic scale against immensely strong forces of evil, the queer gymnastic antics in which he indulged symbolizing his participation in this battle. True, he eventually emerged as conqueror in the heroic fight, and there was thus something of the same grandiose egoistic gratification as in the previous case, but the fact that the obstacles and difficulties against which he had to fight were also greatly magnified, and that he had to endure 'unutterable misery and pain' in the battle, indicates a great departure from the principles of straightforward pleasure seeking. Such a departure is still clearer in the case of some other psychotic disturbances, e.g. in the delusions of persecution so often found in paranoia. Here the patient feels that he is being subjected to constant torments, insults, slights, or suspicions. The element of gratification in such cases lies (as we have seen) in that the patient has used the mechanism of projection to save himself the painful recognition of his own unwelcome tendencies. But the mere fact that these tendencies are unwelcome to him seems to be due to super-ego influence; furthermore, though the process of pro-

[1] C. G. Jung, *The Psychology of Dementia Præcox*, 1909 (originally published 1907). E. Bleuler and C. G. Jung, 'Komplexe und Krankheitsursachen bei Dementia Præcox,' *Centbl. f. Nervenhk. u. Psychiat.* (1908), 19, 220. C. G. Jung. *Collected Papers on Analytical Psychology* (1916), ch. 13.

jection may save him from feelings of guilt, it certainly does not protect him from the sufferings caused by his imagined persecution.

Of all psychotic conditions that of melancholia is most obviously painful and most clearly under the influence of the super-ego. Here, as we have also seen, the patient punishes himself for his own aggression by turning this aggression on himself. Here, too, we have a supreme example of the distortion of reality in the service of the punishing tendencies emanating from the super-ego. This distortion is perhaps clearest when the crime for which punishment is inflicted is one that has been committed in imagination only, as when (to take a well-known instance) the poet Cowper felt himself to be a murderer because he had laughingly lamented the long life of the occupant of a post (the Clerkship of the House of Lords) to which he himself had subsequently been appointed.[1] The id element in such cases is still detectable in the assumed 'omnipotence of thought', but it is the punitive reaction of the super-ego that dominates the picture.

In a similar way **neurotic symptoms,** while they protect the patient from one source of pain (perhaps from two, if we take account of a possible epinosic gain), only expose him to other sources from which he would not otherwise have to suffer. It was, of course, in the field of neurosis that the earliest psycho-analytic discoveries were made, and it was clear from Freud's first formulations that neurotic symptoms represented, not direct, but distorted wishfulfilments, that the distortions were somehow due to moral influences, and that they involved much sacrifice of pleasure and indeed much suffering of pain. Both the distortion of reality and the distortion of the pleasure aim are due ultimately to the same processes—most frequently that of displacement, sometimes others, such as reaction formation. The group of phobias illustrates the operation of both these latter: what was originally an object of desire becomes an object of fear (a change in emotional attitude implying reaction formation) and this fear becomes extended to other associated objects or situations (in virtue of displacement). The characteristic intense unrealism combined with a crippling but entirely

---

[1] This case can also be regarded as one in which mental illness follows, if not success itself, at least the prospect of success. The castration complex, too, was pretty clearly at work, for his first period of melancholia was intimately connected with his fear of an examination, the second with his fear of marriage. See Lord David Cecil, *The Stricken Deer*, 1929, esp. p. 55.

irrational anxiety is interestingly illustrated by the case referred to in Chapter XI of the clergyman who was afraid of falling in Piccadilly. Another of his symptoms was that he was liable to suffer acute anxiety at the sight of omnibuses in the London area. While undergoing treatment he noticed that the amount of fear caused by the proximity of one of these objects varied greatly, and apparently inexplicably, from one instance to another. Endeavouring during a period of some weeks to solve this mystery, he observed that the fear seemed connected in some way with the route numbers on the buses—buses with some numbers causing a much more lively anxiety than those with others. Examination of the data provided by this study eventually showed that those buses which caused him most alarm all passed through or quite near to Piccadilly in the course of their journey! They thus constituted a temptation to visit the dangerous locality, and his quite unconscious association had produced an extension of the original fear to the, in themselves, entirely 'harmless' public vehicles.

Lest it be thought that mechanisms of this sort are confined to individual pathological cases, we may observe that similar extensions of fears through quite irrational displacements can sometimes affect the attitude of sober and erudite public bodies. As an example we might quote the answer given by the Senate of the University of Tübingen to a request that women might be allowed to use the University swimming bath for one hour a week.[1] The request was refused, and the Senate was rash enough to give its reasons, which were to the effect that 'it was impossible to contaminate the minds of the young men swimmers by the knowledge that girls' bodies had shortly before been plunging about in their bath'. This was in 1870, and we can afford to laugh at such an example because, having reduced the taboos on sex in this direction, the fear (and underlying attraction) of the female body is less likely to extend in such an overwhelming manner to the water in which it may happen to have been immersed, but we may remind ourselves that a similar process of irrational displacement underlies the distinction between Aryan and non-Aryan art, science, and even mathematics, that at the moment of writing is still upheld in the same country. The hatred of the Jew has extended to all his works, even in the most abstract of all fields of thought. Our loves, hates, and fears, especially through their extensions

---

[1] The account is taken from Cicely Hamilton, *Modern Germany* (1931), p.76.

by displacement, can all make us suffer from unrealism; but whereas the first-named only casts a more or less harmless glamour over what might otherwise be dull or insignificant, the two latter (and love also when it is repressed) not only distort reality but flavour it with horror and impurity.

To return to individual neurosis, in some cases—to make the situation still more complicated and if possible still more un-realistic—the element of projection may be added. Here the id component may be projected on to someone else, and the patient's fears may relate to the aggression that he might direct on to this other person—as in a case described by Berg [1] where a man was terrified lest he should be compelled by irresistible fury to attack anyone whom he saw whipping a horse. In a remote and forgotten past the patient had himself been guilty of brutally gratifying his sadism on a horse. His attitude had then undergone a threefold change: (1) his sadism had given place to a reaction formation distinguished by an exaggerated intolerance of any infliction of pain on the animal concerned, (2) he projected his own guilt upon a scapegoat (anyone beating a horse) and sought to satisfy his need for punishment by behaving aggressively towards this scapegoat, (3) he developed a phobia of the violence in which this vicari-ously directed need for punishment might involve him. When neuroses are built up on such elaborate transformations we need hardly be astonished at the resultant painful and hampering unrealism of those who suffer from them.

Obsessional neuroses are often less spectacular than phobias and the other manifestations of hysteria, and in them, as is generally recognized, the rôle of the super-ego is more directly manifested. The unrealism of compulsive thoughts and actions is, however, scarcely less obvious than is that of the symptoms of hysteria, and is clearly recognized by the patient himself. When the compulsions are severe and complicated they may involve him in elaborate rituals, which consume an immense amount of time and energy, which are burdensome to carry out, and which may place severe and completely irrational limitations on his freedom and activities.

In neurosis, then, the distortion of reality is attributable both to the id and to the super-ego, or perhaps we should say to the conflict between them and to the displacements and other mechanisms through which a solution of the conflict is sought.

[1] Charles Berg, *War in the Mind* (1941), pp. 70 ff.

The same is true of **dreams,** which, as Freud showed in what is perhaps the most celebrated of all his works,[1] follow closely the pattern of neurosis (although of course distinguished from this latter by their unique hallucinatory character and by their exclusion from waking perceptual and motor activities— features which endow them with a special unrealism of their own). A few dreams, it is true, represent plain undistorted wishfulfilments, thus resembling day-dreams or the cruder forms of wishful thinking. The vast majority, however, are more complex, like neurosis reveal the influence of the super-ego, and are to some extent unpleasant, sometimes extremely so.[2] Here again both the id and the super-ego seem to share responsibility for the autistic nature of the thinking. It is in the much greater predominance of unpleasure and in their hallucinatory character that dreams differ most markedly from day-dreams. The latter difference is doubtless due to the sleeping condition of the dreamer, and the former to the greater rôle of the super-ego; but why the super-ego should in some respects exercise a more vigorous influence when we are asleep than when we are day-dreaming is a problem that has not as yet received a satisfactory answer. It may be because the distinction between reality (albeit here an hallucinatory reality) and phantasy has been lost in sleep—though one might imagine that this would perhaps be compensated by the fact that the power of voluntary movement has also been lost; or it may be because the deeper repressions have been removed in sleep, so that the super-ego is compelled to more energetic intervention at a higher level, whereas in waking life, when these deeper repressions are still functioning, it enjoys a sense of relative security and can consequently afford to be tolerant as regards the special reserved field of day-dreaming.

Myths have sometimes been called the day-dreams of the race. This might seem to indicate that they partake of the character of straightforward pleasure-seeking that distinguishes the day-dreams of the individual. In view of the fact that the content of myths is often far from pleasant, this suggestion appears at first to be palpably untrue, even if we bear in mind that what afforded pleasure to the unknown myth-makers of

---

[1] *The Interpretation of Dreams*, 1913. Originally published 1899.

[2] The intimate relation between pleasure and anxiety in dreams (of the same kind as that shown in phobias) and the liability to rapid change from the one state to the other is particularly well illustrated in nightmares. See Ernest Jones, *On the Nightmare*, 1931.

past times may have been different to that which pleases us
to-day. But there is another difference between myths and
day-dreams that we must take into account. Myths deal with
fictitious persons, or at least with persons who lived in the past,
whereas day-dreams have for the most part an intimate relation
(at most but slightly veiled) to the 'here' and 'now' of the
personal lives of the day-dreamers themselves. There is thus
an element of æsthetic or quasi-æsthetic 'distance'[1] in myths
which is absent in day-dreams, and in virtue of which we can
contemplate with a peculiar pleasure events and things, e.g.
the long trials and tribulations of a hero, that would affect us
most unpleasantly were we experiencing them as part of our
own 'real' and immediate environment. This brings us up
against the great problem of the unpleasant and the tragic in
art, into which we cannot enter here. Owing to this factor of
'distance', however, myths may approximate more closely to
simple pleasure thinking than might at first appear, and we
may hesitate to ascribe the unpleasant element in myths to the
super-ego in the same way and to the same extent as in the case
of dreams and psychopathological symptoms. The super-ego,
especially in its primitive and aggressive manifestations, is no
doubt not without its part in determining the content of myths,[2]
but, as Rank pointed out in one of the early contributions of
psycho-analysis to this field,[3] the majority of myths appear to
be singularly free from overt moral considerations, differing in
this respect from that chronologically later and more morally
sophisticated type of story that we usually call **Märchen,** in
which virtue nearly always meets with its reward. In spite of
the moral influence, or rather just because morality is always
made to pay in the long run, *Märchen* represent autistic thinking
of a pleasure-seeking kind, even though they have undergone
a certain degree of 'secondary elaboration' in the direction of
moral smugness. It would seem that both in myth and *Märchen*
the super-ego stands aloof, or collaborates with the id in such
a way that its demands are met without much sacrifice of
pleasure. It may well be that the factor of 'distance' and the
removal from the field of immediate personal concern and
action are of importance here.[4]

[1] E. Bullough, 'Psychical Distance as a Factor in Art and an Æsthetic
Principle,' *Brit. J. Psychol.* (1912), 5, 87.
[2] See, for instance, Géza Róheim, *The Riddle of the Sphinx* (1934), ch. 3.
[3] Otto Rank, *Psychoanalytische Beiträge zür Mythenforschung* (1914), 382 ff.
[4] Though in so far as myth is, in the way some anthropologists have stressed,

Myth leads us naturally to **religion,** since the metaphysical bases of religion are so intimately connected with mythology. Here, however, the super-ego obviously plays a much bigger part, and it is relatively easy, in view of what has been said in previous chapters, to distinguish between the elements of pleasure thinking and the less agreeable and more awesome aspects in which the aggressive, prohibitive, and punitive elements of the super-ego exercise a predominating influence. The former consist in the gratification of the wish for a protecting, kindly, omnipotent, and omniscient parent, the latter in the exaltation of the sterner moral qualities of the parent and in the projection of such of these qualities as we have previously incorporated by introjection in our super-ego. In both directions there may be a distortion of reality, which may therefore appear to the believer to be both more reassuring and more terrible than it seems to those who do not share his faith. As a consequence the believer may pray or sacrifice to his gods, or may submit in impotent resignation to 'the will of heaven', instead of attempting to do what he can to meet the situation by his own efforts. He may even incidentally be led to actions that aggravate the evil, as when in an epidemic the faithful flock together for prayer, thereby spreading the infection. On the other hand it is only fair to note that, in so far as the view is held (as it often is, either explicitly or implicitly) that 'God helps those who help themselves', a healthy corrective is provided, which tends to bring back the worshipper to realism and to endow him with a greater confidence through the belief that he is fighting with a divine ally by his side.

In the case of higher religions, certain special influences are connected with the beliefs concerning a future individual life. These may, according to circumstances, either increase moral effort, or lead to a certain neglect of all earthly values, but are in any event likely to entail an element of reality distortion. The wishful thinking involved in a belief in a happier hereafter (the particular kind of happiness depending upon the values of the society concerned) is very manifest, and it is probably this aspect of religion that is chiefly in view when it is regarded as an 'opiate of the people,' tending to make them uninterested in any means of improving their present lot. Equally plain,

connected with ritual (much ritual being in the nature of a symbolic dramatization of myths) it is not altogether divorced from action. The ritual involved is, however, of a communal type and therefore not likely to meet with the disapproval of the super-ego.

P

however, is the autistic element in the correlative belief in the torments of hell, so that in notions concerning the future life generally the punitive super-ego, often powerfully reinforced by sado-masochism, reveals itself as no less influential than the pleasure-seeking id.

Magic and superstition constitute another great system of human beliefs which, especially in primitive cultures, is responsible for an immense amount of autistic thought. It differs markedly from religion in the almost complete absence of a moral element, depending as it does upon supposed forces of a more or less constant and mechanical nature. With the aid of these forces it endeavours, as Freud showed,[1] to prolong infantile 'omnipotence of thought' and is indeed mankind's most desperate and thoroughgoing attempt in this direction, actually seeking to convert wishful thinking into something like an exact pseudo-science. In another respect, however, it does resemble religion, namely in the presence on the one hand of a positive element of power and gratification, and on the other of a negative element of fear. The former is represented by active or offensive magic, in which, by means of rites, spells, or talismans, men seek to bring about the fulfilment of their wishes, the latter by defensive magic, in which, through the use of amulets or other appropriate methods, they endeavour to ward off dangerous magical influences emanating from the outer world. The pleasant illusion of unreal power has to be paid for by the fear of unreal dangers; nevertheless, since magic itself provides an imaginary, but to some extent reassuring, means of combating these (equally imaginary) dangers, the autism involved may be regarded as exemplifying the pleasure principle in the narrower and more legitimate meaning of that term. As in the case of religion, moreover, practices that are really efficacious may often traditionally be used in connection with rites and beliefs that have a purely suggestive and reassuring value, as when sowing or ploughing is followed by a swinging festival or by leaping in the air (in both cases to make the crops grow high, on the principle of homœopathic magic) or by human copulation (as it were to set nature an example). It seldom occurs to the magic-users to separate, or distinguish between, the realistic and autistic element in the total situation, while the latter provides them with a degree of hope and confidence that the former by itself would fail to give.

[1] *Totem and Taboo.*

Concerning **taboo,** which in some of its aspects is intimately linked with magic, we need add nothing here, as we have already devoted a long chapter to this subject, in which we had good opportunity to study the unrealism it involved—this time, however, of a predominantly restrictive and pleasure-denying character obviously connected with the super-ego or its social equivalents.

An altogether exceptional position with regard to autistic thinking is occupied by **art** [1] (which we have already briefly touched upon in dealing with myth). In one sense the artist himself is a complete realist, inasmuch as he creates something in the material world (whether this be a poem, a painting, a symphony, a statue—or even a dance)—something moreover that others can enjoy. In these two respects he differs fundamentally from the day-dreamer, who creates nothing in the outer world and who satisfies no one but himself. In some other respects, however, art, especially in its inferior products (we may think of the cruder kinds of fiction or realistic illustration), does little more than provide a day-dream in pictorial or printed form, and even in the highest works of art psycho-analysts have been able to show that certain fundamental human desires constitute the ultimate motives that lead the artist to his choice of theme and his public to the enjoyment of it. [2] A good work of art, however, clearly contains much more than this; otherwise every one of us could be an artist. For one thing it involves an adroit manipulation of the element of 'distance' to which we have already referred; any too intimate concern with our personal desires at once destroys the whole æsthetic attitude, while excessive 'distance' reduces æsthetic interest and enjoyment. For another it involves a technical mastery of the material through which the artistic creation is expressed. Again (and only to be achieved by means of this technique) a good work of art is such that through its pattern or 'significant form' it calls into play a highly stimulating and agreeable exercise of the intellectual powers of those who contemplate it. [3] Finally, as has often been pointed out, art in a sense achieves a deeper insight into reality than mere perception, inasmuch as it abstracts from the uninteresting and

---

[1] Cf. Otto Rank, *Der Künstler,* 1907.

[2] A general consideration of the contributions of psychoanalysis to æsthetics will be found in C. Baudouin, *Psychanalyse de l'Art,* 1929.

[3] One of the most interesting attempts to explain in psychological terms this aspect of æsthetic experience will be found in C. Spearman, *Creative Mind,* 1930.

irrelevant more effectually than perception does (though perception itself goes a long way in this direction) and thus presents
us with a sort of quintessence of the aspect of reality that is
relevant to the artist's theme and purpose. But it is clearly
impossible to enter here on the vast and fascinating problems
of æsthetics. It must suffice to indicate that in some respects
art occupies an intermediate position between autism and reality,
but a position that socially, emotionally, and intellectually
seems to provide a satisfaction of a kind and depth which is
far beyond the reach of the more purely autistic forms of
thought, and which perhaps, in its most exalted aspects, can
provide us with a kind of truth and insight which (without
being confused with the concrete structure of reality) even seems
to transcend the power of strict reality thinking itself.

One last kind of autistic thinking may be mentioned—that involved in **play,** which is generally recognized as having certain
affinities to art. Like art, play involves some manipulation of
the material universe, a manipulation that moreover derives its
value from its symbolic significance. Psycho-analysts have
shown that, as in art, this significance may be derived from the
deeper strivings and complexes of the individual. Like day-
dreaming, play seems to be primarily a pleasure-seeking activity,
in which the super-ego has but little influence. Nevertheless
several of those who have elaborated theories of play have held
that it possesses utilitarian aspects (such as serving as an outlet
for surplus activity, an opportunity for practice of the serious
activities of later life, or a means for abreacting or mastering
emotions) that are not present, or at least not so obvious, in
art or day-dreaming. Such distinctions seem to be of doubtful
validity (a case could be made out for art and day-dreaming
serving at least several of the above-mentioned purposes); but
it remains true that play, with its element of make-believe, has
one unique feature that distinguishes it, not only from art and
day-dreams, but from all other forms of autistic thinking—
namely, that it is found in certain animals, who—as with the
human race—indulge in it principally during the period of
youth.

Advantages of Unrealism

The last-mentioned categories, especially those of art and
play, strongly suggest that at least some forms of autistic
activity may have definite functions of biological value and are

not mere signs of weakness, inefficiency, and maladaptation, as the customary attitude towards 'wishful thinking' and the contemplation of the more grotesque and pathological kinds of autism might suggest. What can we say on the basis of our present knowledge concerning the nature of these functions, supposing they exist?

In the first place there is little doubt that art, play, and perhaps to a lesser extent mere day-dreaming and phantasy, have a very considerable value for the individual mind as providing a sort of reserved territory, perhaps we might say a mental gymnasium, in which, through suitable exercise, mental poise and stability can be achieved, difficult situations mastered, and disharmonies resolved. The theory is, of course, as old as Aristotle, and has received ample corroboration from the psycho-analytic study of the autistic activities of adults and of the play and phantasy life of children, as well as from psycho-therapeutic practice itself. We have to face the fact that for many adults, and for still more children, the frustrations and conflicts aroused by reality are often more than can be borne, and that at least an occasional retreat from reality into some form of autistic thinking is almost inevitable, even if only for the purpose of *reculer pour mieux sauter*. Wherein precisely lies the benefit of this retreat from reality, whether through partial relief of painful tensions and urgent needs, through mastery of and familiarity with trying emotional situations by their presentation in playful or æsthetic form, through practice of difficult activities in a recreational setting, through rest and recuperation by removal from difficulties, or through indulgence in easier activities and the contemplation of a brighter imaginary world— this is a complex problem into which we cannot enter here. Probably all these factors are operative in varying degrees and in different cases; but, whatever the means, the evidence that benefit and relief can be obtained by a temporary retirement from the pressing problems of reality is overwhelming, and even if there were no such evidence of benefit, the tendency of the human mind to indulge in autistic regression is so ingrained, that all we could ever hope to do would be to restrain rather than overcome it, and we should have to resign ourselves to the fact that it is one of the fundamental and ineradicable weaknesses of our nature.

Turning for a moment from the individual to the group manifestations of autistic thinking, we may note that, in the opinion of some anthropologists,[1] beliefs of a magical and animistic kind that we now consider entirely delusory may play an important part in primitive society by helping to produce cohesion of the group and submission to leadership, and by providing the necessary reassurance in the face of a hostile environment during the early stages of human culture (as we have ourselves already noted in the case of myth and religion). It has to be admitted, however, that the case for autism in this field [2] is more speculative and less convincing than that as regards individual autistic thinking—while the evils involved (in the perpetuation of delusions by all the forces of social prestige) are a great deal more apparent.

With regard to the simpler kinds of 'wishful thinking', it would seem fairly easy, in theory at least, to delimit their spheres of usefulness and harmfulness. In so far as unjustified optimism prevents us from taking reasonable precautions to deal with possible disasters, it is unquestionably dangerous, and will sooner or later land us into trouble. No one will excuse a doctor, engineer, or architect who has allowed himself to be lulled by wishful thinking into taking risks, when the means of ensuring safety are well known and within his power. On the other hand there are many matters—including some that may be of life-and-death importance—as regards which both our knowledge and our power are limited, perhaps almost to vanishing point. As regards these matters optimism has survival value even when the prospects are blackest, inasmuch as it gives us strength and confidence to deal successfully with difficulties and dangers to which we might otherwise succumb, and enables us to make full use of any lucky chances that may come our way. The power of confidence in war, sport, personal ambitions, and recovery from illness is universally recognized; it is dangerous only when it leads to gross neglect of difficulties that can easily be foreseen. Not the least of its advantages is that it tends to generate a corresponding doubt or lack of confidence in human opponents. The present war has already illustrated several of these factors: collapse in the face of the confidence displayed by an enemy, the serious under-estimation

---

[1] E.g. Carveth Read, *The Origin of Man and of his Superstitions*, 1920—especially ch. 8; R. R. Marett, *Head, Heart, and Hands in Human Evolution*, 1935.

[2] The argument is similar to that often advanced to-day by those who, although they have no personal need for revealed religion, maintain that it may still be necessary for the relatively uncultured 'masses'.

of dangers and obstacles, and on the other hand the great power of resistance conferred on those who, in more than one part of the world, even after a 'perfect cataract of disasters' and in a period of utmost peril, refused to contemplate emotionally the possibility of ultimate defeat. As regards our own country, we can understand and perhaps even sympathize a little with the irritation of Lord Haw Haw when he complained that the motto of the British seemed to be, 'The more we have retreated, the less we are defeated',[1] and with the predicament of the Goebbels internal propaganda machine when, late in 1940, it felt obliged to warn its listeners that, although of course the war was really over, the British were so stupid that it must be expected that they would take a long time to realize this fact. A stupidity of this kind, based on what was at the moment a legitimate and useful form of wishful thinking (since on a purely objective estimate the outlook was intensely black), clearly makes for strength; as one observer put it, 'The British lack of imagination amounts to nothing less than genius'.

At the present time we know rather more about the psychology of depression and pessimism than about that of optimism—perhaps because those who suffer from the former condition are much more likely to seek psychotherapeutic help. Nevertheless, from such little knowledge as we have, we seem justified in assuming that optimism depends, as regards its degree and depth of confidence, to some extent upon the relation between the super-ego and the id. When wishful thinking is no more than a manifestation of the id in revolt—both against reality and against the super-ego—it is likely to be crude, blatant, and perhaps superficial, i.e. with an underlying distressful element of doubt; it is also liable to fluctuate with periods of depression, much in the way that mania may alternate with melancholia. A deeper kind of confidence and optimism is one that depends upon a fundamental harmony between the id and the super-ego, perhaps of the kind that we discussed in Chapter XIII. If there is any truth in this suggestion, it would not only seem to be of great importance for individual destiny and happiness, but its application to groups and nations should present some fascinating problems [2] to the social psychologist.

[1] It is interesting however to note that, at the moment of writing (August, 1943), the Nazis seem to be adopting a very similar attitude themselves—at any rate in their official propaganda.

[2] It seems likely that the mere length of time during which a nation has preserved its distinctive national and political unity would lead to a certain

Two further considerations should perhaps be borne in mind in assessing the value of 'wishful' as contrasted with 'realistic' thinking. The one relates to the general difficulty of knowing the 'real' and being able to distinguish it from the wishful, the phantastic, the illusory. Psychologists, and perhaps still more psychopathologists, are nearly always anxious to avoid philosophical questions, and when we read the literature on autism, the pleasure principle, the reality principle, etc., we may occasionally harbour justifiable suspicions that the metaphysical and epistemological aspects of the problems involved are being somewhat cavalierly treated—and this in spite of the fact that child analysts have considerably stressed the difficulty in learning to distinguish between the self and the not-self in the early days of life (see Chapter IX). But it remains true that in psychology it is possible to go a long way without coming too obviously and uncomfortably near these questions. In mental science, as in physical science and in ordinary life, we employ the various criteria of truth—'consistency' with our own and others' knowledge, 'correspondence' with supposed objective standards, and the 'pragmatic' test of 'does it work?'—with a somewhat liberal impartiality and a lighthearted reference to our own convenience. On the whole the method serves us fairly well, but the progress of science in recent times has shown the possi-

---

deep national confidence of a kind that suggests internal harmony between id and super-ego and (when the super-ego is projected) might lead to the idea of enjoying some special form of divine protection or approval. Such questions as the following would then arise: How far and in what sense are we justified at all in speaking of the id and the super-ego of groups (clearly this is only a special aspect of the general problem of the 'group mind')? In so far as we are justified, what is the special relation between the super-ego and the id in the case of Britain (with its long continuous traditions), France (with an equally long history but more broken political traditions), Germany and Italy (with their much shorter history as political units, but with an intense and rather strained effort to assert their right to greatness), Japan (with a very long continuous history and, as we have been given to understand, a much deeper moral confidence than Germany, though making the same claims to rightful domination), China (with its long history but incomplete unity), the U.S.A. and U.S.S.R. (both relatively young and with their own special problems)? How far does the strength of the national super-ego itself (as distinct from its relations to the id) depend on long-standing traditions (the efforts of Germany, Italy, and, quite recently, of the U.S.S.R. to hark back to old traditions—in the case of the two former, traditions of a remote past—would seem to suggest such a connection)? How far is a more permanently satisfactory relation between id and super-ego responsible for the relatively quiet confidence of such nations as Britain, as contrasted with the bluster and sabre-rattling of Germany ('that strange gesticulating object across the North Sea', as Wilfred Trotter called it in the last war)? How far does the British preference for understatement or humour, rather than heroics, represent a fundamentally more or less secure moral position? What is there in common between British and Japanese restraint on emotional expression?

bility of so many things that but a little earlier would have been thought impossible that it behoves us to adopt an attitude of caution and humility in dealing with the aspirations of those whom we might be inclined to dismiss as cranks, dreamers, or fanatics, utterly oblivious of the limitations imposed by the real world. Can we be so sure as to what these limitations are? More especially perhaps is this the case when wishful thinking or eccentric behaviour based thereon relate primarily to ethical and social matters. Even those whom we unhesitatingly dub insane may sometimes flout our standards and conventions in a way that, to those not accustomed to these standards, might appear quite sensible. On a very hot day a nurse in a mental hospital complained to the doctor that she was utterly exhausted by her struggles with a patient who insisted on taking off all her clothes the moment she was left to herself. 'Nurse,' replied the doctor, 'I ask you: who is the madder, you or she?' There was obviously much to be said for the doctor's point of view. Turning from the small world of the asylum to the vast canvas of world history, we may remember that Mahomet, Joan of Arc, Adolf Hitler (among many others) were psychopaths, who by the strength given them by the very intensity of their wishes have for good or evil exercised a colossal influence on the fortunes of mankind. To wish wholeheartedly for change, though not in itself sufficient, is yet the most essential require-ment to bring change about. The progressive peoples who have done most to adapt reality to suit their needs are those who, in Varendonck's expressive phrase, are 'continuously tormented by desire'.[1] When a Normanby Islander saw the refrigerator that Róheim had brought with him his comment was, 'O, White Man, your wisdom is like madness', and, enlightened concerning some further wonders of Western civilization, he added that 'he could see no point in making the ships so big or the drinking water so cold'.[2] Contrast this with the advertisers' slogan in present-day United States papers, 'How American, always to want something better!' The realist, with his feet firmly planted on the earth, may sometimes be playing the rôle of the Normanby Islander and the dreamer or wishful thinker that of the American, for under modern conditions his dreams and wishes often have a way of coming true.

We may apply this same lesson to our post-war problems,

---

[1] J. Varendonck, *L'Évolution des Facultés Conscientes* (1921), 171.
[2] G. Róheim, *The Riddle of the Sphinx*, 279.

both national and international. Confronted with the conflict-ing interests, standards, and traditions of different groups, and with the general perversities of human nature, we might well be inclined to resign ourselves to pessimistic 'realism' and to regard the adequate solution of these problems as a hopeless task. But when we remember the success that has eventually rewarded the efforts of some of those who must at first have seemed visionaries of the most unrealistic and fanatic kind (e.g. the early Christians, those who first sought to abolish slavery, the first trade unionists, the early advocates of women's rights, or—in another sphere—those who down the ages have wrestled with the problem of human flight), we may pause to consider whether we have not after all a right, perhaps even a duty, to be optimistic,[1] in spite of the overwhelming nature of the tasks before us. Without optimism we shall certainly fail; with its help we *may* succeed—and meantime, whether we eventually succeed or fail, we shall at least enjoy the undoubted benefit of immediate greater happiness.[2]

The second consideration has to do with the fact that, as culture advances, the rôle of playful and artistic activities (in the widest sense, as distinct from the 'serious business' of life) tends to grow ever greater. The increase of leisure is recognized by most of us as a desirable social aim, but leisure activities usually contain a greater element of autism than do those that come under the heading of work. Much, probably most, of the advance of culture is due to men who during a considerable portion of their time have been comparatively free from the pressure of urgent 'realistic' tasks. Indeed in many of the higher forms of activity it becomes increasingly difficult to distinguish between work and leisure. It may be fairly easy for the worker at a factory bench or in the fields to say exactly how many hours' work he does a day. The manager in his office is less obviously and continuously 'busy' at some immediate job, but his comparatively leisurely activities may be none the less essential, and his work is more likely to continue to occupy

---

[1] Cp. W. B. Curry, 'Is There a Duty of Optimism?' *Monthly Record of the South Place Ethical Society*, August, 1943.

[2] On the very day these words were written Mr F. D. Roosevelt said at the conclusion of the Quebec Conference: 'I am everlastingly angry only at those who assert vociferously that the Four Freedoms of the Atlantic Charter are nonsense because they are unattainable. If they had lived a century and a half ago they would have sneered and said that the Declaration of Independence was utter piffle. If they had lived nearly a thousand years ago they would have laughed uproariously at the ideals of Magna Carta'.

his thoughts when he is at home. Who can say that the philosopher, writer, artist, or scientist is only profitably occupied (even from the realistic point of view) when he is at his desk, his easel, or among his test-tubes ? Beethoven's country walks have enriched the world to a far greater extent than the more obviously laborious activities of many millions of lesser men. And does not 'education for leisure' imply the hope that each of us in our degree, freed for a large portion of our time from the more urgent calls upon our energy, may similarly become occupied in ways that bring out our higher capacities for the pleasure and profit of ourselves and others ? In so far as we succeed in this, the boundaries between work and play, between realistic activities and those in which there is a considerable element of autistic freedom, are likely to become ever more difficult to draw. As Stern correctly emphasized in his doctrine of *Ernstspiel*,[1] our orectic life may vary not only in its intensity but in its 'seriousness', and the range within the latter dimension may be no less than that within the former ; in our own terminology, realism and autism may be mixed in every possible degree.

This last point brings us to a fundamental matter which has perhaps not been adequately stressed, especially in psychotherapeutic literature. When men acquired the power of conception, of imagination, of 'free ideas' and images that could roam at will unfettered by the immediate data provided by the sense organs, they became possessed of a two-edged weapon that could be used for either good or ill. Imagination, by enabling us to foresee possible contingencies before they arise and to study hypothetical situations that are not actually present, provides us with a most potent means for dealing with reality. It became possible for us, without incurring danger and with a minimum expenditure of energy, to avoid errors and devise new methods of satisfying our desires. But the mere imaginary contemplation of situations in which desire is gratified can itself be very pleasant, whereas the steps required before the gratification is obtained in reality may be arduous and painful; sometimes they may even be impossible. There is therefore a temptation to dally long, and even permanently, at the stage of mere imagination. Herein lies very probably the fundamental cause of wishful thinking and of the pleasant forms of autistic thinking generally, though it may be powerfully

---

[1] William Stern, '"Ernstspiel" and the Affective Life,' *Feelings and Emotions* (*The Wittenberg Symposium*), ed. M. L. Reymert, 1928.

supported by certain circumstances of our early life to which psycho-analysts have drawn attention: to wit, the fact that in the first period of our existence our needs were satisfied almost entirely by the ministrations of others, that a little later we used what Ferenczi [1] has called 'magic cries and gestures' to call attention to these needs, and that, as already observed, we only gradually acquired the power of distinguishing the self from the outer world (a power which we hold precariously and only in conditions of clear consciousness and which gradually slips from us every evening as we fall asleep). The ever-present possibility of this short-cut to satisfaction, which tends to make us shirk the harder route of satisfaction through reality (by autoplastic or alloplastic adaptation), is one of the great disadvantages of conception and imagination; the very means of the relatively great control of reality that we human beings possess is also a means by which we can evade reality—often in the long run at our peril. Fortunately, perhaps, severe limits are set to wishful thinking so far as most of our immediate personal bodily needs are concerned.

> O, who can hold a fire in his hands
> By thinking on the frosty Caucasus,
> Or cloy the hungry edge of appetite
> By bare imagination of a feast,
> Or wallow naked in December snow
> By thinking on fantastic summer's heat?

But in less immediately urgent matters, such as those of sex and personal ambition, a rich field is open to the day-dreamer.

The other great drawback of imagination consists in the possibility of dwelling (this time not under the influence of desire but under that of fear and guilt) upon the dangers, pains, and difficulties that life may have in store for us. As Shakespeare has it again:

> Cowards die many times before their deaths;
> The valiant never taste of death but once.

But psycho-analysis has shown us that it is not only conscious wishful or fearful thinking that makes us unrealistic. This may be serious enough, but at least it allows us to retain our fundamental ability to distinguish between desires and fears on the one hand and the properties of reality upon the other. A more thoroughgoing distortion of reality is liable to be produced by the unconscious forces, with their tendency to undergo dis-

[1] S. Ferenczi, 'The Development of the Sense of Reality,' *Contributions to Psycho-analysis*, 1916. First published 1913.

placement, symbolization, projection, etc., and thus to produce an attitude so remote from reality that from the point of view of conscious reason it can only be described as that of a madman. These unconscious forces impelling towards autism are perhaps the heaviest price that human beings have had to pay for their power to free themselves from the thrall of the immediate external environment. The fact, however, that the race has continued to exist for a million years or more, and that during the latter part of this period it has gained an ever-increasing control over the environment, seems to show that the disadvantages of imagination are on the whole more than compensated by its benefits—in other words, that men have not too drastically misused the mental weapon with which they have been endowed.

Nevertheless it is legitimate to ask: What good are the deeper levels of autistic thinking, with their queer symbolisms and unrealisms? Have they any biological or cultural value at all, or are they just an inevitable but burdensome by-product of the faculty of imagination? Though we are hardly yet in a position to give an assured and final answer, it is at least possible to advance a few considerations in favour of the view that they have some useful function. Thus we know that symbolism is used as a delicate means of graduating our emotions, often reducing them when a direct non-symbolic expression would arouse too overwhelming a degree of feeling, sometimes increasing them when it is required to mobilize our energies around some object or idea that would otherwise be too dull or indifferent to impel to action.[1] We know also that, just as on the one hand symbolism and displacement can lead to neurotic symptoms that are unhelpful and unrealistic, they can on the other hand also lead to those biologically and socially useful re-directions of emotional energy that are called sublimations, so that our crude instinctive tendencies are able in this way to be used in the service of the various complex and sophisticated activities that ultimately constitute civilization. It may be too that, as Jung and his followers appear to hold, a temporary regression to a deep level of autistic thinking can sometimes act recuperatively, or perhaps even creatively, in such a way as to enable us to deal more efficiently with grave problems and difficulties,

[1] The most profound study of symbolism from these points of view is to be found in Ernest Jones, 'The Theory of Symbolism' (1916), *Papers on Psychoanalysis*, 2nd ed., 1918.

both those presented by the external world and by our own inner conflicts. But our present knowledge scarcely enables us to say whether these are, as it were, secondary and incidental benefits that we have contrived to extract from the deeper levels of autistic thinking, which in themselves are merely an encumbrance, or whether these levels have a primary function of their own, without which the human mind might not have achieved its unique capacity.

Vindication of Realism

Of the disadvantages of autistic thinking and the disabilities it imposes on our attempts to deal with 'real' problems there can unfortunately be no doubt. Among the most urgent of such problems in the modern world are those connected with our social life and the relations between the large organized national groups into which human populations are now split up. The human intellect, which in other spheres has such vast achievements to its credit, should by itself be quite capable of dealing with these problems. But it is obvious that, in the field of its great triumphs, the intellect has attained the necessary control and evolved the necessary methods to enable it to work more or less unimpeded by autism and wishful thinking. As examples of these methods we can point to the stringent tests and elaborate verificatory techniques that scientists have devised and habitually employ—the purpose of which is to avoid premature conclusions based on insufficient or biased evidence. In social matters however, where our knowledge is less, the phenomena in some respects more complicated, and our emotions and prejudices greater, the attainment of intellectual control has so far proved much more difficult. Even if we were wholeheartedly trying to attain it, the task would be a hard one. But often we do not even want to try; and indeed the Nazis have gone so far as to brand the whole objective attitude in social and political matters as immoral—in much the same way as was done in an earlier epoch by the Church in matters of physical science. Along such lines the world can only be divided into competing groups of madmen, each group armed with all the lethal weapons that the human mind in the spheres where it is allowed to think objectively can so effectually provide. It is difficult to imagine that this unhappy combination of realism and unrealism will not eventually prove suicidal.

To avoid the threatened disaster men must learn to limit

realistically their group ambitions in the same way as they have learnt to limit their personal 'omnipotence', both in their dealings with other individuals and in relation to the physical world. In the conquest of this last, socio-political, citadel of autism, psychology (and in particular psycho-analysis) may prove a useful—indeed an essential—tool. Just as the advance of the physical and biological sciences, through the weight of their cumulative evidence, overcame the moral and theological resistances to an objective appreciation of the extra-human world, so, we may hope, will the progress of scientific social psychology, by revealing something of the nature of the mental forces operating within and between human societies, eventually prove the means of attaining a similar objectivity with regard to social and political problems.

It is clear that such an objective attitude as regards human affairs will demand an immense sacrifice of prejudices that are dear to us, prejudices that spring ultimately from the id (in the form of displacements of personal desires on to the group) or from the super-ego (which in its origin and development is so intimately dependent on the group, and which, as we have seen, can be projected back upon the group). But such was also the case as regards our view of the physical world, where successive discoveries, concerning the place and relative significance of the Earth within the Universe and the position of mankind in the history of the Earth, have done violence, alike to our narcissistic feelings of self-importance and to our religious and moral notions of a God to whom the welfare of the human race (or perhaps even some small part of it) was supposed to be a matter of special interest and concern.[1] Fortunately the discovery of facts about the Universe, the pursuit of science for its own sake and for the sake of the 'real' benefits it can confer, has shown itself to be an activity that can make a profound appeal to the human emotions—which can therefore be enlisted on the side of realism. Popular expositions of the 'wonders' or the 'romance' of science may often seem a little childish and primitive to the trained scientific worker, especially when they touch upon his own field. But both realistically and morally they represent an immense advance upon appeals to theological, political, economic, or racial prejudice. Furthermore, the successful pursuit of science in any field, demanding as it does

[1] Cp. S. Freud, 'One of the Difficulties of Psycho-analysis' (1917), *Collected Papers*, iv, 347.

ingenuity, care, patience, an ability to tolerate uncertainty, and often also to sacrifice cherished theories and beliefs, seems to constitute a far more 'civilized' method of discipline (and, if necessary, of satisfying the 'need for punishment') than the asceticisms of religious penance or of war; while the complex techniques of scientific research represent a similar improvement on the rituals of the cloister or the parade ground. There is ample evidence that human beings can be intensely interested in the 'romance of reality',[1] and we may reasonably hope that with the advance of social and psychological science this romance will extend to the realities of human society and the human mind.[2] But in any case, whether we find the process romantic or otherwise, it is only when we have freed ourselves from the distortions due both to wishful thinking and to fear and guilt, and have become able to think objectively on social and political questions, that we shall be justified in regarding our civilization as reasonably secure. The acquirement of this attitude is the most urgent task of present-day culture. This is the real Riddle of the Sphinx, which, as seems all too likely, the human race must solve or perish.

CHAPTER XVI

THE PSYCHOLOGY OF MORAL PROGRESS

THE time has come to do a little stocktaking. What lessons can we learn from psycho-analysis concerning the general nature of human morality and the general lines of moral progress? We have learnt that morality—in the sense of ideals to be attained, restraints to be exercised, guilt to be felt, and punishment to be endured—is deeply embedded in the human mind. Man is indeed fundamentally a moral animal. But we have

---

[1] As an instance of the arousal of intense and widespread interest in quite a difficult branch of applied science, we may call to mind the popular enthusiasm of a few years ago for the theory and practice of wireless transmission and reception. The considerable success of one or two popular journals on psychology shows that potentially there is a widespread interest in this field also. Unfortunately the lack of an assured basis on many fundamental issues, the fear of the disturbing nature of psychological 'revelations', the divergent approach and varying terminology of the different schools, together with a certain admixture, in some popular expositions, of scientific psychology with 'uplift', superstition, or pure charlatanry, all combine to make a satisfactory popularization of psychology difficult at the present moment.

[2] For an eloquent appeal for the development of this point of view see Janet Chance, *The Romance of Reality*, 1934.

also learnt that much of his morality is crude and primitive, ill adapted to reality, and often at variance both with his intellect and with his higher conscious aspirations.   Just as on the one hand man's bodily structure is not entirely adapted to his physical environment and way of life, but contains primitive features that have outworn such usefulness as they may once have had, while on the other his social institutions and traditions exhibit an inertia that makes them often out of harmony with the requirements of a rapidly changing civilization, so also his moral constitution is in many respects ill suited to his present cultural needs.   Progress in each case demands an abandonment of the old and maladapted features.   As regards his fundamental bodily characteristics, man can at present do little to further his own evolution (though the science of genetics has put some limited means at his disposal, should he care to avail himself of them).   Psychology has taught that even his mental and moral characteristics are far from being completely amenable to conscious will and deliberation and that, since social institutions are ultimately dependent on mental processes, human society also may be less easy to reform than some Utopians have believed.   Our ultimate mental and moral capacities, like our ultimate physical characteristics, can probably be changed only by biological methods.   Nevertheless the purpose to which we put these capacities, like the way in which we use our bodies, depends (even when we make full allowance for the power of the unconscious) to a considerable extent upon our conscious decisions; and the aim of psycho-analysis is indeed to enlarge the sphere of conscious influence by making us aware of mental operations that were previously beyond our knowledge and control.   In this way psycho-analysis (like other branches of psychology) may influence our moral goals in the manner discussed in Chapter I.

If we are to make the most of such control of our moral powers as we possess, or can acquire, we should have at least some guiding notions concerning the main lines of moral progress and development.   How far is it possible to derive such notions from the data with which psycho-analytic study has provided us?   The general implications of the facts that we have passed in review do indeed seem fairly clear, and it is possible to formulate them under a few main headings.   These headings will deal with different aspects of the same basic process of development rather than with independent processes, but for

Q

the sake of simplicity and clarity it may be helpful to consider
them in relative isolation one by one. Proceeding in this way
we may perhaps distinguish eight general tendencies in the
psychology of moral progress. No claim is made on behalf of
these 'tendencies' that they constitute the only possible, or even
the best, basis of classification; they do however seem to emerge
easily and naturally from our preceding discussion of the
relevant psycho-analytic data.

(1) **From Egocentricity to Sociality.**—We mention this
first, as it accords best with the viewpoint of traditional
morality and is in all respects the most generally accepted.
As we grow up, we become increasingly aware of the presence
and claims of others and of the necessity of restraining our own
satisfactions where they conflict with those of others. This
necessity finds traditional expression in such concepts as
'Justice', 'Kindness', 'Tolerance', 'Fair-play', as well as in
such more exalted maxims as 'Do as you would be done by',
'Love thy neighbour as thyself', or 'From each according to his
ability, to each according to his need'. In the beginning this is
largely, or perhaps entirely, a matter of super-ego regulation,
demanding frequent inhibition of egoistic impulses—and to some
extent we have to continue the exercise of such restraints
throughout our lives. With increasing experience, however,
even the most selfish and inconsiderate of us become conditioned
to certain elementary forms of respect for the rights, feelings,
and conveniences of others; the necessary restraints become
habits that assert themselves with a minimum of friction.
Fortunately, moreover, we are by our very nature social as well
as egoistic beings. Dependent as we are on others, we learn
very early in life to interpret the behaviour and expressions of
those about us, in fact to become interested in them. From
the interpretation of their expression it is but a small step for
us to feel sympathy with them—at first perhaps by the direct
contagion of emotion that McDougall has called primitive
passive sympathy, or, as Humphrey [1] has suggested, in virtue of
conditioning (the visual, and perhaps auditory, impressions of
another's pleasure or distress being similar to those of one's
own); later by a fuller and more conscious appreciation of the
feelings of others, so that eventually our needs are satisfied in,
through, and with the satisfactions of others. As development

---

[1] G. Humphrey, 'The Conditioned Reflex and the Elementary Social Reaction,'
J. Abn. and Soc. Psychol. (1922), 17, 113.

—much in the same way as even the most brilliant general is dependent on the faithful following of his instructions by all lesser ranks.

(3) **From Autism to Realism.**—This should be clear enough after what was said in the last chapter. We need perhaps only add by way of a reminder that this transition is largely coincident with that from the Unconscious to the Conscious, since consciousness appears to be capable of a much more accurate and delicate appreciation of reality than is the unconscious.

(4) **From Moral Inhibition to Spontaneous 'Goodness'.**— This is one of the most important tendencies and one to which we ourselves in our review have perhaps paid inadequate attention. Throughout the ages there have been rebellious spirits who have held that the spontaneous human impulses are better than men, misled by their own institutions and traditions, have usually been willing to believe, and that moral control, whether exercised by an external authority or by internal conscience, has tended to suppress and distort much of this natural goodness. With the coming of psycho-analysis important further evidence for the harm done by excessive repression became available and, as noted in Chapter III, the revolt against traditional morality thereby became intensified. A considerable number of more or less 'left-wing' writers (especially those interested in the fields of education and sexology) have set out to combat what they hold to be a vast and pernicious overstressing of guilt and sin, have emphasized man's natural tendencies to love, sympathy, and co-operation, and have suggested that many of the evils (e.g. exaggerated aggression and obsessive preoccupation with matters of sex) which repressive morality seeks to subdue are themselves unhealthy products of this very morality, which has so distorted human nature that we have come to regard as 'normal' what is in reality no more than a gross and cruel caricature.

Although many of these writers freely acknowledge their indebtedness to psycho-analysis, there are some who maintain (though with varying degrees of emphasis) that psycho-analysts themselves have failed to realize the full implications of their own discoveries, have been too ready to accept prevailing social standards, and have lacked the insight or the courage to recognize repressive morality for the evil thing it is. Thus (to mention only a few of the more recent and more psychologically

minded of the writers in question) Suttie [1] has stressed the tragic
consequences of the 'taboo on tenderness' resulting from the
repression of love (both in its infantile and later sexual and
social aspects), and considers that most forms of aggression,
delinquency, anxiety, together with the thirst for power or
admiration, are products of thwarted love. Ranyard West [2]
holds that there are two primary instincts in man, the aggressive
and the social instinct, and that, except for some rare outbursts
and for institutionalized forms of aggression such as war, the
latter nearly always triumphs over the former. He adds,
however, that there is an aggressive-obsessional type of person
(to which certain eminent writers, including Hobbes and Freud,
belong) in whom, owing to unfortunate hereditary or developmental influences, aggression is abnormally strong and has to
be held in check by reaction formations or other mechanisms
of an obsessional kind. It is the latent aggression of such
persons, he suggests, that is liable to stampede the more easy-
going and peaceable majority into war or other manifestations
of mass-criminality. Reich [3] lays more emphasis on the repression of sex, and considers that psycho-analysis in its later
developments has neglected the importance of its early discoveries in this field; he departs however from Freud's own early
formulations in holding that the genital impulse, connected as it
is with the unique phenomenon of orgasm, differs in certain
fundamental respects from the other 'component instincts'.
When, after applying his special therapeutic technique, he had
broken down the repressions and established the full capacity
for the 'orgasm reflex', he observed a great improvement in
the social qualities of his patients. He therefore assumes that
sexual inhibition constitutes one of the most important roots
of our social discontents—a position which in a rather more
generalized form, and with greater emphasis on childhood
factors, had already, though perhaps more tentatively, been
adopted by Money-Kyrle.[4] A number of the writers taking up
this general point of view [5] believe that excessive repression is
connected with the child's attitude to the father, and hold that
the desirable greater degree of freedom involves a more generous
tolerance and encouragement of mother-love and a correspond-

---

[1] Ian D. Suttie, *The Origins of Love and Hate*, 1935.
[2] Ranyard West, *Conscience and Society*, 1942.
[3] Wilhelm Reich, *The Function of the Orgasm*, 1942, and several earlier works.
[4] R. Money-Kyrle, *Aspasia, the Future of Amorality*, 1932.
[5] E.g. Suttie, *op. cit.*; R. Briffault, *The Mothers*, 1927; *Sin and Sex*, 1931.

ing increased emphasis on the matriarchal, as contrasted with the patriarchal, aspects of society (attention being sometimes drawn in this connection to Freud's preoccupation with what might broadly be called patriarchal problems). Recent anthropological work, particularly that of Malinowski, Róheim, Mead, and Benedict, as also that of members of the Diffusionist school such as Elliott Smith and Perry, is at the same time often called upon to prove the importance of early environment and cultural tradition as affecting the relative predominance of peaceable, friendly, and tolerant, as compared with predatory and competitive, social attitudes, both of whole societies and of the individuals composing them.

There is no doubt very considerable truth in the general statement that our moral inhibitions are responsible for the suppression and distortion of much that is good in human nature, and that many of our less amiable characteristics are due not so much to our faulty instinctive equipment as to the extreme crudity of our moral mechanisms. There is perhaps, too, a measure of justice in the contention that psycho-analysis, with its recent absorption in the problems of aggression, has to some extent lost sight of the evils of excessive repression, has drawn in some respects too unflattering a picture of human nature,[1] and has too complacently accepted existing repressive morality.[2] But apart from details—important as many of these may be—the general position advocated by these authors is perfectly in harmony with the main conclusions that emerge from the contributions that psycho-analysis has made to the study of morality and with the recognized therapeutic aim of psycho-analysis itself. Psycho-analysis does in effect seek to reduce guilt and moral conflict and to allow the freest possible use of our instinctive energies in the service of the individual and the community. In doing so, it also tends to lighten the incidence of taboo and the 'need for punishment', as exhibited

[1] Lloyd Morgan once suggested that it was a good rule in animal psychology never to interpret in terms of higher-level mentality what could be satisfactorily accounted for by lower-level processes. The critics we are here considering might perhaps have said (though I do not think they have actually done so) that the psycho-analysts had adopted an analogous rule in the interpretation of human moral conduct, never imputing a higher motive if reason could be found for believing the behaviour in question to be due to a lower one. Of course neither in the sphere of animal intelligence nor in that of human morals can a rule of this kind be regarded as infallible.

[2] It will be noted that this objection to psycho-analysis is the exact opposite of that which, as we mentioned in Chapter III, was formerly brought against it on the ground that it was subversive of morality by undoing repressions and encouraging unsocial tendencies.

in asceticism, the Polycrates complex, and the scapegoat *motif*, while in the doctrine of sublimation it indicates a way in which a satisfactory compromise between the super-ego and the primitive id impulses may be attained, a way in which our instincts can find an unobstructed outlet in harmony with our cultural ideals.[1] Such relatively free and frictionless manifestations of instinct it would regard as ethically far more desirable than reaction formations, obsessional behaviour, or any of the other forms of conduct in which the inhibitory influence of the super-ego obviously plays a major rôle. It would agree that the opposition between the id and the super-ego, though it may be unavoidable and necessary, cannot be regarded as the highest achievement of the moral life, which is much better represented (at the conscious and introspectable level) by smooth coalescence of wish and duty of the kind to which Frenkel's and Weisskopf's subjects often refer in the study with which we dealt in Chapter II. Whatever may be the difference between the detailed views of the majority of psycho-analysts and those of the various writers with whom we have just been dealing, it is safe to say that in general terms the process of development, as seen in the light of psychoanalysis, involves a transition from a relatively crude moral compulsion to a relatively free and spontaneous play of those natural impulses of men that are compatible with, or conduce to, harmonious social life.

(5) **From Aggression to Tolerance and Love.**—This tendency is closely associated with the previous one and also with our No. (1). Since, as we have seen, super-ego action is intimately connected with aggression, either in its nemesistic form (as turned against the self) or as re-projected outwards on to scapegoats, in so far as sublimation or any other form of relatively conflict-free moral behaviour takes the place of more direct super-ego control, there tends to be a reduction in aggression. Even more obviously is such a reduction implied in the transition from egocentricity to sociality. As regards this latter, the ethical desirability of diminishing aggression connected with egoistic self-seeking has been clear to the great moral teachers throughout the ages; but the perhaps equally important connection of aggression with morality itself has been

---

[1] Though it is true that the more detailed theoretical interpretation of sublimation presents us with a number of difficult problems that psychologists are very far from having solved. See J. C. Flugel, 'Sublimation: its Nature and Conditions,' *Brit. J. Ed. Psychol* (1942), 12, 10.

for the most part but dimly and implicitly recognized, and it is one of the great achievements of psycho-analysis that it has made the matter plain (as it is one of the chief aims of the present volume to draw attention to this contribution in its general psychological and moral setting).

But although the general nature of the transition under this heading is so evident, there are a number of outstanding problems with regard to aggression about which there is still uncertainty and dispute among psychologists. In particular there are two rather closely interconnected questions that are in the forefront at the present moment:

(*a*) Is aggression an 'appetitive' or a 'reactive' instinct in Drever's sense of these terms? [1] That is to say, is it—like hunger, thirst, or sex—largely determined by our organic constitution, so that there is something in the nature of a periodic internally generated need to express aggression; or is it—like curiosity or 'wonder' (in McDougall's sense)—only called into operation by certain circumstances or conditions in the outer world? Freud, in most of his writings, seems to take the former view (though he does not use Drever's terms that we have here adopted). McDougall and many other psychologists (including some psycho-analysts) incline rather to the latter, and consider that aggression is in the nature of a biologically determined reaction to a frustrating situation, [2] whereby energy is mobilized for the purpose of overcoming the obstacles that prevent the fulfilment of some desire. The former appears to be a more gloomy view than the latter. If aggression is a need like hunger, men can no more be expected to reduce their aggressiveness than to diminish their desire for food. The most that we could do in the matter would be to discourage the aggressive equivalent of gluttony and to find the least harmful and destructive channel for the remaining irreducible aggression (e.g. some method which would bear a relation to pugnacity similar to that of vegetarianism in the sphere of nutrition). On the other hand, if aggression is purely a reaction to frustration, we can, in theory at least, hope to diminish it by reducing the frequency and intensity of frustration. In actual practice of course, as has been pointed out by several recent writers, the difference is not so great as might at first appear,

---

[1] James Drever, *Instinct in Man*, 1917.
[2] A full discussion of the relations between frustration and aggression will be found in John Dollard *et al.*, *Frustration and Aggression*, 1944.

since a certain amount of frustration is inevitable, especially in early life. Nevertheless, on the second view, we can reasonably hope to produce a very considerable reduction of aggression by the avoidance of unnecessary sources of irritation and frustration (which is what we commonly mean, for instance, by the 'tactful handling of a difficult situation'); and it is this which the writers referred to under the last heading have in mind when they imply that a needlessly frustrating moral code encourages aggression while suppressing natural human kindliness.

(b) What are we ultimately to understand by aggression? How are we to distinguish it from other forms of positive reaction whereby we deal actively with some object or situation? This is a problem implied by the very word 'aggression', which in the last resort means an approach or 'going towards'. At first sight there might seem to be no difficulty in distinguishing between an attitude of love, attraction, or interest on the one hand, and one of hate, combativeness, or destructiveness upon the other; the emotions of a man who wants to get into closer contact with a loved woman, to possess some precious work of art, to learn more of some fascinating branch of scientific study, might seem to differ *toto cœlo* from those of one who seeks to slay his rival, to kill some dangerous beast, or to destroy some hated object, such as the flag of an oppressor nation. And yet on closer inspection there appear to be some elements in common. Did we not see, in dealing with sado-masochism in Chapter VIII, that courtship and sexual approach may involve an appreciable element of aggression? Does not to 'possess' mean to 'sit upon'? And do we not speak of 'getting to grips with' or 'mastering' a scientific problem—the same terms that we might use in describing an attack upon an enemy? In these situations, and in many more, there is an element of forceful self-assertion which seems to be common to reactions of both love and hate, even though the total pattern of behaviour may be very different. Freud might say that we are confronted here with admixtures of Eros and Thanatos in varying degrees. In any case we seem justified in applying the psycho-analytic concept of ambivalence; and this will serve to remind us that psycho-analysts have consistently maintained that more developed attitudes and modes of conduct are less ambivalent than primitive ones. In the latter (as, for instance, the early reactions of the young child that we studied in Chapter IX), love and hate are rather intimately fused; it is only the gradual defusion of the two attitudes (if we may use Ernest Jones's suggestion to which we referred in Chapter VIII) that makes a relatively 'pure' love possible.[1] . Even though the process is seldom if ever complete, this defusion would seem to be an essential element of moral progress and conduces to the possibility and ultimate prevalence of love and tolerance. Perhaps (as some psycho-analysts have definitely stated and still more have implied) at the most primitive levels all stimuli are painful and all are hated as disturbers of the Nirvana state—as would seem also to be the case with one who is forcibly awakened from deep sleep. At higher levels some are pleasant, and we learn indeed that some may be intensely satisfying. In the last resort, perhaps, it is this transition from the attitude of feeling painfully disturbed to that of active joyous welcoming or seeking that constitutes the basis of the change from aggression to love that concerns us here.

(6) **From Fear to Security.**—This general tendency is closely connected with the previous one, inasmuch as a great deal of fear and anxiety arises indirectly from the projection or introjection of aggression. Our own aggression is projected on to other (real or imaginary) beings, who are then feared; or else is incorporated in our own super-ego and then gives rise to the anxiety associated with guilt. The tendency is exemplified in many of the fields we have surveyed. We have seen how, in the early stages of super-ego development, the child is liable to create phantastic bogy figures which are responsible for the characteristic phobias of infancy, and how through the successive introjections and projections of what Baldwin called 'the dialectic of personal growth' these fears are gradually reduced, as the bogy figures give place to a more truthful appreciation of real outer authorities. Similarly, as regards the development of culture and civilization in the race, the savage's fear of magic, ghosts, and spirits gradually succumbs to a growing sense of order and security, while even within the same culture the educated and enlightened person may smile at the superstitions of his more ignorant contemporaries. We have already noted how, in the development of religion, the loving and protecting aspects of divine figures tend to supplant the more fearsome qualities with which they were at first endowed; though we also observed that under the influence of the 'need for punishment' regressive steps might often be made within this sphere. Ethical progress would seem to imply a reduction of just this

---

[1] We referred to the same matter in another connection in Chapter XII.

'need for punishment' and a diminution in the severity of the Polycrates complex, this in itself eliminating one of the most potent sources of unreasonable fear. Similarly the transition from mental disease to mental health often carries with it a deliverance from fear, for, as Freud has pointed out, anxiety is perhaps the most important characteristic and fundamental symptom of all forms of neurosis. In an illuminating recent discussion of the concept of a 'normal' mind Ernest Jones [1] comes indeed to the conclusion that freedom from irrational anxiety is perhaps the best single criterion of 'normality'; only those who have in large measure achieved this condition can be reasonably 'happy', 'efficient', and 'adapted', which are the chief other criteria that have been suggested.

(7) **From Heteronomy to Autonomy.**—This tendency is also exhibited in a number of the fields that we have traversed. In some ways it constitutes perhaps the most fundamental core of the total process of moral development, of which the various 'tendencies' that we have distinguished are but so many aspects. It emerges, however, so plainly from the general trend of our discussion throughout this book that little need be added here. We might perhaps say that there are three chief ways in which the tendency is manifested. First, in the process whereby, as the child grows up, he learns to substitute his own moral judgment for that of the adults around him. The whole growth of the super-ego, as described succinctly in Chapter III and more in detail in Chapters IV to IX, exemplifies this process, as do most other accounts of moral development in the individual, such as that of Piaget, who in his *Moral Judgment of the Child* described a new and very fruitful method of experimentally investigating this development. Secondly, the process is continued, within the individual mind, in the gradual taking over by the ego, with its capacity for reason, discrimination, and delicate adaptation to reality, of the control which at a lower level is exercised more blindly and indiscriminately by the super-ego. In the third place, within society, the individual members come to rely more on their own intelligence and moral judgment and less on taboos, conventions, laws, and the other methods of social restraint that we examined in Chapter X. As we have already indicated there, and elsewhere in this book, one important difference between primitive and civilized society lies in the greater individualization of the latter, the individual

---

[1] Ernest Jones, 'The Concept of a Normal Mind,' *Int. J. Psa.* (1942), 23, 1.

mind taking over functions that were formerly exercised by the group. This process is not without its dangers, difficulties, and disadvantages, exhibited more especially in the less easy group cohesion on the one hand and the greater liability to individual mental conflict (and consequent neurosis) on the other. The disadvantages of the former kind may be so great that in social emergencies, such as war, a certain amount of regression of the sort that we might call increased socialization and lessened individualization may be necessary. Nevertheless the general trend of progress in the direction of individualization is clear enough. The change from autocracy to democracy in politics corresponds to that from parent-figure to individual conscience or from super-ego to ego in the moral development of the individual. In this respect democracy represents a higher stage of evolution than dictatorship or totalitarianism. The latter may be justified in its insistence on the ethical and political necessity for group loyalty, which (as we saw under the first of our eight categories) itself represents an important aspect of moral progress. But such progress demands no less that group loyalty be tempered and held in check by individual moral judgment. Increasing sociality and increasing individualization are complementary aspects of moral evolution. Both are essential. If sociality is cultivated at the cost of individuality (which is the temptation to which totalitarianism is exposed and must indeed almost inevitably in some degree succumb), we are liable to regress to a crude moral uniformity; if individualization outpaces socialization (which is the danger of democracy), we open the door to selfishness, nepotism, sectional interest, and eventually to anarchy. Democracy, properly understood, involves no serious diminution in the loyalty to the larger social groups, including national groups. But it looks upon these groups as groups of individuals, whose welfare, through their collaboration and collective wisdom, is the ultimate goal of all group activity.

Nevertheless it has to be recognized that this last general statement does not take us very far, and that the nature of the compromise to be effected between socialization and individualization remains one of the most acute problems of modern democracy. Totalitarianism would appear to err in one direction as much as *laissez faire* did in the other. Among recent thinkers, K. Mannheim [1] has been particularly concerned

---

[1] Karl Mannheim, *The Diagnosis of Our Time*, 1943.

with this problem, and the solution he suggests—i.e. the formulation of a generally agreed set of basic values, above the level of which individuals should be allowed and encouraged to develop their more personal ideals and points of view—is perhaps as promising as is likely to be found. If this view is correct, the search for such basic values as will secure the necessary measure of agreement and can arouse the necessary loyalty and enthusiasm (as exemplified in such formulations as 'The Atlantic Charter', 'The Rights of Man', etc.) is clearly a work of the very first importance. It may be that the very existence of democracy depends on the success of such a search.

(8) **From Orectic (Moral) Judgment to Cognitive (Psychological) Judgment.**—As regards this last tendency we may refer back to what was said in Chapter I. The tendency has also, in common with our No. (5), the important fact that it is a transition away from aggression; but whereas No. (5) was a transition from aggression to tolerance or love, we have here rather a transition from aggression to understanding. In so far as we achieve insight and understanding as to how we can deal with those who frustrate us, we tend to substitute the surer and more effective methods provided by knowledge and science for the cruder procedures based on anger and moral condemnation, at first in our personal affairs, then as regards social individuals generally (through 'the scientific treatment of delinquency', which is now represented by an important society in this country), and eventually, we may hope, as regards the conflicts between groups. This transition, as we indicated in Chapter I, is a natural consequence of the development of knowledge and of the scientific attitude. Just as we have come to rely on physical science rather than on prayer or magic to bring about the fulfilment of our desires in the material world, so also there is now a great and growing tendency to look to the human sciences (economics, medicine, sociology, psychology, etc.) to solve the difficulties connected with human behaviour and social life—difficulties which, in the absence of the requisite knowledge and attitude, we are otherwise only too prone to meet by simply denouncing as wicked those who irritate us, do not agree with us, or whose interests seem to be opposed to ours. The difference in attitude is, as was also indicated, one that involves a change from the predominance of emotion to the predominance of cognition; instead of feeling angry or indignant, we consider as calmly as we can by what

means we may bring about a change in the offenders' minds and
conduct in the direction we desire (and incidentally, though this
may be more difficult, the same method is applicable when the
offenders happen to be ourselves). But this of course does not
imply that orexis is completely supplanted by cognition. Orexis
still in the last resort supplies the goal at which we aim; cognition only guides us concerning the steps that we must take to
achieve that goal. Here again we can refer to our discussion of
ends and means in Chapter I.

A very important corollary of this change of attitude is that
we seek to alter and control mental processes rather than the
persons who display them, that we direct our disapproval to
the sin rather than the sinner. In the pregnant words of
Graham Wallas,[1] 'anger, previously part of the angry man, is
now separable from him'. It is easy to see what an immense
improvement in human relations would be brought about by
the more general adoption of such an attitude, in which we
substitute a cognitive and psychological approach for an
emotional and moral one.

We have expressed our eight tendencies of moral development
in the form of transitions from one state or condition of a more
primitive kind to another indicative of a higher state of evolution. This series of contrasted conditions would seem (in one
or another of its aspects) to correspond fairly well with a
number of similar distinctions made by other authors. Thus
Bovet distinguishes between 'duty' and 'feeling for good',[2]
corresponding chiefly to our No. (4). Piaget [3] makes several
distinctions of the same kind, e.g. between 'constraint' and
'co-operation', 'unilateral respect' and 'mutual respect',
'justice as law' and 'distributive justice', 'expiatory punishment' and 'restitutive punishment' (with 'retributive punishment' occupying an intermediate position). These all have
something in common with our Nos. (1), (4), (5), (6), and (7). His
further distinction, to which we have already referred in an
earlier chapter, between 'moral realism' and moral judgment
in terms of intention has also some relation to our Nos. (1), (3),
and (8). Adler distinguishes between egoistic instincts and
'social interest',[4] Ranyard West between 'aggressive instincts

---

[1] Graham Wallas, *Human Nature in Politics* (1908), p. 81.
[2] P. Bovet, 'Les Conditions de l'Obligation de la Conscience,' *Année Psycho-
logique* (1912), 18, 55.   [3] *Op. cit.*
[4] Alfred Adler, *Social Interest : A Challenge to Mankind,* 1938.

and 'social instincts',[1] both corresponding chiefly to our No. (1), but with a tincture of Nos. (4) to (7) also.   Anderson, as a result of his experimental studies of the social life of children, comes to the conclusion that there is a fundamental difference between what he calls 'dominative' and 'integrative' behaviour respectively,[2] a difference that Harding has attempted to apply on a large scale to the social life of adults.[3]   This distinction would correspond again to our Nos. (1), (4), (5), (6), and (7).   Integrative behaviour, as understood by Anderson and Harding, would seem to have much in common with that ability for 'collaboration in opposition which, according to Madariaga, is such a happy characteristic of British public life,[4] clearly implying, among other tendencies, something of our Nos. (5) and (8).   Phillips, in her study of sentiment formation, and employing a totally different technique,[5] comes independently to a conclusion that resembles Piaget's in stressing the important difference between unilateral respect (between children and adults or between inferiors and superiors) and mutual respect (between equals), though she also finds that relations implying respect of the latter kind are not at all impossible as between child and adult.[6]

[1] Ranyard West, *Conscience and Society*, 1942.

[2] H. H. Anderson, 'Domination and Social Integration in the Behaviour of Kindergarten Children,' *Genetic Psychol. Mon.* (1939), 31, 3.

[3] D. W. Harding, *The Impulse to Dominate*, 1941.

[4] S. de Madariaga, *Englishmen, Frenchmen, Spaniards*, 1928.

[5] Margaret Phillips, *The Education of the Emotions*, 1938.

[6] Piaget has often been criticized for his tendency to establish dichotomies and to think in terms of too rigid stages of development, and it has been questioned whether these stages are to be found in the development of all children. Thus M. R. Harrower ('Social Status and Moral Development,' *Brit. J. Educ. Psychol.* (1934), 4, 75) and Eugene Lerner (*Constraint Areas and the Moral Judgment of Children*, Menasha, Wisconsin, 1937) have found in England and America respectively that 'moral realism' and certain correlated features are more often present in children of lower social strata than in those who have enjoyed greater cultural privileges, while Ahmed (M. Khalafallah Ahmed, *Moral Reasoning in the Child and its Relation to Mental Age*, 1936. Thesis in University of London Library) has found that liability to moral realism is correlated with lower intelligence.   Lerner, however, discovered that the difference associated with cultural status persisted even when the children compared were matched for age and intelligence, thus creating a very interesting problem concerning the connection between culture and the development of moral thought.   In his study he has well brought out also the intimate relation between the various factors described by Piaget and others who have employed Piaget's methods.   It is perhaps permissible in this connection to quote a passage from this work: 'In developing socialized thinking or communicable forms of language, it is the "shock" of contact with other children of similar age-groups which is considered important.   In contact with "little people" whom he is not afraid to challenge, whom he can defy and who can defy him, the child is gradually led to reciprocally intelligible arguments with his social equals, and thus to true verification of ideas.   His "autistic" language (exemplified in extreme forms of unintelligible baby prattle, which may persist quite long and be understood by omniscient parents only) becomes socialized or communicable, as understanding and being

Finally, Isaacs, in her prolonged observations on the daily life of children at the Malting House School, gives many examples of all the tendencies we have described, including our Nos. (2) and 3 (e.g. transitions from magical and autistic to realistic procedures).[1]

Having seen that our eight tendencies of progress are reasonably in harmony with the suggestions of other authors dealing with some of the more specific problems on which we have touched, we may conclude this chapter by noting how our criteria appear in the light of wider and more cosmic views of ethical development. We shall, however, confine ourselves to two examples of such views—those of the great nineteenth-century philosopher of evolution, Herbert Spencer, and those recently put forward by C. H. Waddington, which formed the basis of an interesting discussion in which philosophers, biologists, and others, including psycho-analysts, took part.[2]

For Spencer the whole of evolution, in the sphere of physics, as in that of biology, psychology, sociology, and ethics, can be regarded as a twin process of integration and differentiation. An object that is evolving, whether it be a nebula, a planet, a living organism, or a society, becomes at one and the same time more integrated, i.e. more closely interrelated and co-ordinated within itself, and more differentiated, i.e. more specialized in its different parts, this double process applying both to the structure and the function of the object. In his famous formula: 'Evolution is a change from a relatively indefinite incoherent homogeneity to a relatively definite coherent heterogeneity through continuous integrations and differentiations'. In the case of living organisms this process may be regarded as one of adaptation, whereby the organism seeks to adapt itself as well as possible to the various forces impinging on it. Life is 'a continuous adjustment of internal relations to external

understood by other children becomes desirable. Similarly in the field of moral reasoning, it is such reciprocal relations of co-operating equals which would conduce to a sense of self-imposed, actively felt, desire for fair play, team spirit, I'll help you and you'll help me, etc.' (p. 8).

With regard to the general criticism of Piaget's stages, it is only fair to suggest that Piaget himself often seems well aware that these are in reality no more than the extreme ends of a series with continuous transitions, and on one occasion when the doctrine of relatively discrete stages was imputed to him in discussion he is reputed to have replied: 'I am much less of a Piagetist than you would think'.

[1] Susan Isaacs, *Intellectual Growth in Young Children*, 1930; *Social Development in Young Children*, 1933.

[2] C. H. Waddington *et al.*, *Science and Ethics*, 1943.

R

relations'. In the sphere of ethics, good conduct is conduct which is relatively more evolved in this sense, bad conduct that which is relatively less evolved.

It is, I venture to think, sufficiently clear that our eight tendencies are generally in close agreement with the Spencerian formula, both when we contemplate the development of the individual in isolation and when we consider the relations between individuals that in their totality make up social life. Nor is the correspondence any less evident when we examine the tendencies one by one in turn. No. (1) (Egocentricity to Sociality) clearly makes for greater adaptation of the individual to his social environment and for greater social integration within the group. No. (2) (Unconscious to Conscious) makes for greater integration within the mind of the individual, as illustrated in the effects of successful psychotherapy in breaking down repressions and dissociations and in increasing the sphere of conscious control. This last also produces a greater capacity for delicate discrimination (in contrast with the all-or-none methods of the unconscious) and in this conduces to more differentiated and adapted behaviour. Much the same holds of No. (3) (Autism to Realism), though here the accent is primarily on increased adaptation. The child, the savage, the neurotic, the insane are all distinguished by a higher degree of autism, are less well adapted to reality, than the adult, the civilized, the 'normal', the sane. At the same time they exhibit both less integration and less differentiation of behaviour and mentality. With No. (4) (Moral Inhibition to Spontaneous 'Goodness') the gain is chiefly as regards integration. All manifestations of voluntary control and inhibition involve some mental conflict and friction, which is reduced in the proportion in which wish and duty coincide. Not to speak of the more complex conditions revealed by psycho-analysis, we need only call to mind once more Frenkel's and Weisskopf's findings on this point. No. (5) (Aggression to Tolerance and Love) clearly makes on the whole for better individual adaptation and greater social integration, and also—in virtue of nemesism—for greater individual integration; and the same is true of No. (6) (Fear to Security). No. 7 (Heteronomy to Autonomy) makes for greater individual and social differentiation, being, as we have already in effect observed, complementary in this respect to No. (1), which latter corresponds to 'integration' in the Spencerian formula. Finally, No. (8) (Moral to Psychological Judgment) promotes better individual adaptation to the social environment and better social integration.

The discussion in *Science and Ethics* has much in common with Spencer's point of view, inasmuch as it starts from the position, stated by Waddington, that ethical conduct is conduct that is fundamentally in harmony with the evolutionary process. T. H. Huxley, the great Victorian biologist, in a famous essay on 'Evolution and Ethics' had indicated a certain discontinuity or even contradiction between this process as it takes place below the level of ethical reflection and as it occurs after the attainment of this level. As moral beings, it was, he suggested, our duty, not so much to follow the crude and cruel methods of nature, as to modify and correct them in the light of insight, sympathy, and moral principle. In the discussion under review, J. B. S. Haldane suggests that the problem can be treated dialectically. In a sense the cosmic process that is responsible for human evolution negates itself by generating the ethical process. But in virtue of a higher synthesis ethical behaviour itself carries on the process of evolution at a more advanced level and by more efficient methods.

The primitive and unadapted nature of the super-ego was then brought into the discussion. As Karin Stephen said, it is the super-ego's 'fantastic, slapdash character (that) has rendered man's social evolution so miserably slow and full of setbacks'. Julian Huxley, however, seeks to justify it biologically as an example of the all-or-none mechanisms by which the higher animals avoid conflict, mechanisms that are exemplified on a lower level by the interactions of antagonistic muscles and competing reflexes. 'Man', he says, 'is the only animal in which conflict is normal and habitual, so that some form of minimizing its effects is essential; and this will be of the greatest importance in early childhood before sufficient experience has been accumulated to enable conflict to be dealt with empirically and rationally'. But the more empirical and rational method of control, as was amply brought out in the discussion, is the method of advance. It constitutes the spearhead of ethical, as of evolutionary progress, and if Julian Huxley is right in his view that further biological advance can be achieved only by man, the development of these more delicate methods of control is man's unique responsibility as the sole guardian of further evolution on this planet. The cruder methods of the unconscious super-ego can be justified, as Huxley suggests, as a sort of temporary or emergency measure, such as the scaffolding that is used for the erection of a building or the harness with which children are sometimes taught to walk. In so far as its basis is fundamentally sound (as we have seen, a condition that is unfortunately by no means so easy to fulfil), the super-ego can also be entrusted with the enforcement of what might be called moral routine. But it is clearly unsuited to serve (as it is often expected to do) as the supreme court of moral appeal. If, as seems indeed to be the case, man is by his very nature doomed to conflict, we must seek the ultimate solution of conflict at the higher level of reason rather than at the lower one of conscience or tradition. If we adopt the older view of T. H. Huxley we can, in so doing, regard ourselves as combating the primitive brutality of Nature 'red in tooth and claw' (so long as we remember in all humility that man—especially primitively moral man—can be at least as 'brutal' as Nature at her worst). If we adopt the more embracing view we can hold that, in this very act of combating Nature, we are furthering her process in our own specifically human way. This may prove an inspiring and ennobling thought to those who are disturbed by the apparent disloyalty to ancient traditions and ideals that seems involved in each new moral revolution, in each new attempt at the solution of the different problems presented by the rapidly changing conditions of human life. If, in dealing with these problems, we make the fullest use of the powers of reason with which Nature has endowed us, we are still carrying on the purposes of Nature, still working within the framework of the great cosmic whole of which we form a part.

CHAPTER XVII

THE PROBLEM OF RELIGION

STRICTLY speaking, our task is now accomplished. We have studied the nature and development of the chief psychological factors in morality, and have traced the influence of these factors in a variety of fields. In so doing, our exposition has been determined for the most part by the particular aspect or kind of psychological process (if we allow the term, the particular psychological mechanism) with which we happened to be dealing, and we have sought illustrations of this process from observations made in the consulting-room, the nursery, or the experimentalist's laboratory, from the facts of religion and of the political arena, the data of the anthropologist, and so on in kaleidoscopic sequence. It may be that the reader will experience some relief from these rapid and perhaps bewildering transitions if, in conclusion, we devote one or two chapters to the study of the same phenomena by a somewhat different method, taking as our starting point, not a particular kind of mental process, but a definite group of social phenomena, and endeavouring to see how these phenomena appear when regarded in the light of our psychological formulations. The choice of theme along these lines is of course almost endless, but since we are only seeking examples with the help of which to clarify and illustrate what has already been said, we will confine ourselves to three subjects, all of them in the forefront of discussion and interest at the present day: religion; conservatism and radicalism in political and social life; and finally, what are at the moment the most absorbing of all human phenomena, war and peace. In each of these fields we shall endeavour to confine ourselves to aspects that seem germane to our previous findings and shall make no attempt at a complete survey of the vast and complicated problems involved.

Recapitulation

With regard to religion, we have already said so much that it may be well to start with a brief recapitulation. In Chapter V we encountered, though no more than incidentally, the most fundamental contribution of psycho-analysis to this field, viz. that the attitude of man to his gods is determined to a large extent by displacement of his attitude towards his parents, either in their original form as dominating external figures or as incorporated in the super-ego; in which latter case there is a projection of the internal super-ego on to the external figure of God, as in the notion of the 'all-seeing eye of God'. In Chapter VII, in dealing with nemesism, we were reminded that asceticism, the deliberate restriction of enjoyment and submission to hardship, plays an important part in religion, and that sacrifice can be regarded as a form of asceticism. In sacrifice the worshipper suffers indirectly by depriving himself of something valuable and offering it to his God, while in other forms of religious asceticism he inflicts suffering directly on himself to appease or pay homage to his God. In Chapter X we met another form of restriction connected with religion, that of taboo. At the religious level (as distinct from the levels of magic and of purely social disapproval) a taboo on certain persons, things, acts, or words is imposed, supposedly as the result of a divine injunction. In this chapter we also studied the fundamental ambivalence underlying taboo, an attitude that applies to the religious aspects of taboo as to all others. In Chapter XI we dealt with the Polycrates complex and the notion of 'hubris', the dim fear that the gods are jealous of pleasure and success enjoyed by mortals and (unless appeased by sacrifice) will signify their disapproval by the infliction of disasters. In Chapter XII we saw that the possibilities of vicarious punishment for guilt could extend to divine victims, and we had an opportunity to realize the strangely ambivalent attitude towards such victims. In Chapter XIII we returned to deal at greater length with the projection of the super-ego on to God, and gained some understanding of the peculiar conditions of religious exaltation that may arise from a sense of unity with the divine, a unity that seems to correspond psychologically to some condition of fusion between the ego and the super-ego. We saw, too, that in the idea of God we are able to recapture that sense of reliance on an all-good, all-wise parent which we enjoyed in our early years and which, we had regretfully come to realize, could not be permanently and completely satisfied in reference to any purely human figure. But, as we also saw, the problem of ambivalence still remains; there is still a struggle between the good, helpful, and protective, and the cruel, frustrating aspects of the parents, and this sometimes leads to a 'decomposition' of the Godhead into good and evil deities. In any case the attempt to purify the Deity of all elements of anger, cruelty, and hatred leaves unsatisfied the nemesistic urge incorporated in the super-ego, so that there is a strong tendency to return to the notion of a fierce, punishing, and jealous God. So strong is this urge that even if the metaphysical belief in a cruel God is abandoned, the super-ego often continues to demand a standard no less severe than that which such a God would be likely to impose. Finally in Chapter XV we briefly considered the 'unrealistic' aspects of religion, both on their pleasant (simple wishfulfilment) and unpleasant (severe and punitive) sides, in their relation to our conduct in this life and our notions concerning life beyond the grave. In our treatment of autistic thinking in general we discovered grounds for believing that unrealism was not without advantages—chiefly in the direction of affording an outlet for frustrated tendencies and of inspiring confidence that might help to overcome real obstacles—but that in the long run reality thinking constitutes the line of progress. And we gave no indication that in the sphere of religion there exists an exception to this rule.

Psycho-analysis and Religious Values

With this last point we have reached the fundamental and very delicate problem of the bearing of psycho-analysis upon religion. It is here more than anywhere else that we meet with that resentment against psychology as an illegitimate and vandalistic intruder in the world of values of which we spoke in our first chapter. This resentment clearly springs from a deep fear. It is feared that psycho-analysis especially, by revealing so much concerning the motives that find satisfaction in religious beliefs and the mechanisms (e.g. projection) that produce them, has undermined religion, or indeed 'disproved' it. Now a distinction must, I think, be made between undermining and disproof. As has been pointed out by a number of writers, including Freud himself, to show that a thing is ardently desired (even to show that it is desired from deep-lying motives that have not hitherto been fully recognized) does not prove that such a thing does not or cannot exist. Throughout the ages men have ardently desired to fly, and in recent years it has been demonstrated that human flight *is* possible (though it has not proved the unmixed blessing that had perhaps been imagined). Even—to take Freud's example—the dream of a poor girl that a prince will come to fetch her home is not necessarily untrue; 'some such cases have occurred'. The existence or possibility of Cinderella's prince, of the flying machine, or of God himself, must all be proved or disproved by independent evidence. But what psycho-analysis has done has been to make us suspicious of our wishes when they are likely to affect our appreciation of reality. In our dreams, in the delusions of the insane, in slips of the tongue, eye, ear, hand, and pen, in the scientist's welcome to facts that support a favourite theory and his reluctance to admit or remember those that seem against it (a tendency to which Darwin freely admitted and which he took steps to counteract), even in the queer unrealistic anxieties and obsessions of the neurotic, and in many other ways, psycho-analysis has revealed the potent but disturbing influence of 'wishful thinking'. And the very popularity of this last term indicates that we have to some extent taken the lesson to heart—for instance with reference to the present war. In estimating the actual military situation, when a belligerent confesses to severe losses, withdrawal, or defeat we feel we can safely believe all that he admits, but when he claims a victory, or even a successful 'elastic defence', we usually consider it wise to wait for further evidence before assessing the full nature and import of the events described. So also when those who assert the existence of a God at the same time reveal that they ardently desire Him to exist, we are justified in feeling a little sceptical (as we should be also with regard to the opposite assertion from an embittered atheist). Our scepticism is likely to be heightened by the fact that the religious have so often regarded want of faith as itself a sign of wickedness which they resent or punish; just as our doubts concerning war communiqués are liable to be increased if it is made a criminal offence to listen to those from the other side. In this way, as Cattell has well brought out,[1] the psycho-analytic doctrine of wishfulfilment has to a large extent reversed the old 'ontological argument', which deduced the existence of God from our idea of Him. This idea, being shown to satisfy an earnest wish, is, we now hold, less, rather than more, likely to be true than one that men accept with indifference or reluctance, and in all the greater need of being treated with the utmost caution— especially as scientific evidence from independent sources seems to speak so strongly against the truth of this idea, at least in the forms in which it has most frequently been held. If a princess claims she has a princely lover, we are more likely to believe her than we should a peasant girl, for we know that princes marry princesses far more often than they marry peasants. In this respect science seems somewhat in the position of the princess, religion in that of the peasant girl. The claims of the peasant girl and of the religious believer are not *ipso facto* proved untrue, but we feel more justified in waiting for a confirmation of their 'good news' than we should do in the case of the princess or the scientist, who can point to the frequent triumphant vindication of comparable claims made by members of their class in the past. Unfortunately, however, neither confirmation nor confutation is so easily forthcoming for the believer as for the peasant girl.

[1] R. B. Cattell, *Psychology and the Religious Quest* (1938), p. 31.

In this way psycho-analysis has in truth done much to under-mine religion; by its own methods it has continued the work in this direction that the physical and biological sciences had begun. But it has no more 'disproved' religion than have these other sciences. Indeed, in so far as religious beliefs concern themselves (as in their more primitive forms they often do) with the nature and origin of the physical universe and of mankind, it is a less formidable enemy than these other sciences, which have so often been able to show that the know-ledge gained from scientific study is grossly at variance with the prevailing forms of such beliefs. In certain ways it may even be said to have held out a helping hand to religion in its desperate struggle against the successive devastating attacks of science. It has done this in two ways, which however, as we shall see, are not altogether unconnected.

In the first place it has provided some indirect assistance (or at the very least some respite or consolation) to religion by raising in a more acute form than the other sciences do certain problems connected with the nature of truth and reality. Psychology is always a little nearer to the problems of episte-mology and metaphysics than are its sister disciplines; often indeed it is uncomfortably near. As Pear has recently emphasized [1] it is, for instance, intimately concerned with such delicate questions as the 'reality' distinction between percept, image, eidetic image, and hallucination, the 'reality' equivalents of concept, instinct, need, emotion, value; while the advent of psycho-analysis brought into the foreground the perhaps still more disturbing question as to the sense in which reality is to be attributed to unconscious mental processes. In what sense, if any, for instance, is the 'latent content' of dreams more or less real than the 'manifest content'? And in what way does 'psychological reality', which many psycho-analysts have stressed, differ from physical reality? A science that possesses so many vulnerable glass frontages of its own can perhaps ill afford to throw stones at the exposed windows of religion. Being concerned also, as it is, with so many and so varied claims to 'reality' of one sort or another, it might well hesitate before it banishes even the crudest metaphysical assumptions of religion to the limbo of utter unreality.

The second, and more direct, way in which psychology (and

[1] T. H. Pear, 'The Sense of Reality,' *Riddell Memorial Lectures*, University of Durham, 1936. (Published 1937.)

with it psycho-analysis) may be said to be helpful to religion is by taking seriously the emotions and attitudes involved. Here indeed it is under an obligation that does not affect the other sciences. From the early days of the psychological study of religion it was clear that there were two elements in religion that could profitably be distinguished—on the one hand a series of intellectual beliefs concerning the nature of the universe and the powers that govern it, and on the other the provision of means for the mobilization and canalization of emotion— and as this study progressed it became increasingly evident that, even though the beliefs may all be false, the emotional aspects may still be of great importance. In the eyes of some psychologists, indeed, the emotions are so important that they afford a sort of pragmatic justification for the beliefs, however erroneous or absurd these might appear when judged by a purely intellectual standard. Such psychologists occupy a position obviously akin to that of the pragmatist philosophers, who are also inclined to be tolerant to the 'truths' of religion so long as these appear to 'work'. To others the same emotions, just because they are attached to beliefs that are intellectually suspect, appear to be unhealthy and in need of redirection— though of course not for that reason any less worthy of attention. Jung is an example of the first of these classes, Freud of the second. To Jung, a religious dogma may indeed be at least psychologically truer than a scientific theory, for the very reason of its greater emotional investment. 'In itself', he says, 'any scientific theory, no matter how subtle, has, I think, less value from the standpoint of psychological truth than the religious dogma, for the simple reason that a theory is necessarily highly abstract and exclusively rational, whereas the dogma expresses an irrational entity through the image. This method guarantees a much better rendering of an irrational fact such as the psyche'.[1] To Freud, on the other hand, religion is 'the universal obsessional neurosis of humanity', which it should outgrow, just as a child outgrows the seemingly inevitable neuroses of infancy; and he looks forward to an admittedly remote future when mankind will be able to enjoy a 'primacy of the intellect', as the result of which emotion will no longer be able to distort the appreciation of reality.[2]

In their ultimate metaphysical positions the two writers are

[1] C. G. Jung, *Psychology and Religion* (1938), p. 56.
[2] S. Freud, *The Future of an Illusion*, 1928.

not perhaps so very far apart, for Jung himself, in the work just quoted, goes on to say that 'it would be a very regrettable mistake if anybody should understand my observations to be a kind of proof of the existence of God. They prove only the existence of an archetypal image of the Deity, which is the most we can assert psychologically about God'. The difference lies rather in the nature of their satisfaction with 'psychological truth' or 'psychological reality'. To both it is no doubt satisfying as an object for the contemplation and study of the psychologist, but to Jung it is so satisfying that he appears to be undisturbed by its frequent lack of agreement with 'truth' or 'reality' as judged by other standards, whereas to Freud such lack of agreement makes it an 'illusion' and brings it into the category of the primitive or pathological. In becoming a psychologist Freud has not been willing to sacrifice the general criteria of truth observed by other sciences, while Jung on his part has become so enthralled by the psychological significance of religious dogma and symbolism that he seems to some extent to have lost interest in these criteria.[1]

As regards the reality and significance of the religious emotions as such, however, there can be no doubt. The general nature of the satisfaction found in religion is briefly summarized by Freud in his *Future of an Illusion*, and after what has been said earlier in this book we need do little more than recapitulate this summary. The advantage that religion shares with all animistic beliefs is that we can deal with the forces of nature as we can with people; we can bribe, flatter, implore, cajole, or perhaps even threaten, them. At the stage of religion proper, i.e. when

---

[1] In this connection it is perhaps well to draw attention to the ambiguous nature of such terms as 'psychological truth' and 'psychological reality', which may be taken to imply: (1) merely the existence of the mental states or processes concerned (conscious or unconscious), or (2) that these states or processes point to some further reality outside themselves, or again (3) that they are peculiarly satisfying—perhaps in ways that other forms of 'reality' are not. It would seem to be in this last sense that, as we noticed in Chapter XV, a great artistic production is sometimes said to be truer than ordinary perception of the external world. It assembles or re-creates in a single entity (e.g. a picture) aspects of reality that may be widely separated in space and time, and thus presents them in a more comprehensible, enlightening, and satisfying manner. But the artist makes no claim that there is any corresponding single entity in outer reality in which these varied aspects are combined in the way depicted, whereas religious dogma does so. We can no more argue from 'artistic truth' to 'scientific truth' than we can from the 'psychological truth' of religious dogma to the existence of God as an entity outside the mind of the believer.

Alike as regards 'artistic', 'psychological' and 'religious' 'truths' or 'realities', it might save much confusion if such terms as 'value' or 'significance' were substituted, where no reference to a closely corresponding extra-psychical reality is intended.

spirits become exalted into gods, we can (as we have seen) enjoy a continuation of the protection and guidance that was given to us by our parents in our infancy. We need not feel that we are weak and helpless puppets of Chance or Destiny, forlorn orphans in a vast and heedless universe; on the contrary, we can enjoy the sense of playing an important part in a scheme of things run by an omnipotent Creator who watches over us lovingly as we play the rôle He has allotted to us. Our puny efforts acquire dignity and meaning as part of a Higher Purpose. The seeming hardships and injustices of life lose their sting when we believe that they only appear to us in this light because of the shortness of our vision, or at least that divine justice will recompense us amply for the sufferings we have endured. When belief in personal immortality is added to our belief in God, the ever-present threat of death loses its horror when confronted with the prospect of an eternity of bliss. Finally, our intellectual curiosity is gratified by an explanation of the origin, nature, and purpose of the universe so far as our limited intellects are capable of grasping problems of this magnitude, and our moral perplexities can be resolved with a minimum of trouble or conflict by a reference to the Divine Will in so far as this has been made manifest to us. The attractions of all this are clear enough and we need hardly wonder that men grasp eagerly at the 'illusion'.

As against all these advantages there are two serious drawbacks. First the 'illusory' quality of the belief itself, as manifested in the painful impact of the visible and tangible world, from which the protecting hand of the Super-Parent seems so often to be lacking. Secondly the fact that the divine love and mercy are offset by the divine restrictions on human desires and the divine wrath when these restrictions are infringed—corresponding to the frustrating and punishing aspects of the infantile parent-figures, themselves magnified upon a cosmic scale. These drawbacks need not necessarily, and indeed do not usually, reduce the religious emotion. As we saw at the end of Chapter XI, a variety of highly complex factors determines whether guilt is increased or decreased by disaster, and in the former case evil and suffering may only lead to an increased dependence on, and submission to, the Deity. Indeed it may be said to be the general rule that men have most need of God when they feel themselves most helpless in the face of evil. Although the very existence of this evil might seem to belie the divine love, it yet creates so great a need for superhuman help that men will cling all the more desperately to the belief in such a love. The situation of helplessness naturally induces a tendency to regression to the infantile position when we were dependent upon our earthly parents. Alternatively, the existence of overwhelming evil may be interpreted as a manifestation of the power of the divine displeasure, in which case the need for placating the angry Deity becomes all the more insistent. It makes no difference if the evil springs manifestly from the heart of man himself, for then we only regress to the infantile need of a parent to restrain us in our wickedness (in the manner indicated in Chapter IX).[1] On the whole, men feel they can dispense with the Deity more easily on fair days than on foul, whether the foulness be due to human agency or to the inclemency of Nature. It is when they fall on evil times that they tend to turn back with repentance and relief to ancestral creeds that perhaps before had seemed to them outmoded.

As regards the characteristics of the emotion involved, both Freud and Jung are agreed that the influence of the past is of very great importance. To Freud this influence is to be found largely in a 'return of the repressed' or of the 'surmounted' (such as animism or magic), a feature as regards which the religious emotion has something in common with the peculiar condition we describe as the 'uncanny'.[2] The repressed or surmounted elements in question may derive either from individual experience or from the past history of the race. This second alternative is made more explicit in Freud's last book, *Moses and Monotheism* (1939), which brings his position into greater harmony with that of Jung, who had for long maintained that racial 'archetypes' play an extremely important part in religious beliefs and account for the remarkable similarities of dogma and symbolism found in many different parts of the world. The views of both authors in this respect encounter the difficulty that they seem to imply the inheritance of acquired

[1] This last consideration is well illustrated by the public pronouncement made by a well-known philosopher on the occasion of his conversion from agnosticism consequent upon the horrors of the present day. 'Evil', he says, '—there seems no escape from the conclusion—is endemic in the heart of man. But to believe in the reality of evil and to have no recourse against it save such as lies in the sporadic efforts of one's own will and the slender integrity of one's own judgment, this is for me a quite intolerable position' (C. E. M. Joad in *The Evening Standard*, August 28, 1942). He takes this step, moreover, with full recognition of the disadvantages of what he calls the 'shadow' of belief (as contrasted with the 'sunshine' of agnosticism).

[2] S. Freud, 'The Uncanny,' *Collected Papers* (1919), iv, 368; *The Future of an Illusion*, 1928.

characters (in this case something in the nature of 'innate ideas'), which runs counter to a vast preponderance of the evidence at present available from biology and genetics. Jung's position implies the further great assumption of the 'Collective Unconscious', concerning which the majority of psychologists still display a justifiable scepticism, though the attractiveness of the view for the purpose of explaining such feelings as that of being 'in tune with the infinite' cannot be denied.

This last consideration may serve to remind us that full justice can scarcely be done to the emotional satisfaction of religious experience at its highest by any bare enumeration of the advantages to be obtained from it, of the circumstances in which it is sought, or of the regressive tendencies that it may involve. Such highest satisfaction is rather to be found in the peculiar exaltation connected with the fusion of ego and super-ego that we discussed in Chapter XIII. At its best, religious experience produces not a humbling but an elevation of the spirit, the ego being somehow raised to the position of the super-ego, the child to that of the parent, the worshipper to that of his God. But, as we saw in the same chapter, an exaltation of this kind may be experienced, if not in the same degree, at least with something of the same quality, in connection with experiences that would not usually be termed religious. These latter experiences exhibit what we might perhaps regard as a dissociation of the characteristic religious emotion from religious belief—indicating that the metaphysical aspects of religion are not absolutely necessary for the achievement of its most valuable emotional satisfactions. Emotion and belief can in fact be separated. And this in turn prepares us for the fact that there is at the present time an increasing tendency to look for 'religious' emotion elsewhere than in the company of meta-physical belief, in 'religions' of 'humanity' or 'nature', or even in the high 'devotion' of the scientist, artist, or social reformer to their respective tasks.

To sum up the discussion of the bearings of psycho-analysis upon religious belief contained in the present and previous chapters of this book we may say:

(1) That, by revealing religious beliefs as elaborate social forms of 'autistic' thinking, psycho-analysis has reinforced the objections to the metaphysical implications of these beliefs that were already so plentifully forthcoming from the other sciences. But although it is calculated to make us additionally

suspicious of the validity of these beliefs, it has no power to 'disprove' them.

(2) That, on the other hand, by demonstrating the fundamental nature and infantile origin of the needs underlying religion, by revealing something of the intimate meaning and complex over-determination of its symbolism, by drawing attention to its value from the point of view of mental and social hygiene as a prophylactic against individual neurosis, and by raising certain subtle problems as to the 'reality' of different kinds of mental content, psycho-analysis endows religious belief with a significance far greater than that which we should be inclined to attribute to it from the standpoint of physical science.

(3) That it reveals, above all, the great significance of the higher types of emotional attitude involved in religious experience, but at the same time indicates the possibility of attaining at least a comparable emotional attitude apart from metaphysical religious beliefs, the attitude thereby acquiring perhaps a greater 'reality' value.

(4) That it shows at the same time that, alongside of its beneficent functions, religion in its cruder forms can exercise a severe crippling and inhibiting effect upon the human mind, by fostering irrational anxiety and guilt, and by hampering the free play of the intellect. In this respect religion mirrors the evil effects of the primitive internal super-ego, and in the long run even an increase in individual neurosis may not be too high a price to pay for the removal of the restrictions it imposes.

Psycho-analysis and Christianity

So far, we have dealt only with religion in general. But it is clear that there are religions and religions—some being of a higher quality than others. To trace the evolution of religion in terms of psycho-analytic conceptions would be a fascinating study, but would obviously require a volume for itself. All we can do by way of further illustration is to say a few more words concerning that form of religion which has played the greatest part in the development of the modern Western world—Christianity.

Christianity emerged from a people, the Jews, who had already developed an exalted religion of their own, all power in the universe being attributed to a single divine being, who, while he accorded a unique distinction on his Chosen People, demanded from them at the same time a strict obedience.[1]   He was in fact a Jealous God, and inspired much guilt in his worshippers, who had indeed some cause for feeling guilty, as a result of their considerable transgressions of his rules.   Among the numerous ways in which Christianity differed from Judaism, one that is especially important to us here is its attempt to diminish this sense of guilt, associated with which are certain other very significant characteristics: its condemnation of violence, its universality, and its appeal to the lowly—the 'underdog'.

It displays in fact many of the characteristics of moral progress that we considered in the previous chapter, and Pfister has in this connection drawn an interesting parallel between the aims of Christianity and those of psycho-analysis, which he summarizes as follows [2]:

(1) Both aim at reducing guilt.

(2) In both there is a tendency to look upon suffering as a punishment for infringing the commands of some stern authority (God and the super-ego respectively).

(3) In both this stern, implacable, punishing authority is replaced by a mild, kindly, healing authority, with a view to eventual individual moral autonomy.

(4) This transition implies some degree of regression from emphasis on a stern father-figure (such as that represented in the exquisitely patriarchal Jahveh worship) to reliance on a kindlier, more tolerant mother-'imago'.   Pfister admits, however, that the actual figure of the mother was seldom allowed to emerge with full clarity and that only the founder of Christianity himself was apparently able to maintain an attitude consistently free from guilt and anxiety in relation to the father, with the result that anxiety-laden ritual soon began to be reintroduced by his followers.

(5) The satisfactory solution of conflict can only be found in love, as inculcated and represented by Jesus in the case of Christianity and as implied in the endeavour to remove the mental obstacles to loving in the case of psycho-analysis.

(6) The rôle of Christ as heavenly-earthly intermediary may

---

[1] We may note, in anticipation of the considerations advanced in the next section, that the same is true of the Chosen People of that new political religion, Nazism, who by a cruel irony of fate are at this moment so outrageously persecuting the Chosen People of the older régime.

[2] O. Pfister, 'Neutestamentliche Seelsorge und Psychoanalytische Therapie,' *Imago* (1934), 20, 425.

be compared to that played by the psycho-analyst, who, in his turn, cannot escape some degree of idealization and who serves as a father-surrogate with whose help aggression is worked off, guilt and fear alleviated, and a greater sense of love and reality-appreciation attained.

(7) Both Christian teaching and psycho-analytic therapy involve some degree of regression to an infantile situation ('except ye be converted and become as little children . . .') as a necessary condition of readjustment.

There are, of course, also important differences, which Pfister does not fail to point out; above all the fact that Christianity still speaks in terms of the projected divine father-figure, while psycho-analysis concerns itself with the internal father representative, the super-ego. Christianity, moreover, is concerned with social and religious values, whereas psycho-analysis as a method of treatment has primarily a more modest, therapeutic aim. A point, moreover, that is perhaps inadequately stressed by Pfister in the paper referred to is the element of universal companionship and equality that plays so important a part in Christianity and that brings it into the left-wing pattern of matriarchal brotherhood movements—of the kind with which we shall be concerned in the next chapter.

Christianity then is a great attempt to escape from the authoritarian father-figure and the archaic aspects of the super-ego. It is pre-eminently a son and brother religion rather than a father religion. But the central drama of Christianity shows that it was not possible to surmount the guilt of rebellion against the father without the sacrifice of atonement whereby the great revolutionary leader was himself slain in the rôle of the divine scapegoat. This great act of aggression itself implied a process of regression, for the Jews had long been hankering after the sacrifice of the first-born [1] which Moses and the prophets had forbidden them—a sacrifice to which, if we follow Freud in his last thoughts on the subject, they were probably impelled by the dim sense of guilt connected with the slaying of their own great leader and earthly father-figure, Moses himself. Christianity in fact, as Philpott has suggested in a recent stimulating paper, [2] was in some important respects a return to a pre-Mosaic order, to a sort of 'neo-totemism' in

---

[1] On this point see Sir J. G. Frazer, *The Dying God*, 168 ff.
[2] S. J. F. Philpott, 'Unconscious Mechanisms in Religion,' *Brit. J. Med. Psychol.* (1942), 19, 292.

which there was both a slaying of the god and an eating of him (the Last Supper)—only now the slain divinity represented the son rather than the father.[1] Putting together the ideas of Freud and Philpott on this subject, we may say that Moses had himself forbidden the only effective means of atoning for his own murder and hence condemned his people to an unrelieved tension of their guilt, which found unsatisfactory expression in endless petty restrictions and observances. Christianity relieved this tension by consummating the sacrifice, at the same time indicating that this was in accordance with the will of the Father (now the divine Father himself), thus removing the Mosaic taboo. Three advantages were thus obtained. A double guilt (that of the original father-murder and that of the forbidden atoning son-sacrifice) was removed and at the same time by the one supreme and final act of expiation the necessity for further sacrifice of the first-born was abolished.

With this wiping out of guilt connected with the past there went the injunction of non-violence, which, if followed, should have prevented the incurring of fresh guilt. Such at least, we may surmise, was the intention—an intention which, alas, humanity, with its all too deeply ingrained guilt and aggressiveness, has been unable to fulfil. Notwithstanding the magnificence of its vision and the nobility of its purpose, Christianity (like the other great religions) has been in most respects a failure, and this in spite of its nominal and worldly triumphs. It has failed both to remove internal guilt and to abolish external aggression—largely, as we have seen in this book, two aspects of the same problem. Hence, as we noted in Chapter XIII, the continual backslidings towards a renewed sense of sin—backslidings which have resulted in the all too familiar fusion of guilt with sado-masochism, as revealed in religious wars, religious persecutions, and the savage glorification of hell-fire, all of which involve the most phantastic travesties and perversions of the master's teaching.

As regards external aggression, as Waddington has pointed out,[2] a great forward step was taken by Christianity when it indicated a way in which individuality could be cultivated and the worth of the individual stressed without at the same time insisting upon individual dominance. This was perhaps especi-

---

[1] Though it is true that in primitive totemism also the totem animal often represents a sort of elder brother as well as a paternal or ancestral figure.
[2] C. H. Waddington et al., Science and Ethics, 1943.

ally suited to a religion of the 'underdog', who had few means of exercising dominance and who believed that this world would in any case shortly be destroyed. But the ideal of kindness and tolerance combined with a cultivation of the individual spirit, admirable as it was so far as it went, was clearly insufficient when this religion itself became a dominating influence in a world that obstinately continued to exist.

The great weakness of Christianity would seem to be that it had indicated neither a suitable outlet for the energies of aggressive extraverted individuals nor an adequate and positive goal for social and political endeavour; indeed, by its attitude of indifference to the larger social problems, it fostered the divorce between ethics and politics which many thinkers have in recent years deplored. In the absence of any guidance concerning such goals and outlets, Christianity has probably never seemed entirely satisfying to the man of action, and has in modern times incurred the reproach of being no better than a 'slave morality', with ideals that are contemptible from the point of view of strong and energetic individuals and societies. The path along which this reaction leads has become painfully apparent, especially during the last few years. Hence an increasing realization that the religious emotions must in their turn be canalized along active and social lines, if they are to serve (and perhaps to save) humanity. Indeed they have to a large extent already been so canalized, but unfortunately all too often under the influence of a crude reaction against Christianity that has idealized force, worshipped the state, and made a virtue of brutality. Such reactions show that other-worldliness and tolerance are not enough, if this world is to be other than a roaring chaos, and recent events have made it clear in which direction the next step in religious development must lie. The religious emotions must be largely or entirely secularized and be put in the service of humanity. The religion of humanity is surely the religion of the nearer future.

The Religion of Humanity

Of the modern psychologists of religion Cattell [1] would seem to have given by far the most thoroughgoing, consistent, and courageous exposition of this view. He endeavours to show in some detail that our relations to Humanity (or, as he prefers to put it, to the Group Mind, which looked at in this way can,

[1] *Op. cit.*

he suggests, be appropriately called the Theopsyche [1]) are in many all-important ways similar to our relations to God, and that we can find in them an adequate outlet for our 'religious' needs and aspirations without recourse to any form of supernaturalism. His main contentions with regard to this can perhaps be summarized as follows:

(1) The individual depends upon his fellows, upon his social group, in much the same way as, according to revealed religion, he depends ultimately upon the will of God. Without the co-operation of his fellows he would soon cease to exist, just as, on the other view, his continuance depends upon the protection and benevolence of his divine Creator.

(2) He is to a very large extent spiritually created by the Group Mind, i.e. his ideals, his goals, his frames of intellectual reference, his whole outlook upon life are profoundly influenced by the 'mental atmosphere' of the society in which he grows up and in which he lives, just as, according to the supernaturalist view, his spiritual being is guided and influenced by God. Even his physical existence is largely determined by the social conditions of his group, his actual parents, essential as they are, being indeed on both views only the immediate instruments of a greater creative purpose.

(3) The group, as the 'cumulative reservoir of super-individual wisdom', provides the ultimate commands of morality (incorporated in the super-ego), just as God does on the theological hypothesis.

(4) The individual can find his own purpose in life in service of the group, just as he can in service of God's will. His 'need to be needed', his desire for co-operation in something larger and higher than his own immediate and personal concerns, can be satisfied in this way perhaps even more effectively than in trying to fulfil the often mystifying and inscrutable intentions of a supernatural God.

(5) This service may often call for personal sacrifice (even for the 'supreme sacrifice' of life itself) in ways that are at least intellectually more satisfying than the sacrifices usually demanded by the religious rituals of the past.

---

[1] In using thus the concept of the Group Mind we are not, I think, necessarily committed to any view of its ultimate nature, e.g. that it exists as a mind over, above, and in addition to, all the individual minds, a view which has its attractions but which raises many difficulties. It may signify only the sum of the minds of the individuals composing the group, as they are influenced by one another and as they express themselves through the instruments and channels giving effect to their collective organization.

(6) The continuance of the group after the individual's death gives him the necessary faith to carry on with the tasks valuable to the community which personal chance or accident may interrupt.

(7) The fact that the individual has during his life influenced the group—for good or ill, and of course in varying degree according to his abilities and eminence—inevitably confers on him a sort of immortality, which is independent of any strictly personal survival.[1] He lives on through the ages through his effect on human society, even although his individual soul or body may not be rejoicing in heaven or suffering in hell.

(8) If he has children, he gains a further and more direct immortality through them and their descendants—both in virtue of his physical parenthood and of his special moral influence as parent.[2]

As Cattell fully recognizes, such a substitution of the group 'Theopsyche' for the God of revealed religion can hardly function satisfactorily without some provision for the aim or purpose of the group. The mere maintenance of the group as such, or the mere preservation of its present status and traditions, is less satisfying than trustful reliance on God's will—perhaps because of the inevitable realization of the pettiness and transience of human affairs as compared with the might and majesty of a Being who is supposed to rule the universe. Such an aim or purpose he finds (as no doubt most other moderns would do) in Progress, the gradually increasing realization of the aspirations of mankind. To Cattell human progress has both a biological and a social aspect: on the one hand the deliberate eugenic cultivation of the best human types based on scientific knowledge and experiment (without, of course, the exercise of cruelty such as has been inflicted on supposedly inferior types under the Nazi régime), on the other hand the determination and establishment, also by experiment, of the optimal conditions of human social life and individual development. Such a view involves no insistence on any dull uniformity, but on the contrary demands an impartial study of the possibilities of every type. Mankind will, in fact, engage in an applied science of itself, especially of

---

[1] The case for this kind of immortality has been whimsically but very cogently put by Samuel Butler in chapter eleven ('The Physics of Vicarious Existence') of *Erewhon Revisited*.

[2] Cattell does not stress this factor in the book in question. But his lively interest in eugenics shows that he is keenly aware of it. In any case it is sufficiently obvious, and does of course actually receive a great emphasis in some cultures other than our own.

its own mental qualities, and this science, in Cattell's somewhat startling but quite consistent terminology, may be called 'the experimental study of God'.

It is clear that any attempt to establish a religion of this sort is not without very formidable difficulties. In particular it involves two great interconnected problems, of the existence of which Cattell is certainly not unaware but which he can hardly be said to have treated adequately in his small but most suggestive book:

(a) The relations of humanity as a whole to the various racial, national, and other groups of which it is composed, and of these groups to one another. The 'Theopsyche' is ultimately the Group Mind of all humanity, past, present, and to come, but it would seem that loyalty to the minor groups will, on his view, itself take on something of a religious character (one might perhaps compare it to the attitude of the Roman Catholic to his saints or of the polytheist to his minor deities). The formation of a proper hierarchy of loyalties, so as to facilitate co-operation and prevent conflict, is therefore a matter of very great importance. That such a hierarchy is not impossible is indicated (if there is any relevance in our above analogies) by the fact that the saints seldom squabbled and that Jove usually contrived to keep the minor members of the pantheon firmly in their place. We shall return to this question in its more political aspects in our last chapter.

(b) The necessity of arriving at some degree of consent as to the nature of human progress and the goals at which it aims (a problem to which the previous chapter of the present book was devoted [1]). This problem is all the more important because, in the absence of a goal in accordance with enlightened morality, the tendencies to moral degradation in group action are only too likely to assert themselves, as we have seen in the terrible examples of narrow and fanatical group 'religion' afforded by modern Germany and Japan.

The substitution of such a Theopsyche for the more personal God of revealed religion also inevitably entails certain sacrifices and renunciations, and it would be well that these should be clearly realized and admitted from the start. Perhaps the first and most obvious of such renunciations is the narcissistic trauma

[1] We may note especially the importance of attaining a due balance between general agreement as to fundamental values and individual freedom at higher and more detailed levels—a point that we considered in connection with our seventh 'tendency' in that chapter.

occasioned by the loss of the prospect of personal immortality. It requires a certain philosophic exaltation, or at least detachment, before immortality through works manifested in the lives of later generations can be regarded as a satisfactory substitute for personal participation in the delights of a heaven in which virtue is given its reward and suffering its compensation. Nevertheless, since the sense of unity with a larger whole (the psychological implications of which we considered in Chapter XIII) is such an essential element in all the more highly developed forms of religious experience, it would seem that the renunciation in question is not one which is altogether too great for humanity to bear. To-day it is doubtful whether the belief in personal survival is a real force in the lives of more than a small minority of people, and there is of course compensation in the fact that, though the hope of heaven may be lost, so also is the fear of hell. Even in more primitive cultures it is the survival of kings and chiefs that is stressed rather than that of common folk; and in some of the most exalted religious thought of the East not merely the hope, but the very desire, for personal immortality seems to have been overcome.

In many ways more important is the fact that Humanity or the Theopsyche serves as a sublimation for the primitive feelings relating to the mother or the idea of brotherhood rather than for those relating to the father. The Western world, with its strongly patriarchal traditions, will perhaps not easily forgo the father. How to cater for the archetypal need for a father-figure in a world society is indeed a problem. The age-long institution of the Popes, as figures whose authority transcends the boundaries of state or race, suggests however that the problem in itself is not insoluble; it suggests also that the authority or dignity concerned is likely to attach more to the office than to the man who holds it at any given moment. Alternatively recourse may perhaps be made to a small Senate or Council of Elders, e.g. a Big Three or Big Six, thus returning to the well-tried principle of gerontocracy, which can also boast of considerable success in the past history of human government. But whether a single father-figure be maintained, or whether his power and honour be divided among a small number of figures (a procedure for which the spectacle of a few great national leaders working in collaboration may perhaps afford a favourable preparation), some concession will almost certainly have to be made to the longing for an all-wise, all-powerful father.

Even the supreme representatives of humanity, however, must appear relatively small and insignificant when compared with an Almighty Being.   And here the final ineluctable renunciation must be made.   Men must abandon the last shred of that longed-for but illusory 'omnipotence' to which, even after the relinquishing of magic, they sought to cling through their relation with a divine ruler of the universe.   Prayer and sacrifice, the hope for miracles, are, as usually understood, useless, if our gods themselves are only human and enjoy no jurisdiction beyond the range of human power.   The vaster universe around us appears to be indifferent to human hopes and sufferings, and we must, it seems, resign ourselves to accept the teaching of Omar Khayyám:

> And that inverted Bowl we call The Sky,
> Whereunder crawling coop'd we live and die,
>   Lift not thy hands to *It* for help—for It
> Rolls impotently on as Thou or I.

A terrible lesson, which cannot perhaps be learnt without incurring a bitter sense of loss and loneliness.   Men are in fact thrown back upon themselves and must rely on their own efforts to improve their lot.   But this very sense of loneliness and isolation may well serve to bring them closer together than would otherwise be possible; and they have the consolation of knowing that in the human heart and brain they possess instruments which, faulty though they be, have brought them far along the path of evolution, and, if wisely used, may bring them almost infinitely farther.   We have ample proof that courage and intelligence, though they never perform miracles, will yet achieve what a generation or two earlier would have been considered miracles.   Within his sphere of influence (which is so rapidly expanding) man himself is far from being impotent and, as Freud reminds us in the last passage of his earlier book on religion,[1] science at least has no appearance of being an 'illusion'.   And if this view should still seem intolerably bleak, we can, as was indicated at the end of the last chapter, perhaps derive some comfort from the thought that man, with all his powers and possibilities (as yet so largely unexploited), is himself a product of evolution.   If there is a purpose in evolution, we have no means of understanding it except in and through the mind of man.   There is no guidance

---

[1] *The Future of an Illusion*, p. 93.

as to the nature of this purpose and our place in it save such as we ourselves provide through the free use of human faculty.

CHAPTER XVIII

'LEFT' AND 'RIGHT' AS SOCIAL ATTITUDES[1]

THE divine has led us by a natural transition to the human; for that seems to be the cultural trend of modern religious thought. Let us for the remainder of our examples confine ourselves to human society and let us seek our next instances from the internal politics of states and nations. In many times and places, whenever there has been some degree of democratic government, there has also been a tendency for two major parties to arise, a party desirous of change and of greater power and privilege for the 'underdog', and a party whose aim was the conservation of existing practice and traditional status. Correspondingly the individual members of the community, in virtue of their dispositions, upbringings, and interests, exhibit a predominant sympathy with one party or the other. In W. S. Gilbert's well-known words:

> I often think it's comical
> How nature always does contrive
> That every boy and every gal
> That's born into this world alive
> Is either a little Liberal
> Or a little Conservative.

Recent experimental work on 'attitudes,' mostly in America,[2] has provided considerable statistical confirmation of the existence of what has generally been called a 'radical-conservative' factor, in virtue of which an individual tends to hold views that accord with a radical or conservative pattern, and that apply to a number of distinct fields which at first sight might appear to be logically independent but which are connected in social

[1] The substance of this chapter is to some extent an expansion of an article entitled 'Why Do We Oppose Socialism?' in *Science and Society* (February–May, 1937), vol. i.

[2] The most convenient summary of the American work for British readers will perhaps be found in P. E. Vernon, *The Assessment of Psychological Qualities by Verbal Methods. Industrial Health Research Board Report No. 83*, 1938 (especially sections 29 and 65). Relevant data from England will be found in the work of S. Brahmachari, to which extensive reference was made in Chapter VI, and S. P. Adinarayaniah, *The Psychology of Colour Prejudice*, 1939 (Thesis in the University of London Library).

and political tradition. The fields studied in these investigations relate mostly to religion, politics, economics, sex, penology,
and education. The radicals tend to be unorthodox or freethinkers in religion, progressives and internationalists in politics,
socialistically inclined in economics, liberal in regard to sexual
matters, and in favour of freedom and the arousal of good will
as against coercive discipline in penal methods and in education;
while the conservatives tend to the opposite views in all these
fields.[1] In addition then to the evidence afforded by history
and by the platforms of political parties, experimental psychology
also seems to show that there exist what might be called radical
or conservative 'patterns', rather similar perhaps to the
'patterns of culture' in terms of which Ruth Benedict has
endeavoured to describe primitive communities,[2] but which
here manifest themselves primarily in individuals and groups of
individuals within a given community.

As regards individuals it would perhaps be more correct to
speak of a single bipolar radical-conservative factor, for the
evidence seems to show that here, as is usual in psychology, we
have to do, not with two distinct types, as Gilbert's verse might
suggest, but rather with a continuous and statistically 'normal'
distribution, the majority of people occupying a more or less
intermediate position with a few extreme 'radicals' or 'conservatives' at either end. But the interesting fact remains that
those who incline to radicalism or conservatism in one of the
above-mentioned fields tend to exhibit a corresponding attitude
in the other fields also. In virtue of this tendency we are
therefore still justified in speaking of radical and conservative
(or, if we prefer the shorter terms so much in vogue to-day,
'left' and 'right') patterns, so long as we bear in mind that—
as with most other types that psychologists have endeavoured
to distinguish—individuals may exhibit the characteristics of
these patterns in very varying degrees.

Though experimental psychology shows the existence of these
patterns and gives some indication of the fields over which they
extend, it has so far thrown but little light upon their cause and

---

[1] From the data available it would seem that this radical-conservative factor
exhibits a fairly high degree of 'invariance', i.e. it is found in much the same form
in differently selected populations, contrasting in this respect with some of the
other factors brought to light by the same method of investigation, many of
which are found in some groups but not in others. Writing of the radical-
conservative factor, Vernon says: 'So far this is the only dimension of attitudes
which can definitely claim to be established' (*op. cit.* p. 38).

[2] Ruth Benedict, *Patterns of Culture*, 1935.

origin. Why should people tend to fall into these two classes and why should the left and right attitudes take the shape they do in these separate and, as it might seem, independent fields? The problem here is the same in form as that in the case of other psychological factors, where the isolation of a factor by experimental and statistical means does little to explain its psychological nature and origin. There may be one single major cause of all the manifestations concerned (analogous to that which holds in the sphere of intellectual abilities, if we accept Spearman's suggested explanation of 'g' in terms of mental energy). An explanation of this sort is the one that springs most naturally to mind. The effect might, however, possibly be produced by several overlapping causes, or even by a more or less chance arrangement of many of them. In the present case, moreover (unlike that of most other psychological factors that have been brought to light by experimental tests and factor analysis), we have to reckon with the consolidating influence of history and tradition, which has obviously played a part, for instance, in the programmes of political parties and the aims of propagandist societies. There can be little doubt indeed that the left and right patterns, as we meet them in our own Western culture, are to a considerable extent determined in this way. This, however, need not (and perhaps should not) deter us from seeking a deeper-lying psychological influence which may itself have helped to mould the social and political traditions and which, even independently of them, may be at work within the mind of the individual, determining his general tendency to fall into one or other of the two patterns. If there is such a deep-lying psychological influence, psycho-analysis would appear to be the method most likely to reveal it, and, as a matter of fact, psycho-analytical work in its social applications does seem to point to the existence of just such an influence. This lies in the parent-regarding, especially the father-regarding, attitude, and in the continuation of this attitude in introjected form in the super-ego; the 'right' or conservative attitude resulting from a predominance of, obedience to, admiration of, and identification with the parental figure or its substitutes in the external world or as introjected in the super-ego; the 'left' or radical attitude resulting from a rebellion against this figure, from an adoption of the child's standpoint as contrasted with that of the parent, of that of the ego as contrasted with that of the super-ego. The influence in question is therefore of a kind that is very relevant to the main theme of the present book—and this is our justification for devoting a chapter to the subject.

To study the way in which this influence would appear to manifest itself in the various fields, we will consider ten contrasted 'right' and 'left' attitudes, first listing them in tabular form and then dealing with them one by one.

Right	Left
1. Loyalty to a single Father-figure (Leader).	Loyalty to Group.
2. Upholds Family.	Regards Family with suspicion.
3. Stresses Discipline in education, penology, etc.	Stresses Freedom.
4. Anti-feminist.	Feminist.
5. Stresses Sexual Restraint.	Tends to Sexual Freedom.
6. Patriotic.	Cosmopolitan.
7. Upholds Class Distinctions.	Tends to 'Classless' Society.
8. Upholds Conventions and Traditions.	Critical of Conventions and Traditions.
9. Upholds Religion.	Anti-religious.
10. Upholds Private Property.	Socialistic.

(1) Attitude to Leader and Group

As regards this we are in direct contact with Freud's line of thought, as outlined in *Totem and Taboo, Group Psychology and Analysis of the Ego* and elsewhere, and as elaborated in certain directions by other psycho-analysts.[1] We may also refer to what has been said on the subject of kings and rulers in Chapters X and XIII of the present book. The leader of the group, tribe, or nation is inevitably regarded with feelings that are to a large extent displacements of those which in earlier life were directed to the parents, and especially the father. In a word, the leader is a father-figure, towards whom his followers have the same ambivalent attitude of love, homage, respect, combined with envy, hatred and rebelliousness, that they had towards their own fathers. All children share to some extent these feelings, and this fact may bring them together either in

[1] What may perhaps prove a convenient summary of earlier psycho-analytic formulations in this field will be found in chapter twelve of the author's *Psycho-analytic Study of the Family*, 1921. See also M. D. Eder's chapter on 'Politics' in *Social Aspects of Psycho-analysis*, ed. by Ernest Jones, 1924.

loyalty or in revolt. In the latter case they tend to form a league of young rebels united against what seems to them adult, parental, or governmental tyranny. Such an attitude in its extreme form may lead to the overthrow of the father-figure, and this of course is the basis of Freud's famous theory of the slaying of the primal father by the band of brothers—a 'just-so story', as he himself has called it, which, with endless variations on the central theme, has been constantly repeated throughout the long history of human society. It is therefore with justice that Hopkins has given the title *Father or Sons?* to his interesting study of certain modern versions of this story.[1] The leader represents the father, the group represents the sons, and the slogan 'Liberty, Equality, Fraternity' of one of the mightiest of modern revolutions does but express more explicitly than usual the ideals dimly apprehended by rebels of all time. The attitude of the 'right' thus corresponds to the universal human tendency to loyalty towards parents and parent substitutes, that of the left represents the no less ubiquitous conspiracy of the young against the old. Since both attitudes are inevitable, it is not surprising that parties crystallize around them, calling to their banner those in whom one or other attitude happens to preponderate, and that, just as revolution follows tyranny, so counter-revolution follows revolution. It is important, however, to realize the difference in the nature of the sentiments involved. With the 'right', loyalty to the leader and all he represents (or in some rarer cases loyalty to a few leaders, as in an aristocracy, oligarchy, or gerontocracy) is paramount and loyalty to the group is secondary (the group being primarily cemented by the common loyalty of all concerned to the leader), whereas with the 'left' the chief accent is on community and brotherhood within the group, and the leader is regarded not so much as in an altogether different class from that of ordinary men but as *primus inter pares*, his presence being a concession at once to the real needs of social organization and to the psychological requirement of submission to, and veneration of, a father-figure.

(2) Attitude to the Family

In our own patriarchal culture the institution of the family is closely linked with the power of the father, and the endeavour of the children to free themselves from the father's power often

[1] P. Hopkins, *Father or Sons?* 1927.

takes the form of attempting to escape from the narrow family circle into the wider social world where this influence of the father is less directly felt. Loyalty to the family when it persists strongly into later life may also compete with loyalty towards wider social groups, and it is this fact that has led group-minded thinkers (from Plato onwards) to look upon the family with suspicion and to suggest restrictions on what they considered to be its anti-social influence. The family is, of course, a biologically determined social unit, but the adaptability of human nature is such that the functions of this unit can be largely taken over by other agencies, and its actual social importance has varied considerably from one period or culture to another. Some anthropologists have endeavoured to distinguish certain main stages in the history of human civilization which bring out clearly the fluctuation in this relative significance of the family. Thus Wundt [1] and Müller-Lyer,[2] though using a different terminology, seem to agree as to the existence of four such stages, which, stated in tabular form, are as follows:

Wundt	Müller-Lyer
A. Primitive age.	Primitive phase.
B. Totemic age.	Clan (*verwandtschaftlich*) phase.
C. Age of heroes and gods.	Family phase.
D. Transition to humanity.	Personal phase.

In A, the biological family constitutes the essential social unit in a scattered population, and the influence of the father as the head of the family is therefore great. In B, which corresponds to the stage of the majority of primitive societies as we know them, a larger group—the clan—has to a great extent taken over the social functions of the family. Descent is often traced in the female line, and the father as an individual authoritarian figure has given place to a group of elders (in so far as an individual authority is still important in early life, this authority being often the maternal uncle). Freud's theory of the origin of totemism [3] following the overthrow of the primal father relates of course to the transition from A to B (though he

[1] W. Wundt, *Elements of Folk Psychology*, 1916.
[2] F. Müller-Lyer, *Phasen der Kultur*, 1920; *Phasen der Liebe*, 1921; *Formen der Ehe*, 1922.
[3] This theory is admittedly based upon the previously formulated theories of Darwin and Atkinson and was greatly influenced by the work of Robertson Smith. Interesting supplements to Freud's theory, with special reference to the developments of early totemic culture, will be found in G. Róheim, 'Nach dem Tode des Urvaters,' *Imago* (1923), 9, 83.

envisages the 'primitive' condition as one of a patriarchal 'horde' in which the overlord rules over all the sons and grandsons and possesses all the women). With growing culture and denser populations B gives place to C, which is essentially the age of *patria potestas*. The biological family exists as a smaller unit within the larger one of the tribe or state, and the father once again comes into his own as the head of this smaller unit. We ourselves are living in an age which represents a transition from C to D. In this latter the individual tends increasingly to find his loyalties, duties, and privileges connected with the wider social group rather than in and through the family, while the wider group in turn becomes increasingly related to the rest of mankind. Hence the justification at once for Wundt's 'transition to humanity' and for Müller-Lyer's 'personal phase'; both the individual as such and also the wider community (eventually perhaps itself widening to include all the human race) increase in importance, while the family recedes (and with it the power of the individual father). In our own times it is easy to recognize some of the influences—economic (e.g. the industrial revolution), political (e.g. socialism, communism, fascism), and cultural (e.g. the printed word, radio, films, improved means of transport)—which work in this direction; it is easy to see also that, whereas left-wing thought favours this transition, that of the 'right' on the whole opposes it, and hence lays greater stress on the value of the family. Turning to psychology, we can understand that, since the super-ego is in its origin so largely bound up with the father-figure, the 'right' tends to uphold this embodiment of the super-ego in its original and primitive form, whereas the 'left' favours a projection of the super-ego on the social group. In so far as it lays greater emphasis upon the individual also, as distinct from the family (Müller-Lyer's 'personal' element), it favours the ego in its opposition to the super-ego. On the whole, then, phases B and D represent swings to the 'left' after a preceding phase in which the 'right' attitude has predominated.

(3) Attitude to Discipline in Education, etc.

Here we have the conflict of child with parent, of the ego with the super-ego, in one of its purest forms. In this conflict those of the 'left' identify themselves with the child, those of the 'right' with the parent. The former constantly extol the benefits of freedom, the latter the advantages of discipline; and

this attitude towards authority in general is mirrored in their
attitude towards the treatment of the child at home and at
school, of the offender in the law court and the prison.   In this
connection we may also refer back to what we have said about
the Polycrates complex and the need for punishment (especially
in its projected or extrapunitive form) in earlier chapters.   For
a variety of reasons there is a vague but potent fear that calamity
will follow any relaxation of discipline, any removal of hardship,
any mitigation of punishment, and this fear plays a significant
part in determining the attitude of the 'right' to all questions
concerned with discipline or punishment, whereas the attitude
of the 'left' is governed rather by the hope of spontaneous
'goodness' which was discussed in connection with our fourth
'tendency' in the last chapter.[1]

(4) Attitude to Feminism

In our patriarchal society authority is predominantly
masculine and the father is the essential prototype and external
representative of the super-ego.   Women must therefore (like
children, though in lesser degree) be kept in subjection.   For
the preservation of the family and the *patria potestas*, moreover,
chastity of women is essential, alike to ensure the legitimacy
of offspring, to satisfy the husband's possessiveness, and to
preserve the 'sanctity' of home life.   The 'right' therefore
tends to treat women as inferiors or as chattels, though often
under the pretence of shielding them from danger.   The 'left',
on the other hand, tends to treat them as individuals entitled
to equal rights with men.   Feminism springs essentially from
the ego-assertiveness of women themselves, aided by men who
see in the 'subjection of women' another manifestation of
oppressive patriarchal power and who (consciously or unconsciously) rebel against the exclusive sexual rights of married

---

[1] The following words of Joseph C. Grew, American Ambassador in Tokyo
till the outbreak of war, well express the connection between the three headings
we have just discussed (Leader, Family, Discipline) as exemplified by Japan:
'The whole concept of Japanese education has been built upon the military
formula of obeying commands.   The spirit of free inquiry and intelligent criticism
that we consider fundamental in education is not encouraged in Japan.   It is
the student's duty to receive without question what the professor provides, and
to hand it back at examination times.   This attitude in education stems from
the idea of paternal authority in the family and in the state.   For Japan has
seized upon the authority of the family system, with its deference to the head
of the house, and has taught its people to revere the authority of the Emperor
on a national plane as the father of the household is honoured and obeyed within
the home' (*Report from Tokyo* (1942), p. 67)

men—this last being as a rule based on reverberations of the infantile Œdipus complex.

(5) Attitude to Sex

This last point leads us naturally to sex. Since some of the main authoritarian taboos relate to sex, in its infantile, adolescent, and adult forms, it is natural that those who uphold authority should seek to preserve these taboos and that those who oppose it should seek to overthrow them. Hence at least some measures towards greater sexual freedom figure in all the more thoroughgoing 'leftist' programmes, and hence the remarkable attempt at a purely 'rational' sex law and sex morality in the early days of the U.S.S.R. The sexual inhibitions are, however, so deeply rooted in human nature [1] that very few left-wing reformers are able to be thoroughgoing in this respect. As Reich has pointed out,[2] opponents of socialism and communism correctly diagnose the sexual rebelliousness of the 'left' and sometimes use this knowledge as a political weapon by playing on the sexual anxieties of those whom they address,[3] while the 'leftists' on their part are hampered by not being able either satisfactorily to rebut the charges or openly to come forward as champions of 'sexual reform'. The courageous adoption of this latter attitude would, Reich suggests (on the basis of his own experience), greatly strengthen their position as providing both a straightforward reply to their

[1] In view of the large modern literature on sexology and the great importance attributed to sexual repression by psycho-analysis, it is perhaps curious how few attempts have been made to discuss the origin, cause, and fundamental rôle of sexual inhibitions in general. Among the few such attempts may be mentioned: E. Bleuler, 'Der Sexualwiderstand,' *Jahrbuch für Psychoanalytische und Psychopathologische Forschungen* (1913), 5, 442; J. C. Flugel, 'The Biological Basis of Sexual Repression and its Sociological Significance,' *Brit. J. Med. Psychol.* (1921), 1, 225; J. D. Unwin, *Sex and Culture*, 1934; W. Reich, *Der Einbruch der Sexualmoral*, 2nd ed., 1935. These may be said to stress psychological, biological, cultural, and economic factors respectively.

[2] W. Reich, *Zur Massenpsychologie des Fascismus*, 1933; and elsewhere.

[3] Reich quotes the following example from a manifesto issued by the (German) 'Association for Combating Bolshevism', issued in 1918: 'German Women, do you realize in what way Bolshevism threatens you? Bolshevism seeks to socialize women'. The manifesto goes on to state certain alleged Bolshevik rules as follows:

'1. The property rights of women between 17 and 32 are abolished.
2. All women are the property of the state.
3. Any man who desires to make use of any particular piece of this state property must obtain a ticket from the Workers' Committee.
4. No man has a right to take away any particular woman for more than 3 times a week and more than 3 hours at a time.
5. It is the duty of everyone to report cases of women who offer resistance.
6. Any man who does not belong to the working class must pay 100 R. for the privilege of using this state property'.

T

opponents' insinuations and an attractive and glamorous
supplement to the in itself somewhat drab insistence upon
purely economic factors which plays such a large part in socialist
propaganda.   But even though radicals may seldom be willing
to 'go the whole hog' (as some might think, an appropriate
metaphor in this case) with regard to sexual liberty, they
nevertheless tend on the whole to adopt a more liberal attitude
towards such questions as those of divorce, birth-control, extra-
marital intercourse, abortion, etc., than those of the opposite
political and social persuasion.

A complicating circumstance here (as also perhaps in some
other of our ten categories) is to be found in the process of
'increase of satisfaction through inhibition' to which we referred
in Chapter VII.   On the whole, those of the 'right' are more
liable to obtain satisfaction of this kind, which thus sweetens
restrictions and inhibitions that might otherwise be burdensome,
and which may even make it appear that the abolition of such
restrictions, as advocated by the 'left', would signify a return
to crudity and barbarism and a destruction, not only of the
foundations of morality, but of all the refinements and subtle
pleasures that have grown up round the numerous taboos on
sex.

(6) Attitude to Patriotism and Cosmopolitanism

At the present stage of political evolution the nation-state
has the great advantage of being a going concern supported by
strong traditions of loyalty, which themselves have during the
last century or so been further buttressed by certain schools of
philosophic thought, by economic and social development which
has tended to confer greatly increased power and responsibility
on the state, and by the widespread use of symbols (such as
those connected with flags, coins, postage stamps, uniforms,
anthems, etc.).   Under these circumstances it would be natural
for those who place their trust in existing authorities to uphold
the state as one of the great supports of morality and order.
Furthermore, as psycho-analysts have insisted, our state or
country makes a great appeal to the unconscious, inasmuch as
it stands in a symbolic relationship to the parent-figures of our
infancy, as is revealed in the very words 'patriotism', 'motherland', 'fatherland', etc.   Our earlier loyalty and obedience to
the parents are thus very easily transferred to the state.   When
we are exhorted to fight (and perhaps to die) for 'king and

country', we are in effect asked to defend a person and a social organization which in large part derive their emotional appeal from displacements of this earlier loyalty, and the proverbial question put to conscientious objectors, 'What would you do if a German (or whoever the enemy happens to be) attacked your mother?' is therefore psychologically sound. Small wonder then that those of her 'sons' who refuse to rise in defence of their 'motherland' are often looked upon as traitors. Resistance to such an appeal implies rebellion against one of the most powerfully entrenched forms of traditional authority, and the few who offer such resistance (whether as regards the urgent demand for active service in war or the milder claim for a patriotic attitude in time of peace) may perhaps be said to fall into four main categories: (a) those who rely primarily on their own conscience, which forbids them to participate in the peculiarly widespread and violent form of aggression that is war, (b) those who are acutely aware of the apparent inconsistency between Christian (and other religious) injunctions of 'non-violence' and the brutal exercise of power involved in war and aggressive patriotism generally, (c) those who find in 'class consciousness' or some other comparable social loyalty a substitute for loyalty to the state—one that compels them to direct both their love and their hate into channels other than those used by the patriot, (d) those who connect their ideals with the concept of humanity as a whole and who seek to regard all men as their brothers. These categories are, of course, not mutually exclusive but correspond rather to varieties of emphasis. As Glover [1] in particular has pointed out, pacifism does not necessarily imply a lack of aggressiveness. Indeed those who fall into categories (a) and (b) may often do so in virtue of a reaction-formation to a strong individual aggressiveness, which may often manifest itself openly in other directions. Nevertheless it has to be admitted that their attitude represents an attempt (albeit perhaps sometimes an unhappy and unhealthy one) to control their violence in conformity with the precepts of most of the great religious and moral teachers throughout the ages.

Here, as in many other comparable matters, the upholding of a minority view which opposes a strongly held moral position is hardly possible without a considerable aggressiveness directed into rebellious or 'leftist' channels. Even the 'crank' or 'eccentric' (if he is not definitely insane) may be useful to

[1] E. Glover, *War, Sadism, and Pacifism*, 1933.

society, for there is often a degree of reasonableness in his ideals, even though it requires a considerable amount, and an unusual direction, of aggression for him to espouse a cause which to others seems trivial, absurd, or contemptible.

Those who belong to (c) make little or no pretence of hiding their aggressiveness. Their attitude corresponds to that of the band of rebellious brothers who seek to slay the father-figure, who for them however is to be found not so much in an enemy ruler or country as in 'capitalists' or some other class of oppressors. Both their friends (their brothers or 'comrades') and their enemies (now embodied in a 'have' as opposed to a 'have-not' class) transcend national boundaries. The old conflict is still there, but differently orientated, and in this conflict rebelliousness triumphs over the older traditional loyalties. In (d), which is still seldom found in anything approaching a pure form (in spite of the fact that Christianity is a religion of 'humanity'), 'mankind', 'cosmopolis', 'the world', would seem to represent a fusion of the brotherhood and mother ideals. Cosmopolitanism stands in somewhat the same relation to the nation-state as the matriarchal clan or tribe does to the patriarchal family or 'horde'. In either case there is a move away from father-loyalty to 'brotherly love' and mother love; while the world-mother of cosmopolis represents a more satisfying and all-embracing mother than the narrower one of the 'motherland', in somewhat the same way as the divine parent represents a more powerful and satisfying protector than the human one, though in both cases there is also the same disadvantage, that of greater remoteness and lesser 'warmth and intimacy'.

(7) Attitude to Class

Existing social classes, like existing national states, tend to arouse loyalty and obedience in virtue of their mere permanence and their traditions. But, except where there is a rigid caste system, classes differ from states in that they are less well defined units, having fluid boundaries which can be crossed with the help of the social ladder. These boundaries moreover are, in the more complex civilizations, to some extent transected by those of numerous other social groups, to wit the countless societies and associations, political, occupational, topological, recreational, etc., which make such considerable calls upon the resources, energies, and interests of most adult individuals.

Moreover the mutual dependence of the classes into which the inhabitants of a state may be divided is much more obvious to all concerned than is the interdependence of states; classes are clearly less self-sufficient and all-embracing than are states. These facts make it more difficult to enlist a constant loyalty to a class (as envisaged for instance in the doctrine of 'class war') than to a state, so that in a conflict between the two the latter is usually triumphant, and class wars tend to be suspended at the threat of any serious danger to the state.

Nevertheless, within these limitations, an upper class can play the rôle of authoritarian parent or projected super-ego in much the same way as the country or state itself. Those of the 'right' will therefore tend to see the ruling class as an embodiment of an ideal, to be obeyed, admired, and perhaps attained, whereas those of the 'left' will regard it rather as an oppressive power to be overthrown or shattered. But identification and the vicarious enjoyment associated with 'altruistic surrender' may also play an important part in the respect for, and support of, upper classes by those who do not actually belong to them, as is shown for instance in the somewhat snobbish pride of servants of the 'old retainer' kind (now however a rapidly disappearing social type), and, more significantly, in the wide popularity in this country of newspaper columns, and indeed of whole newspapers, largely devoted to the doings of the 'upper ten' and their associates. Ridiculous, or even contemptible, as many of such manifestations of vicarious satisfaction may appear, they yet contribute an element of stability to society and may carry out certain social functions in a way that is preferable to that of some of the possible alternatives. 'In England', says McDougall, 'the social nexus takes the place of the official nexus', thus to some extent freeing us from the more rigid (if more logical) subservience to dictators or bureaucrats, while Madariaga finds in this country 'not an aristocracy with a people, but a people with an aristocracy of which it is proud'. The successful working of such a system implies, of course, that the aristocracy is itself imbued with a certain sense of responsibility and a spirit of *noblesse oblige*. The absence of such a spirit has in its time led to the downfall of the aristocracy of France, Russia, and other countries, since a manifestly degenerate upper class can no longer play the rôle of super-ego. Apart from this, however, it is clear that the existence of an upper class that can inspire admiration and respect (even if to some extent unreasonably) does in fact tend to gratify the super-ego craving of the 'right', while the 'classless society' which is the aim of the 'left' represents as near an approach as possible to the goal of egalitarian brotherhood from which the authoritarian father-figure has been successfully eliminated.

(8) Attitude to Conventional Morality

Conventional morality, and indeed convention generally, represent the crystallization of ethical and social thought as it manifests itself in tradition and as it is handed down from the super-ego of the parent to that of the child in the manner indicated in Chapter VI. It is therefore not surprising that, both in big matters and in small, the 'left' should revolt against traditional authority and should express itself in a flouting of convention; as manifested for instance in the frequent 'leftish' tendency to some symbolic unorthodoxy of dress or some neglect of prevailing etiquette. As we saw moreover, in the same chapter, the conscious ego-ideal may often itself be in conflict with the deeper layers of the super-ego in matters of conventional morality, while in Chapter X we also noted the by no means unimportant connection between the maintenance of class distinctions and the observance of certain conventions and taboos.

(9) Attitude to Religion

This is sufficiently obvious after what has been said on the subject in the last chapter and in earlier portions of this book. God as the super-father is the supreme representative of the super-ego, and revolt against Him is in some respects the supreme rebellion. Nevertheless it is well to bear in mind what we had to say at the conclusion of Chapter XIII as to the persistence of guilt and the need for punishment even among those who have intellectually discarded the belief in God. Atheism may in some circumstances only throw the disbeliever back upon complete dependence on his own perhaps more rigid super-ego. In actual practice, however, to judge from recent tendencies, when traditional religious belief is abandoned, an emotional substitute is now most likely to be found along the lines indicated in the last chapter, i.e. in some form of the religion of humanity. In obedience to the state or party man finds an alternative to obedience to God, while *Mein Kampf* or *Das Kapital* replaces the Bible.

(10) Attitude to Property

As has often been pointed out, those who possess property (especially in a society in which property is highly esteemed) are naturally more inclined to be conservative than those who do not. The former have something to lose by any change of régime, the latter may reasonably hope to gain. In capitalist society, moreover, property confers prestige, while being 'without visible means of support' is itself regarded as a crime. The capitalist therefore tends to become the respectable, authoritarian father-figure, against whom the 'have-nots' and the 'under-privileged' rebel. In Suttie's words, 'the capitalist aims to play parent to other people and the communist aims to be children together'. But clearly there is no complete correspondence between economic or social position and attitude to 'right' or 'left'; partly because in any given individual this latter attitude may be determined with reference to one or more of the other fields we have passed in review, partly because he may, even within the economic sphere, identify himself predominantly with the opposite group—perhaps, if he is 'over-privileged', by a sense of guilt at possessing more than others (a rapidly and, as many will think, fortunately, increasing tendency); if he is 'under-privileged', in virtue of 'altruistic surrender', through which he enjoys vicariously the pleasures of the rich. This last factor may very well co-operate with others, some of which are themselves economic, as when a member of a lower socio-economic class is himself a capitalist on a small scale (as is the case with millions in this country); others more of the nature of traditional loyalties, as in the respect for 'The Old Lady of Threadneedle Street', which is surely a mother-figure. In fact a whole series of anxieties, many of them infantile in origin, can be aroused at any threats to property, such as those associated with 'Communism' or 'Bolshevism'. There is the 'oral' fear of going hungry, which leads to great emphasis on the importance of savings and an assured income. Glover [1] and Róheim,[2] among psycho-analysts, have drawn attention to the probable influence in this direction of early feeding experiences upon economic attitude in later life. There is the 'anal' fear connected with that strange but psychologically very important equation money = fæces, for the existence of which

---

[1] E. Glover, 'Notes on Oral Character Traits,' *Int. J. Psa.* (1923), 4, 131.

[2] Actually reported (from a paper read by Róheim at the British Psycho-analytical Society) in R. Money-Kyrle, *Superstition and Society* (1939), 126.

psycho-analysts have brought forward very striking evidence.[1] As the child was once deprived of what he considered valuable, his excreta, so the capitalist, large or small, in virtue of the unconscious persistence of this equation, fears that he will once more suffer a similar deprivation, this time of possessions which society had hitherto agreed to be legitimate and worthy of esteem. There is the 'genital' fear connected with the castration complex; loss of money (which we are often told is 'power') may symbolize a dreaded sexual mutilation or loss of sexual potency. There is fear at the level of 'object love' connected with the arousal of childish jealousies and envies at the possibility of other children (particularly our brothers and sisters) receiving more privileges than ourselves; those in whose favour we may be dispossessed may arouse feelings associated with these figures from our early life. Finally there are certain moral factors that are more directly germane to our present theme, the duty of 'self-help' and of acquiring property—as contrasted with the wickedness of the 'spendthrift' and the 'improvident'[2] (these duties, as Hopkins[3] has well brought out, being in themselves very often based on 'sphincter morality'), perhaps even a fear, connected with the Polycrates complex, that the abolition of poverty, through its reduction of human suffering, will in some vaguely conceived way bring about disaster or incur divine displeasure.

Of course those of the 'left' are likewise subject to their own infantile sources of irrationalism, linking on to childish revolts, jealousies, and tantrums connected with early experiences of adult tyrannies and frustrations. The prevalence of such motives often leads to an excessive emphasis on destruction, which is the danger of all rebellious movements and which (besides making the movement unattractive and alarming to those inspired by lesser hate) soon leads to efforts at restitution and perhaps to the reinstatement of a father-figure in the form of a dictator.

This last observation will serve as a salutary reminder that our pictures of the 'right' and 'left' are really abstractions,

---

[1] See especially Ernest Jones, 'Anal Erotic Character Traits,' *Papers on Psychoanalysis* (2nd ed., 1918), 664.

[2] The religious and ethical implications of this attitude have been studied in detail by Max Weber, *The Protestant Ethic and the Spirit of Capitalism*, 1930.

[3] Pryns Hopkins, *The Psychology of Social Movements* (1938), pp. 160 ff. The whole volume contains much that is important from the point of view of the present chapter.

representing only general tendencies which few if any 'right' or 'left' parties or individuals exemplify to the full. The tendencies underlying conservatism and radicalism are both fundamental to human nature and, while the attitude of the left in general represents the path of progress,[1] any excessive sway in that direction tends to bring about in time (sometimes a surprisingly short time) a reactionary movement towards the right. Revolt must in fact be stabilized by authority and obedience if it is to succeed; just as authoritarian discipline must be tempered by some compensating advantages in the way of protection, responsibility, or tactful indulgence in certain directions, if it is to be safe from the danger of revolt. This is perhaps the reason why the two great successful new political movements of the twentieth century, fascism and communism, do not entirely fit the pure patterns of either 'right' or 'left' as we have drawn them. Moreover in the short history of the fascist and communist régimes there is clearly discernible a swing away from some of the more extreme positions that were occupied at first. The fascist rule in particular (as exemplified by Nazi Germany), though in the main it is distinctly reactionary and conservative, nevertheless has some elements that are characteristic rather of the revolutionary 'left'. Indeed, with its policy of completely opportunist propaganda, which in its appeal (though not in its outcome) aims at being 'all things to all men', this is only to be expected. Communism was more consistent in its initial radicalism, but almost from the start there has been some swing towards the 'right' and this has recently been considerably intensified. It may be of interest to attempt to classify the attitudes of fascism and communism to the ten criteria of 'right' and 'left' that we have just considered, though such an attempt, by revealing that neither attitude falls consistently into our 'right' and 'left' patterns, may seem to detract considerably from the practical usefulness of these

---

[1] The reader may perhaps legitimately demand that we should attempt a detailed confrontation of our 'right' and 'left' characteristics with the eight psychological 'tendencies" of moral development that we distinguished in Chapter XVI. This would be an interesting and useful task, but would take too long and require too many qualifications to be undertaken here. But I think it should be generally clear that in so far as the 'left' aims at an escape from blind authority and a social adjustment in the light of conscious ego-functions, it does on the whole correspond to the 'tendencies' of progress. When, however, rebellion is so intense as to become dominated by aggression, and hence mainly destructive in character, it represents rather an overcoming of the ego by the id, and therefore ceases to exhibit any orderly progress. The quantitative factor is therefore of very great importance.

patterns, however justified they may be from the point of view
of theoretical orientation.

		Fascism	Communism
1.	Leader.	R	L, then towards R
2.	Family.	R, then towards L	L
3.	Discipline.	R	L, then towards R
4.	Feminism.	R	L
5.	Sex.	R, then towards L	L, then towards R
6.	Patriotism.	R	L, then towards R
7.	Class.	L (but new 'party' distinctions)	L (but new 'party' distinctions)
8.	Convention.	L (but new conventions)	L (but new conventions)
9.	Religion.	L (but new religion of state or race)	L, then towards R
10.	Property.	L	L

A few comments on this bald but still, I think, suggestive
table may be in order. As regards No. 1, fascism from the
first was very definitely 'right' in its insistence on the person
of the 'leader', whose supposed almost superhuman qualities
have been so magnified that he may be said to have undergone
something very near to an apotheosis. Russian communism
also has its leader, whose actual power is perhaps no less than
that of the fascist dictators. There would seem, however,
to be a subtle difference in the attitude towards the leader,
Stalin being something more of a *primus inter pares* than Hitler
or Mussolini. He is still 'Comrade Stalin', his innumerable
portraits appear alongside those of a few others, while behind
him lie the remoter and more shadowy figures of Lenin and
Marx. Nevertheless the leader principle has undoubtedly been
of immense help in giving stability to the communist régime
in Russia, and Eder [1] may very well be right in his early surmise
that it was owing to the adoption of this principle, and to the
provision of a father-figure (as testified in the very beginning
by the popularity of busts of Marx), that the Russian revolution
was able to succeed in ways in which the French revolution
failed. Marx, though dead, was able to give a comfort and
confidence that statues of Liberty and Reason (at once more
abstract and more feminine figures) were unable to provide.

[1] M. D. Eder in *Social Aspects of Psycho-analysis*, ed. Ernest Jones (1924),
p. 149.

As regards No. 2, communism adopted the traditional 'left' anti-family pattern from the start. It was recognized that the care of children was largely a concern of the state and that the allegiance of children should be to the state rather than to the family. Fascism ultimately adopted the same principle, but did so less wholeheartedly in its early days when there was a (perhaps psychologically sound) attempt to link the idea of the family, and particularly that of the mother, with that of the state.[1] Later on, however, the policy was altered, as exemplified in the encouragement given to children to spy upon their parents and report any ideological shortcomings, such as might be implied by grumbling, criticism, or listening to foreign broadcasts. As regards No. 3, comparison is made difficult by the difference between the immediately preceding régimes. As compared with war-time Tsarist Russia, the Soviet régime was in some respects free and lenient, whereas the Nazis at once introduced a disciplinary system that was strict in comparison with the easy-going conditions that prevailed under the peace-time Weimar republic. In Russia, however, discipline rapidly became more severe, partly no doubt under the stress of civil war and foreign attempts at interference. With regard to No. 4 (Feminism), the difference has been clear cut and well maintained from the start. So far as No. 5 (Sex) is concerned, both sides have swung back a good way from their original positions. Nazism was at first hostile to the sexual freedom enjoyed under the republic and, as we have seen,[2] was at pains to emphasize the maternal aspect of women as guardians of the home. Russia, on the other hand, as we have also noticed, sought to abolish all unnecessary sexual taboos and to establish purely rational systems of sexual law and ethics. This attitude, however, has been progressively undermined, with increasing restrictions upon divorce, abortion, homosexuality, etc., while the Nazis on their side have in recent years in many ways encouraged sexual

---

[1] This is well exemplified in an exhortation relating to 'Mother Day' published in *Der Angriff* in 1933: 'The National Revolution has brushed aside everything that is small and petty. Ideas lead us once more, and lead us together. Family, Society, People! The idea of Mother Day is intended to honour that which is the symbol of the German Idea—the German Mother. Nowhere has the Woman and the Mother such a profound significance as in modern Germany. She is the protection of a family life from which the German people cull the strength which shall lead them upwards. She—the German Mother—is the sole carrier of the German folk thought. The concept of Germany is eternally united with that of Mother. Nothing is more capable of uniting us than the idea of coming together in common homage to our Mothers.'

[2] In the preceding note.

laxity, by abolishing the stigma on extra-marital intercourse and illegitimacy and (as we have been given to understand) by the more or less official provision of pornographic literature and art. With regard to No. 6, it is the Nazis who have been consistent in their patriotism and their doctrine of the 'master race', while the Russians, who were at first cosmopolitan, have become increasingly nationalistic, endeavouring quite recently to encourage this point of view by dissolving the Comintern and by linking up present Russian achievements with the traditions of the Tsarist past.

A statement of the fascist and communist attitudes to our last four categories is more difficult, as is indeed also the distinction between the two régimes themselves, which is quantitative rather than qualitative. Both of them have tended to abolish existing class distinctions, the communists however much more thoroughly than the fascists; but in both cases the rise of a new kind of aristocracy related to membership of the 'party' has to some extent replaced the old divisions. Both régimes, too, have largely abolished old conventions (the Russians once again more thoroughly), but substituted new ones of their own. With regard to No. 9, in both cases a new and political channel has been provided for the emotions that were formerly satisfied in the field of traditional and theological religion. In both régimes the older religions have been discouraged, though much more actively and consistently in Russia, where however, after a period of growing toleration, the remarkable step has recently been taken of according official recognition to the Orthodox Church. Finally, as regards No. 10, in both cases there have been measures aiming at the dispossession of the existing 'plutocrats'; both régimes have very largely eliminated the profit motive and have made political power the condition of wealth, instead of wealth being a road to political power, as it has been in the democracies. Of course dispossession and redistribution of wealth have been far more consistent and thoroughgoing in the case of Russia; nevertheless the original extreme economic egalitarianism was soon modified, and in one way or another (from the days of the 'New Economic Policy' onwards) a good many features of capitalism have returned.

Thus, considering the list of categories as a whole, though neither communism nor fascism fits completely into the 'left' or 'right' pattern respectively, the former, as we might expect, does so to a considerably greater extent than does the latter. The feature in which it departs most from what appears to be the line of progress consists in its totalitarian character, which it shares with fascism. But even here there is a difference, at least so far as theory is concerned. Whereas Hitler seems to envisage no change from authoritarian and party rule for the thousand years' duration which he has predicted for the Third Reich, the communists have for the most part drawn a distinction between emergency or transition measures and those which it is hoped will prevail when the régime has become more firmly established; and they can fairly claim that the period from 1917 to the present day has been throughout one of greater or less emergency. Both fascism and communism appear to enjoy a distinct superiority over most recent democratic régimes in respect of the first of the 'tendencies' of moral development that we considered in Chapter XVI (the tendency from ego-centricity to sociality). It is here, as we have seen, that democracy has much to learn from the success of both political systems. Russian communism, however, is greatly superior to fascism as regards the more embracing character of its sociality, which is not confined within the narrow and phantastic limits of a supposedly higher race, but which on the contrary has in its successful fusion (or at least co-operation) of many different races and cultures a most remarkable achievement to its credit. Fascism moreover appears diametrically opposed to progress as regards our fifth 'tendency' (aggression to tolerance and love). But both fascism and communism as they exist to-day are inferior to democracy as regards our seventh 'tendency' (heteronomy to autonomy). In this field lies indeed the great achievement of democracy.

With these brief and perhaps unsatisfying indications we must leave this fascinating subject, since this is not a treatise on the relative merits of rival political systems, and our whole excursion into this field aims only at illustrating the scope and possible application of the psychological principles which have been our main concern.

CHAPTER XIX

THE PROBLEM OF WAR AND PEACE

THE APPEAL OF WAR

We now come to our last problem—that of war and peace. More than once in this book we have found ourselves touching the fringes of this mighty and, as it may well seem to us at the present moment, quite outstanding human theme. We will now in this final chapter endeavour to survey it a little more thoroughly in the light of some of the concepts with which we have been dealing.[1]

In this country it has for long been customary to speak of war as one of the greatest evils that can befall humanity, and this attitude has led us unduly (and very dangerously) to neglect or disparage the views of those who think differently upon the subject. The soldiers, statesmen, and philosophers who openly glorify war and extol its virtues have some right upon their side, and it would be foolish to ignore them because they come mostly from those countries which are, or have been recently, our enemies. They surely err in treating with contempt the teachings of those great moral and religious leaders who have condemned all unnecessary violence, and therefore *a fortiori* the supreme form of organized violence that is war; these teachings have made too deep an impression on humanity to be lightly brushed aside. But the apologists for violence are justified when they imply that war also makes a strong appeal, one moreover that is no less powerful in its moral than in its instinctive elements. Here we shall spend no time in discussing the horrors and depravities of war; we have all in recent years had ample opportunity to realize them. It will be more helpful to examine in some little detail the psychological appeal of war, for an understanding of the nature of this appeal is likely to put us in a more favourable position for dealing with the practical problem of diminishing or eliminating war. Here as elsewhere we may reasonably hope that psychological knowledge will be more effective than lamentation, exhortation, or moral indigna-

---

[1] Much of the material of this chapter has already appeared (some of it in more expanded form) in *The Moral Paradox of Peace and War* (*Conway Memorial Lecture*, 1941), and 'The Psychological Appeal of Federation,' *New Commonwealth Quarterly* (1940), 6, 102.

tion. War can from certain points of view be looked upon as mass-delinquency, and if psychology can be of use in dealing with the misdemeanours of the individual it may not impossibly be helpful in dealing also with the more grandiose immoralities of nations. We can at least fairly say that religion and ethics have proved singularly impotent in this respect. Christianity, which is a religion of non-violence, has held nominal sway over Europe for over 1500 years, during which Christians have been almost continually waging war, for the most part with one another. Whether psychological knowledge will prove any more effective is still an open question. At any rate we can but try.

The psychological appeal of war can perhaps best be summarized under four main heads, dealing respectively with: adventure, the increase of social unity, freedom from certain individual worries and restrictions, and the provision of certain outlets for aggression—each head permitting of certain subdivisions.

Adventure

Here we may make four subdivisions, the first three and more obvious of which are closely interconnected:

(1) War, especially modern 'total' war, opens up unknown possibilities and opportunities. It changes the course of life for nearly all of us, fighters and civilians alike, though more especially for the former. Civilization, we are often told, demands a dull routine to which we do not all take kindly, and the eagerness with which we read 'thrillers' and adventure stories shows that many of us retain throughout life some of that zest for adventure, for a life that is less settled and secure, which all but the most timid of us had in youth and which has been so successfully exploited by the Boy Scout Movement. This lure of the unknown, this opportunity of witnessing, and perhaps actively participating in, unforeseeable, exciting, and world-shattering events, may be a very potent influence with those who find the daily life in field, factory, or office all too drab and uninspiring.

(2) Closely connected with this is the further possibility that these unpredictable events may make a bigger call upon our bodily and mental powers than is demanded by the everyday routine of peace—which perhaps, except in the case of the young and inexperienced and of the relatively few who hold responsible positions, demands little more than the efficient

functioning of habits. In war we feel that we may each and
all be called upon to perform some noble or heroic deed, to
emulate at least in some small measure the exploits of the great
figures of history, of romantic fiction, or the screen—a possibility that is denied to most of us in the secure conditions of
civilized existence. This in turn is closely connected with:

(3) The increased possibility of risk and danger. The motto
'Safety First', reasonable enough as it may be in some matters,
such as the management of the useful but deadly motor-car or
(as is less often recognized) the framing of sweeping generalizations upon slender evidence, is not one that makes a strong
appeal to bolder and more enterprising minds. Risks must
often be taken if progress is to be made, and a 'spice of danger'
(as the very phrase indicates) is indeed to such minds often in
itself a source of additional attraction. Fear in low or moderate
intensities can certainly be pleasant. We do not fully understand the reason why—perhaps, as McDougall's theory of
emotion would seem to imply, because it is the inevitable
accompaniment of the exercise of an important instinct (that
of escape), perhaps, as psycho-analytic evidence so clearly
indicates, because it has some very intimate connection with
sex, especially in its more masochistic aspects. In ordinary
peace-time life we can for the most part gratify this tendency,
if at all, only in our sports and (vicariously) through our
'thrillers'. In war the possibilities of a more realistic gratification are greatly increased and, especially since the advent of
long-distance air raids, may be said to have been brought
within the reach of all.

These first three factors in their relation with war are all
admirably expressed by F. S. Chapman, the traveller and
explorer, in a passage which is well worth quoting in this
connection. 'It is curious', he says, 'what vicarious pleasure
one derives from physical exhaustion and discomfort. It is a
strange paradox that the more intolerable a journey is at the
same time the more satisfying does it become in retrospect.
Our responsibilities and characters were made to be sharpened
against the hard forces of Nature. But how few people get the
chance to test their physical endurance to breaking-point, to
feel cold fear gnawing at their hearts or to have to make decisions
that hold life and death in the balance? That is why men
flock so easily to war: to test a manhood that is perverted by
the present state of civilization. Rugby football, mountaineer-

ing, ski-ing, even motoring,[1] are but makeshifts for this vanished birthright, narcotics to alleviate the monotony of existence that has grown too soft and easy'. [2]

(4) A fourth factor, one the full implications of which have only become apparent as the result of psycho-analysis, consists in the satisfaction of the nemesistic urge and of the need for punishment so often associated with it—in that deep-seated inability of man to enjoy himself and to make full use of his powers except for ends that themselves involve an element of pain. The appeal of war has here something in common with the motives that lead to sacrifice or asceticism. As we saw in Chapters VII and XI, such motives may have an element of reasonableness, as manifested in what we have called the utilitarian, disciplinary, and epicurean forms of asceticism; it is often necessary to undergo pain, hardship, and exertion for some distant end; it may even be desirable to discipline ourselves in a general way, so that we are capable of making an exceptional effort when called upon to do so. But the need for punishment is apt to drive us far beyond the bounds of reason and makes suffering appear a self-sufficient end. And it is largely to this tendency that the appeal is made when we are asked to believe that guns are in themselves better things than butter. Though in far more sinister guise, it is at bottom the same tendency as that which makes the British Public School man feel that somehow football and fox-hunting are nobler sports than tennis because they involve a greater risk of injury. In war, moreover, there is always the hopeful possibility that the larger share of the punishment may be enjoyed vicariously through the sufferings of the enemy (see Chapter XII).

Social Unity

Let us turn now to our second main heading, that of social unity. Here we can perhaps distinguish five factors, though the first four are so closely allied as not always to be easily distinguishable.

(1) War brings together all the members of a nation, inasmuch as it gives them a greatly increased number of thoughts, interests, emotions, and purposes in common. They all (with the possible exception of a few quislings) ardently desire victory

[1] What price 'Safety First'? But perhaps he is thinking of the racing track.
[2] F. S. Chapman, *Lhasa, The Holy City* (1938), p. 287. By permission of Messrs. Chatto & Windus., publishers.

U

—or, failing that, survival—and this sense of having great common interests at stake, of harbouring the same great common purpose, produces a sense of social harmony that is very hard to achieve in peace-time when, in the absence of a common danger and a common and absorbing purpose, each individual's personal, professional, and local concerns are apt to loom far larger than the interests that are shared by all alike. As McDougall has so well brought out in his *Group Mind*, the existence of a common purpose is one of the great forces that unite a group, and since in war the common purpose is one that applies to the whole nation, it is as members of their nation that individuals feel themselves knit together in a mighty fellowship.

(2) Simultaneously another factor much stressed by McDougall comes into operation: a great increase in the vividness and power of the idea of the nation itself. In war we become more acutely conscious of the history and traditions of our country, as an entity that transcends the existing generation of its citizens. Its soil, its landscape, its language, its literature, its institutions, its historic buildings, all become precious to us as symbols of this enduring entity and we feel ourselves at one with its heroes of the past. It is not merely our own lives and those of our contemporaries that are threatened; it is the existence of this higher entity that is at stake—an entity that links us alike to our forefathers and our descendants.

At the same time as the nation as a whole is exalted, the smaller groups within it tend to diminish in significance, or at any rate to be fitted, mentally and socially, into the larger framework of the nation. A sort of spontaneous *Gleichschaltung* occurs, not one that is dictated by authority from above, but one that springs naturally from the prevailing loyalties and interests. Unless a society or organization can be shown to play its part in the total national scheme of values it ceases to make any strong appeal to us; and, as Harding has emphasized,[1] those in charge of minor mutually competing associations are, in self-defence if for no higher motive, compelled to reconcile many of their differences and to make it appear that the activities of these associations are all in some way contributing to the total national welfare and thus, at least indirectly, to the national effort.

(3) The greater sense of national unity brought about by

[1] D. W. Harding, *The Impulse to Dominate*, 1941.

these first two factors is powerfully reinforced by the substitution of a sense of co-operation for one of competition between the individuals, groups, and classes of a nation. Since all are engaged, in some way and in some degree, in the common task, everyone tends to feel himself a member of a team. Perhaps again we may be permitted to make a quotation which puts the matter better than the present writer could hope to do. In one of his 'Postscripts' broadcast in 1940, J. B. Priestley read a letter he had received that ran as follows: 'My son was formerly a salesman; he resigned to join the Air Force. On a recent visit home he said: "I shall never go back to the old business life—that life of what I call the survival of the slickest; I now know a better way. Our lads in the R.A.F. would, and do, willingly give their lives for each other; the whole outlook of the force is one of 'give', not one of 'get'. If to-morrow the war ended and I returned to business, I would need to sneak, cheat, and pry in order to get hold of orders which otherwise would have gone to one of my R.A.F. friends if one of them returned to commercial life with a competing firm. Instead of co-operating, as we do in war, we would each use all the craft we possessed with which to confound each other. I would never do it".' [1]

(4) Closely allied again with the last-mentioned factor is the increased satisfaction of 'the need to be needed' that war provides. In war-time almost every citizen is both able and glad to 'do his bit'. This in turn is brought about first by the realization of the great common worth-while purpose in which all can participate according to their positions and abilities, secondly by the fact that war (or at least the preparation for war) has proved the most effective means of overcoming the economic problem of unemployment and of actually providing jobs for all. These two influences—psychological and economic respectively—are of course not unconnected, since it is ultimately the sense of national urgency that sets the economic machinery in motion. But this is a matter into which we cannot enter here. [2]

(5) Underlying all the previous social factors there is one great psychological factor at work within the individual mind: war makes the activities of the individual more ego-syntonic,

---

[1] J. B. Priestley, *Postscripts* (1940), p. 43. By permission of the author and the publishers, Messrs. Heinemann.

[2] It is dealt with in chapters four and five of E. H. Carr's *Conditions of Peace*, 1941, a book to which we have already referred.

it reduces the tension between the ego and the super-ego, and tends to raise the ego to the level of the super-ego in the way discussed in Chapter XIII. Participation in a great collective enterprise, strenuous and dangerous exertion, identification with a greater social whole, the substitution of co-operation for competition, the sense that one is really needed—all these produce a satisfying mixture of humility and happy pride, in which the ego willingly submits to the super-ego and the individual is no less willing to sacrifice himself in the service of his country. Herein lies, I think, the most essential element in the *moral* appeal of war. It is this that makes war, in spite of its horrors, cruelties, and crudities, seem noble and uplifting and makes so many peace-time activities seem in comparison trivial and insignificant.

Freedom from Individual Worries and Restrictions

(1) If we look upon the ego from the standpoint of the super-ego, our individual weal or woe becomes automatically of less account and our own petty concerns seen in the light of mighty social events cause us less worry and embarrassment. The great common concern, even the great common danger, drives out our individual anxieties, both because they appear in themselves to be relatively unimportant and because we have less time and energy to think about them—and this in spite of the very real and manifold sacrifices, perils, difficulties, and disturbances that war brings in its train. To this general factor there are added a number of more special ones, of which at least three should perhaps be mentioned:

(2) The lessened economic worry resulting from greater security of employment.

(3) The lessened anxiety—partly financial and partly connected with prestige—concerning social 'face' and class distinctions. When all alike are exposed to the same dangers, compelled by the same necessities and submitted to the same restrictions, the tiresome snobbish form of competition that consists in trying to 'keep up with the Joneses' becomes pointless or downright impossible. A drastic reduction in class privileges and class differences is indeed one of the most striking results of 'total' war—one that, in spite of some nostalgic regrets for the old values that have gone, especially (but not perhaps exclusively) on the part of the former 'over-privileged', most of us feel on the whole to be purifying and ennobling; it

brings us, at any rate in one respect, a little nearer to the Christian principles which for so many centuries we have been professing but not practising. And this in turn, together with the general emergency and the pressure on our time and energy, has freed us also from many small conventions and taboos that we are glad to throw aside and forget now that we have the opportunity.

(4) In this way we are led back to the considerations we raised in Chapters XI and XIV concerning the relaxation of super-ego control that may follow upon suffering. Because of our sacrifices, our anxieties, our danger, and the general sense of urgency, we feel that we are justified in enjoying with a good conscience such pleasures as may be within our reach. This tendency, as we have seen, will not always bear the test of closer moral scrutiny. Nevertheless, amid much that is ethically questionable, it does help to relieve us of some unreasonable restrictions, gives us a wider freedom, and in any case for the time being holds out a prospect of id gratification without incurring guilt, and thus constitutes one of the subtler but none the less significant aspects of the manifold appeal of war.

This allusion to the less morally edifying side of war's attractiveness leads us naturally to our last main heading:

Aggression

(1) War above all provides an outlet for moralized aggression, and psycho-analysts, who in their more recent work have attached so much significance to the aggressive tendencies and their incorporation in the super-ego, have been inclined to see in the unsatisfied aggression of the individual the ultimate source of the strange and sinister appeal of war.[1] Individual aggressiveness, whether it be in the nature of an 'appetite' or a natural 'reaction' to the inevitable frustrations of life,[2] is itself constantly frustrated, and in its cruder manifestations is normally condemned, alike by the law, by the conventions of polite society, and by the super-ego. In war, however, aggression is provided with a channel that is ego-syntonic and socially approved, indeed socially demanded, and the individual is therefore willing and even eager to make use of it. How far

[1] See for instance Edward Glover, *War, Sadism, and Pacifism*, 1933; E. F. M. Durbin and John Bowlby, *Personal Aggressiveness and War*, 1939 (probably the most valuable book dealing with the psychology of war from this point of view); Mark A. May, *A Social Psychology of War and Peace*, 1943.

[2] The reader may be reminded of the brief discussion of this problem in Chapter XVI.

this theory really takes us is still a matter of discussion.[1] But that it has some considerable degree of truth can hardly be doubted. And in any case, whatever degree of aggression be involved and whatever be its source, the fact that it is moralized is beyond all dispute. In war we all acquire, in so far as our behaviour to the enemy is concerned, what in other circumstances might legitimately be called a criminal super-ego. We regard it not only as permissible but as supremely right to kill, maim, and destroy, so long as our violence is directed to the foe. Within this limited sphere there is a complete 'transvaluation of all values', what are otherwise the greatest crimes becoming now the highest virtues. War provides the most thoroughgoing and morally satisfactory rationalization for unsocial conduct that has yet been discovered. To the members of each side the rightness of their cause is obvious and the standpoint of their opponents utterly perverse and wicked. At the present moment in the stress of war it is hard to comprehend how our enemies, the Germans and the Japanese, can be for the most part no less convinced (indeed perhaps more so) of the utter perversity of our aims than we are of theirs. Such is the tragic moral relativity of war. But here we are concerned not so much with the tragedy, as with the appeal, of the unique combination of morality and aggressiveness that war is able to provide. As a means of doing evil and of feeling good while doing it, war is

[1] It has been objected in particular: (a) That the vast majority of the activities of modern war do not seem particularly suitable as channels of aggression. Actual fighting only occupies a small part of the time even of those on 'active service', what there is of it consists largely in the skilled manipulation of complicated machines, while the still larger numbers of people engaged in organizing the war or in making and transporting its vast and cumbrous equipment themselves may never fight at all. The reply to this is clearly that the end justifies and inspires the means and that aggression through displacement or conditioning can find some considerable degree of expression through 'war work' of any kind, though the home-front workers recognize that it would be emotionally more satisfying to 'have a smack' at the enemy themselves instead of having to do it vicariously through the fighting forces; (b) That even the fighters themselves do not often display anger or any other easily recognizable manifestations of aggressiveness. Neither, it might be replied, does a mother constantly experience maternal feeling towards her infant; but this does not prove that it is not a driving force behind her varied and self-sacrificing activities on its behalf. Again, psycho-analysis has shown pretty conclusively that in virtue of displacement the sexual urge may underlie a great number of interests that certainly fail to arouse any white heat of sexual passion but that possess at most a dimly discernible sexual background. It may be similarly with aggression; (c) That not all frustrated populations are warlike. Here admittedly questions of social organization and tradition are important. War, in the words of Durbin and Bowlby, is 'organized fighting between large groups of adult human beings' and as such undoubtedly requires the necessary degree of social organization, as also a tradition or some other powerful influence (such as that of a militarily-minded leader) which will set the organized social activity working for a warlike aim.

without a parallel. Even the hunting of witches, heretics, and traitors, which to some extent provides a similar satisfaction, sinks into relative insignificance beside it, both in scope and in the completeness of its apparent moral justification. This element of moral justification is increased by two further closely related factors:

(2) The general direction of all aggression towards the enemy, who in war-time is apt to become something of a universal scapegoat, enables us to be relatively free of aggression towards the other members of our own group. Inter-group aggression becomes a condition of intra-group co-operation; all our hostility being directed outwards, friendly feelings can have unimpeded play in our relations with our fellow-fighters. Here again we see at work that process of 'decomposition' that we have already studied in certain other connections. This factor is complementary to, or perhaps we should even say only another aspect of, the first four factors that we considered under the heading of 'Social Unity'.

(3) In his rôle of scapegoat the enemy serves us as an object upon which we can project our own vices, especially our vices of aggression. It is indeed this which often makes him appear a veritable monster of iniquity. In our own opinion it is nearly always the enemy who has provoked the conflict; we ourselves enter into it unwillingly and in self-defence. Even modern Germany and Japan, in spite of their view that they deserve to rule the earth in virtue of their superiority over other nations or races, have recourse to their supposed 'encirclement' by less worthy peoples, i.e. they project their own aggressiveness upon those whom they attack. Perhaps, as Money-Kyrle [1] has suggested, the capacity for the outward displacement and projection of his own hostile feelings is the only condition on which man could have successfully combined two of his chief characteristics which at first sight might appear to be incompatible—his aggressiveness and his gregariousness. On this view he became 'exoctonous', to avoid conflict within the social group, much as he became exogamous, to ensure peace within the family. The same 'exoctony' is perhaps to some extent true of wolves, as would appear from Wilfred Trotter's well-known parallel between the wolf pack and the aggressive human nation.[2]

---

[1] R. Money-Kyrle, 'The Development of War,' *Brit. J. Med. Psychol.* (1937), 16, 219.   [2] W. Trotter, *Instincts of the Herd in Peace and War*, 1st ed., 1918.

THE CONDITIONS OF PEACE

Hitherto the attempts to combat war have been made along two main lines, moral and political respectively. The first seeks to bring about 'a change of heart' by producing a vivid realization of the horrors of war and its utter incompatibility with the ethical standards recognized in other spheres. The second aims at providing political machinery for preventing international disputes or for settling them without recourse to arms. Our psychological considerations in this chapter and in the earlier portions of this book suggest a certain extension and reorientation of both these methods of approach, while at the same time they indicate a third that would seem to be no less important, i.e. the attempt to provide the advantages that, as we have just seen, may accrue from war, otherwise than through the destructive process of war itself. This last method corresponds in the main to the provision of what William James in a celebrated essay [1] has called a 'moral equivalent of war'. In the remainder of this chapter we will briefly consider these three methods of approach.

The Moral Approach.—This method seems so far to have been singularly ineffective, chiefly perhaps for the reason that it has scarcely begun to touch the point at issue. The moral values with which war is at variance are by tradition individual moral values and these, as we have seen, are abrogated when the individual conscience is handed over to the group, as is usually the case in war. This suggests that the moral emphasis, so far as this particular end is concerned, must be displaced from the individual to the state. It is the more difficult and so far but little attempted moralization of the state that is required, the transference to the state of the moral obligations that have long been recognized as incumbent on the individual. It would be foolish to under-estimate the magnitude of this task and the very considerable changes in our views that it seeks to bring about. We have long recognized that the individual must in many ways sacrifice himself for the community and that un-adulterated egoism is incompatible with social life. We have only begun to recognize at all clearly the necessity for a similar limitation of the egoism of states—for in the past it has usually been thought that any restriction, self-abnegation, or self-sacrifice is a reflection on the honour and glory of the nation,

[1] William James, *The Moral Equivalent of War.* Association for International Conciliation: Leaflet No. 27, 1910. Reprinted in *Memories and Studies,* 1911.

whose sovereign power, it was implicitly assumed, could only be vindicated by the most crude and ruthless self-assertion and by complete disregard of the claims of other national units; altruism might be virtuous in the case of individuals, but was dishonourable and humiliating in the case of states. As several psycho-analysts have pointed out, this retention of an 'immoral' attitude on the part of the state is determined, not only by the projection of the individual super-ego on to the state, but also by the fact that the complete 'sovereignty' of the state represents a last attempt to preserve the original infantile 'omnipotence' (in some respects similar to that which we enjoy vicariously in contemplating the power of an 'Almighty God'). Hence the abandonment of this sovereignty constitutes a narcissistic trauma as well as a submission to the super-ego in a sphere (that of international politics) in which its influence has hitherto been successfully evaded.

How far-reaching is the change of attitude required can be seen from a glance at just one of the many delicate problems involved—that of population. It is commonly implied that any nation with a high birth rate, and therefore a real or potential rapid increase of population, has a right (if it has the necessary power) to demand fresh territories for its overflow. Except in the rare cases where unexploited land is actually available, such a notion must inevitably lead to war. Self-sacrifice and mutual accommodation among nations on the other hand will demand something like a rationing of territory as of other goods; and this in turn, if over-population is to be avoided, will demand a rationing of population—a proposal that seems only too likely to arouse the most fiery indignation on the part of those affected; probably because the ever-latent castration complex is liable to be 'touched off' by anything that may appear to diminish the fertility and 'virility' of the race.[1] The Nazis and the Japanese are not alone in thinking that their 'race' and culture are superior to others, though at the moment it is they who proclaim this belief most shamelessly. Every people that harbours such a notion is likely to consider any proposed restriction on its numbers as an attempted emasculation of the finest human stock. A genuine and equitable rationing of the world's resources would, however, take no more immediate account of the supposed superiority or inferiority of races than does a

[1] For a detailed discussion of the psychological factors involved in this see J. C. Flugel, 'The Psychology of Birth Control,' in *Men and Their Motives*, 1934.

rationing scheme within a nation of the differences in rank or ability between the individual citizens. It is only fair to add that there is, of course, nothing in either sort of rationing that is necessarily antagonistic to a long-term eugenic encouragement of those who are agreed to be the better types. But we can foresee that agreement will be more readily reached concerning individuals (not that it is easy here) than concerning states or races. Truly, from this point of view alone the task of pacifism is much harder than is commonly believed.

Fortunately, and somewhat paradoxically, it would seem that this task can be made somewhat easier by another simultaneous readjustment, viz. a change of emphasis from the welfare of the state to that of the individuals composing it. If we wholeheartedly adopt the democratic point of view, and assume that the ultimate end and purpose of the state is to ensure a good life for its individual citizens, we shall be much less liable to be misled by the often phantastic claims of national pride and glory —phantastic, that is, so far as any improvement in the lot of the average individual is concerned. In so far as this is done, the foreign policy of a state is likely to become much more hedonistically realistic than it is at present. Our attitude towards other states should also become less ruthless, bellicose, and 'touchy' if we could think of them in terms of their component individuals, many of whom, we agree, may be pleasant enough people, not unlike ourselves. It is with the hostile collectivity, the enemy nation, that we are at war, and it is largely because we think in terms of collectivities that it becomes possible to look upon our enemies as utterly abandoned to every form of wickedness (which indeed *as collectivities* they often are). It is in our capacity to form an abstract concept of an enemy nation (perhaps aided by a concrete stereotyped image rigged out with all the characteristics we have learned to hate) that there lies one of the great moral dangers of war.[1] To bear in mind consistently that nations (both our own and others) are composed of individuals, whose fears and hopes and longings, whose capacity for joy and suffering, are not unlike our own, should help to give us pause before we lightheartedly hand over our individual conscience to the state and proceed to commit those enormities that appear ethically justified in war. The *applica-*

---

[1] Here, as in the case of wishful thinking, we learn that one of the most important of human mental powers—in this case that of forming abstract concepts—is not without its drawbacks as well as its advantages.

tion of the notion of moral responsibility to the state should therefore, it would seem (and here is the paradox), go hand in hand
with an *insistence on the ultimate value of the individual,* if we
would facilitate our task—and as this task in any case involves
so drastic a revision of our ways of thinking in the field of international politics, we can hardly afford to neglect any means of
help that may be within our reach.

The Political Approach.—The attempt to combat war along
these lines lies in the provision of super- or inter-national
machinery for the settlement of disputes between nations and
for the general political guidance of the world or some large
part of it. The League of Nations was by far the most outstanding of all such attempts. Why did this great effort fail
to prevent war? Various answers have been given, among the
most plausible being that it was divorced from power, that it
had no armed police force of its own to implement its decisions
—the kind of force upon which the administration of justice
between states, no less than within a given state, must in the
last resort depend. But underlying this question of power there
would seem to be a still more fundamental matter, that of
loyalty. In spite of the work of the League of Nations Union
and of other bodies, of the devoted labours of many of the
League's own servants, and of the enthusiastic support of many
isolated individuals in all parts of the globe, it is clear that
the general amount of loyalty, interest, and enthusiasm aroused
in connection with the League in the different countries of the
world was insufficient for its purpose. In any new organization
of the kind, whether a resuscitated League, an Alliance between
a few great nations, a Federal Union, or what not, this grave
deficiency must be put right, and we must recognize that here
again there is no easy problem. The nation-state is an entity
that we have learnt to trust and honour (no matter if sometimes
with insufficient reason). The older nation-states are strong in
their age-long traditions. Now the successful functioning of a
super-national organization implies that some of the loyalty that
men have been accustomed to feel for their own states must be
transferred to a new and politically 'higher' body. It is unreasonable to expect that this will happen unless very active
steps are taken to ensure it. The League of Nations had no
universally recognized flag, anthem, emblem, or other symbol,
of the kind that we are accustomed to use for the purpose of
mobilizing our political loyalties. The very appearance of the

League of Nations building was unfamiliar to most people, though in view of its significance it should have been as well known as the Pyramids or the Leaning Tower of Pisa. In fact there was a lamentable failure to realize the importance of creating and maintaining the strong new loyalty that was necessary if the grandiose scheme was to have any weight in competition with the well-established older loyalties.

If a super-national body (we will for the sake of simplicity call it the Federation, though the same general considerations will apply whatever be its form) is successfully to take over some of the functions of the present nation-states, it must almost certainly come to be regarded with something like the same feelings as those now directed to these states. The state, as we have reminded the reader (though we have not in this book presented the full evidence), is a father and/or mother symbol. Like a parent, it is expected to guide, direct, enforce obedience, and at the same time nourish and protect. Within the sphere of its influence and responsibility the Federation must fulfil the same fundamental rôle and must have the necessary authority, prestige, and will to do so. Intellectually at least it should be easy to demonstrate that a properly organized and equipped Federation can protect and nourish better than any nation-state, its potential military strength and economic resources being greater. Nevertheless, apart from questions of loyalty, the League of Nations failed to inspire any confidence in this respect. The Federation, if it is to be more successful, must show that it can and will enforce obedience, protect from outer aggression or inside revolt, and provide for economic welfare. For the purpose of protection, of course, it must above all be certain of the loyalty and obedience of such armed forces as it has at its disposal, and these forces themselves can hardly be other than the main armies, navies, and air fleets supplied by the federated nations, but united under a supreme command directly responsible to the Federation, and not to the nation from which any particular detachment has been drawn. Under any other arrangement the ancient national loyalties would surely reassert themselves at the slightest suspicion of a conflict of interests between the Federation as a whole and one of its constituent nations.

Since it is not proposed to do away with nations and establish at one stroke anything resembling a completely centralized world government, the nations should naturally retain some of the loyalty at present directed to them, which however will need to be properly subordinated to the loyalty to the Federation as a whole. There is nothing impossible about this; there exist numerous hierarchies of loyalties in many individual minds, such as that of family, school, town, county, nation, empire. There is no reason why such hierarchically arranged loyalties should stop at a man's country and should not be extended to embrace a larger whole. But again the necessary steps must be taken to bring about the hierarchy; the interest of country and Federation must be felt, not as antagonistic, but as bound up with one another, much as, for instance, the interests of the various colleges at Oxford and Cambridge are connected with those of their respective universities. The flags and anthems of country and of Federation should be seen or heard together; every opportunity should be taken of driving home the lesson that the federated nations are co-operating in a common task, and the more each nation knows about the others and their contribution to this task the better. The experience gained from the successful fusion produced in the U.S.S.R. may be invaluable here, though much that is useful (both to imitate and to avoid) can no doubt also be learnt from the history of the British Empire, the United States, China, and other great political units.[1]

One of the difficulties to be encountered by any Federation is that the glory of national states is by tradition so largely linked up with their military history. Here also a great change of emphasis will be required, and nations must learn to glory in such things as their contribution to literature, art, science, hygiene, education, social service, and their treatment of delinquents and of backward peoples. In terms of the rehabilitation of individual miscreants, we may say that the criminal super-ego of the nations must be replaced by a normal one. All this will be helped if we can substitute a forward-looking view for the nostalgic yearning for a past which was lived under conditions very different from those that hold to-day. Not that in so doing we shall be untrue to the great traditions of our ancestors; we should rather look upon ourselves as carrying on in new ways and new fields the work so well begun by them. It is indeed only by carrying forward the banner of Progress,

---

[1] The work of such bodies as The New Commonwealth Institute of World Affairs contains of course many valuable preliminary studies in this direction.

and not leaving it where they were compelled to drop it, that
we can live up to these traditions and prove ourselves worthy
of our heritage.

Two great dangers will confront us at the end of the present
war (dangers that occur in the case of all wars involving many
nations), that of falling out with our friends and that of failing
to become reconciled with our enemies.   Much the same prophylactic measure is perhaps applicable to both dangers, i.e. an
urgent realization of the necessity for co-operation in a common
task of reconstruction.   The world will largely need to be
rebuilt.   We and our allies must assuredly co-operate in this,
and (as already indicated, for instance at the end of Chapter V)
it will probably be well if at the earliest possible moment we
enlist the co-operation also of our late enemies.   As Carr so well
puts it: 'People become like-minded by doing things together
and by sharing the same experiences; and the way to create a
psychology of co-operation is not by preaching co-operation but
to co-operate.   This is particularly true of the younger generation.   Hitler appealed to the youth of Germany by demanding
service to a narrowly national cause.   Anyone who is to sway
the destinies of Europe after the war must have the imagination
to make an equally cogent appeal to the youth of Europe for
service in a larger cause'.   And again, stressing the common
task confronting all belligerents: 'We can "re-educate" the
Germans only if we are prepared in the course of the same
process to re-educate ourselves'.[1]   We may add that in so far
as, in spite of its moralization, war is capable of arousing guilt
in the belligerents (and it is more likely to do so in the vanquished
than in the victors); in so far too as, in accordance with the
views of Melanie Klein, guilt can be most satisfactorily and
rationally wiped out by reparation; then, association in a
common work of reconstruction to make good as far as possible
the vast havoc of the war is most likely to extinguish a smoulder-
ing guilt which, by a process of projection, could so easily be
turned again into aggression.   Co-operation may be not only the
best method for immediate purposes but the safest in the long
run.

The Provision of 'Moral Equivalents'.—If we glance
through the list of sub-headings in the first part of this chapter
we can at once realize that here again our problem, in this
case the provision of a substitute for war that shall have some-

[1] E. H. Carr, op. cit., ch. 9.

thing approaching war's peculiar combination of moral and instinctive appeal, is far from easy. In its danger, its hazards, its call for heroism, effort, and sacrifice on the part of whole communities, war is without a parallel—as also in the sense of social cohesion that it brings and the amount of aggression it permits.

At first sight it is only as regards the question of employment and the 'need to be needed' that the prospect of finding 'moral equivalents' without resort to war itself appears to be reasonably hopeful. Economists tell us that the mass-unemployment in democracies in pre-war years is totally unnecessary and that the adoption of a well-considered plan for the utilization of the world's resources to meet human needs could easily bring to an end the miserable and humiliating spectacle of millions crying out for work while millions more are craving for the things that this work would produce. The psychological problem of satisfaction in work is also not insoluble. A further development and use of vocational guidance and selection, an extension of the methods of industrial psychology to make work itself more productive and more pleasant, and perhaps above all a wider realization of the fact that an individual through his work performs a service to his fellows, should go very far towards fulfilling that 'need to be needed' that is gratified in war. As revealed by Mass Observation and by other methods, most people in this country in days before the present war regarded their work primarily, or indeed exclusively, as a means of gaining a livelihood for themselves or their families or (what was even less inspiring) as a means of putting money into their employers' pockets; the nobler satisfaction to be obtained from a sense of service to the community was for the most part denied them, largely because there was nothing in the organization of society or in their social outlook to make them look upon their work in such a light. True, lip-service was sometimes paid to the 'dignity of labour', but the phrase had a hollow ring; it smacked of discipline and submission rather than of service, and in actual fact many forms of labour carried a stigma of inferiority. The war, with its urgent appeal for the help of every willing hand, has changed all that; and it should not be hard by means of suitable—and very justifiable—propaganda to produce a continuance of the new attitude into times of peace. Here also we may learn something from the totalitarian countries and above all from Russia. The joy of co-operation in a larger common purpose must be preserved if we are to find a peaceful 'equivalent' of war.

But where are we to find such a purpose? Here, I think, lies the real core of the problem of discovering a substitute for the great but sinister appeal of war. So far, I believe, but one suggestion has been made. It has been put forward from many quarters, but often perhaps without a realization of the full depth of its implications; and it is the same as that to which the argument in our own chapter on moral progress has led us and to which we referred again at the end of our chapter on religion. According to this view, it is man's duty and destiny to carry on the process of evolution by utilizing all his powers for the betterment of himself, for the improvement of his spiritual and physical welfare, for the increase of his knowledge and of the power with which this knowledge can endow him, for the reshaping of the world into a fitter place for human beings to live in, for the attainment of more exalted and more fundamentally satisfying experience—in a word, for what we mean by Progress in the widest sense. This Progress can from our present point of view be looked upon as a battle of man against nature, as a call upon man's 'aggression' in the larger and more sublimated meaning of the word.[1] Here we have the vision of a battle, bigger and better than any dreamt about by our old Nordic ancestors or by their modern successors who are so enthralled by what they hold to be the essential nobility of conflict. It is a battle, too, that can and will continue as long as man exists; the problems of science, art, philosophy are inexhaustible; the Universe presents endless possibilities for the exercise of human daring, skill, and ingenuity. Finally it is a battle that can and must be fought on many fronts: by the statesman whose business it is to organize society, by the sociologist who endeavours to understand the laws of its development, by the doctor who fights against disease, by the research worker who wrestles with the secrets of nature in his laboratory, by the technician, engineer, and farmer who apply the knowledge thus gained to make nature fulfil our needs, by the factory worker who provides the tools for them to do so, by the artist who satisfies our longing for æsthetic experience (that unique craving of the human mind), by the psychologist who tries to penetrate the mysteries of man's own soul—and by many more, a vast

---

[1] See the discussion under the heading of our fifth 'tendency' in Chapter XVI.

army of specialist fighters, that exceeds even our present huge military organizations in numbers and complexity.

But have men not been doing this, it may be asked, since the very beginning of human culture? In a sense, yes; but again, and in a very important sense, no. They have not done so in the light of a clearly formulated ideal (if we like to call it so, a religious ideal) that applies to all the human race as such; they have not done so in the full consciousness of co-operating in one vast human team. Indeed much of man's progress is due to isolated individuals here and there, working for their private ends or to satisfy some personal urge or curiosity; and the greater pioneers among them have, more often than not, been feared or persecuted by their fellows. For did not the attempt to improve man's lot or to extend the boundaries of his power and knowledge excite the ancient fear of 'hubris'? Was it not likely to arouse divine displeasure? Hitherto the influence of morals and religion has been largely such as to deter men from any effort of the kind. It has been chiefly in war that they have sought and found the sense of high adventure; and brotherhood in arms has up to now been the supreme form of co-operation. It is only in quite recent times that they have been able to see at all clearly the possibilities and implications of the goal of Progress; and even now they have hardly begun to realize that Progress can be an ideal embracing and inspiring all mankind—an ideal that still calls upon men to be brothers-in-arms, not against their fellows, but against the forces of nature which, in so far as they threaten, restrict, and embitter human life, are the enemies of all. If we wish to be dramatic (and it is perhaps well that we should be so, if we would compete against the lure of war), we can say that the stage is set for the epic struggle of Man versus the Universe—a spectacle surely no less breath-taking in its audacity and splendour than the most famous exploits of purely interhuman warfare. In the great conflict of the latter kind in the midst of which these words are written we have seen heroism unsurpassed, on land, on sea, and in the air—heroism not only of trained fighters but of common men and women in all parts of the earth. Will such people also have the courage and the insight to cast aside their old traditions of fighting with each other, to advance a further step upon what appears to be their path of destiny and to enter with set purpose upon the larger and nobler struggle in which all mankind can be allied?

x

Much that is primitive and sinister in human nature—including much that we have had to deal with in this book—may make us hesitate before we say that such a thing is possible. Yet here again we can but try. In the words of a philosopher recently departed from among us, 'Human beings are too fine in their highest achievements to justify despair'.[1]

[1] L. Susan Stebbing, *Ideals and Illusions* (1941), p. 205.

INDEX

AUTHOR INDEX